The Earl is too easy... ...on Mistress Road.

A year has passed since I began work on this series. Seriously, I never expected it to last so long. (Hey, now…) But I'm very happy. I'd like to thank my editor, my assistants, and all the staff. And I'd also like to thank my readers. I love you!

—Katsura Hoshino

Shiga Prefecture native Katsura Hoshino's hit manga series *D.Gray-man* has been serialized in *Weekly Shonen Jump* since 2004. Katsura's debut manga, "Continue," appeared for the first time in *Weekly Shonen Jump* in 2003.

Katsura adores cats.

GRAPH HOSHI NO V. 5

D.GRAY-MAN
VOL. 5
SHONEN JUMP ADVANCED
Manga Edition

STORY AND ART BY
KATSURA HOSHINO

English Adaptation/Lance Caselman
Translation/Toshifumi Yoshida
Touch-up Art & Lettering/Kelle Han
Design/Yukiko Whitley
Editor/Gary Leach

D.GRAY-MAN © 2004 by Katsura Hoshino. All rights reserved.
First published in Japan in 2004 by SHUEISHA Inc., Tokyo.
English translation rights arranged by SHUEISHA Inc.

Printed in the U.S.A.

Published by VIZ Media, LLC
P.O. Box 77010
San Francisco, CA 94107

10 9 8 7 6
First printing, May 2007
Sixth printing, December 2010

THE WORLD'S MOST CUTTING-EDGE MANGA

SHONEN JUMP ADVANCED

www.viz.com

www.shonenjump.com

SHONEN JUMP ADVANCED MANGA EDITION

STORY & ART BY
Katsura Hoshino

vol. 5

D.Gray-man

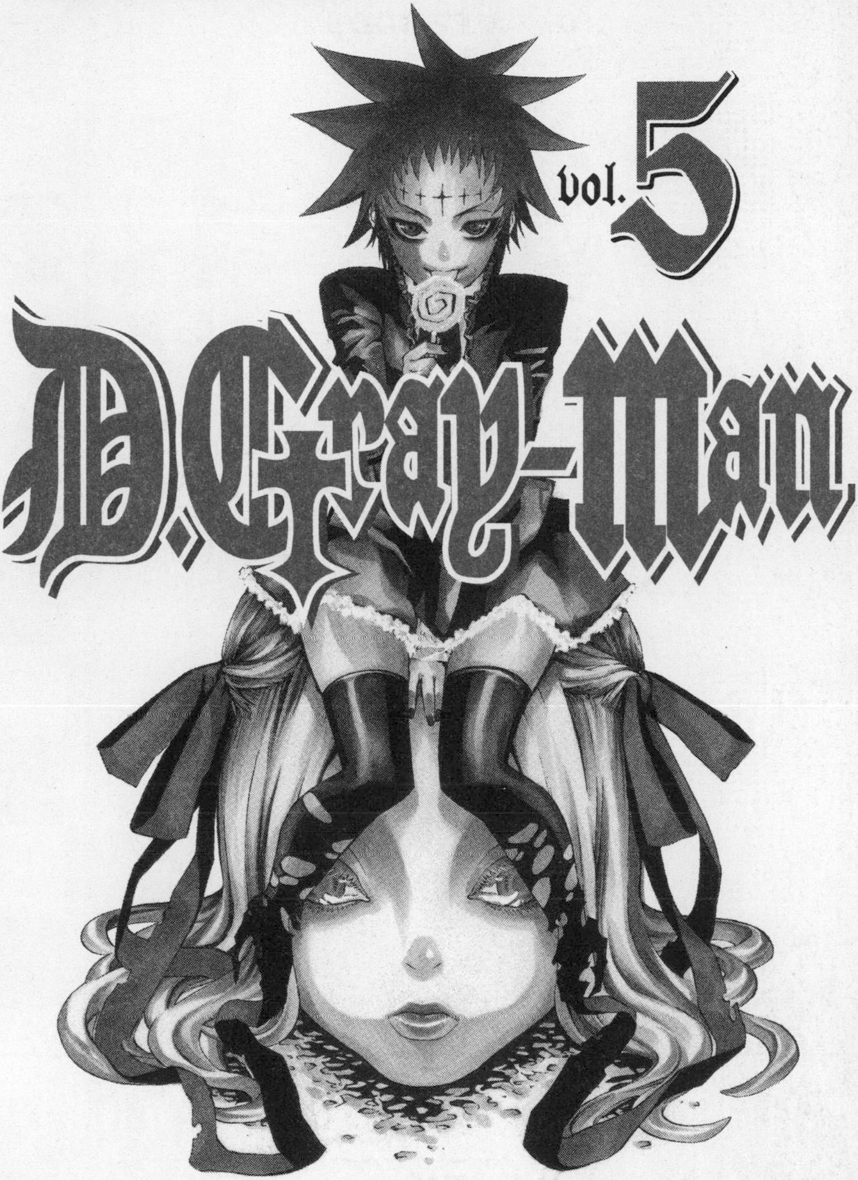

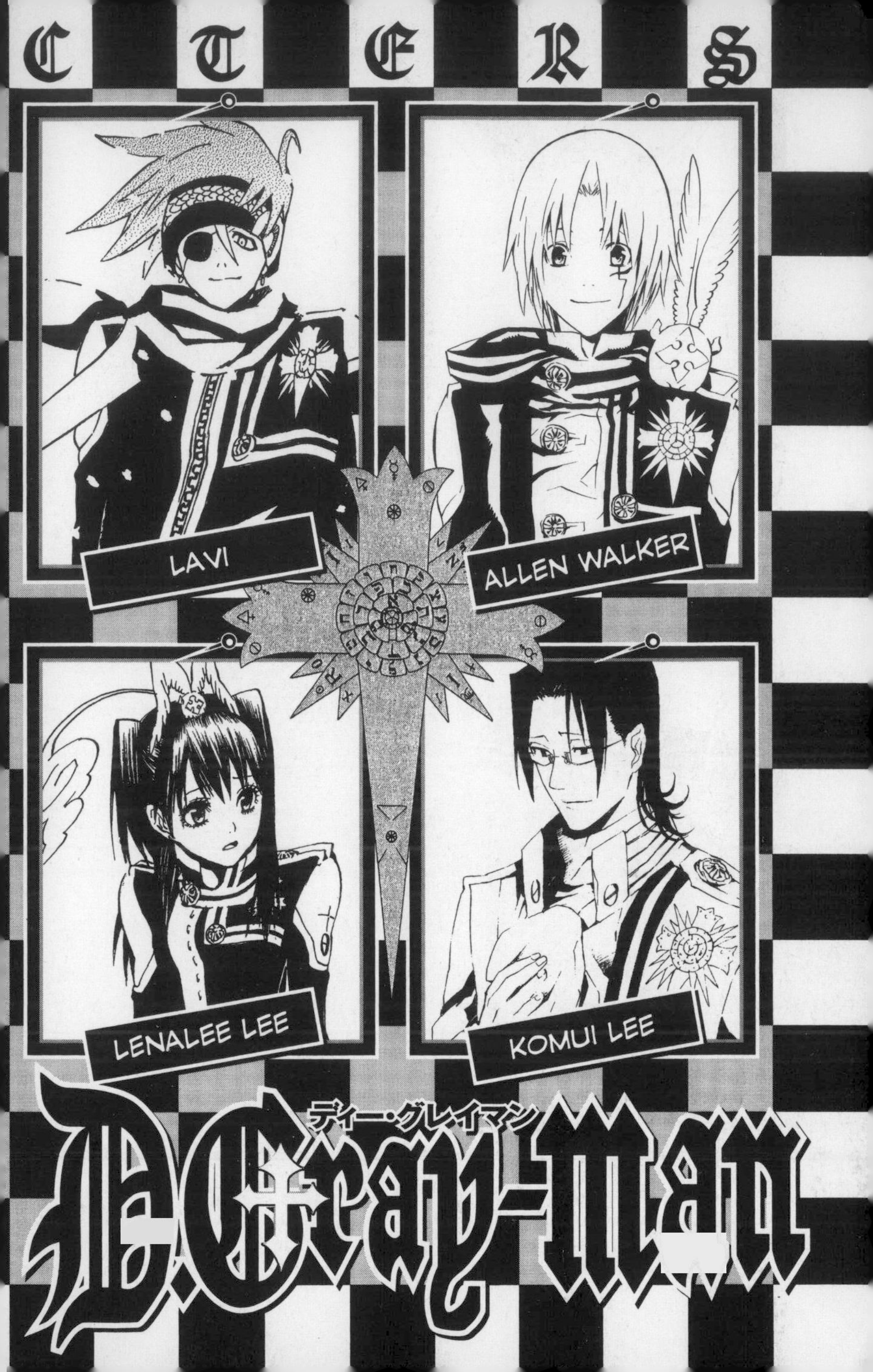
C T E R S
LAVI
ALLEN WALKER
LENALEE LEE
KOMUI LEE
ディー・グレイマン
D.Gray-man

CHARA

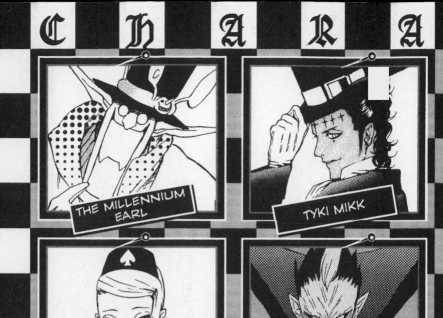

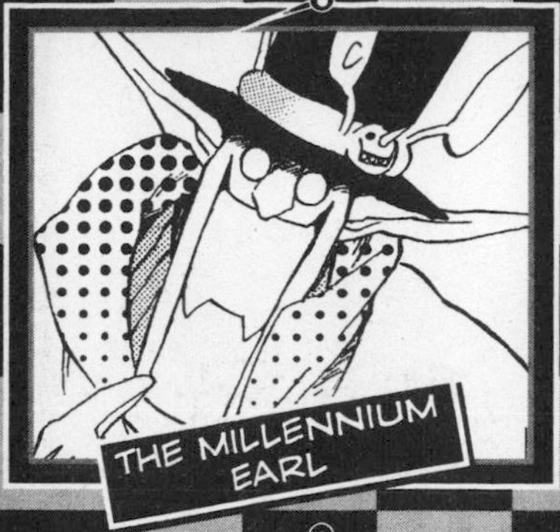
THE MILLENNIUM EARL

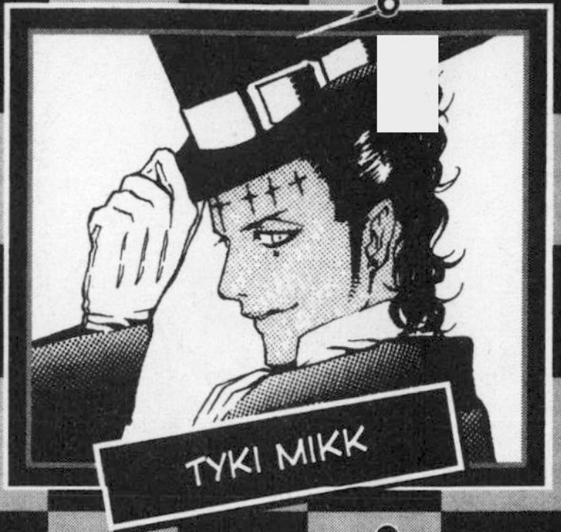
TYKI MIKK

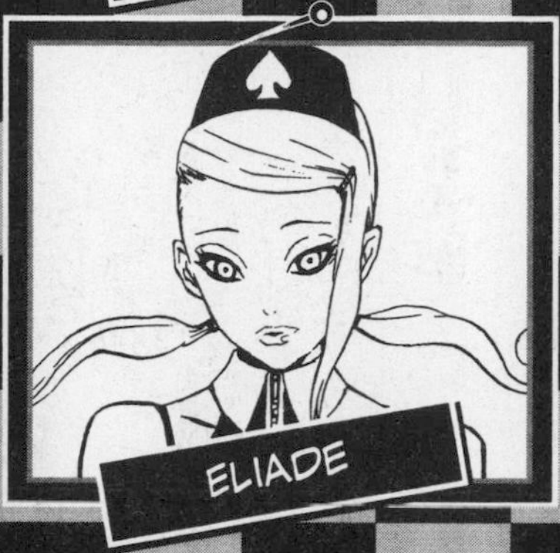
ELIADE

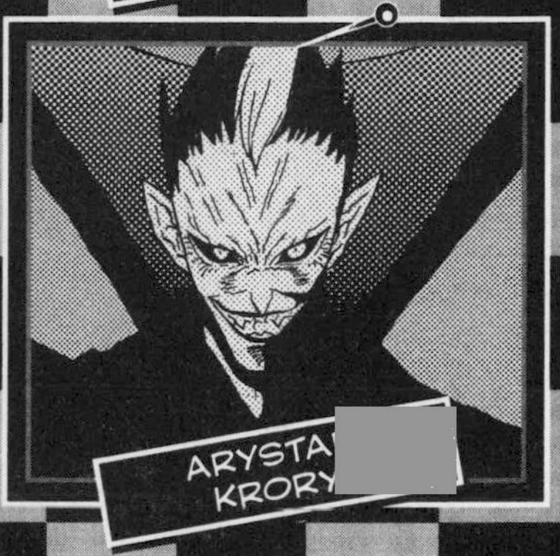
ARYSTA
KRORY

STORY

IT ALL BEGAN CENTURIES AGO WITH THE DISCOVERY OF A CUBE CONTAINING AN APOCALYPTIC PROPHECY FROM AN ANCIENT CIVILIZATION, AND INSTRUCTIONS IN THE USE OF INNOCENCE, A CRYSTALLINE SUBSTANCE OF WONDROUS SUPERNATURAL POWER. THE CREATORS OF THE CUBE CLAIMED TO HAVE DEFEATED AN EVIL KNOWN AS THE MILLENNIUM EARL USING THE INNOCENCE. NEVERTHELESS, THE WORLD WAS DESTROYED BY THE GREAT FLOOD OF THE OLD TESTAMENT. NOW TO AVERT A SECOND END OF THE WORLD, A GROUP OF EXORCISTS WIELDING WEAPONS MADE OF INNOCENCE MUST BATTLE THE MILLENNIUM EARL AND HIS TERRIBLE MINIONS, THE AKUMA.

WITH ONE GENERAL ALREADY DEAD, AND ITS FORCES UNDER CONSTANT ATTACK, THE BLACK ORDER MUST FIND A SPECIAL INNOCENCE CALLED THE "HEART" BEFORE THE MILLENNIUM EARL DOES. ALLEN IS ASSIGNED TO FIND AND PROTECT GENERAL CROSS, BUT FIRST HE MUST DEAL WITH A VERY UNUSUAL VAMPIRE!

D.GRAY-MAN
Vol. 5

CONTENTS

THE 37TH NIGHT: VAMPIRE OF THE CASTLE (PART 7) MERGE

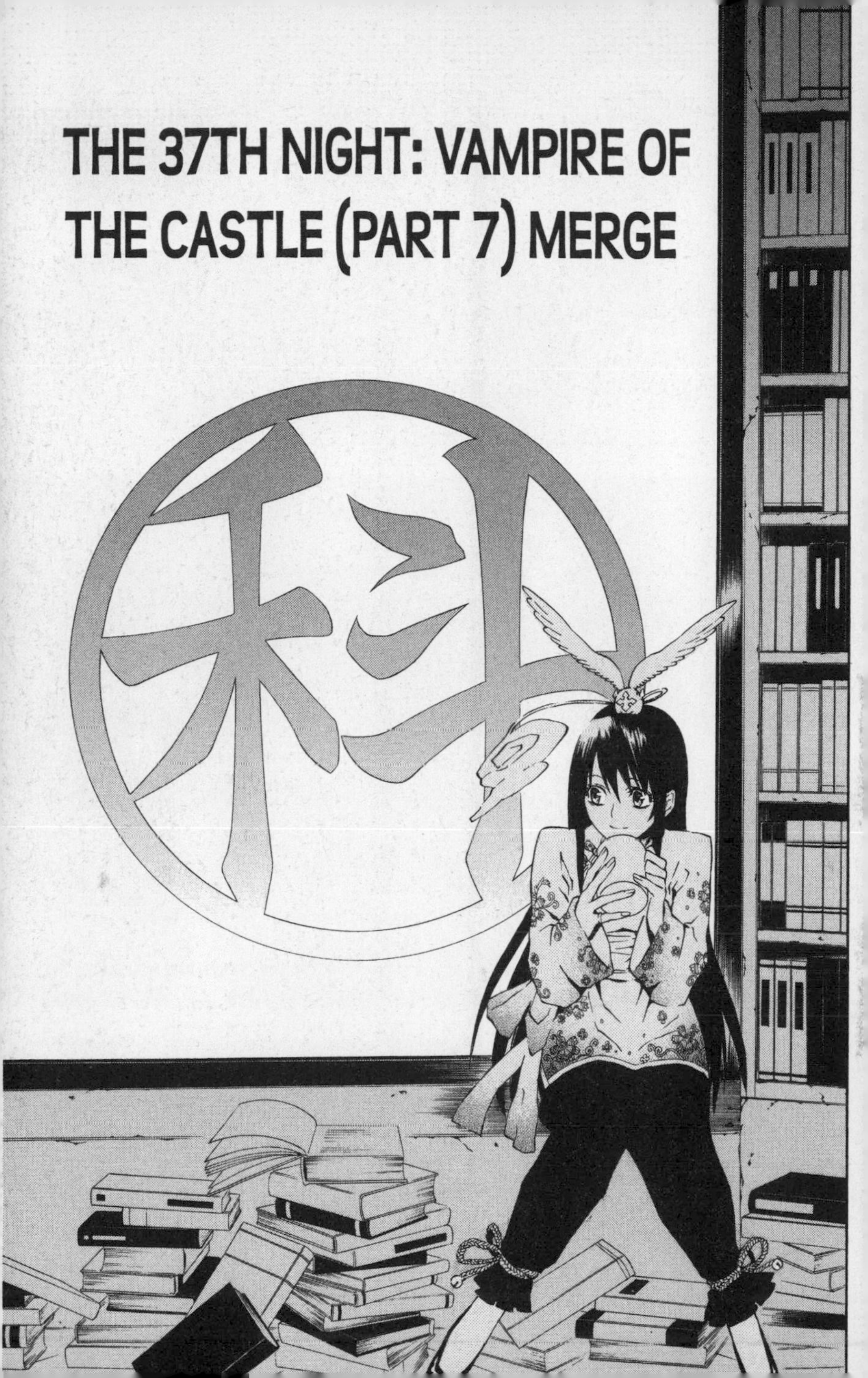

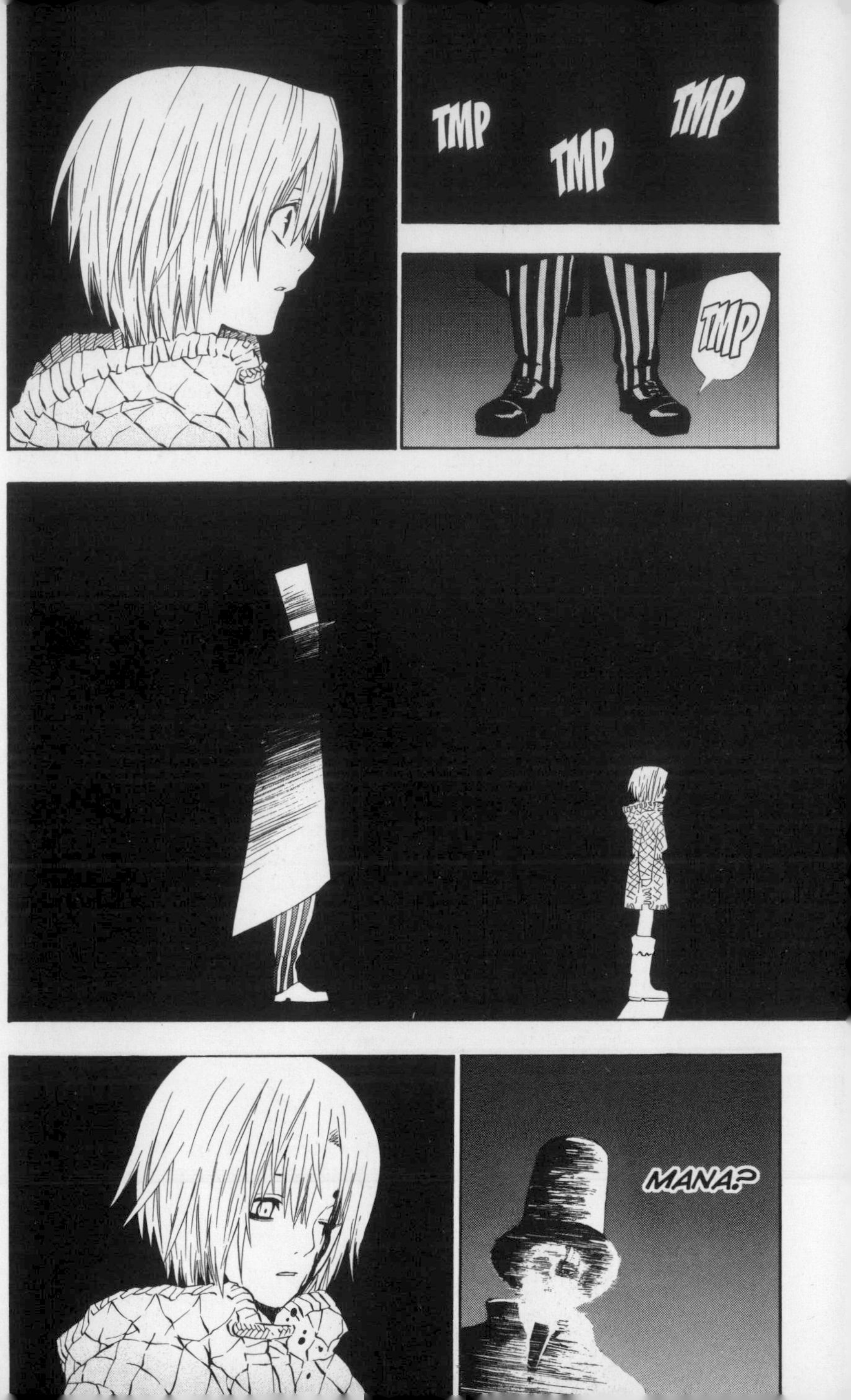
TMP
TMP
TMP
TMP
MANA?

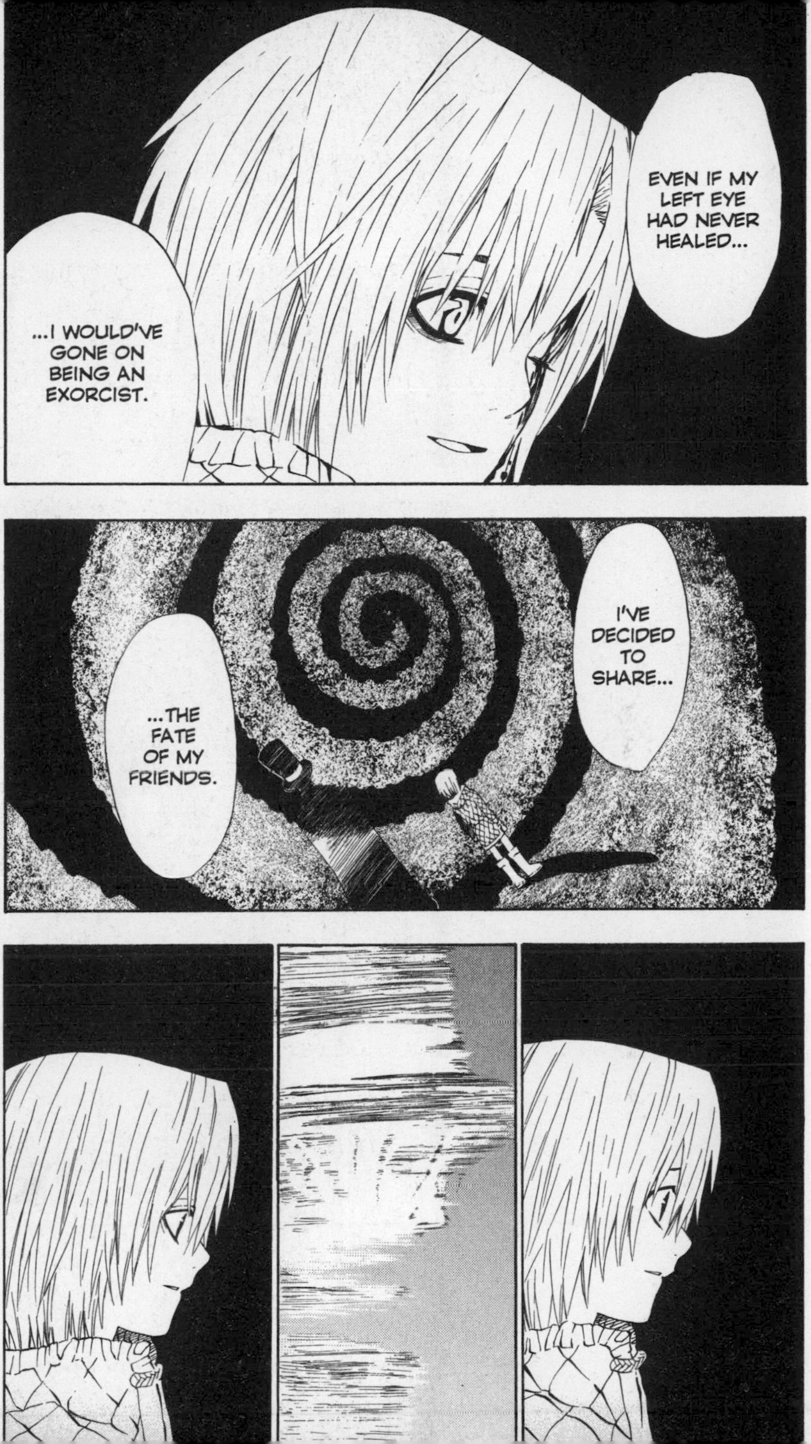
EVEN IF MY LEFT EYE HAD NEVER HEALED...
...I WOULD'VE GONE ON BEING AN EXORCIST.
I'VE DECIDED TO SHARE...
...THE FATE OF MY FRIENDS.

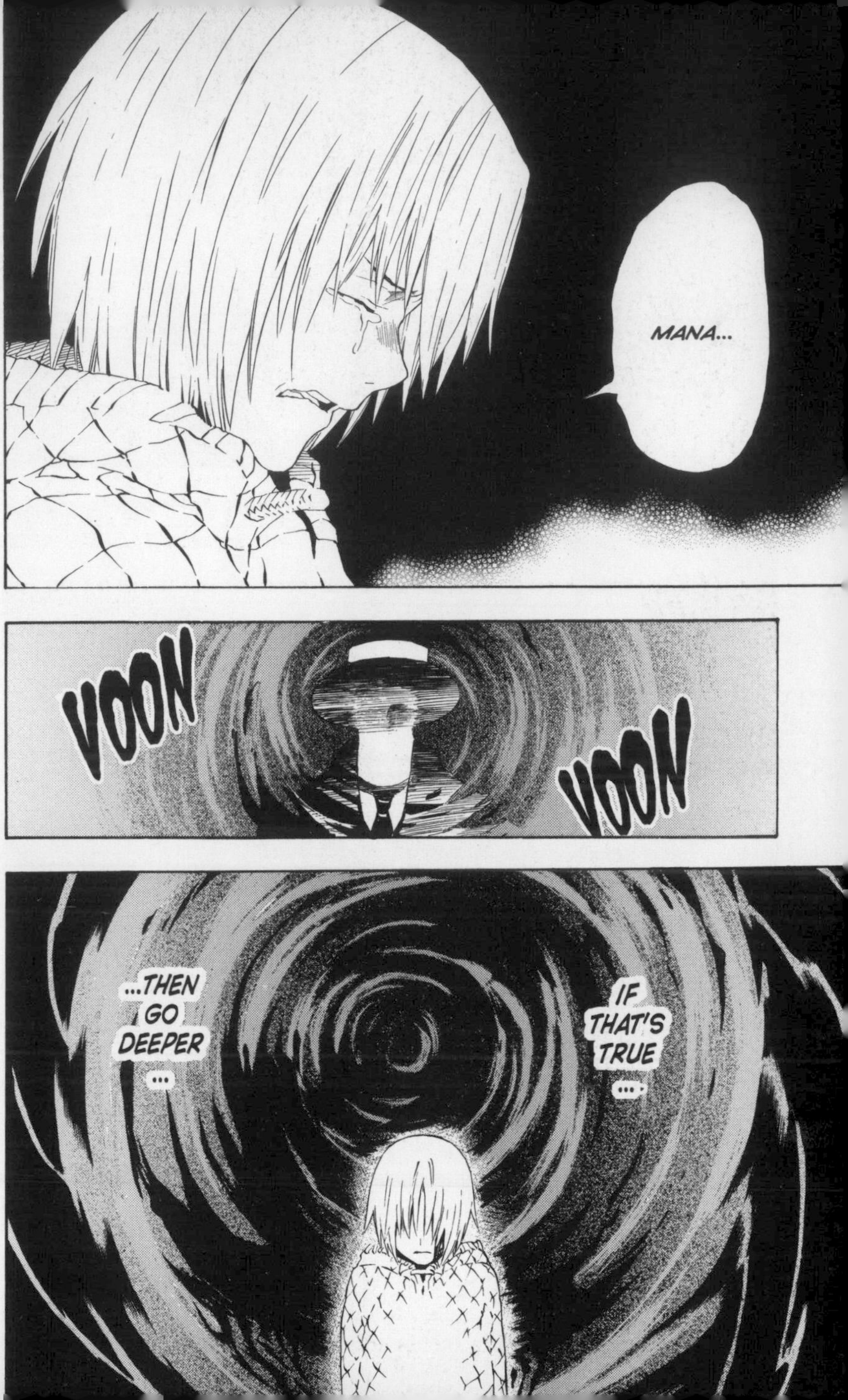
MANA...
VOON
VOON
IF THAT'S TRUE ...
...THEN GO DEEPER ...

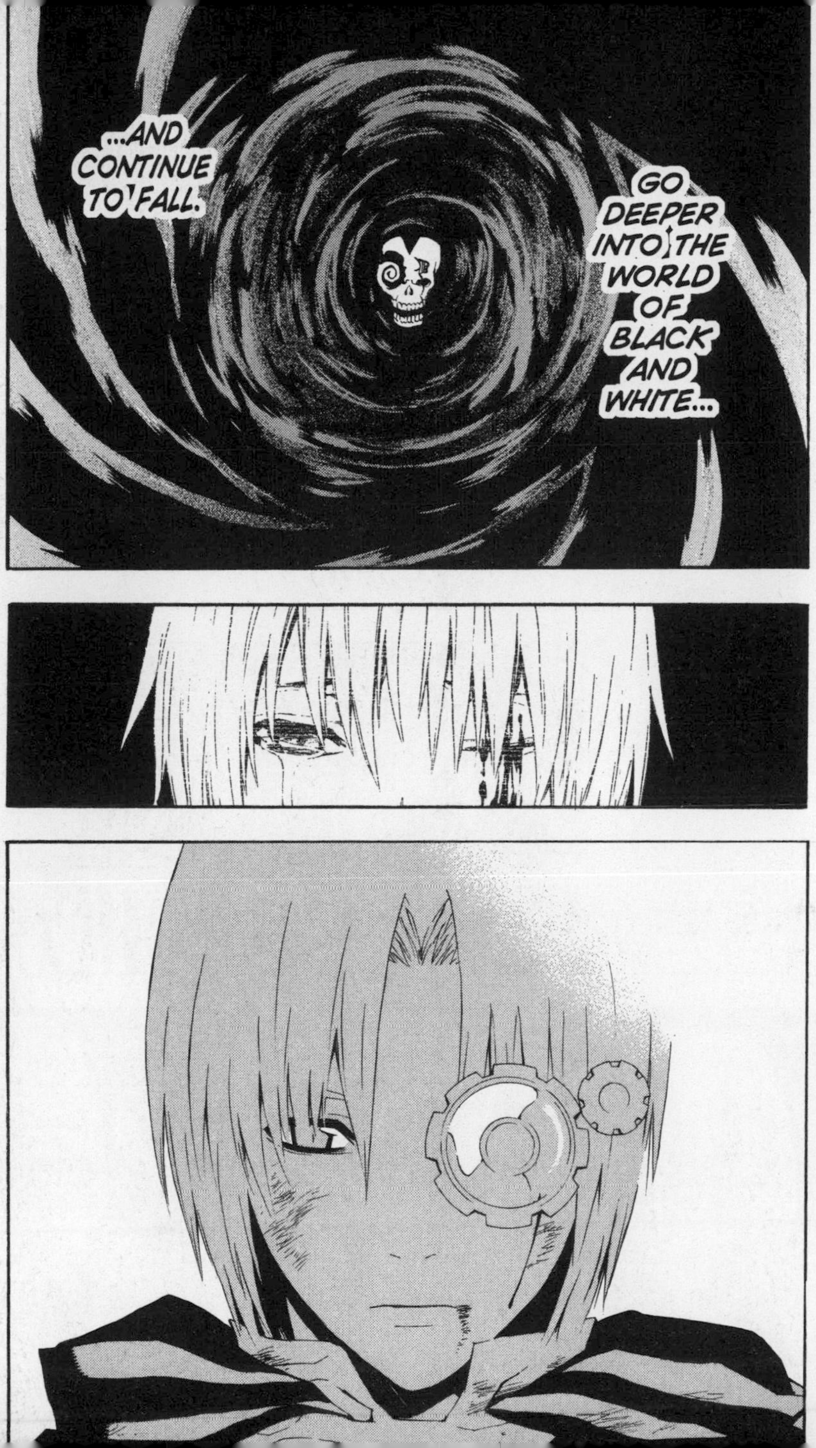
GO DEEPER INTO THE WORLD OF BLACK AND WHITE...
...AND CONTINUE TO FALL.

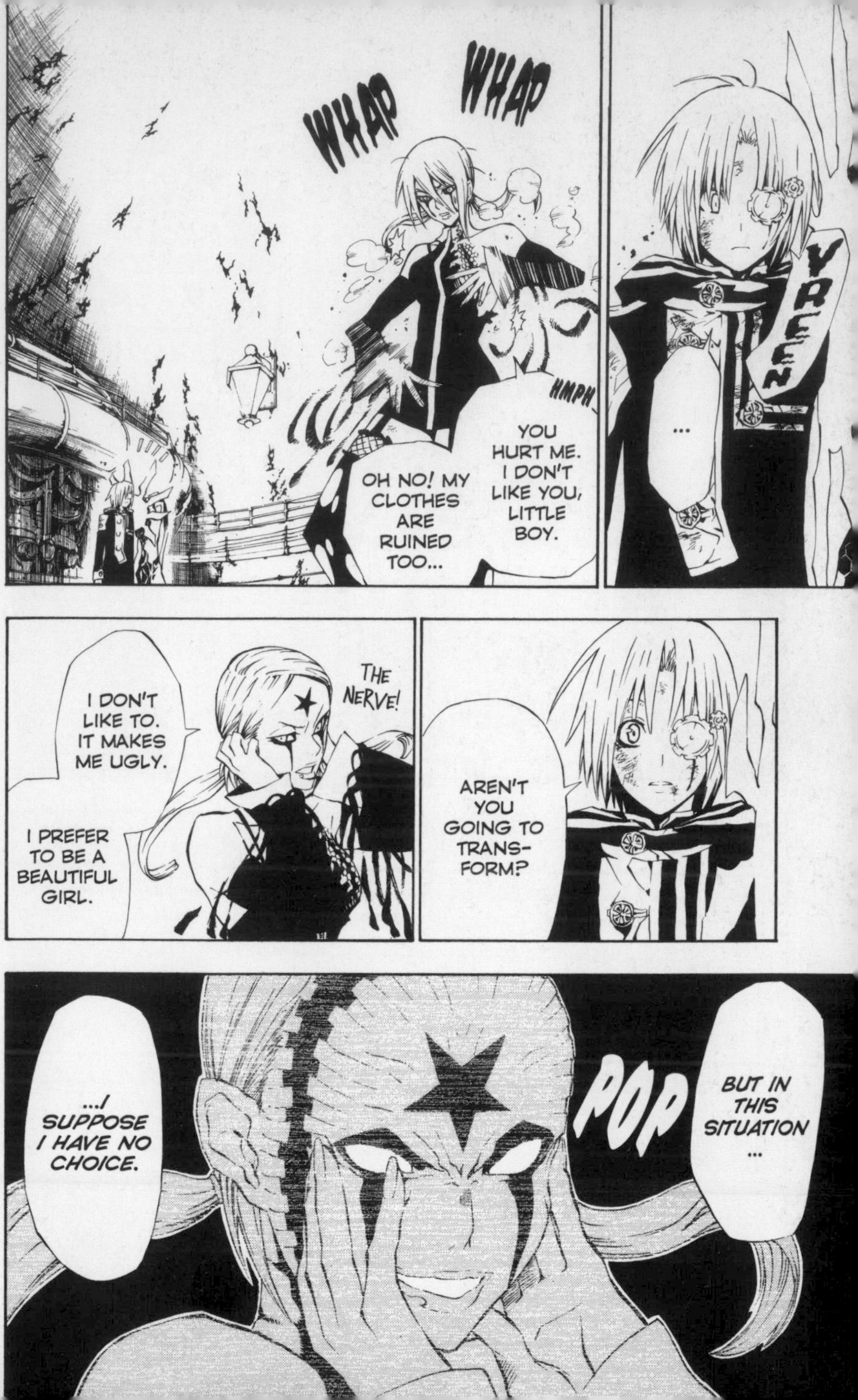
VREEN
...
WHAP
WHAP
HMPH
YOU HURT ME. I DON'T LIKE YOU, LITTLE BOY.
OH NO! MY CLOTHES ARE RUINED TOO...
AREN'T YOU GOING TO TRANS-FORM?
THE NERVE!
I DON'T LIKE TO. IT MAKES ME UGLY.
I PREFER TO BE A BEAUTIFUL GIRL.
BUT IN THIS SITUATION ...
POP
...I SUPPOSE I HAVE NO CHOICE.

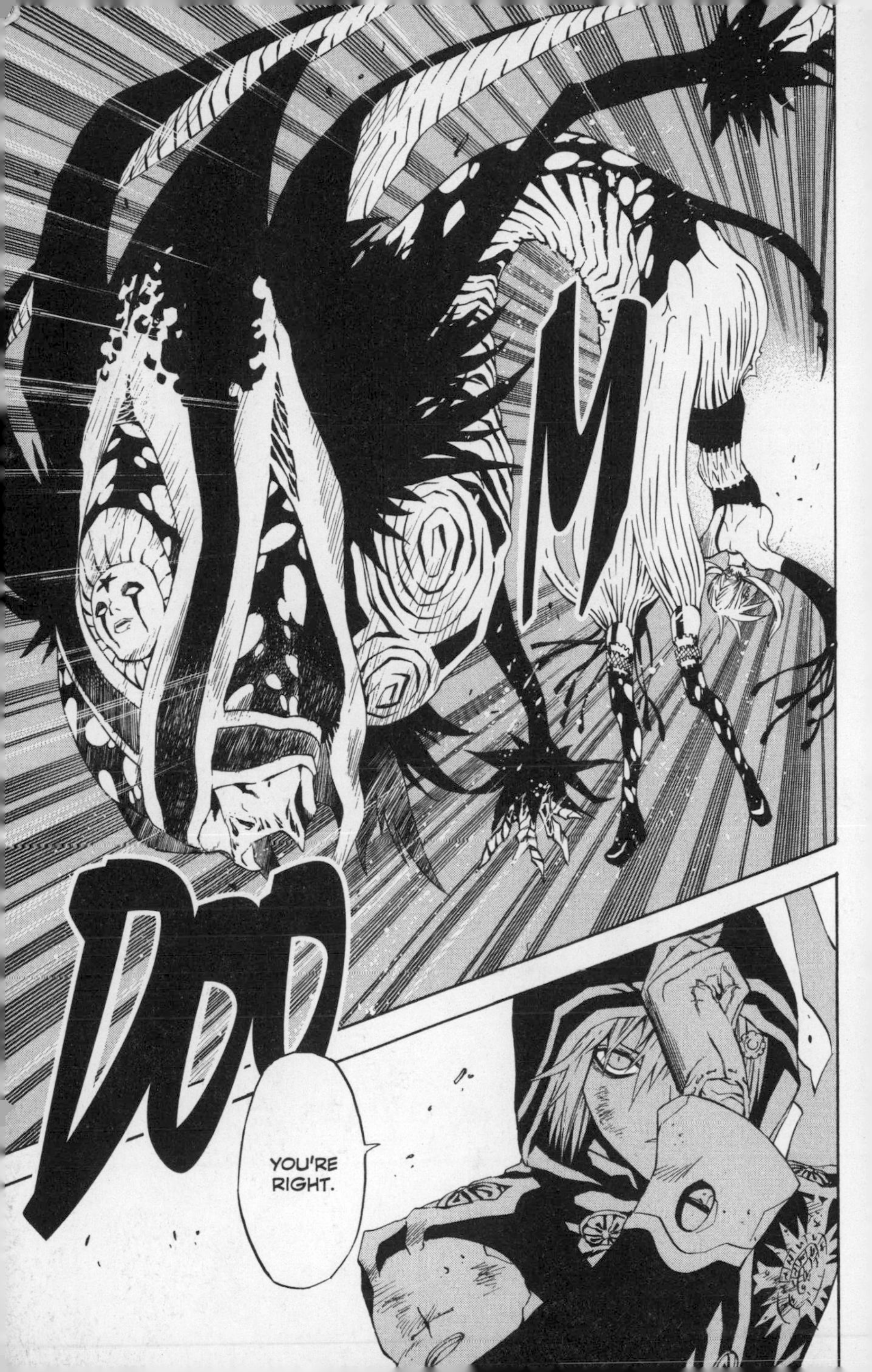
YOU'RE RIGHT.

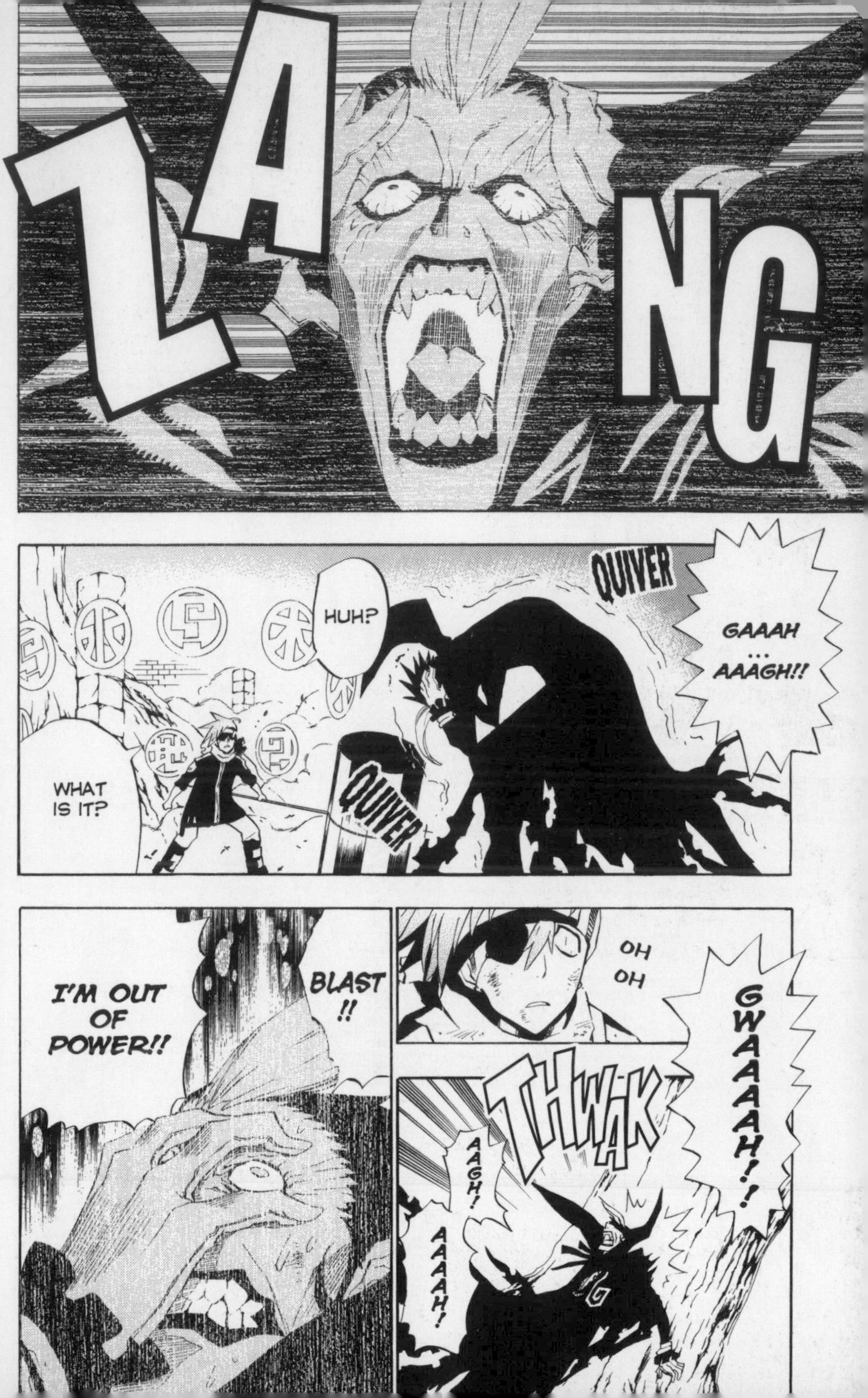
ZANG
QUIVER
GAAAH ... AAAGH!!
HUH?
QUIVER
WHAT IS IT?
OH OH
GWAAAAAH!!
THWAK
AAGH!
AAAAH!
BLAST!!
I'M OUT OF POWER!!

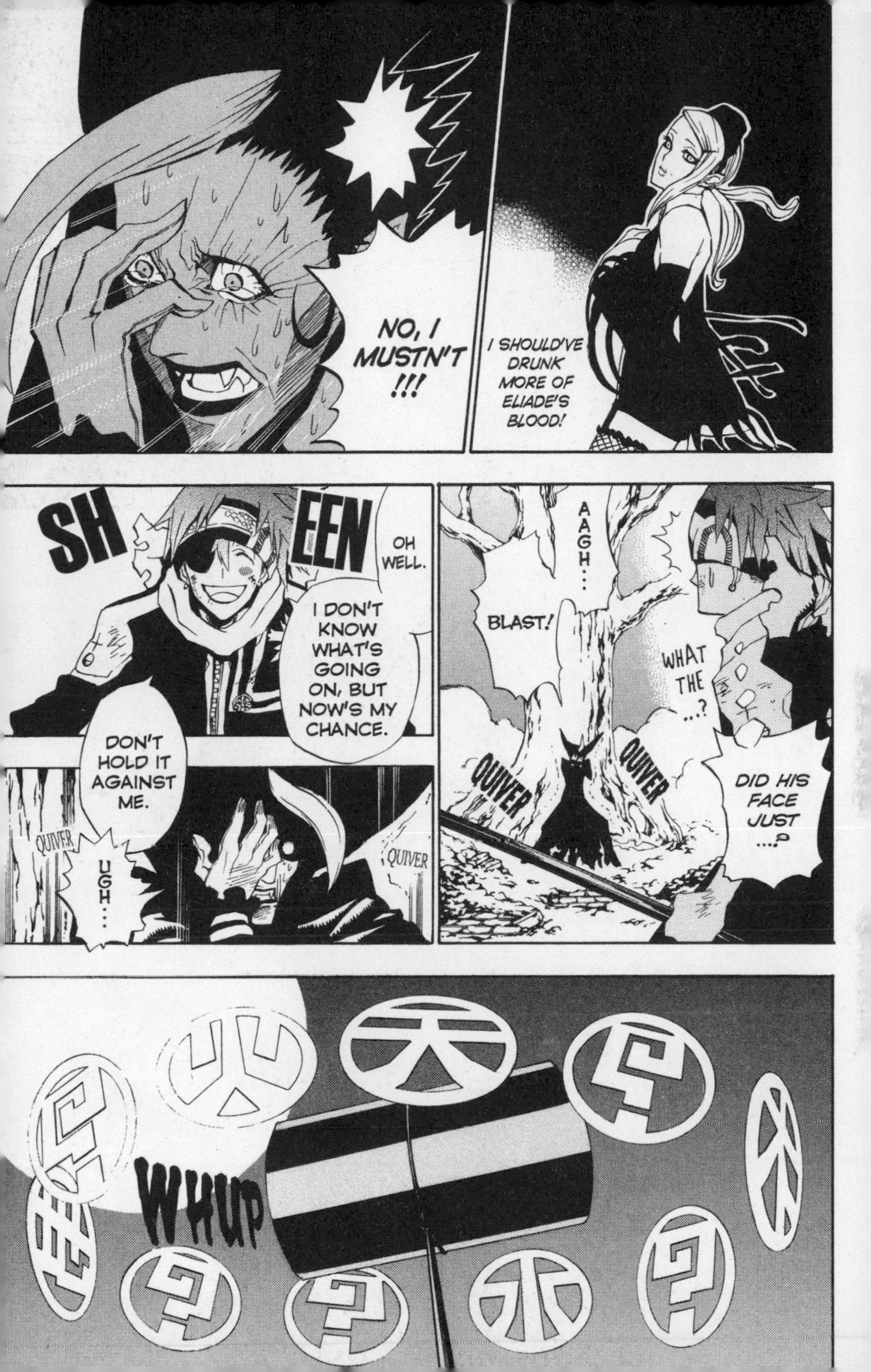
I SHOULD'VE DRUNK MORE OF ELIADE'S BLOOD!
NO, I MUSTN'T !!!
AAGH...
BLAST!
WHAT THE ...?
QUIVER
DID HIS FACE JUST ...?
QUIVER
SHEEN
OH WELL.
I DON'T KNOW WHAT'S GOING ON, BUT NOW'S MY CHANCE.
DON'T HOLD IT AGAINST ME.
QUIVER
UGH...
QUIVER
WHUP

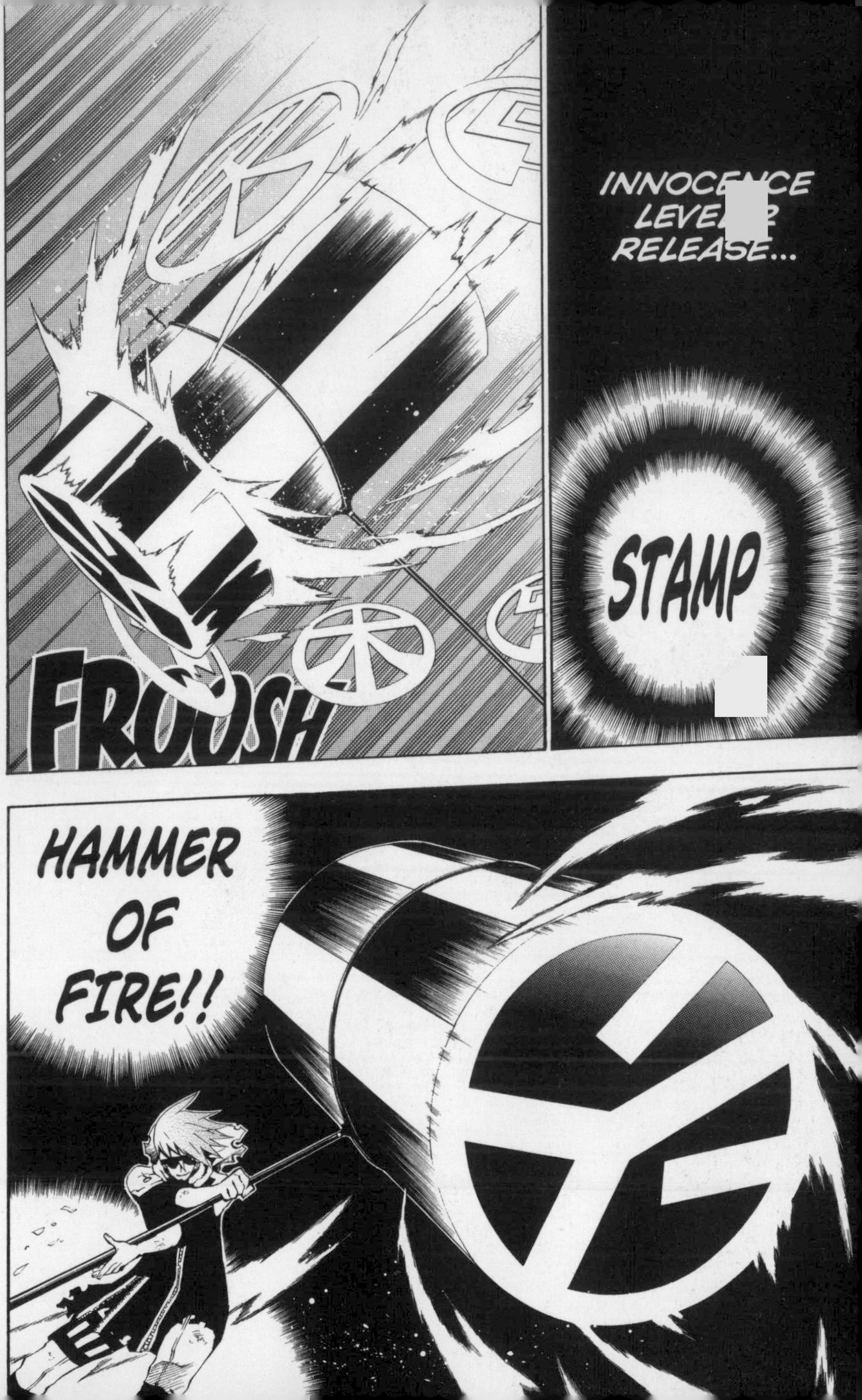
INNOCENCE LEVEL 2 RELEASE...
STAMP
FROOSH
HAMMER OF FIRE!!

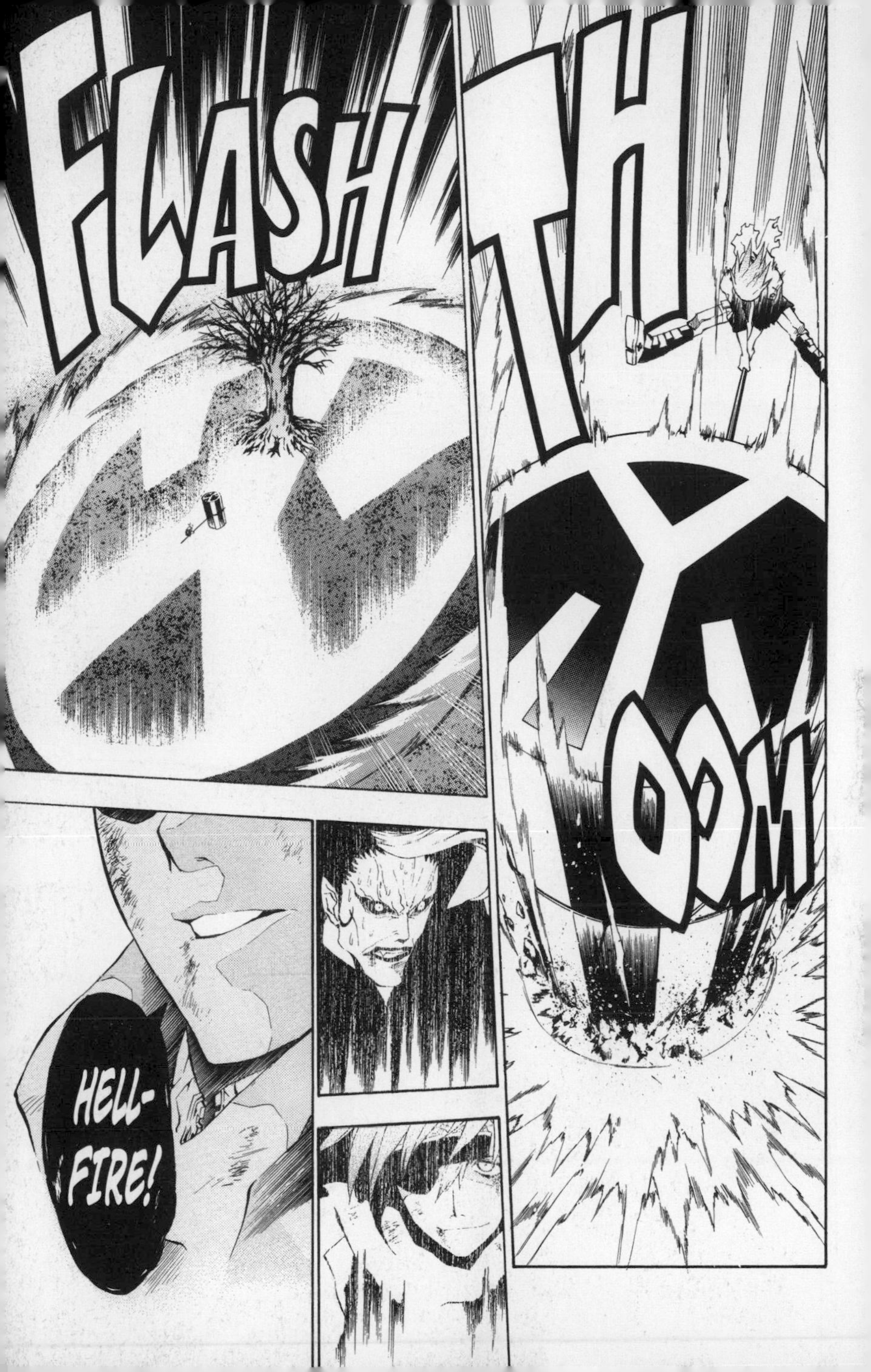
THOOM
FLASH
HELL-FIRE!

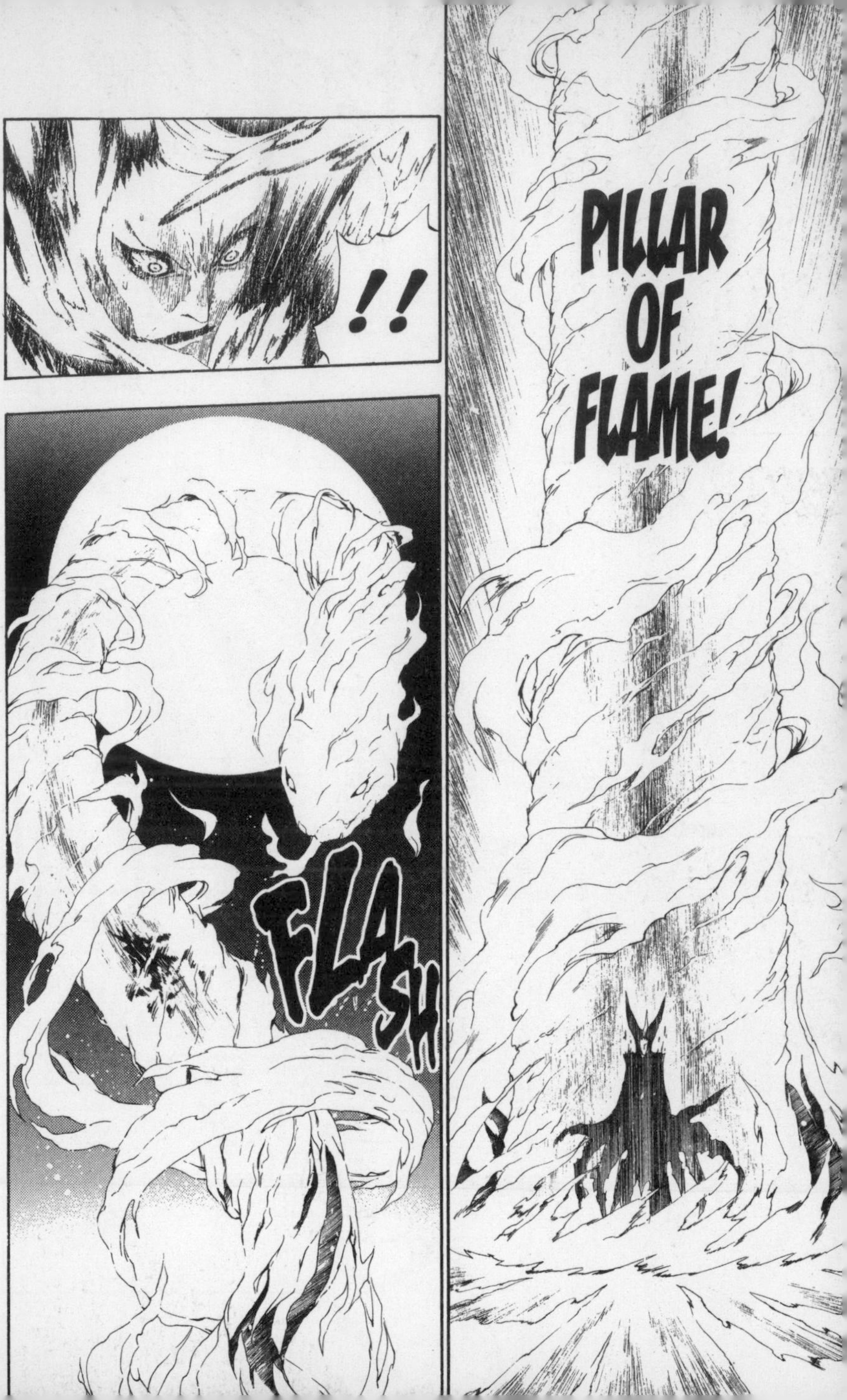
PILLAR OF FLAME!
!!
FLASH

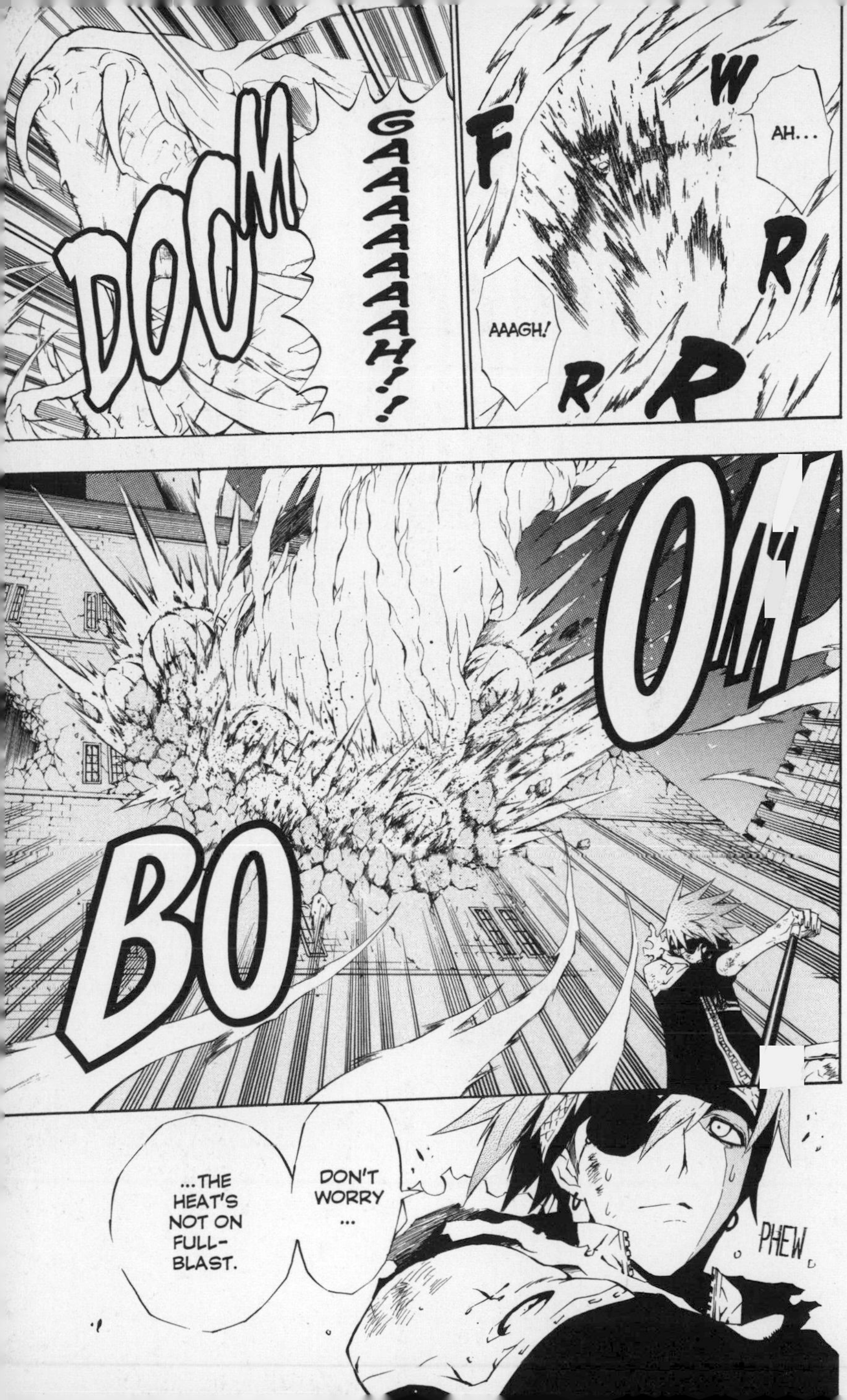

AH...
FWRRR
AAAGH!
GAAAAAAAAAH!!
DOOM
BOOM
DON'T WORRY ...
...THE HEAT'S NOT ON FULL-BLAST.
PHEW

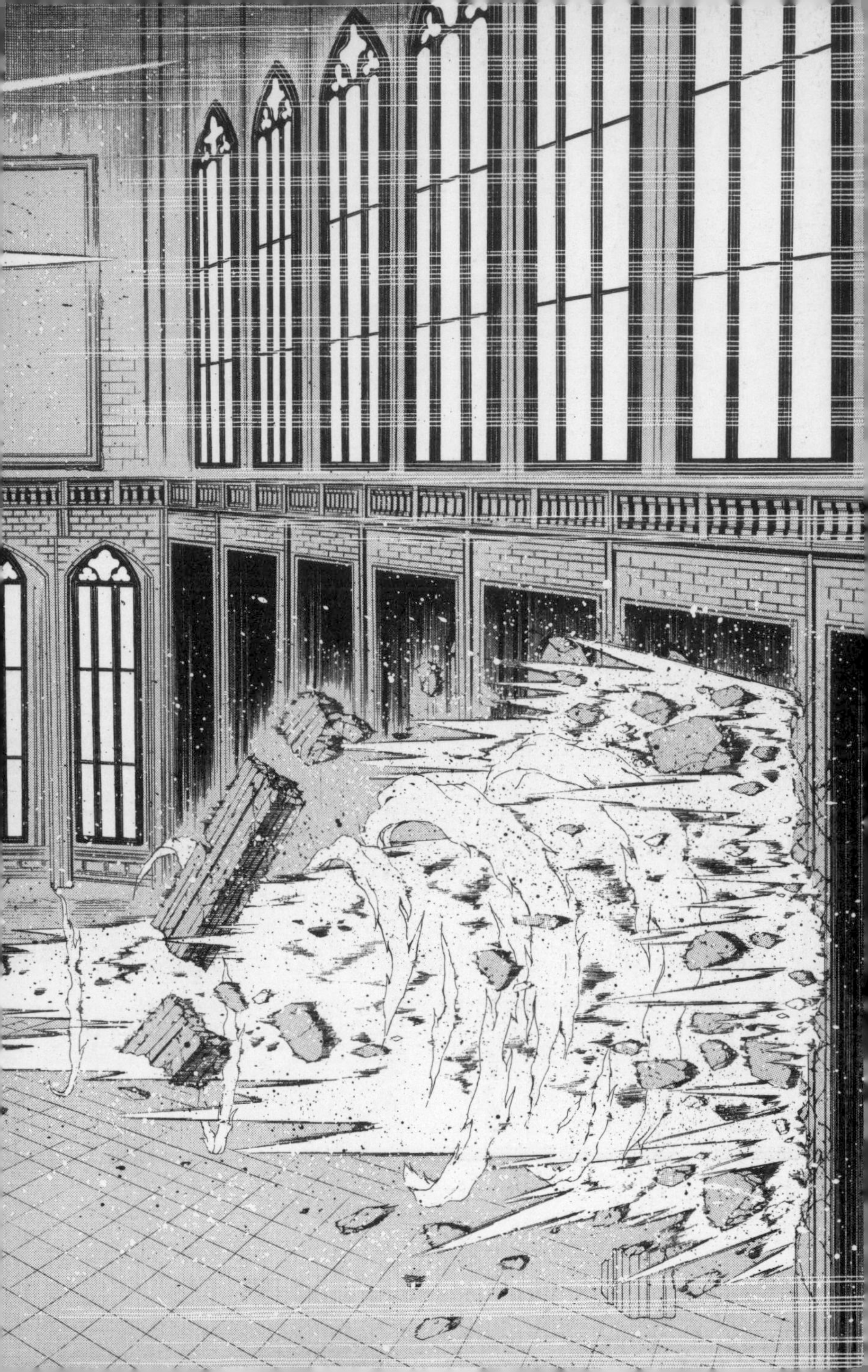

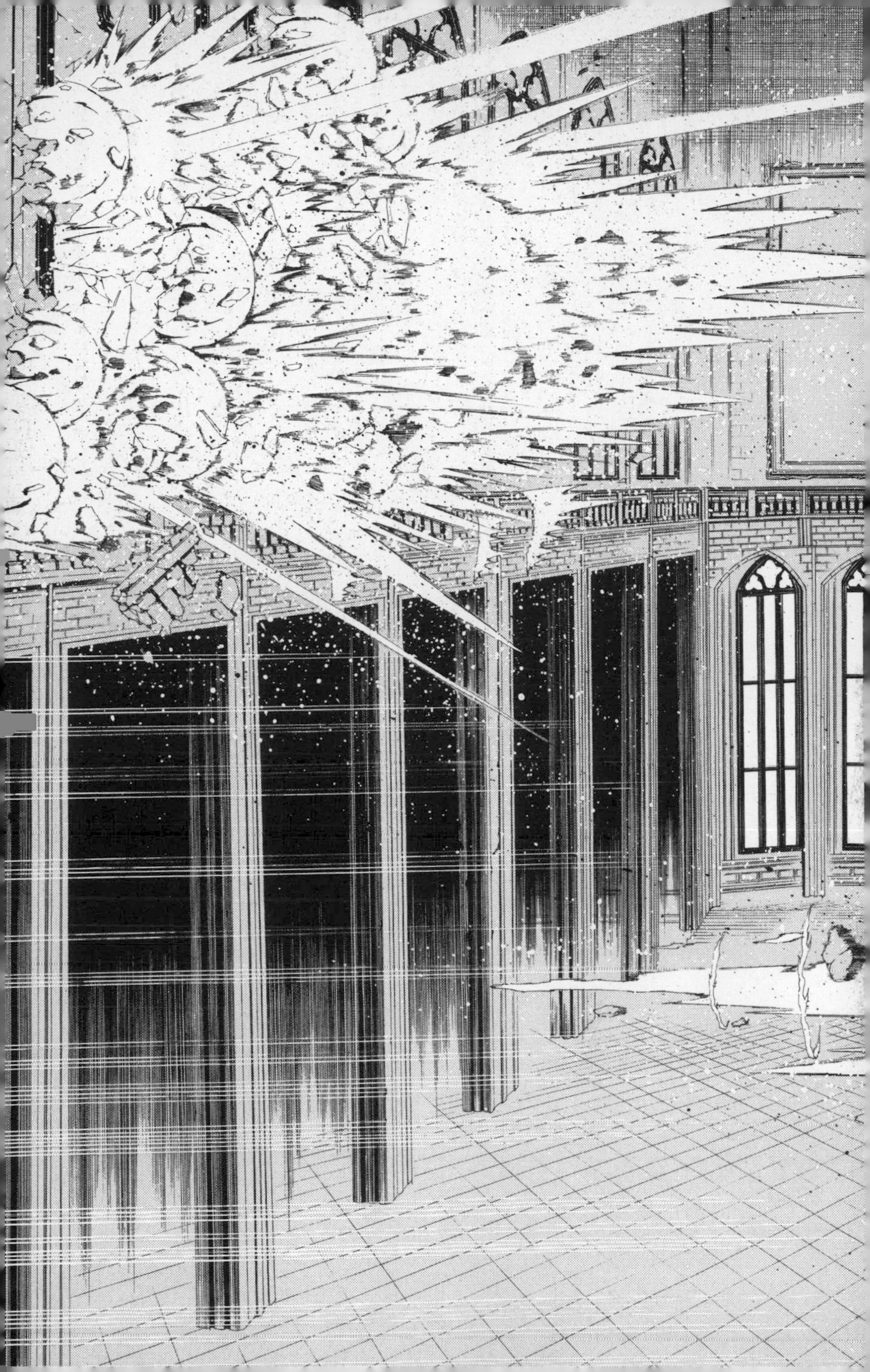

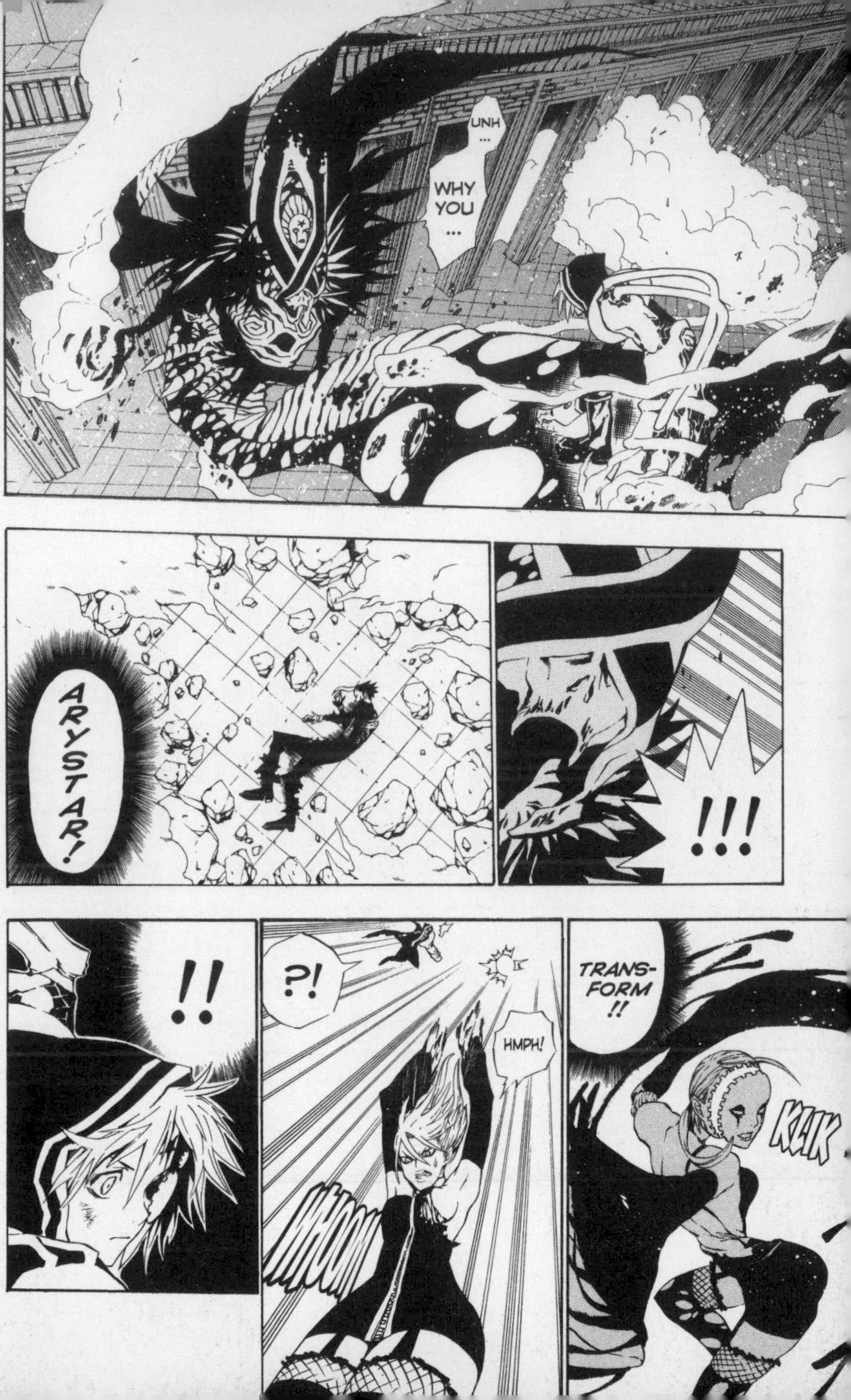
UNH ...
WHY YOU ...
!!!
ARYSTAR!
TRANS-FORM !!
KLIK
?!
HMPH!
!!

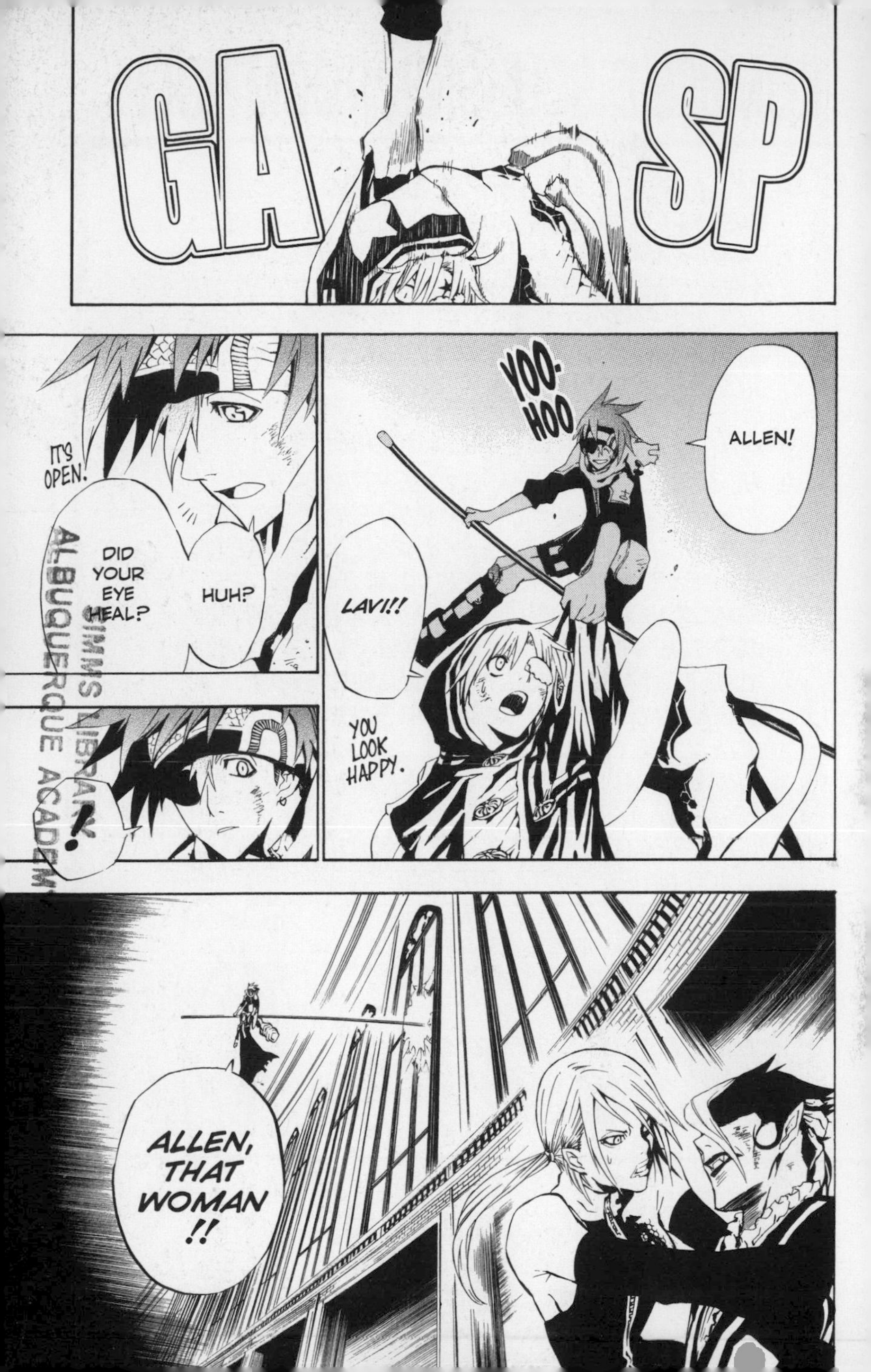
GASP
ALLEN!
YOO-HOO
LAVI!!
YOU LOOK HAPPY.
IT'S OPEN.
HUH?
DID YOUR EYE HEAL?
!
ALLEN, THAT WOMAN!!

KOMUI'S DISCUSSION ROOM VOL. 1

★ HELLO, REEVER WENHAM, SECTION LEADER OF THE BLACK ORDER'S SCIENCE DIVISION HERE. THIS IS ACTUALLY KOMUI'S JOB, ~~BUT THAT SON OF A GUN DUMPED IT ON ME!~~ UNFORTUNATELY, HE HAD OTHER COMMITMENTS, ~~THOUGH I'M JUST AS BUSY AS HE IS,~~ SO THE DUTY HAS FALLEN TO ME. SHALL WE BEGIN?

Q. WHY IS CHIEF KOMUI CALLED "CHIEF"?

A. AN EXCELLENT QUESTION. CENTURIES AGO, WHEN THE BLACK ORDER WAS FIRST FORMED, THE STAFF WASN'T VERY LARGE, AND THERE WERENT AS MANY SECTIONS AS THERE ARE NOW. THERE WAS JUST A COMMAND CENTER, AND THE MAN IN CHARGE WAS CALLED THE "CHIEF." THAT TITLE IS STILL USED TODAY, EVEN THOUGH THE ORDER IS ENORMOUS NOW. GIVEN OUR CURRENT CHIEF, YOU MIGHT NOT THINK THAT THIS IS A VERY HIGH POSITION, BUT IF YOU LOOK AT THE HIERARCHY CHART OF THE BLACK ORDER, YOU'LL SEE THE IMPORTANCE OF THE CHIEF. HAVE A LOOK AT THE CHART IN VOL. 2 OF THE DISCUSSION ROOM! (SEE PAGE 42!)
NOW IF ONLY CHIEF KOMUI WOULD BEHAVE LIKE AN OFFICER. (MUMBLE MUMBLE...)

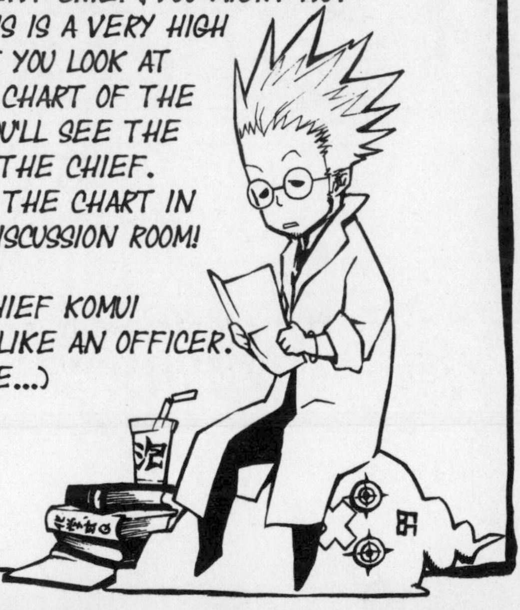

THE 38TH NIGHT: VAMPIRE OF THE CASTLE (PART 8)
BROKEN HEARTS, BROKEN ROSES

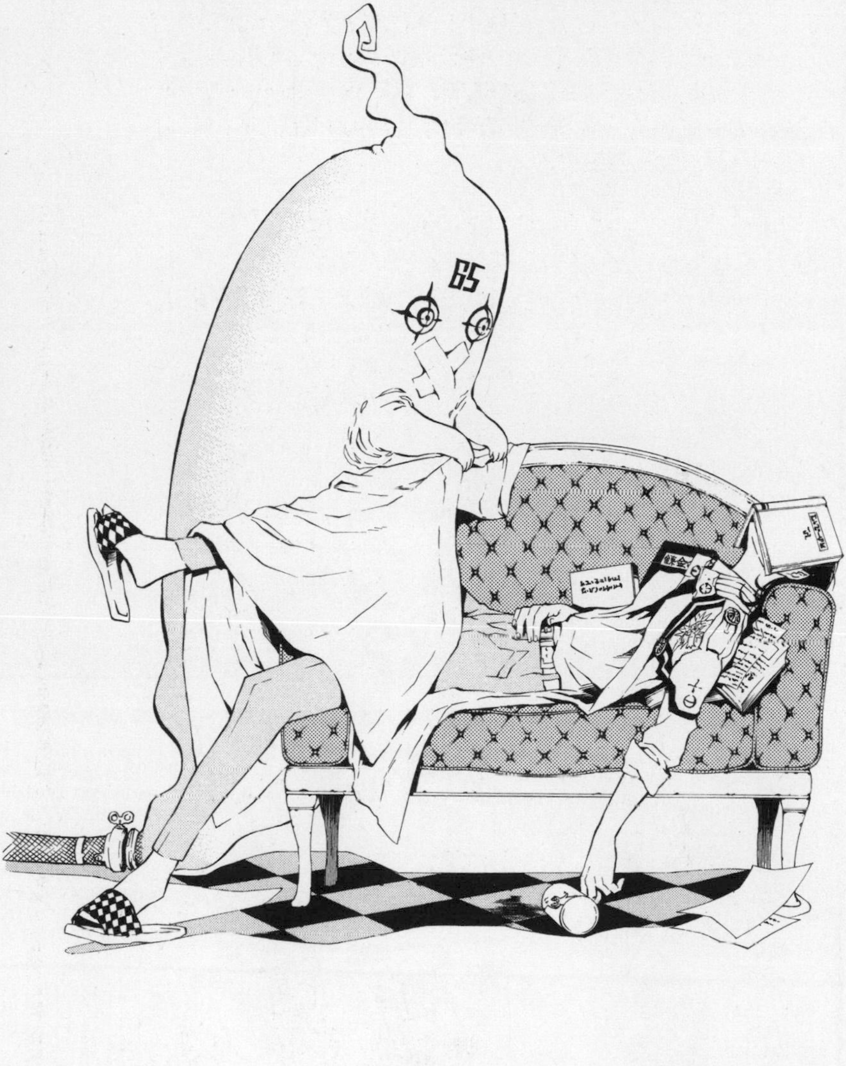
65

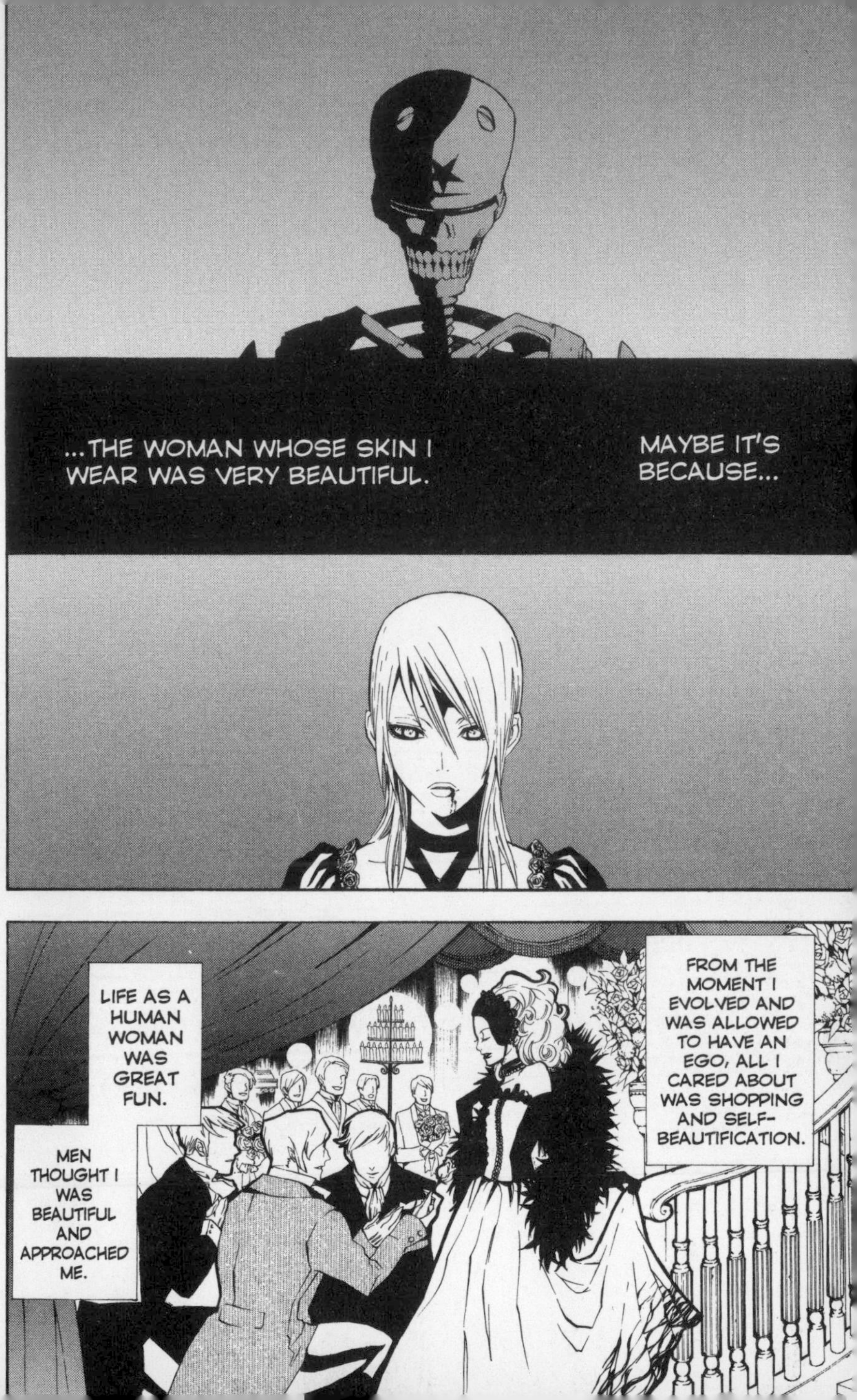
MAYBE IT'S BECAUSE...
...THE WOMAN WHOSE SKIN I WEAR WAS VERY BEAUTIFUL.
FROM THE MOMENT I EVOLVED AND WAS ALLOWED TO HAVE AN EGO, ALL I CARED ABOUT WAS SHOPPING AND SELF-BEAUTIFICATION.
LIFE AS A HUMAN WOMAN WAS GREAT FUN.
MEN THOUGHT I WAS BEAUTIFUL AND APPROACHED ME.

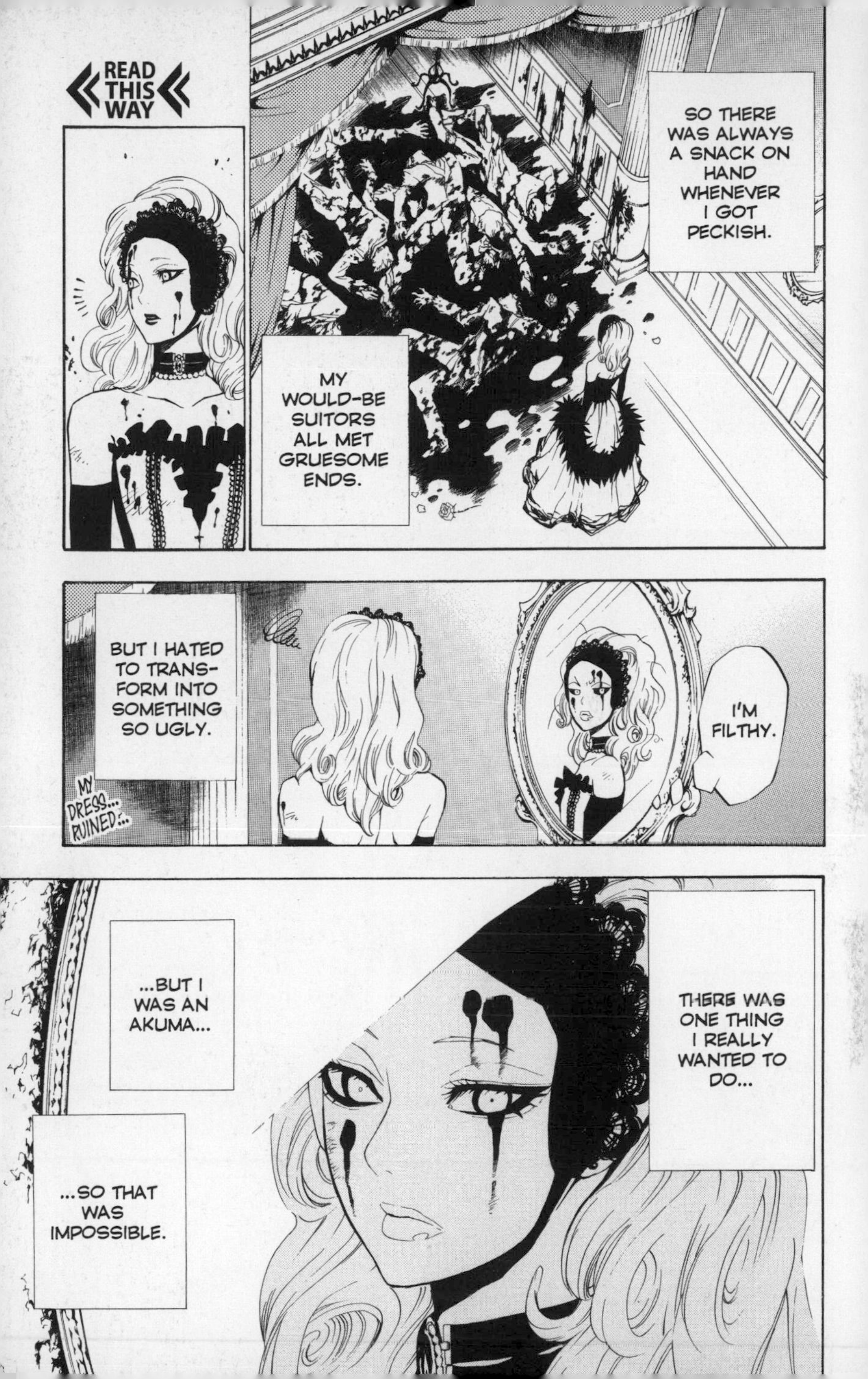
READ THIS WAY
SO THERE WAS ALWAYS A SNACK ON HAND WHENEVER I GOT PECKISH.
MY WOULD-BE SUITORS ALL MET GRUESOME ENDS.
I'M FILTHY.
BUT I HATED TO TRANS-FORM INTO SOMETHING SO UGLY.
MY DRESS... RUINED...
THERE WAS ONE THING I REALLY WANTED TO DO...
...BUT I WAS AN AKUMA...
...SO THAT WAS IMPOSSIBLE.

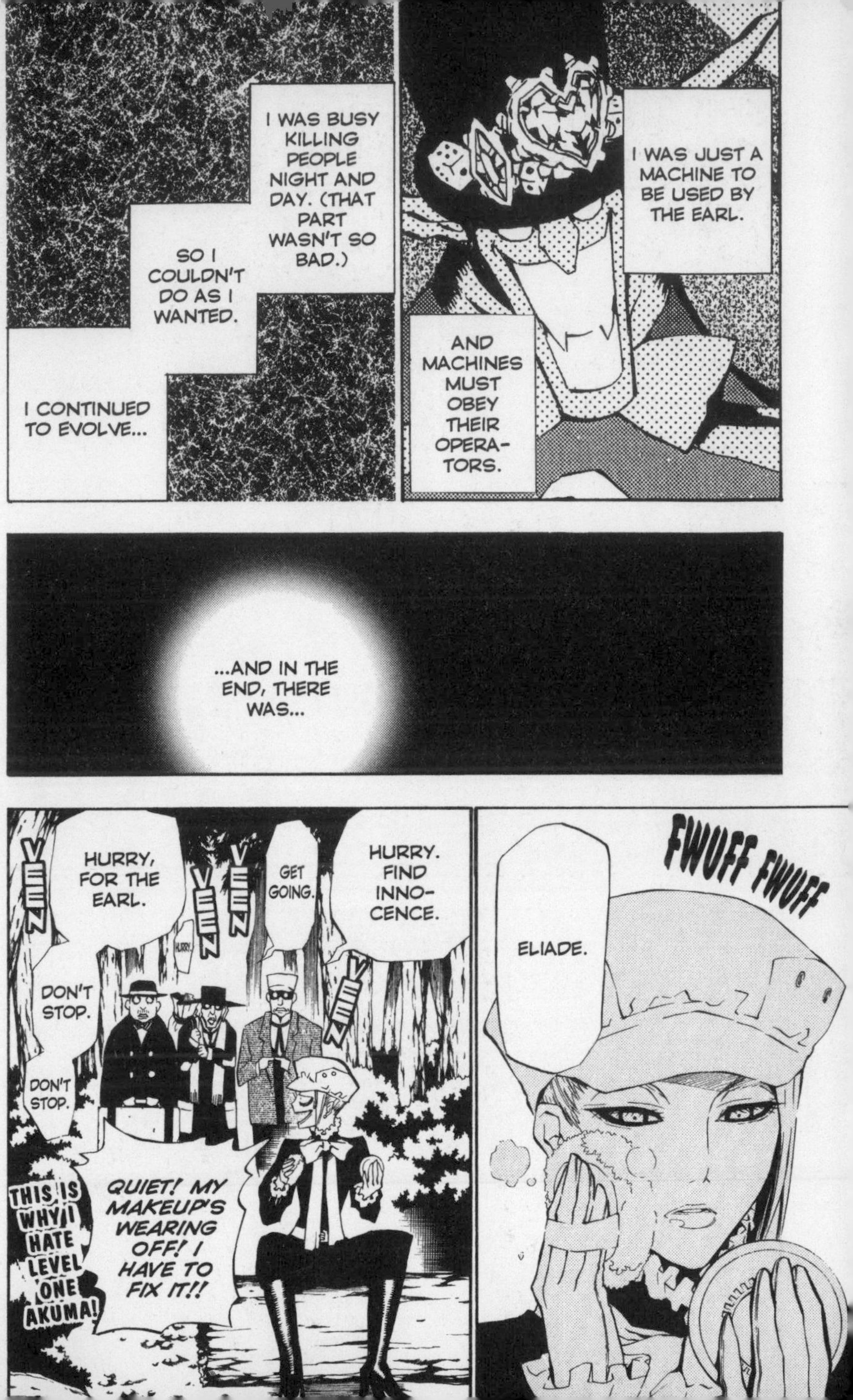
I WAS JUST A MACHINE TO BE USED BY THE EARL.
AND MACHINES MUST OBEY THEIR OPERA-TORS.
I WAS BUSY KILLING PEOPLE NIGHT AND DAY. (THAT PART WASN'T SO BAD.)
SO I COULDN'T DO AS I WANTED.
I CONTINUED TO EVOLVE...
...AND IN THE END, THERE WAS...
FWUFF FWUFF
ELIADE.
HURRY. FIND INNO-CENCE.
GET GOING.
VEEN
VEEN
VEEN
HURRY, FOR THE EARL.
VEEN
HURRY.
DON'T STOP.
DON'T STOP.
QUIET! MY MAKEUP'S WEARING OFF! I HAVE TO FIX IT!!
THIS IS WHY I HATE LEVEL ONE AKUMA!

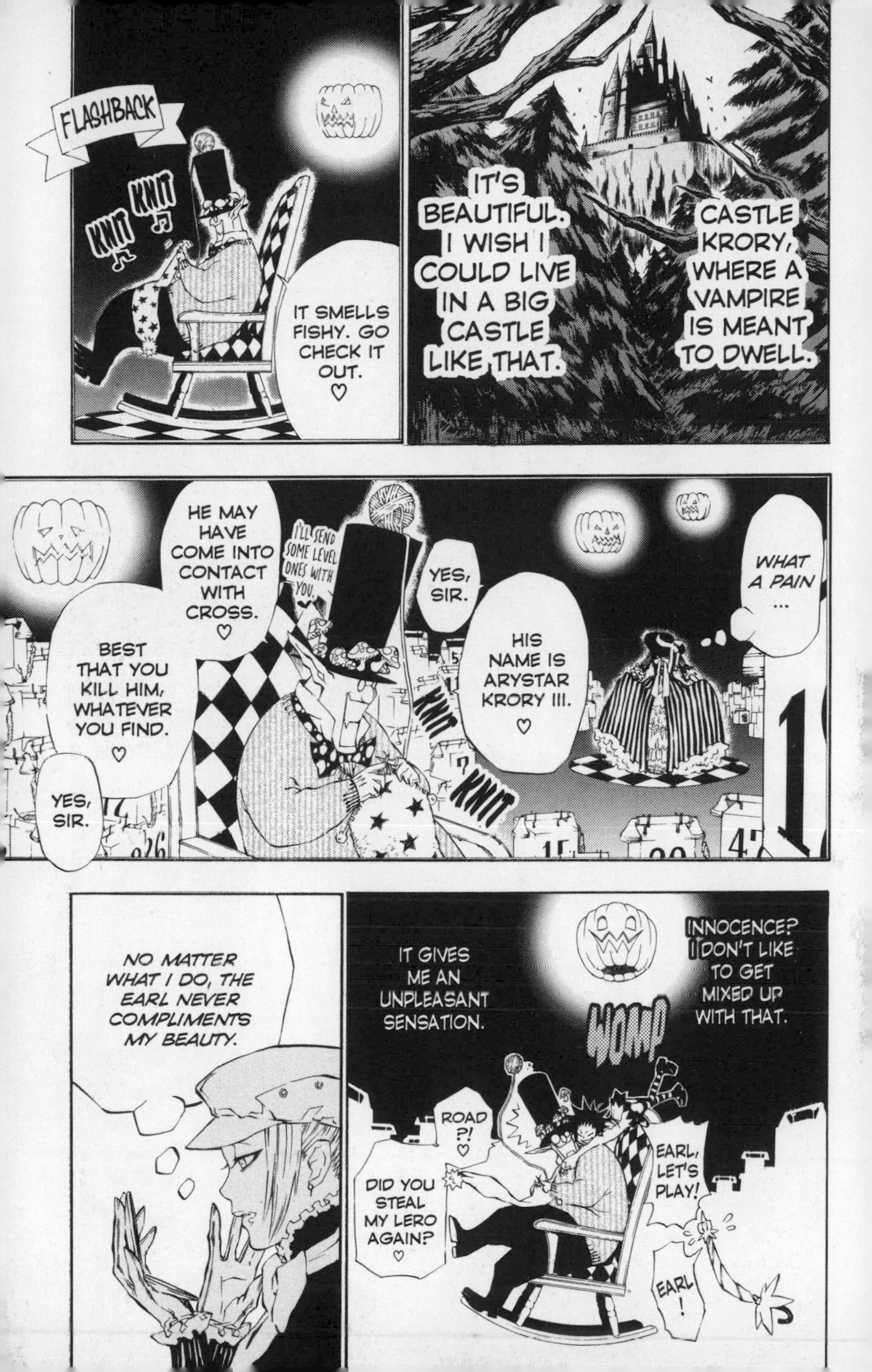
CASTLE KRORY, WHERE A VAMPIRE IS MEANT TO DWELL.
IT'S BEAUTIFUL. I WISH I COULD LIVE IN A BIG CASTLE LIKE THAT.
FLASHBACK
KNIT KNIT
IT SMELLS FISHY. GO CHECK IT OUT. ♡
WHAT A PAIN ...
HIS NAME IS ARYSTAR KRORY III. ♡
YES, SIR.
I'LL SEND SOME LEVEL ONES WITH YOU.
KNIT KNIT
HE MAY HAVE COME INTO CONTACT WITH CROSS. ♡
BEST THAT YOU KILL HIM, WHATEVER YOU FIND. ♡
YES, SIR.
INNOCENCE? I DON'T LIKE TO GET MIXED UP WITH THAT.
IT GIVES ME AN UNPLEASANT SENSATION.
WOMP
EARL, LET'S PLAY!
ROAD?! ♡
DID YOU STEAL MY LERO AGAIN? ♡
EARL!
NO MATTER WHAT I DO, THE EARL NEVER COMPLIMENTS MY BEAUTY.

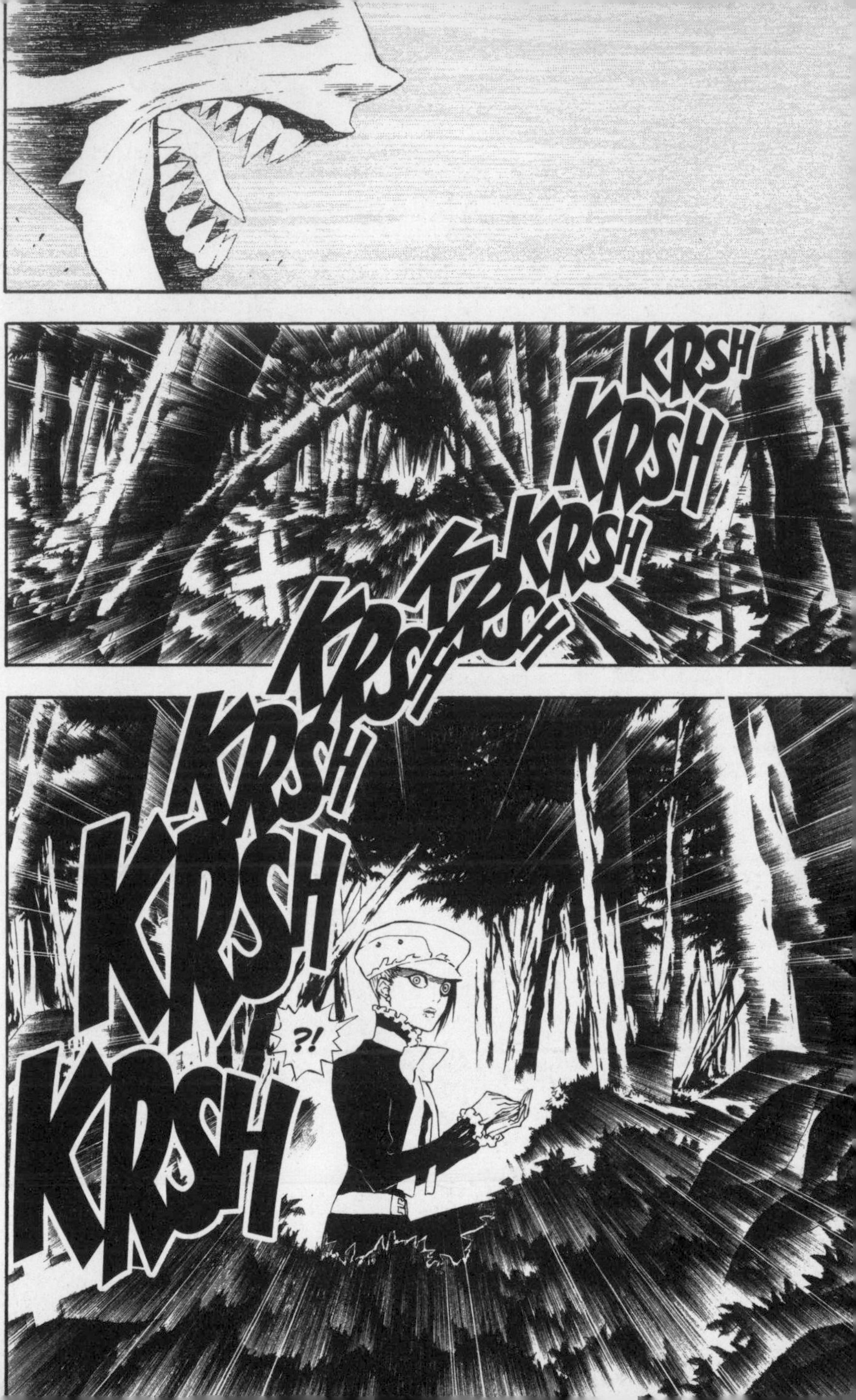
KRSH
KRSH
KRSH
KRSH
KRSH
KRSH
KRSH!
?!
KRSH

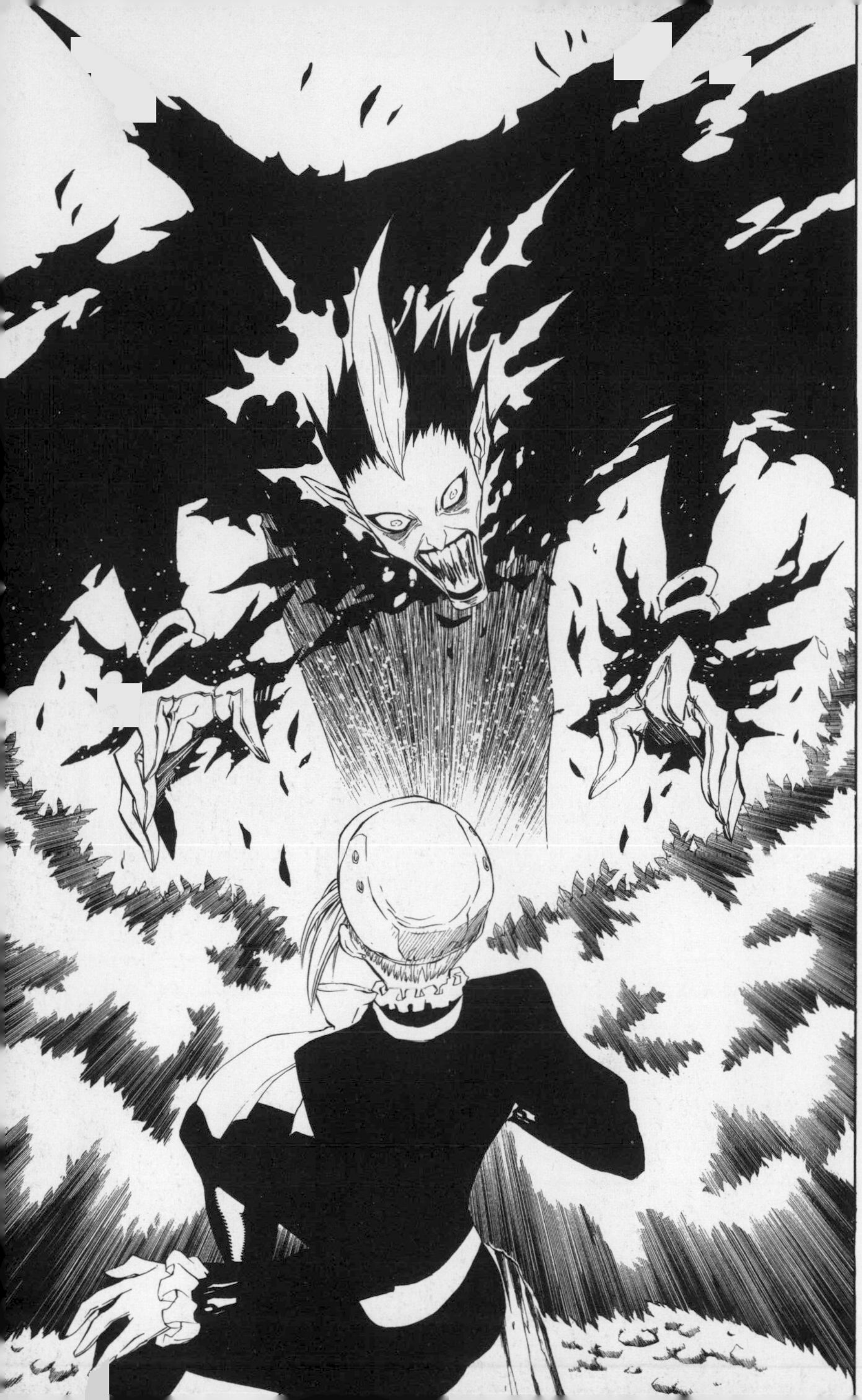

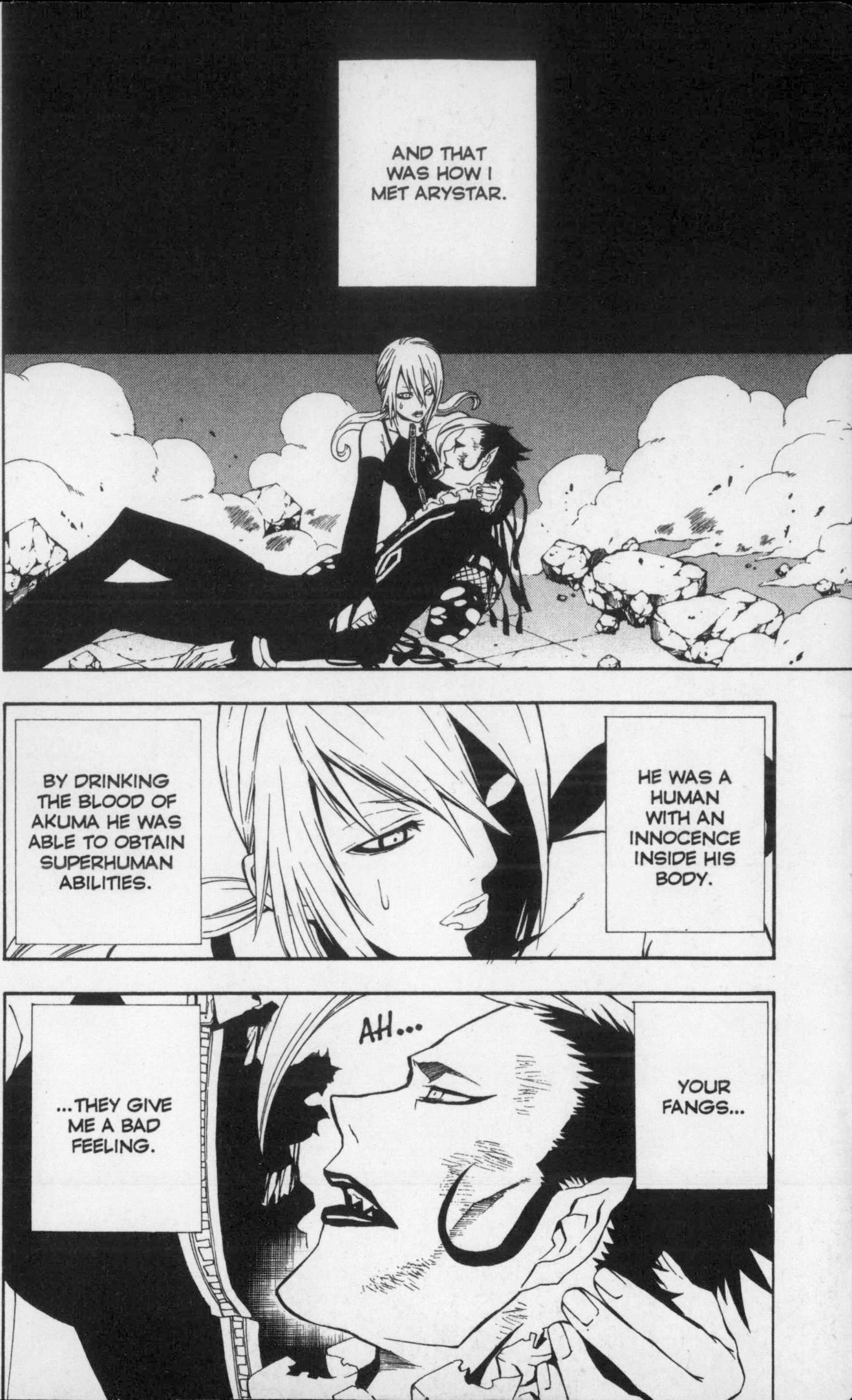
AND THAT WAS HOW I MET ARYSTAR.
HE WAS A HUMAN WITH AN INNOCENCE INSIDE HIS BODY.
BY DRINKING THE BLOOD OF AKUMA HE WAS ABLE TO OBTAIN SUPERHUMAN ABILITIES.
AH...
YOUR FANGS...
...THEY GIVE ME A BAD FEELING.

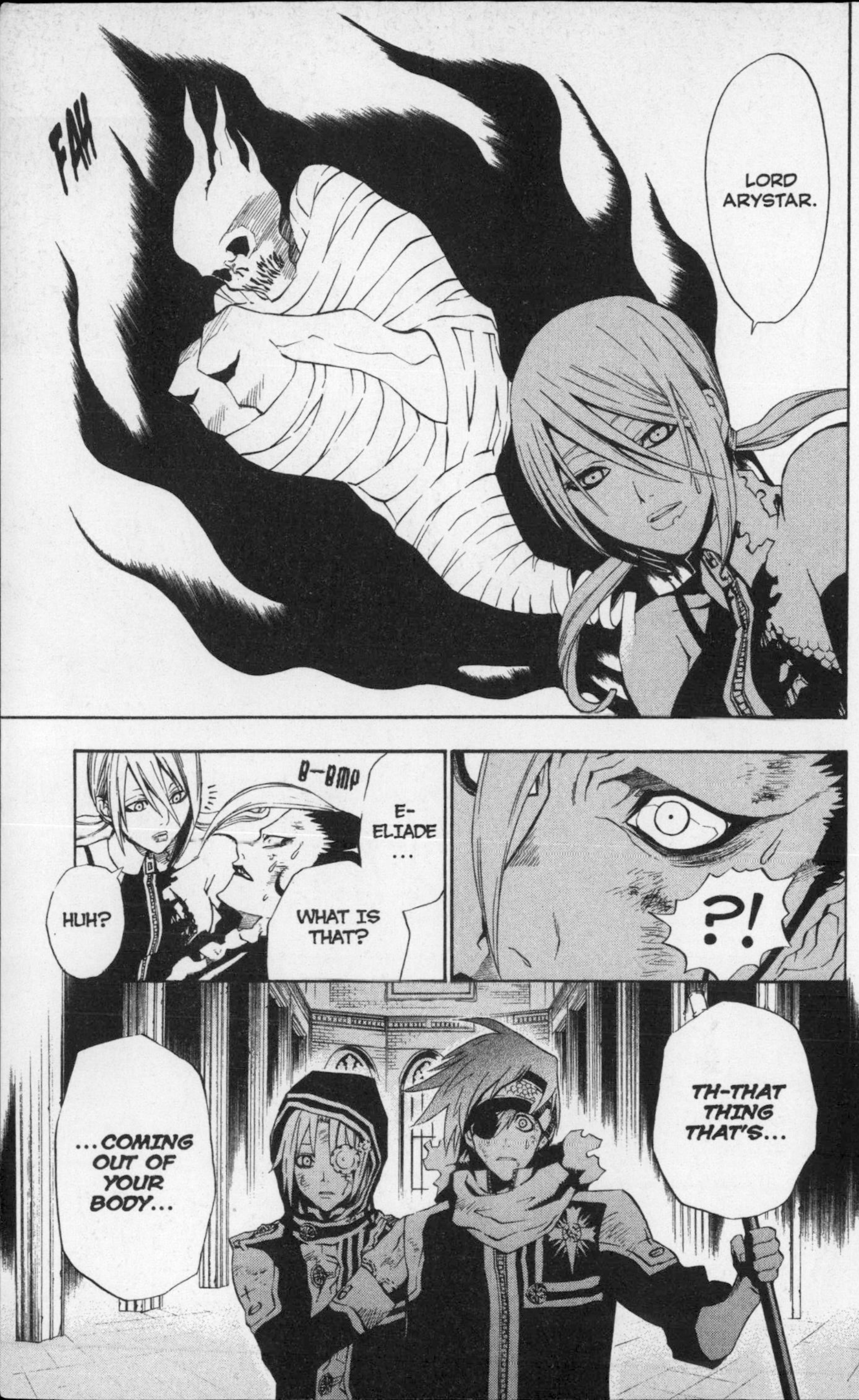
LORD ARYSTAR.
FAH
?!
B-BMP
E-ELIADE...
WHAT IS THAT?
HUH?
TH-THAT THING THAT'S...
...COMING OUT OF YOUR BODY...

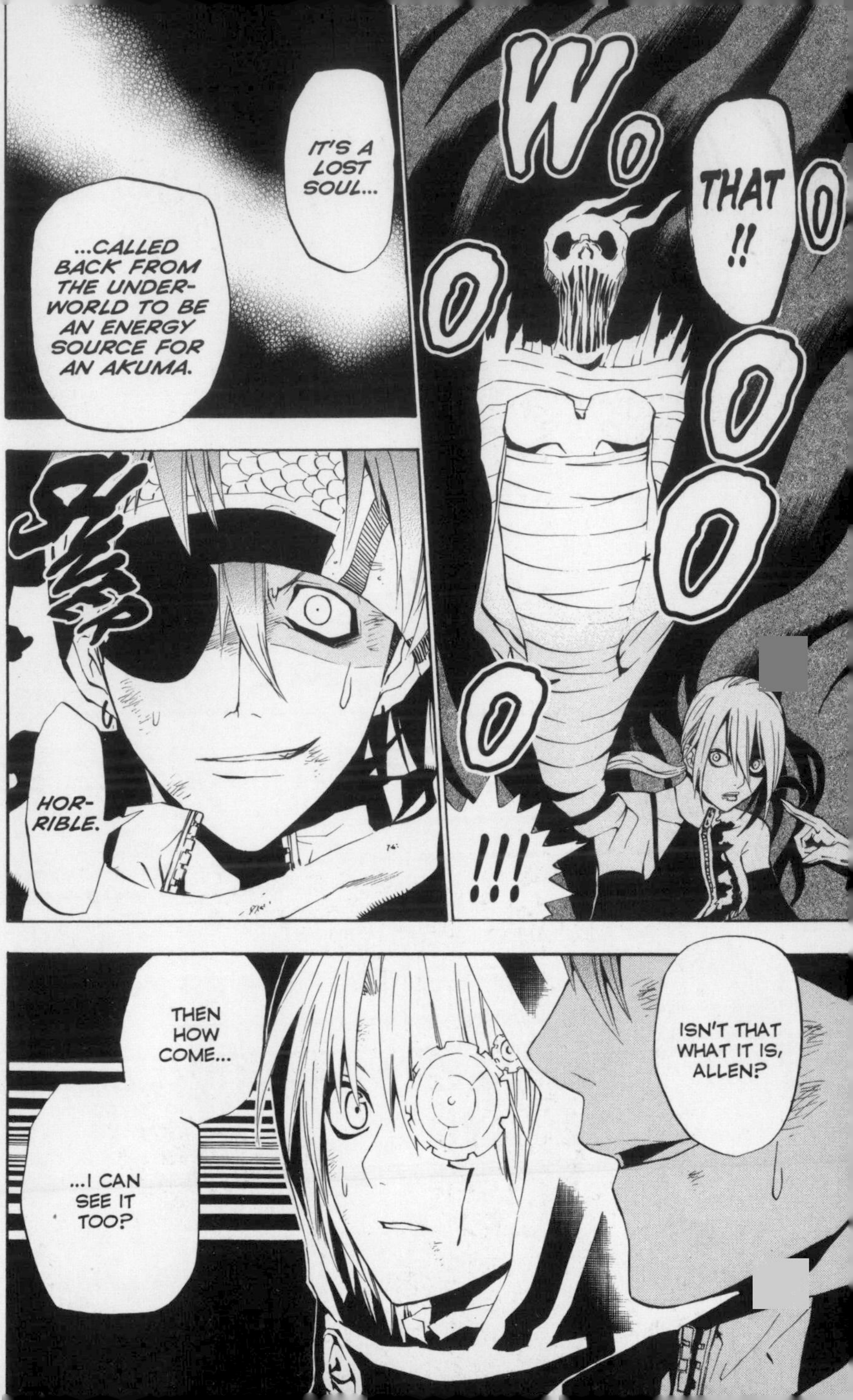
THAT !!
WOOOOOOOO
!!!
IT'S A LOST SOUL...
...CALLED BACK FROM THE UNDER-WORLD TO BE AN ENERGY SOURCE FOR AN AKUMA.
SHIVER
HOR-RIBLE.
ISN'T THAT WHAT IT IS, ALLEN?
THEN HOW COME...
...I CAN SEE IT TOO?

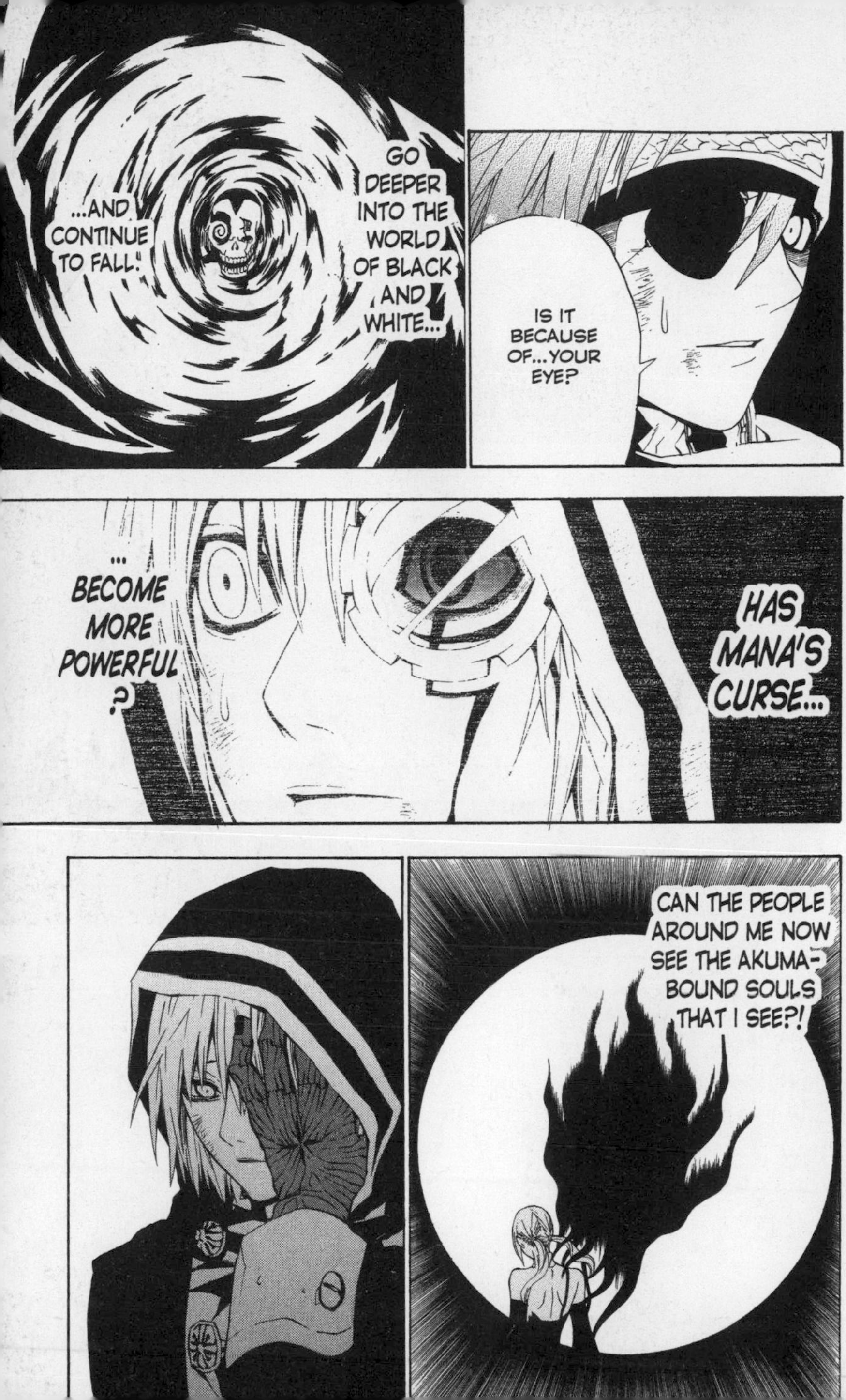
IS IT BECAUSE OF...YOUR EYE?
GO DEEPER INTO THE WORLD OF BLACK AND WHITE...
...AND CONTINUE TO FALL.
HAS MANA'S CURSE...
...BECOME MORE POWERFUL?
CAN THE PEOPLE AROUND ME NOW SEE THE AKUMA-BOUND SOULS THAT I SEE?!

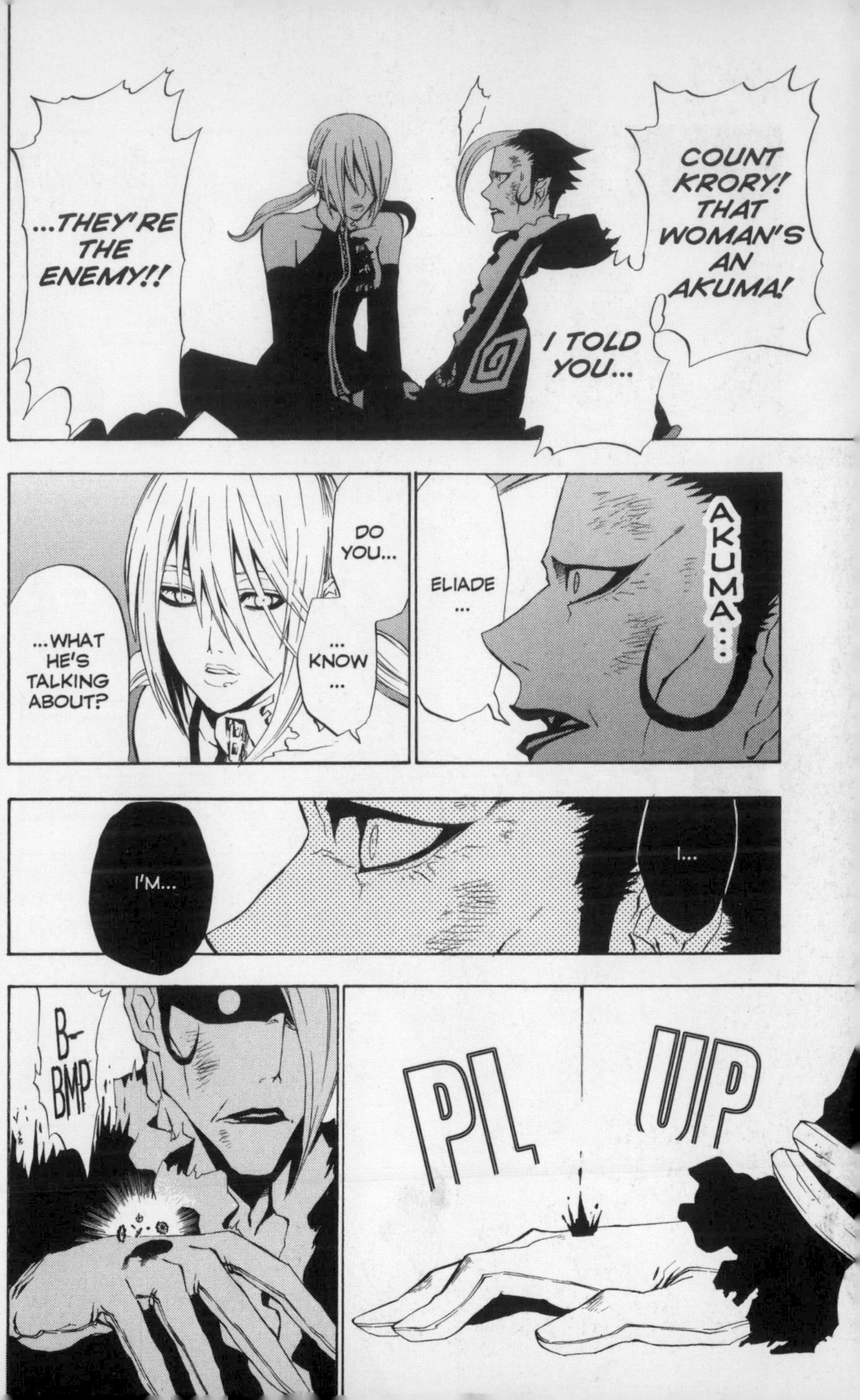
COUNT KRORY! THAT WOMAN'S AN AKUMA!
I TOLD YOU...
...THEY'RE THE ENEMY!!
AKUMA...
ELIADE ...
DO YOU...
... KNOW ...
...WHAT HE'S TALKING ABOUT?
I...
I'M...
PLUP
B-BMP

READ THIS WAY

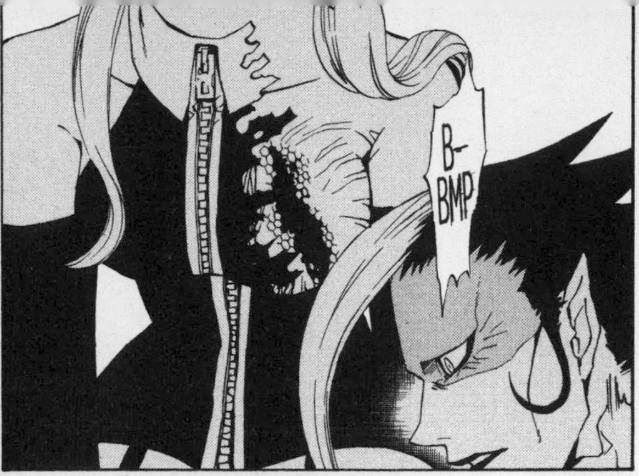
B-BMP

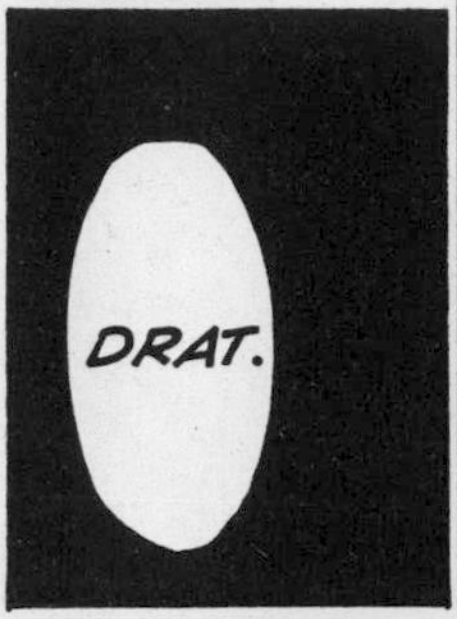
DRAT.

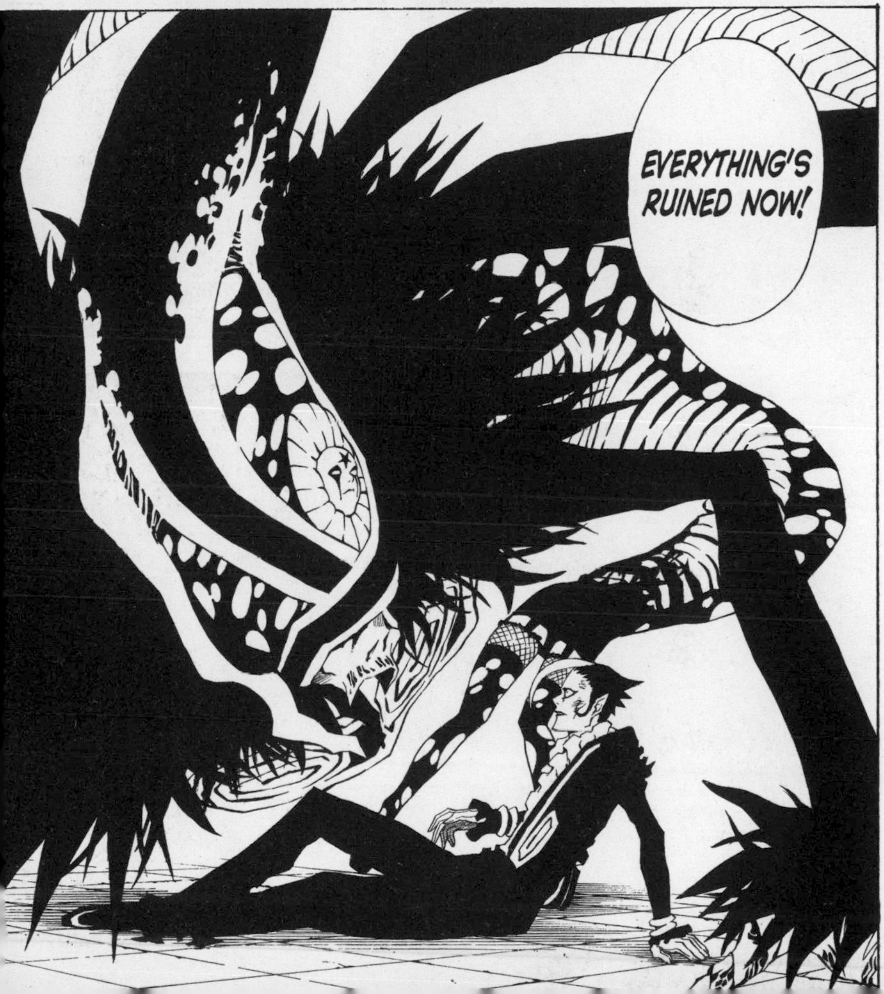
EVERYTHING'S RUINED NOW!

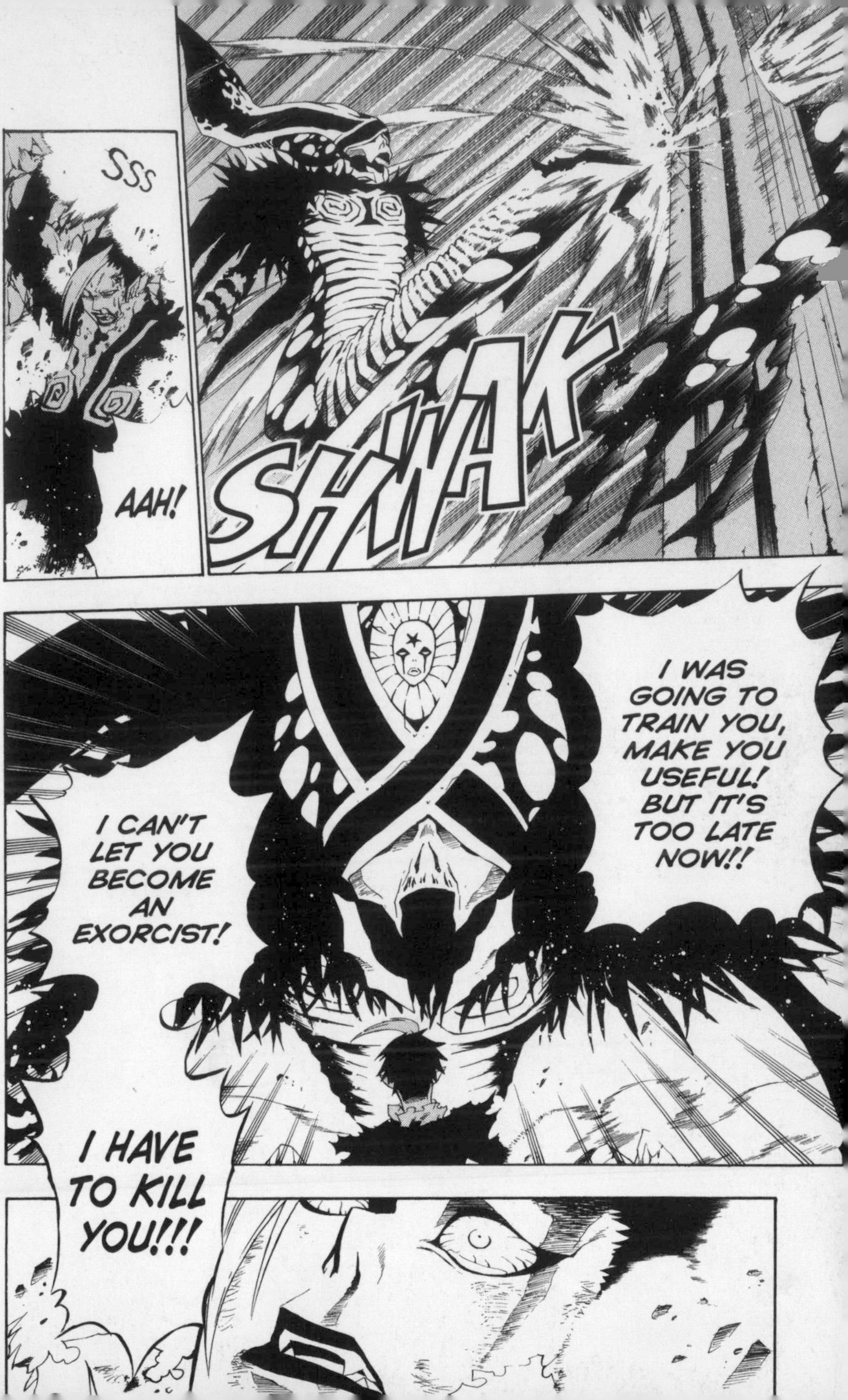
SHWAK
SSS
AAH!
I WAS GOING TO TRAIN YOU, MAKE YOU USEFUL! BUT IT'S TOO LATE NOW!!
I CAN'T LET YOU BECOME AN EXORCIST!
I HAVE TO KILL YOU!!!

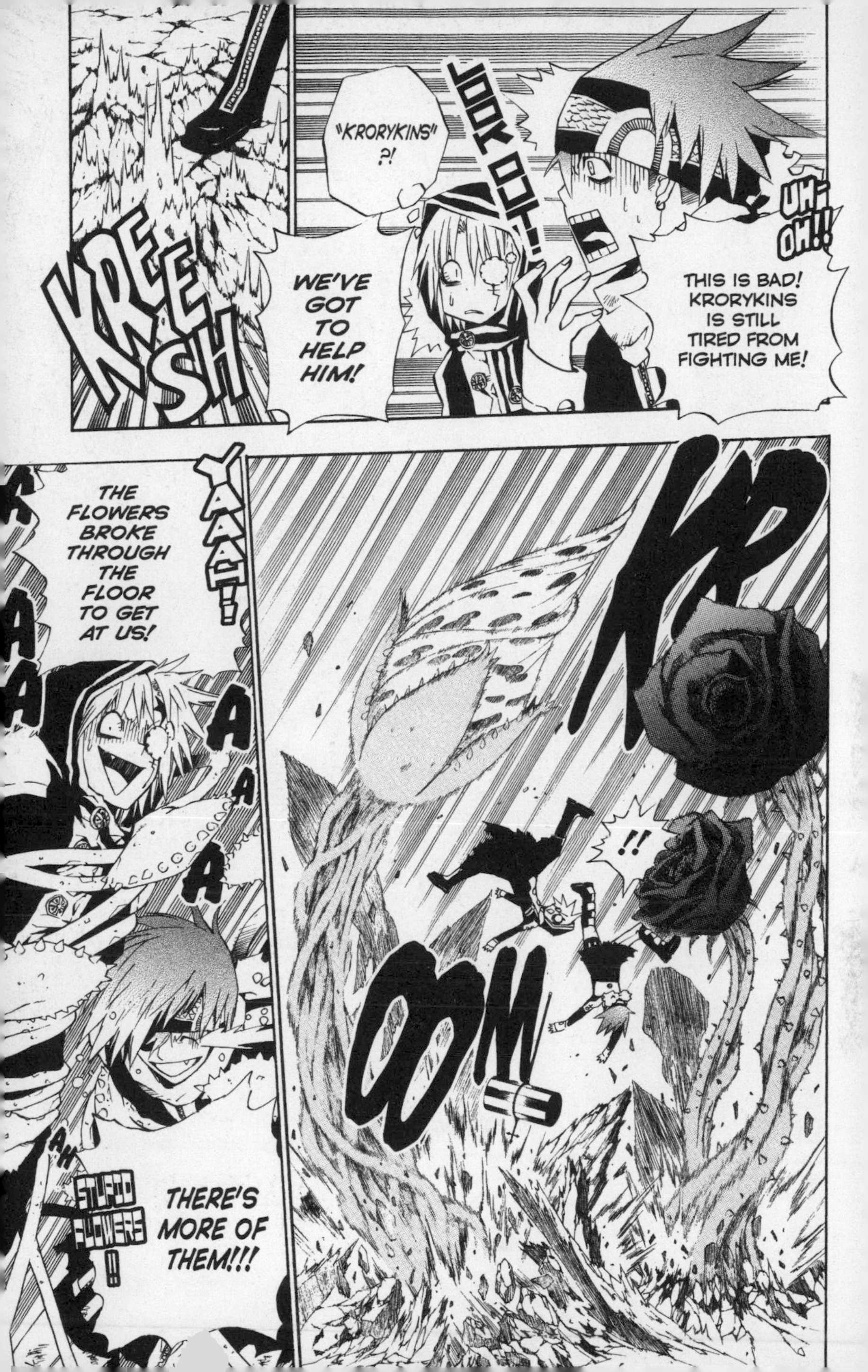
UH-OH!!
LOOK OUT!!
"KRORYKINS" ?!
THIS IS BAD! KRORYKINS IS STILL TIRED FROM FIGHTING ME!
WE'VE GOT TO HELP HIM!
KREESH
KR
!!
OOM
YAAAAH!
THE FLOWERS BROKE THROUGH THE FLOOR TO GET AT US!
AAAAAAA
THERE'S MORE OF THEM!!!
STUPID FLOWERS!!
AH

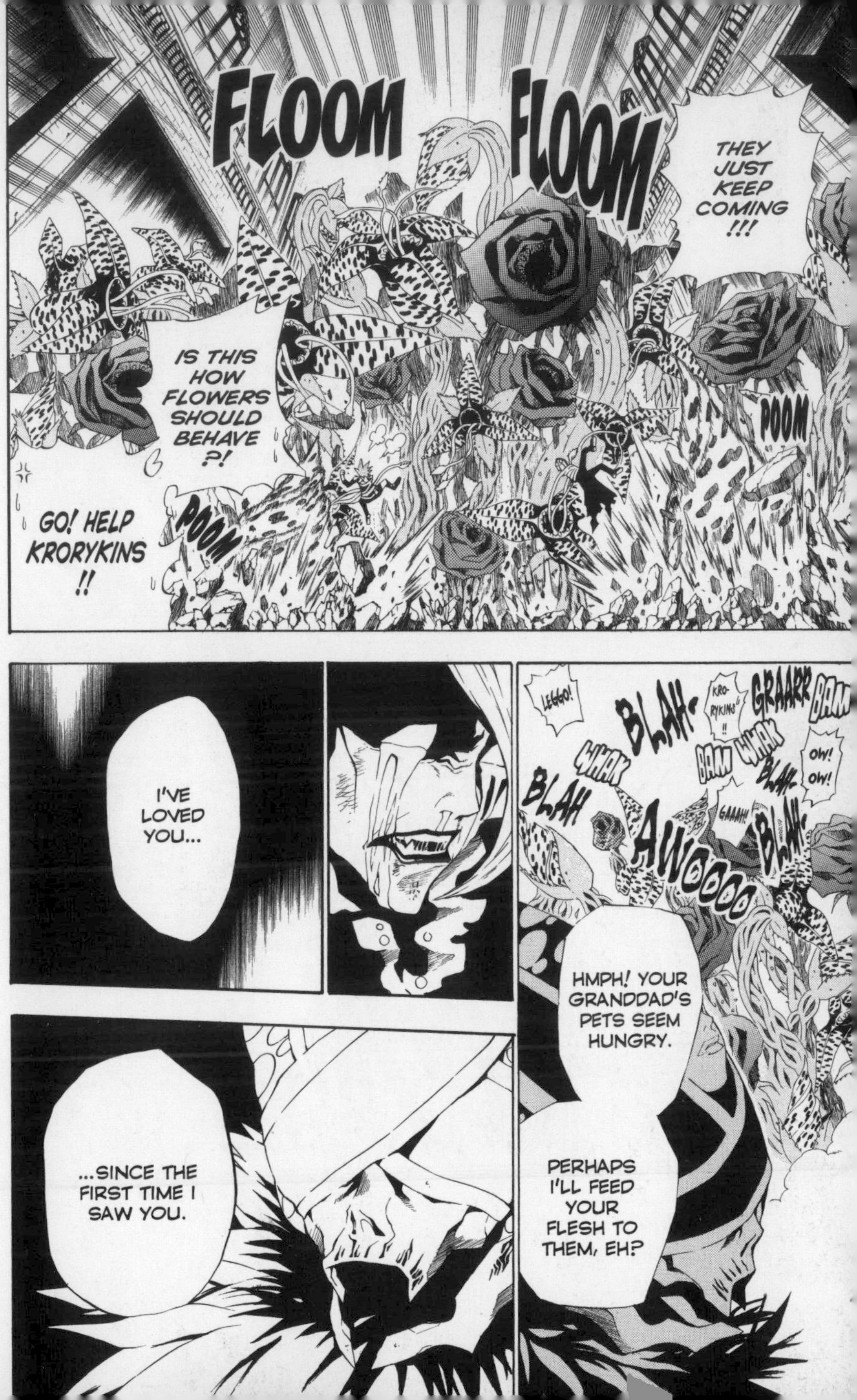
FLOOM
FLOOM
THEY JUST KEEP COMING!!!
POOM
IS THIS HOW FLOWERS SHOULD BEHAVE?!
GO! HELP KRORYKINS!!
POOM
BAM
GRAARR
KRO-RYKINS!!
BLAH
LEGGO!
OW! OW!
BLAH
WHAK
BAM
BLAH
WHAK
BLAH
BLAH
GAAAH!
AWOOOO
HMPH! YOUR GRANDDAD'S PETS SEEM HUNGRY.
PERHAPS I'LL FEED YOUR FLESH TO THEM, EH?
I'VE LOVED YOU...
...SINCE THE FIRST TIME I SAW YOU.

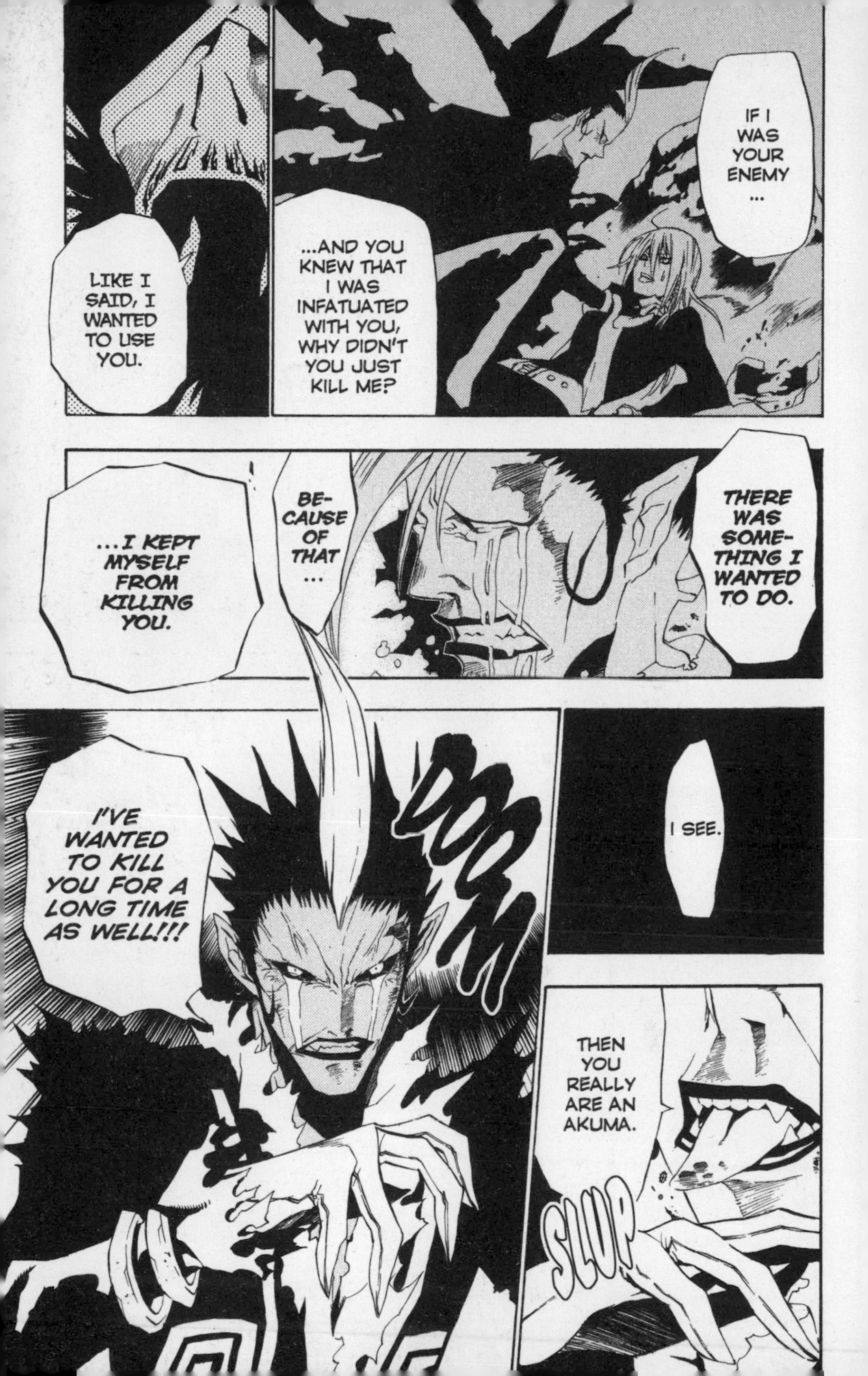
IF I WAS YOUR ENEMY ...
...AND YOU KNEW THAT I WAS INFATUATED WITH YOU, WHY DIDN'T YOU JUST KILL ME?
LIKE I SAID, I WANTED TO USE YOU.
THERE WAS SOMETHING I WANTED TO DO.
BECAUSE OF THAT ...
...I KEPT MYSELF FROM KILLING YOU.
I SEE.
THEN YOU REALLY ARE AN AKUMA.
SLUP
DOOM
I'VE WANTED TO KILL YOU FOR A LONG TIME AS WELL!!!

KOMUI'S DISCUSSION ROOM VOL. 2

THIS CHART SHOWS THE HIERARCHY OF THE BLACK ORDER. OVER THE CENTURIES OF FIGHTING THE MILLENNIUM EARL, IT'S GROWN VERY LARGE.

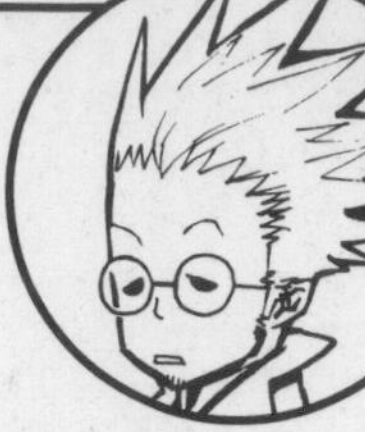

THE BLACK ORDER'S ORGANIZATIONAL HIERARCHY REVEALED!!

WHAT IS THE BLACK ORDER?!

CENTURIES AGO, WHEN THE CUBE WAS DISCOVERED IN NORTHERN EUROPE, THE VATICAN FORMED AN ORGANIZATION OF PEOPLE ATTUNED TO INNOCENCE CALLED "ACCOMMODATORS." THESE PEOPLE SCOUR THE WORLD FOR INNOCENCE. WITHIN THE ORGANIZATION ARE AGENTS OF THE VATICAN SENT TO OBSERVE THE ORDER.

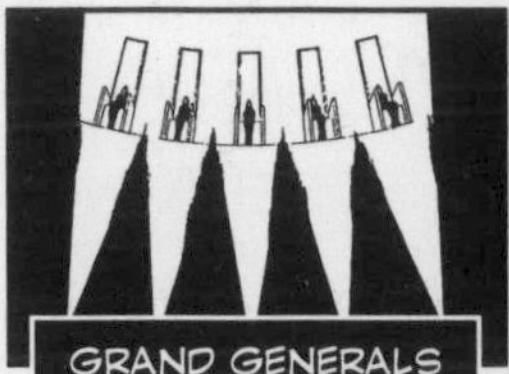

GRAND GENERALS

THEY GIVE THE ORDERS TO THE GENERALS AND OTHER OFFICERS. RUMOR HAS IT THEY HAVE LINKS TO THE VATICAN.

ACTIVE SERVICES

GENERALS

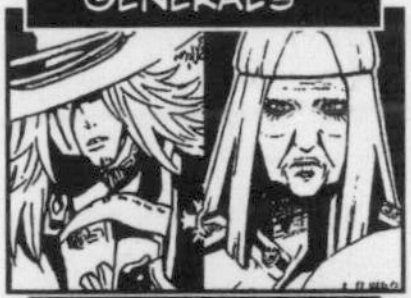

GENERALS RANK HIGHER THAN STANDARD EXORCISTS AND OFTEN GO ON SOLO MISSIONS.

EXORCISTS

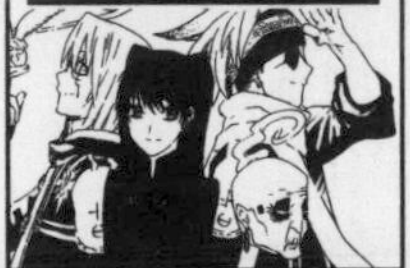

THOUGH NOMINALLY UNDER ONE OF THE GENERALS, DAY-TO-DAY ORDERS COME FROM KOMUI.

SECRET A COVERT GROUP MAY EXIST IN THE ACTIVE SERVICES...

SUPPORT SERVICES

CHIEF

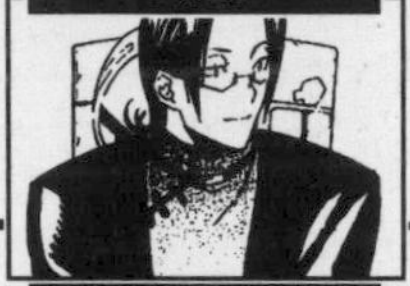

HE IS THE CHIEF OFFICER AND BRAINS OF THE ORDER, AND DIRECTS THE EXORCISTS.

WITHIN THE ORDER

THERE ARE SEVEN DEPARTMENTS WITHIN THE ORDER, EACH LED BY A SECTION CHIEF. MAIN DUTIES ARE OVERSEEING EUROPE AND COORDINATING THE VARIOUS WORLDWIDE BRANCHES.

- **SCIENCE SECTION** — RESPONSIBLE FOR R&D OF THE INNOCENCE, AND DESIGNING ORDER UNIFORMS.
- **INTELLIGENCE SECTION** — IN CHARGE OF THE FINDERS, WHO GATHER INFORMATION FROM AROUND THE WORLD.
- **MEDICAL SECTION** — RESPONSIBLE FOR THE GENERAL HEALTH AND WELFARE OF BLACK ORDER PERSONNEL.
- **SIGNAL SECTIONS** — IN CHARGE OF ALL COMMUNICATIONS BETWEEN EXORCISTS, FINDERS, AND THE ORDER.
- **SECURITY SECTION** — THEY GUARD ALL ENTRY POINTS (GATES, WATERWAYS, ETC.) INTO THE FACILITY.
- **DIPLOMATIC SECTION** — THEY HANDLE AFFAIRS WITH VARIOUS COUNTRIES AND ARRANGE FOR SUPPORT AND COOPERATION.
- **LOGISTICS SECTIONS** — IN CHARGE OF THE DAY-TO-DAY FUNCTIONING OF THE ORDER, INCLUDING MEALS, CLEANING, AND ACCOUNTING.

OUTSIDE THE ORDER

THE BLACK ORDER HAS BRANCHES THROUGHOUT THE WORLD TO SUPPORT THE EXORCISTS WHEREVER THEY MAY GO. EACH BRANCH IS OVERSEEN BY A BRANCH CHIEF.

- ASIA BRANCH
- MIDDLE EAST BRANCH
- AFRICA BRANCH
- NORTH AMERICA BRANCH
- SOUTH AMERICA BRANCH
- OCEANIA BRANCH

THE 39TH NIGHT: VAMPIRE OF THE CASTLE (PART 9) AFFECTION

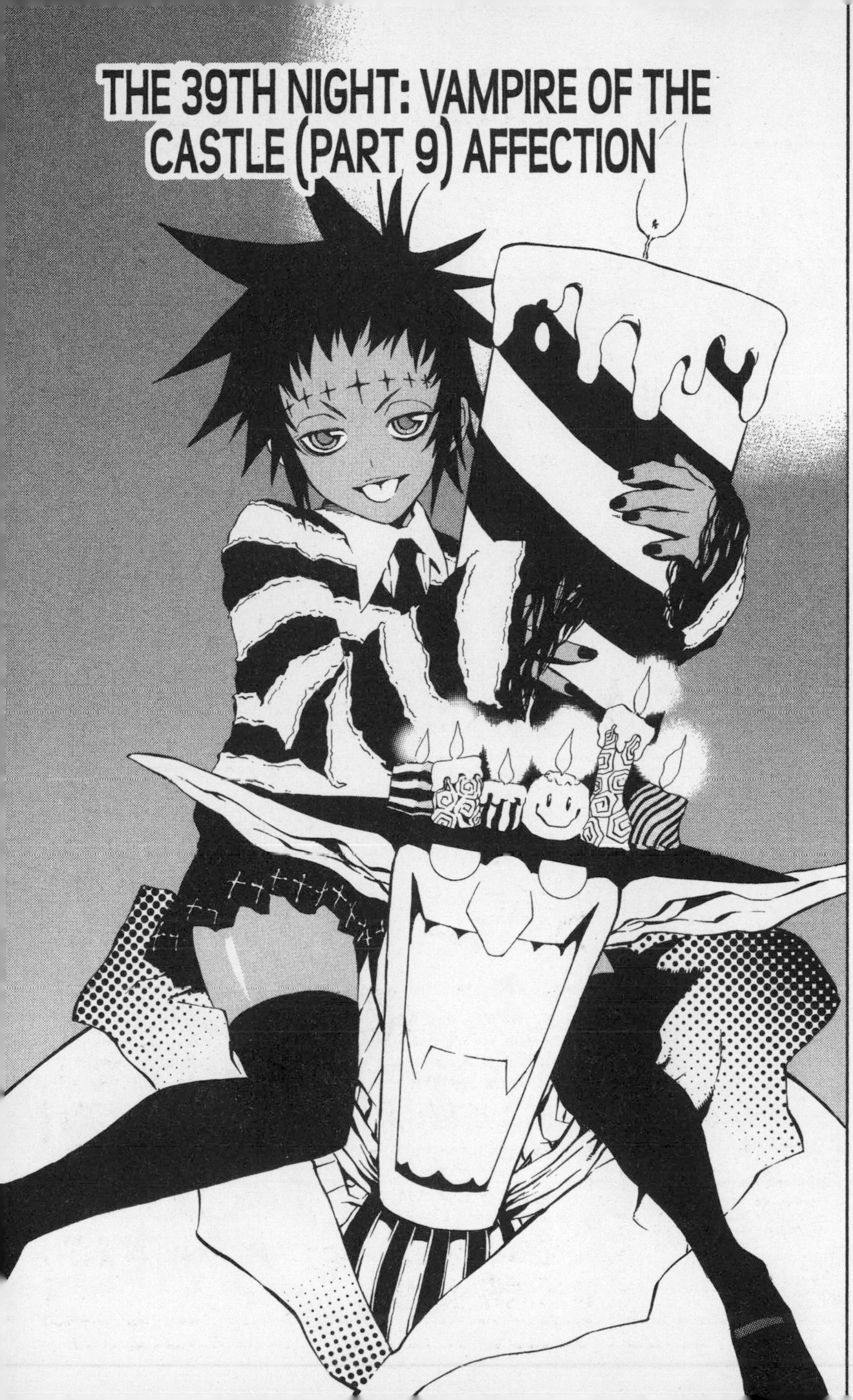

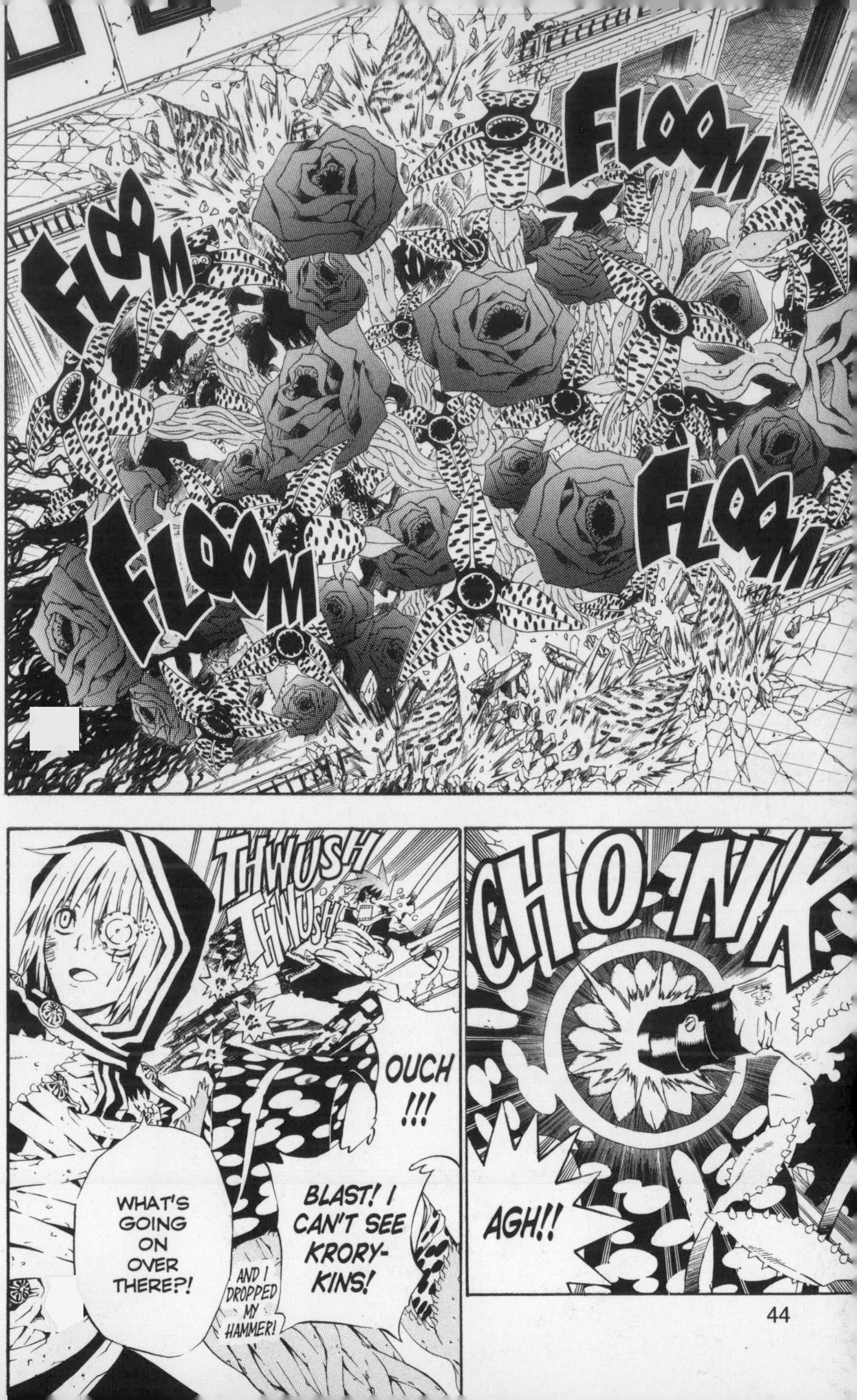
FLOOM
FLOOM
FLOOM
FLOOM
CHO-NK
AGH!!
THWUSH
THWUSH
OUCH!!!
BLAST! I CAN'T SEE KRORY-KINS!
AND I DROPPED MY HAMMER!
WHAT'S GOING ON OVER THERE?!

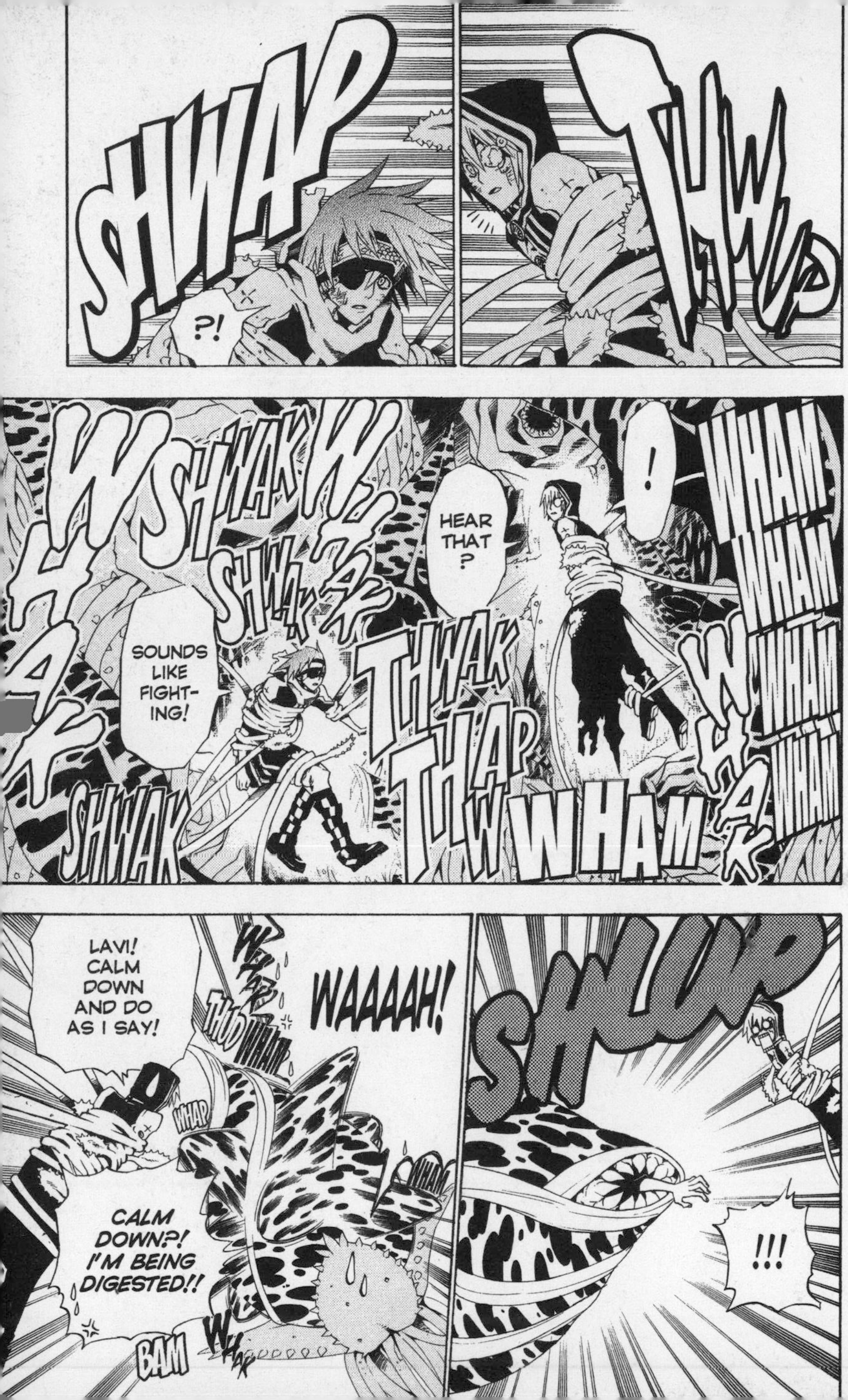
THWUP
SHWAP
?!
WHAM
WHAM
WHAM
WHAM
!
HEAR THAT?
WHAK
THWAK
THAP
THW
WHAM
SHWAK
SHWAK
SOUNDS LIKE FIGHT-ING!
SHWAK
SHWAK
SHLUP
!!!
WAAAAH!
THUD
WHAM
LAVI! CALM DOWN AND DO AS I SAY!
WHAP
WHAM
CALM DOWN?! I'M BEING DIGESTED!!
BAM

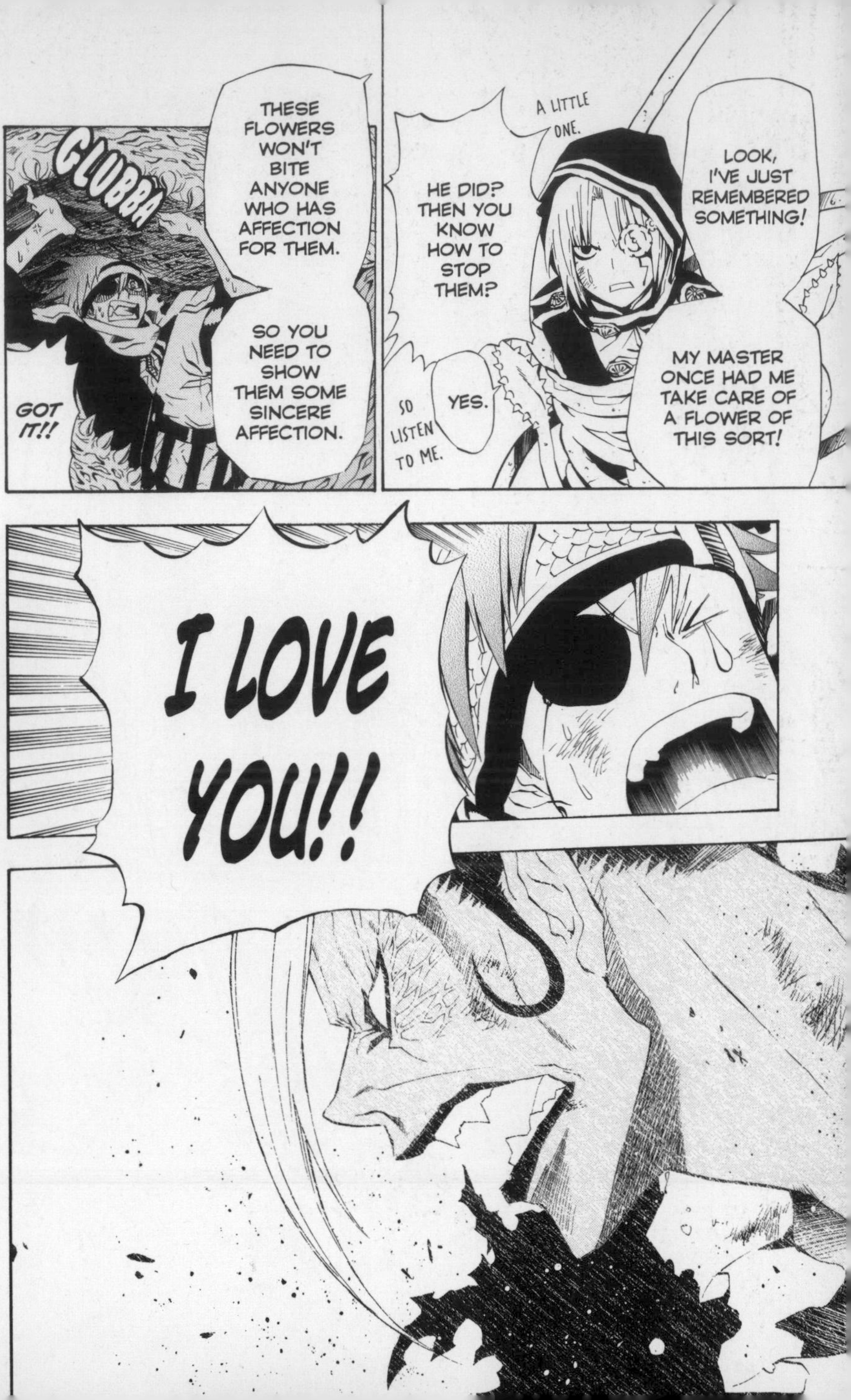
LOOK, I'VE JUST REMEMBERED SOMETHING!
MY MASTER ONCE HAD ME TAKE CARE OF A FLOWER OF THIS SORT!
A LITTLE ONE.
HE DID? THEN YOU KNOW HOW TO STOP THEM?
YES.
SO LISTEN TO ME.
THESE FLOWERS WON'T BITE ANYONE WHO HAS AFFECTION FOR THEM.
SO YOU NEED TO SHOW THEM SOME SINCERE AFFECTION.
GLUBBA
GOT IT!!
I LOVE YOU!!

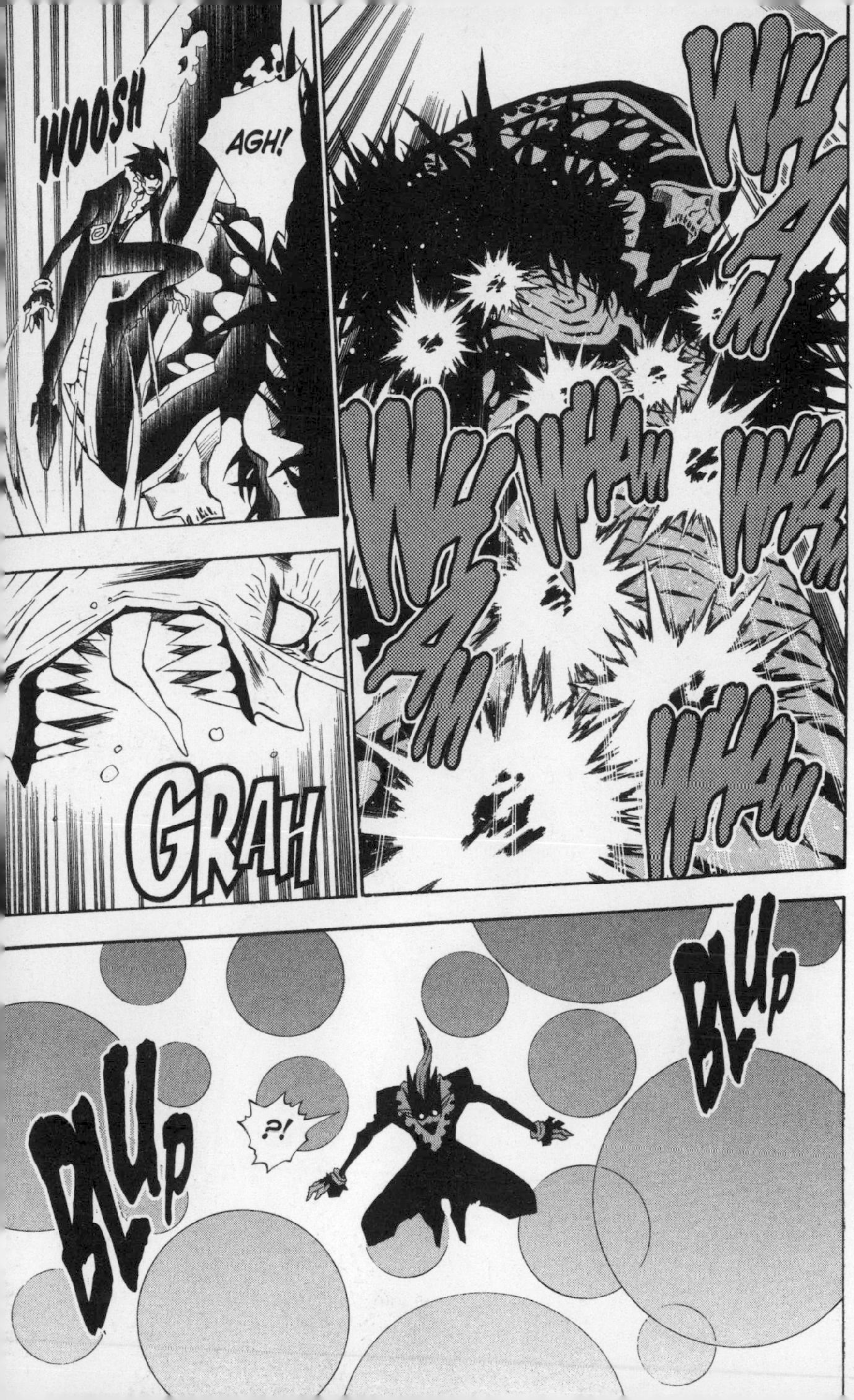
WHAM
WHAM
WHAM
WHAM
WHAM
WOOSH
AGH!
GRAH
BLUP
?!
BLUP

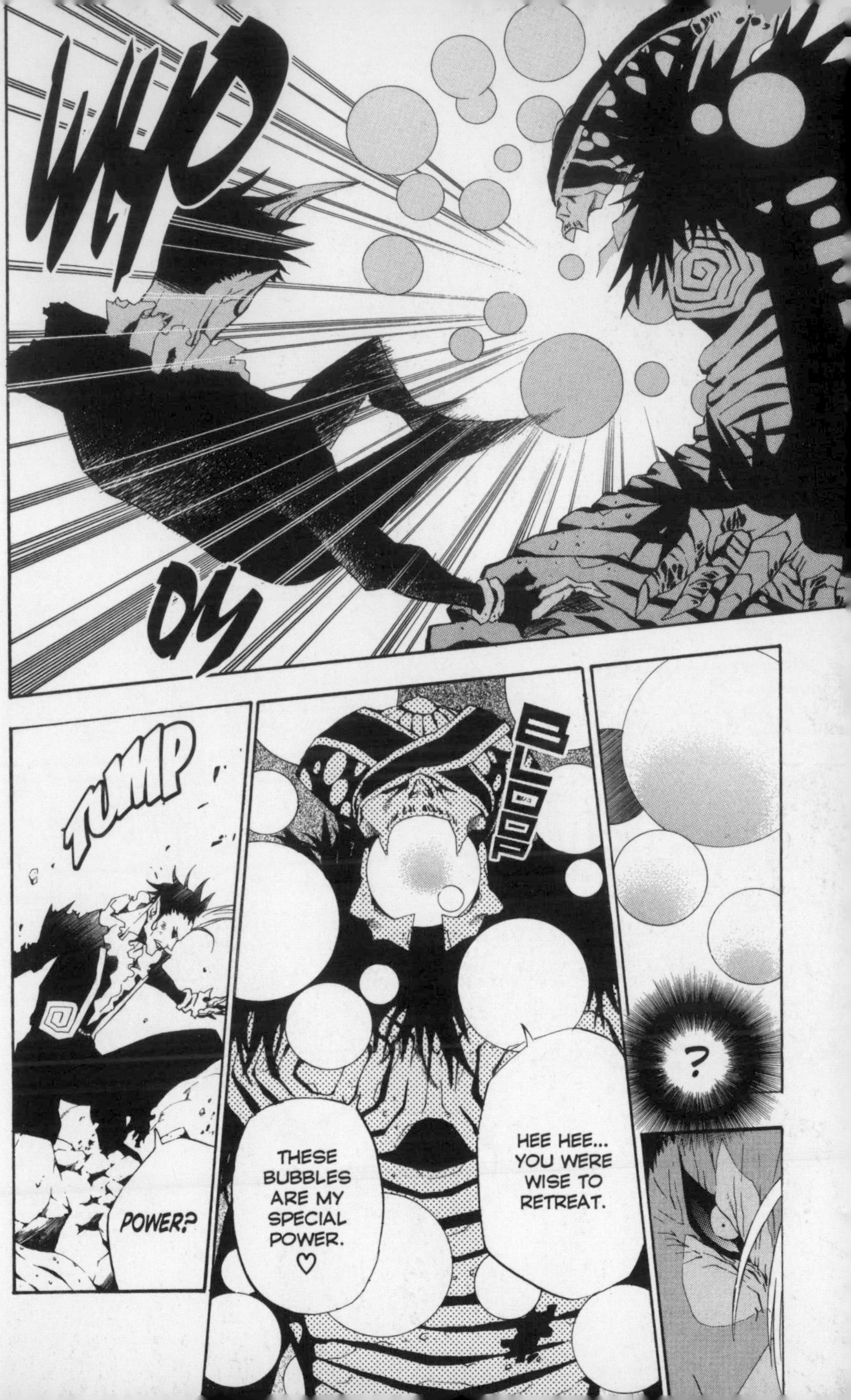
WAP
OY
?
BLOOP
HEE HEE... YOU WERE WISE TO RETREAT.
THESE BUBBLES ARE MY SPECIAL POWER. ♡
TUMP
POWER?

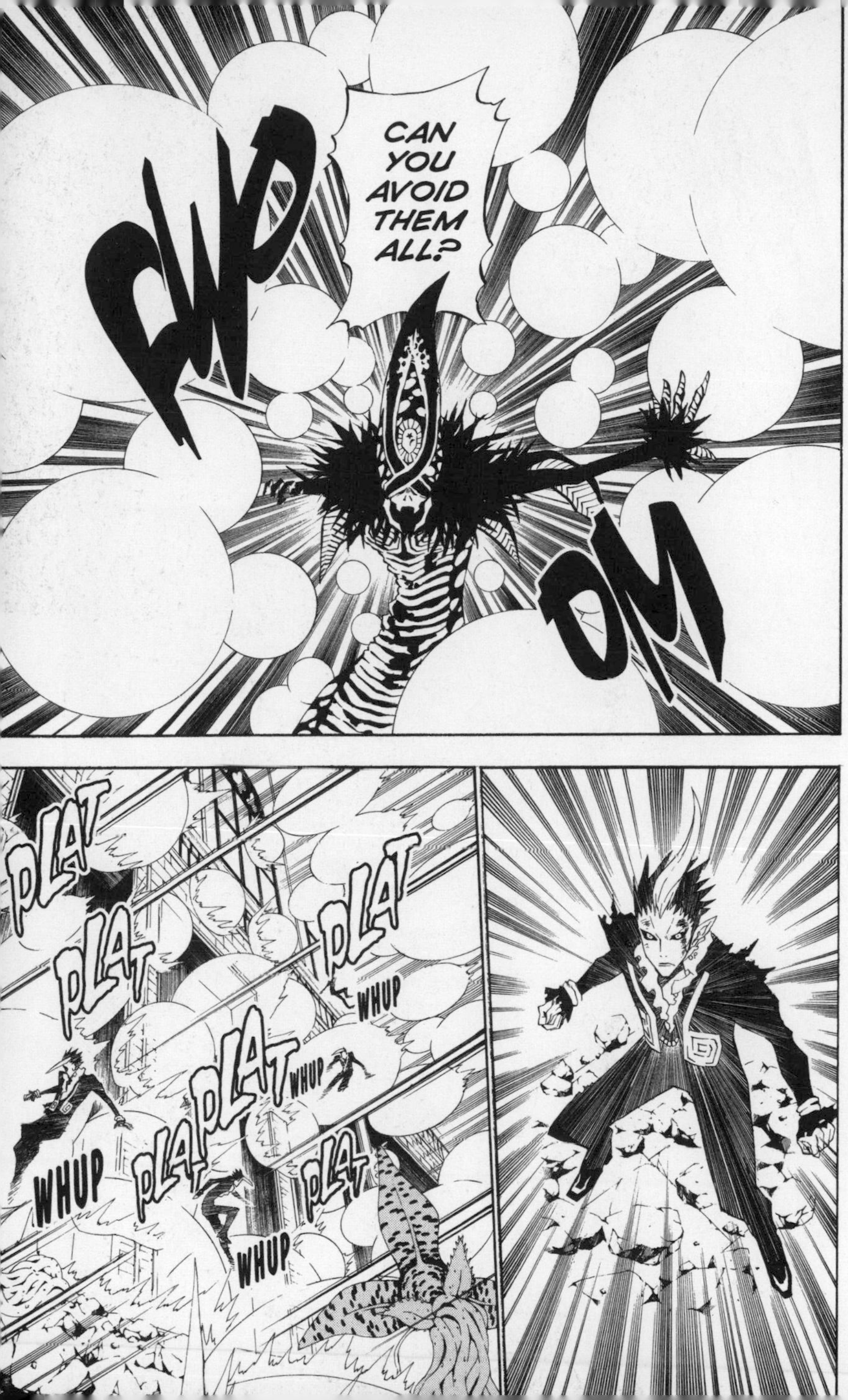
CAN YOU AVOID THEM ALL?
PLAT
WHUP
PLAT
PLAT
PLAPLAT
WHUP
PLAT
WHUP
WHUP

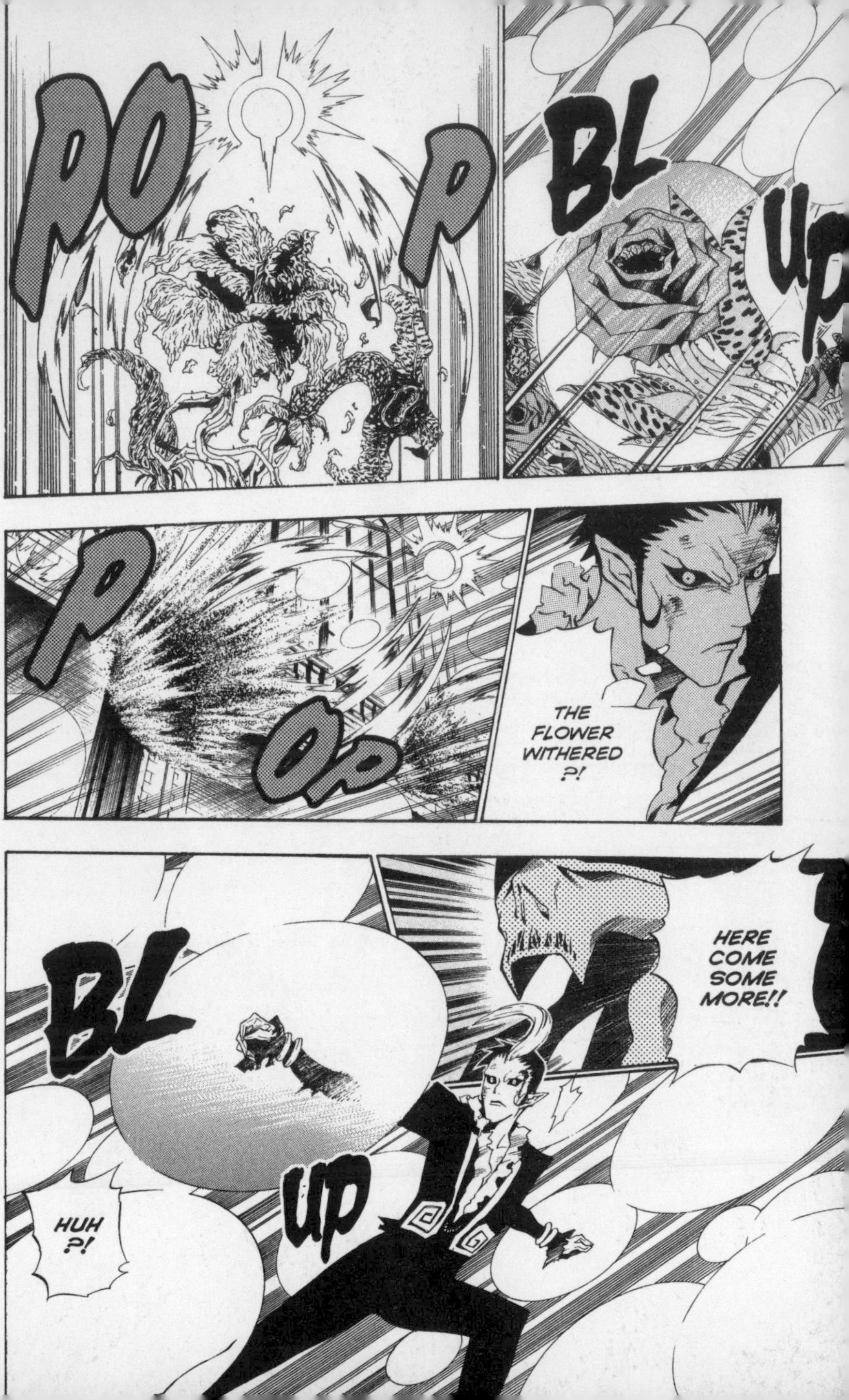
BL
UP
PO
P
THE FLOWER WITHERED ?!
P
OP
HERE COME SOME MORE!!
BL
UP
HUH ?!

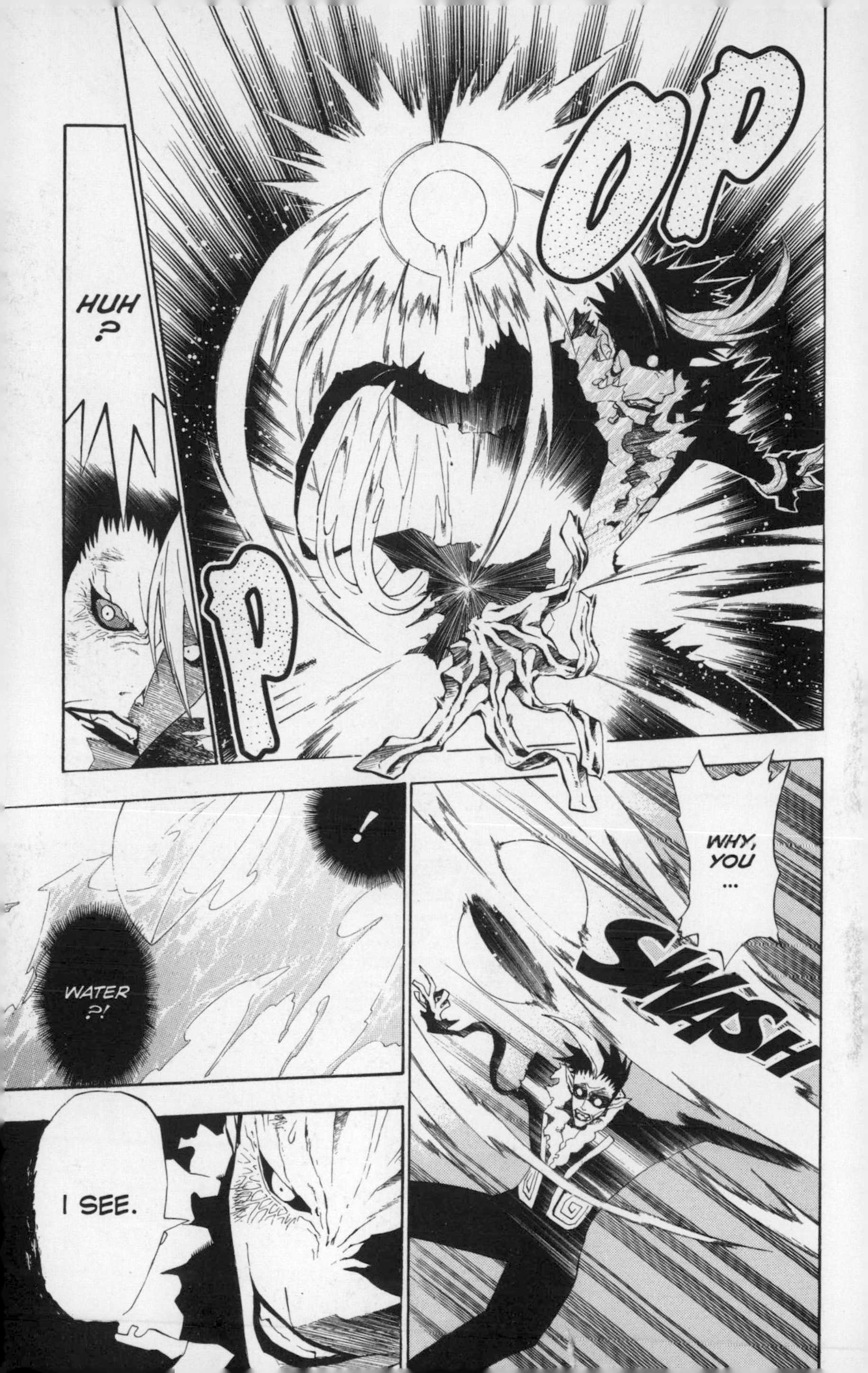
POP
HUH?
WHY, YOU ...
SWISH
!
WATER?!
I SEE.

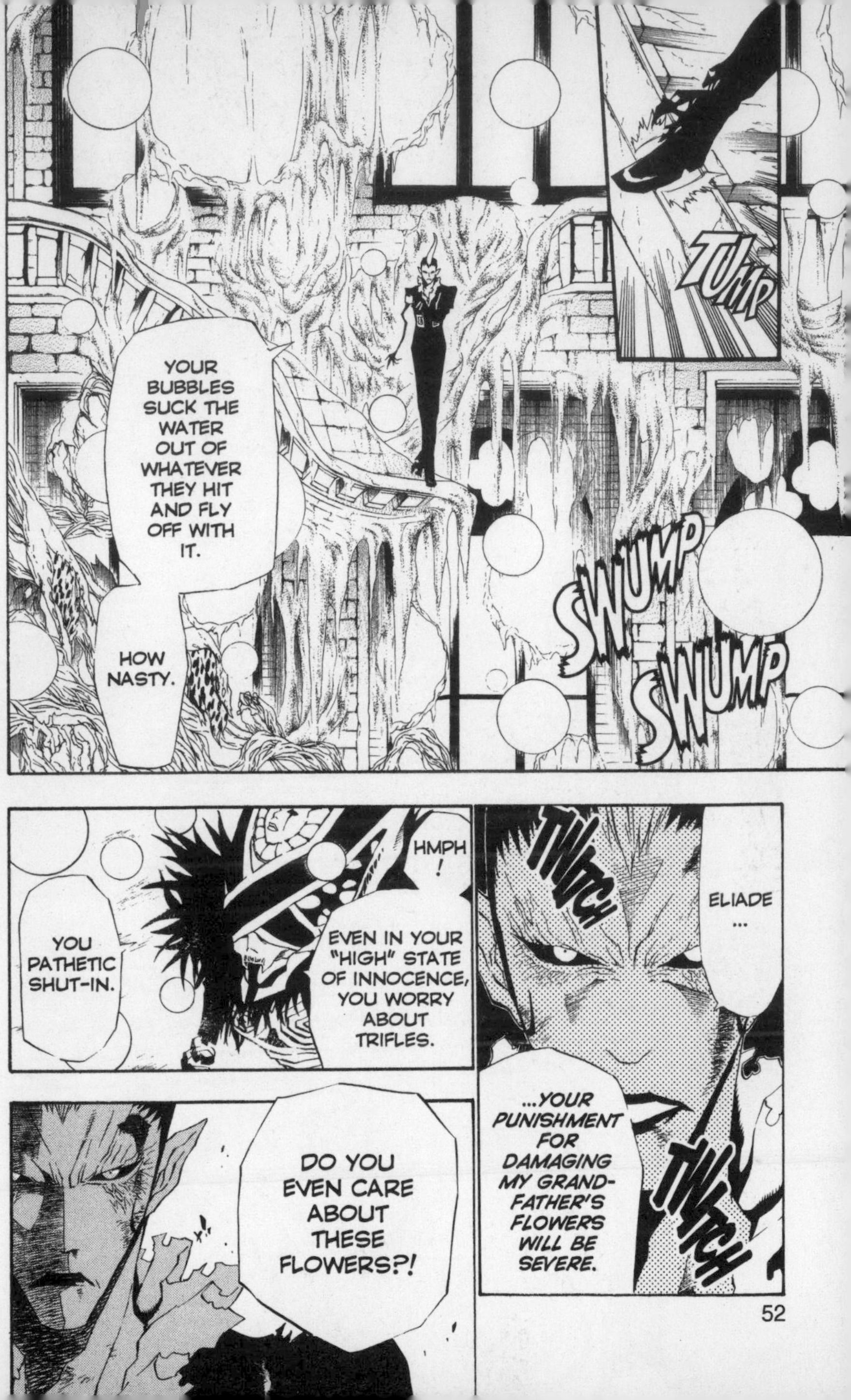

TUMP
SWUMP
SWUMP
YOUR BUBBLES SUCK THE WATER OUT OF WHATEVER THEY HIT AND FLY OFF WITH IT.
HOW NASTY.
TWITCH
ELIADE...
...YOUR PUNISHMENT FOR DAMAGING MY GRAND-FATHER'S FLOWERS WILL BE SEVERE.
TWITCH
HMPH!
EVEN IN YOUR "HIGH" STATE OF INNOCENCE, YOU WORRY ABOUT TRIFLES.
YOU PATHETIC SHUT-IN.
DO YOU EVEN CARE ABOUT THESE FLOWERS?!

READ THIS WAY

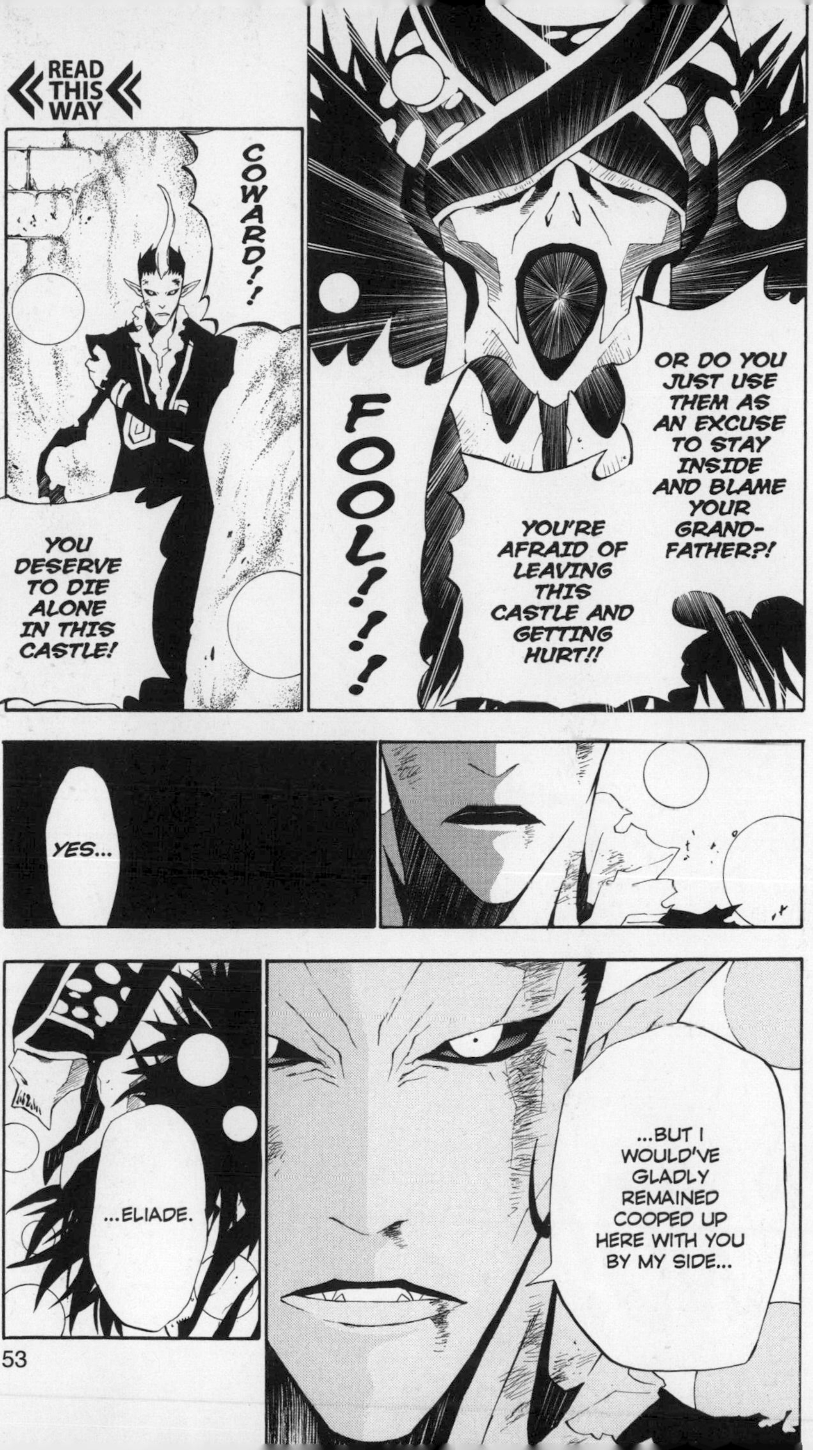
FOOL!!!
YOU'RE AFRAID OF LEAVING THIS CASTLE AND GETTING HURT!!
OR DO YOU JUST USE THEM AS AN EXCUSE TO STAY INSIDE AND BLAME YOUR GRAND-FATHER?!
COWARD!!
YOU DESERVE TO DIE ALONE IN THIS CASTLE!
YES...
...BUT I WOULD'VE GLADLY REMAINED COOPED UP HERE WITH YOU BY MY SIDE...
...ELIADE.

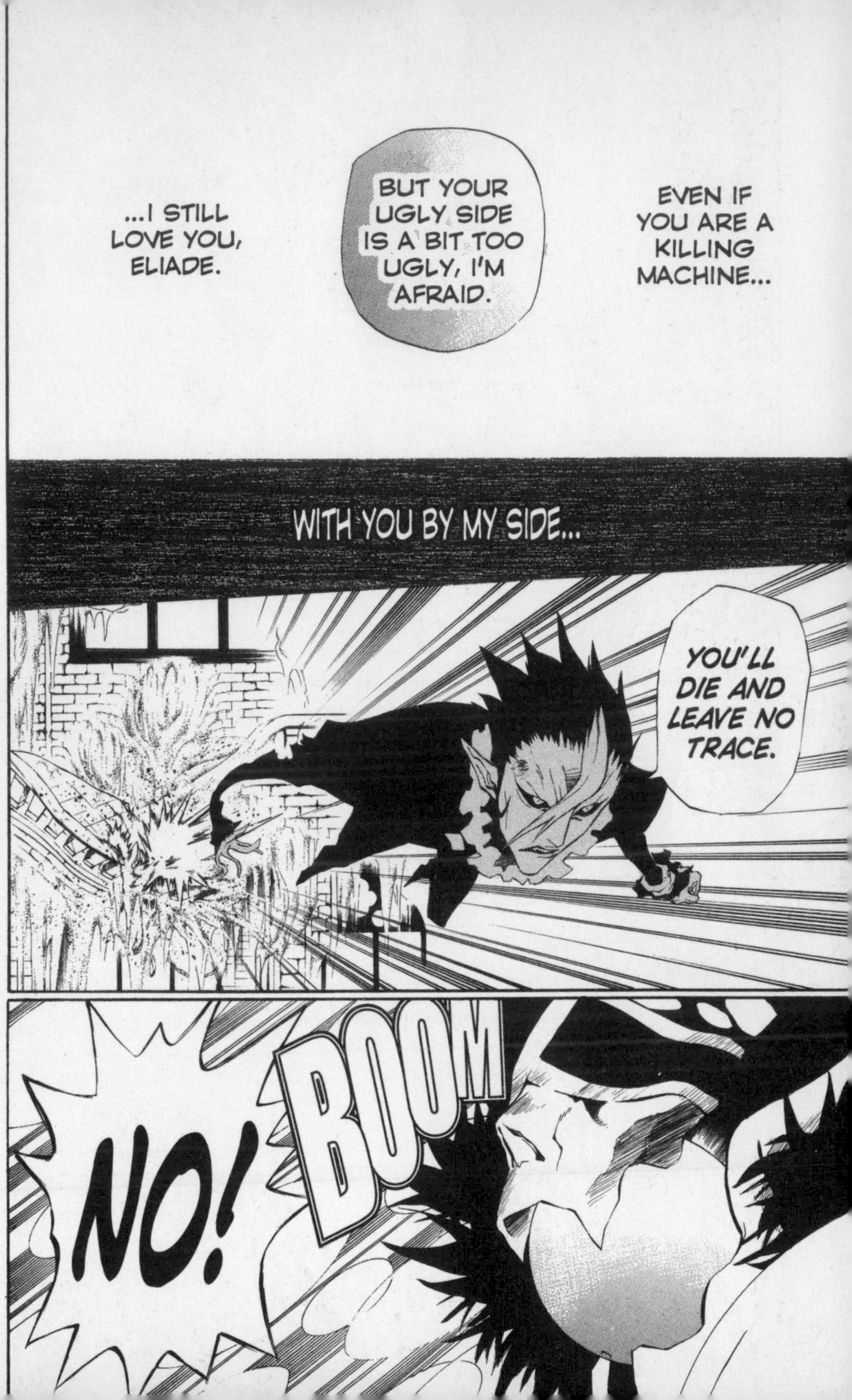
EVEN IF YOU ARE A KILLING MACHINE...
BUT YOUR UGLY SIDE IS A BIT TOO UGLY, I'M AFRAID.
...I STILL LOVE YOU, ELIADE.
WITH YOU BY MY SIDE...
YOU'LL DIE AND LEAVE NO TRACE.
BOOM
NO!

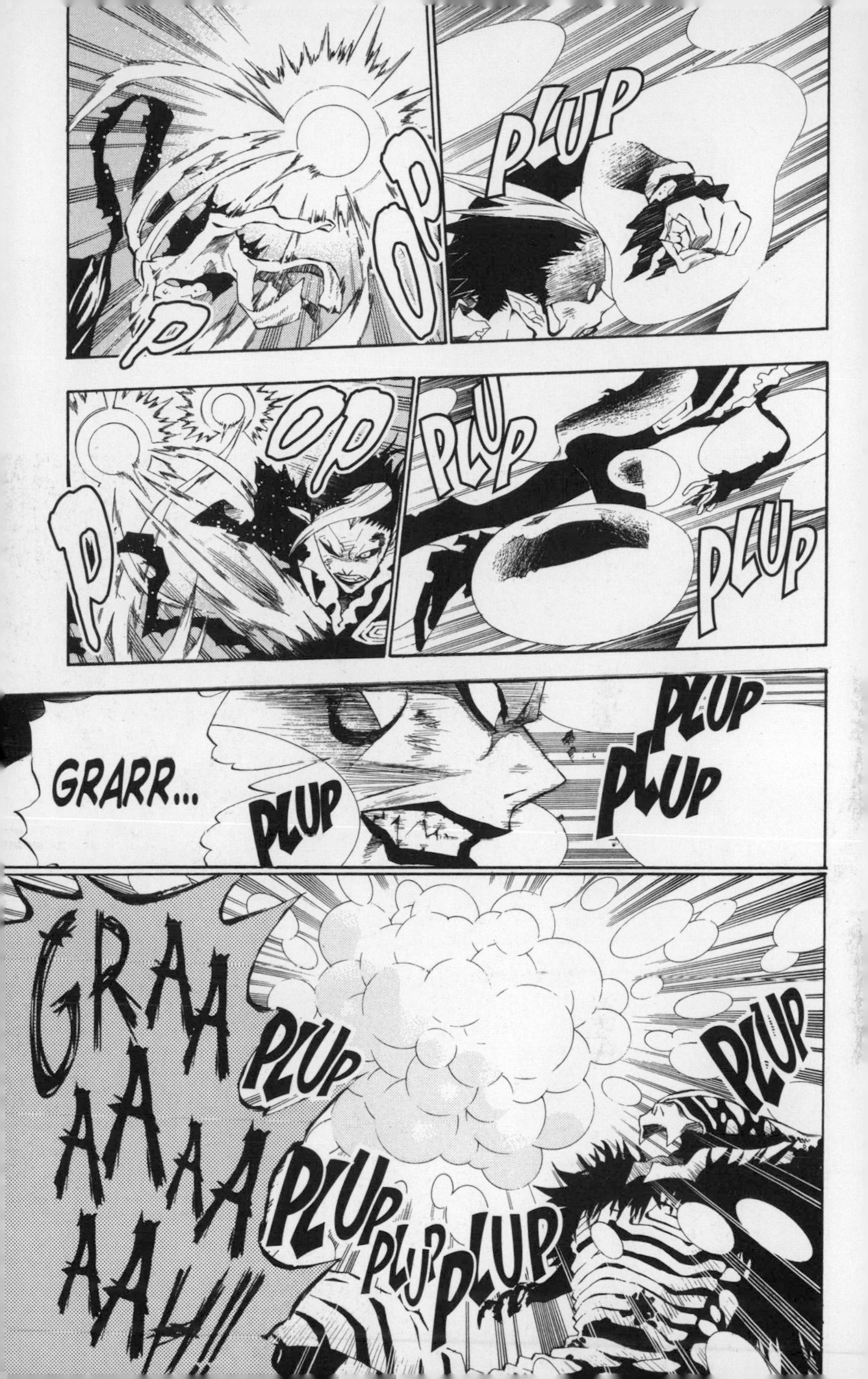
PLUP
POP
PLUP
PLUP
POP
PLUP
PLUP
PLUP
GRARR...
PLUP
PLUP
PLUP
PLUP
PLUP
GRAAAAAAAAH!!

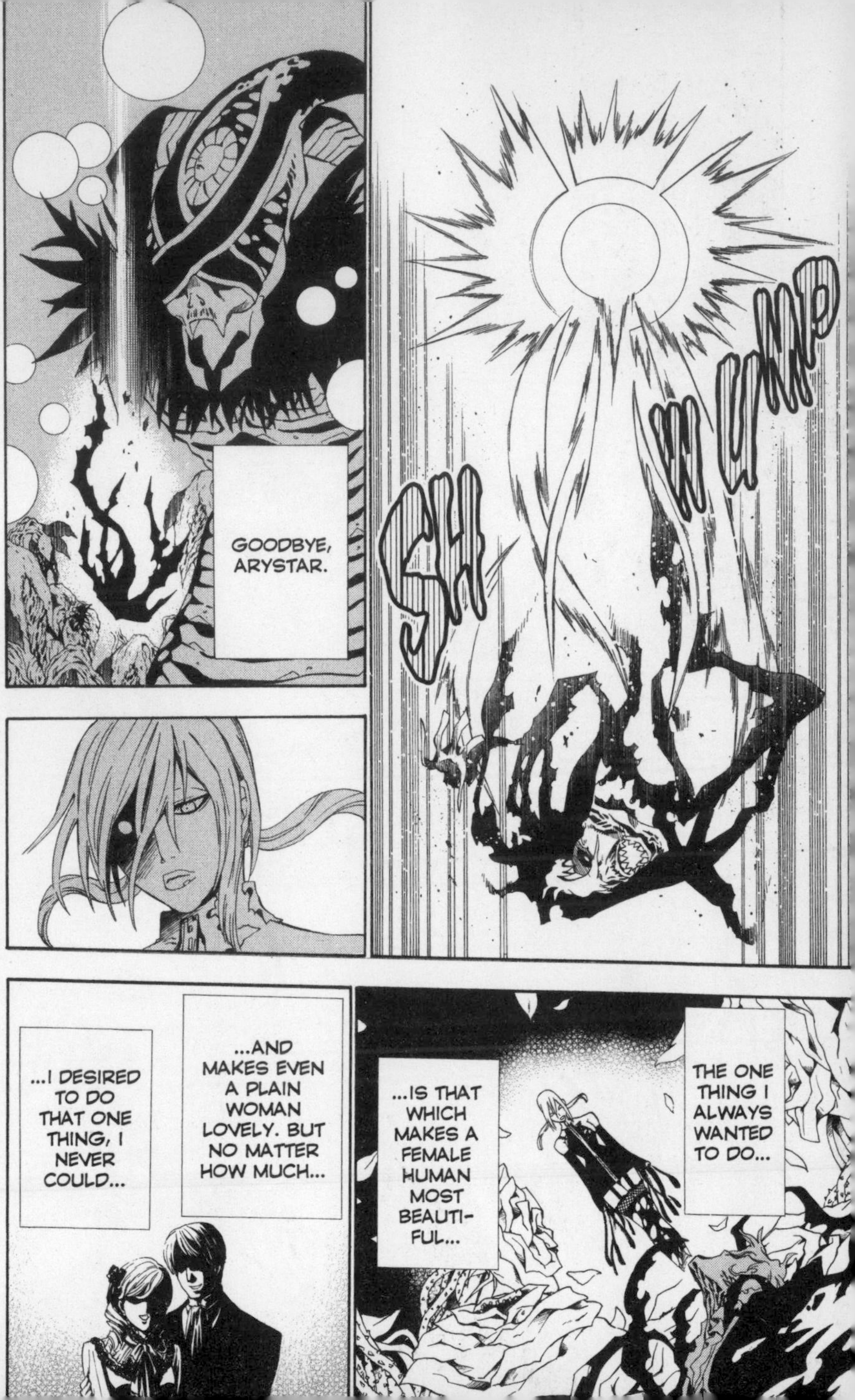
SHWUMP
GOODBYE, ARYSTAR.
THE ONE THING I ALWAYS WANTED TO DO...
...IS THAT WHICH MAKES A FEMALE HUMAN MOST BEAUTI-FUL...
...AND MAKES EVEN A PLAIN WOMAN LOVELY. BUT NO MATTER HOW MUCH...
...I DESIRED TO DO THAT ONE THING, I NEVER COULD...

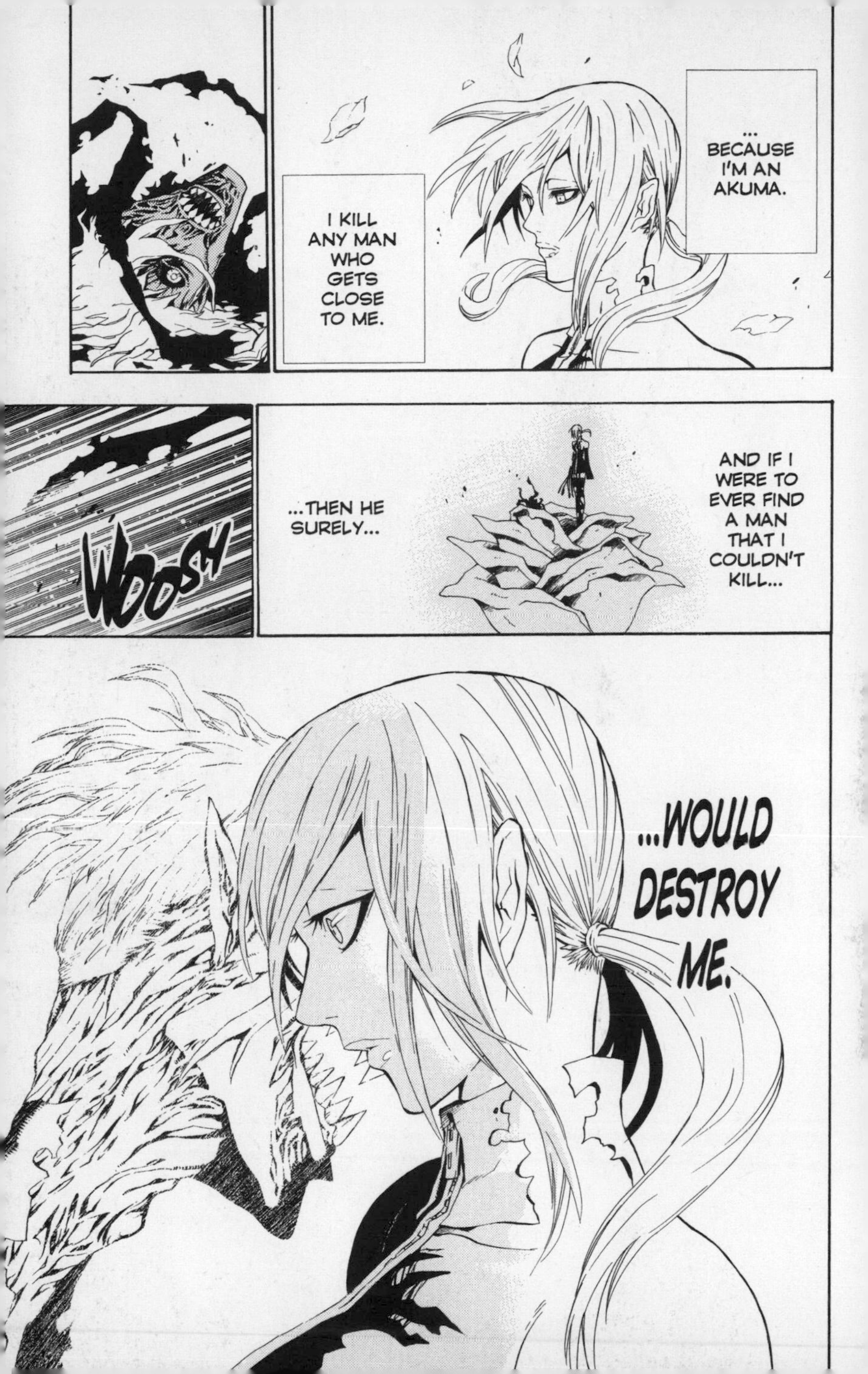
...BECAUSE I'M AN AKUMA.
I KILL ANY MAN WHO GETS CLOSE TO ME.
AND IF I WERE TO EVER FIND A MAN THAT I COULDN'T KILL...
...THEN HE SURELY...
WOOSH
...WOULD DESTROY ME.

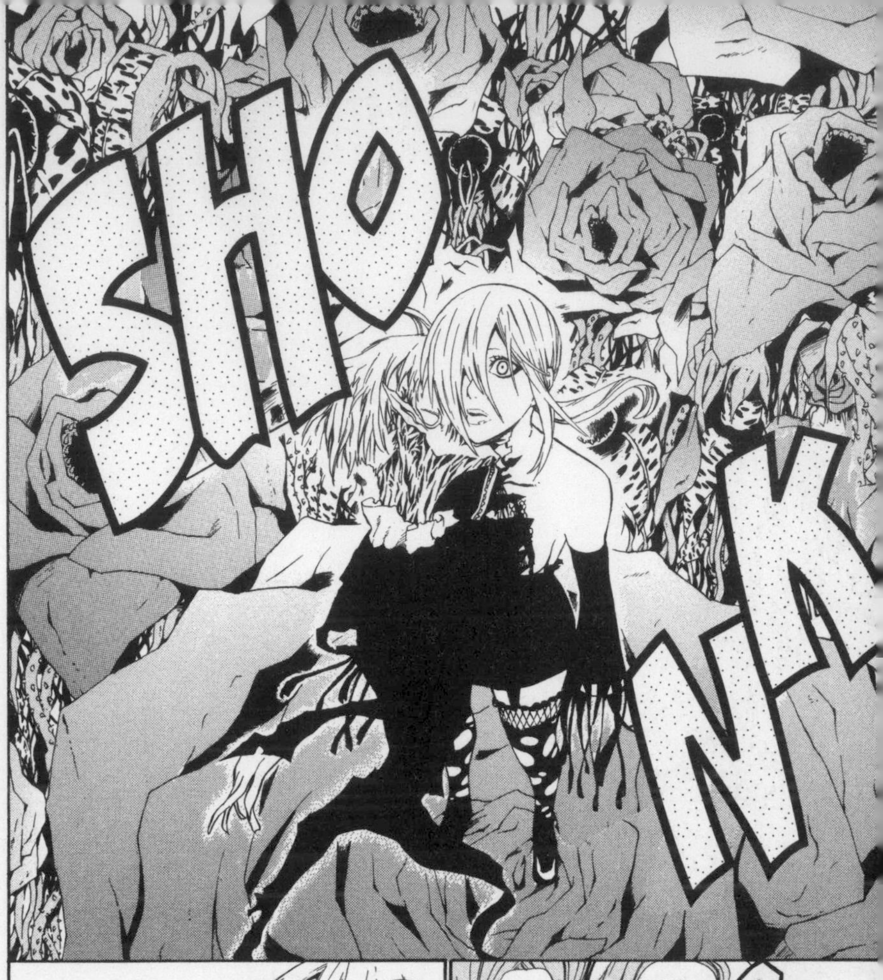
SHOONK
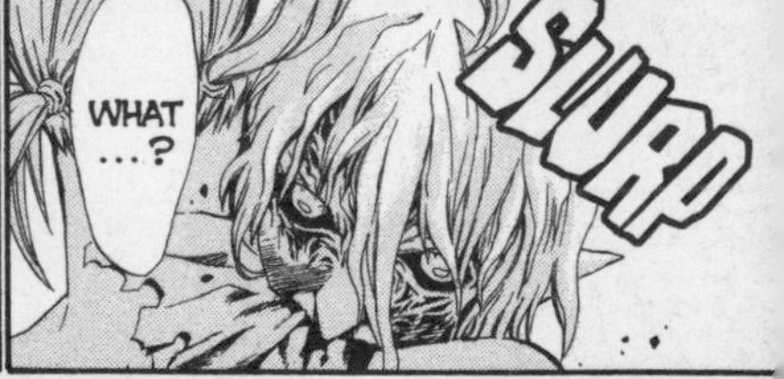
SLURP
WHAT . . . ?
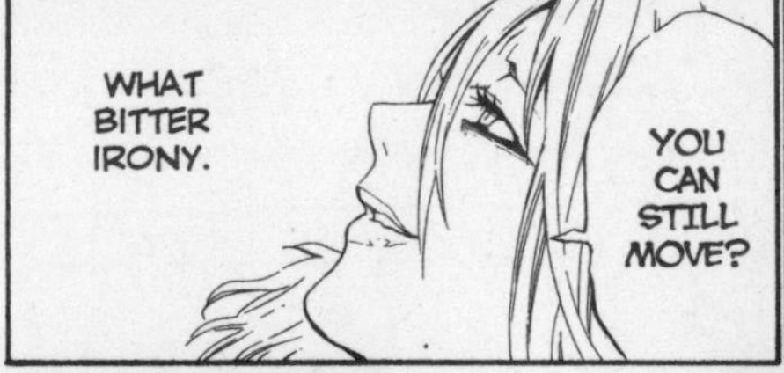
YOU CAN STILL MOVE?
WHAT BITTER IRONY.
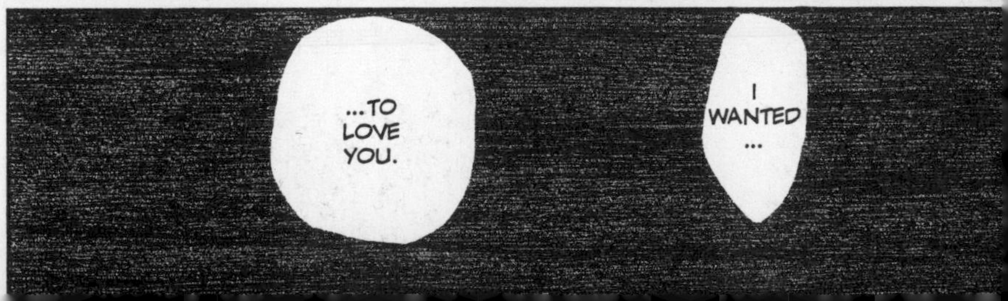
I WANTED ...
...TO LOVE YOU.

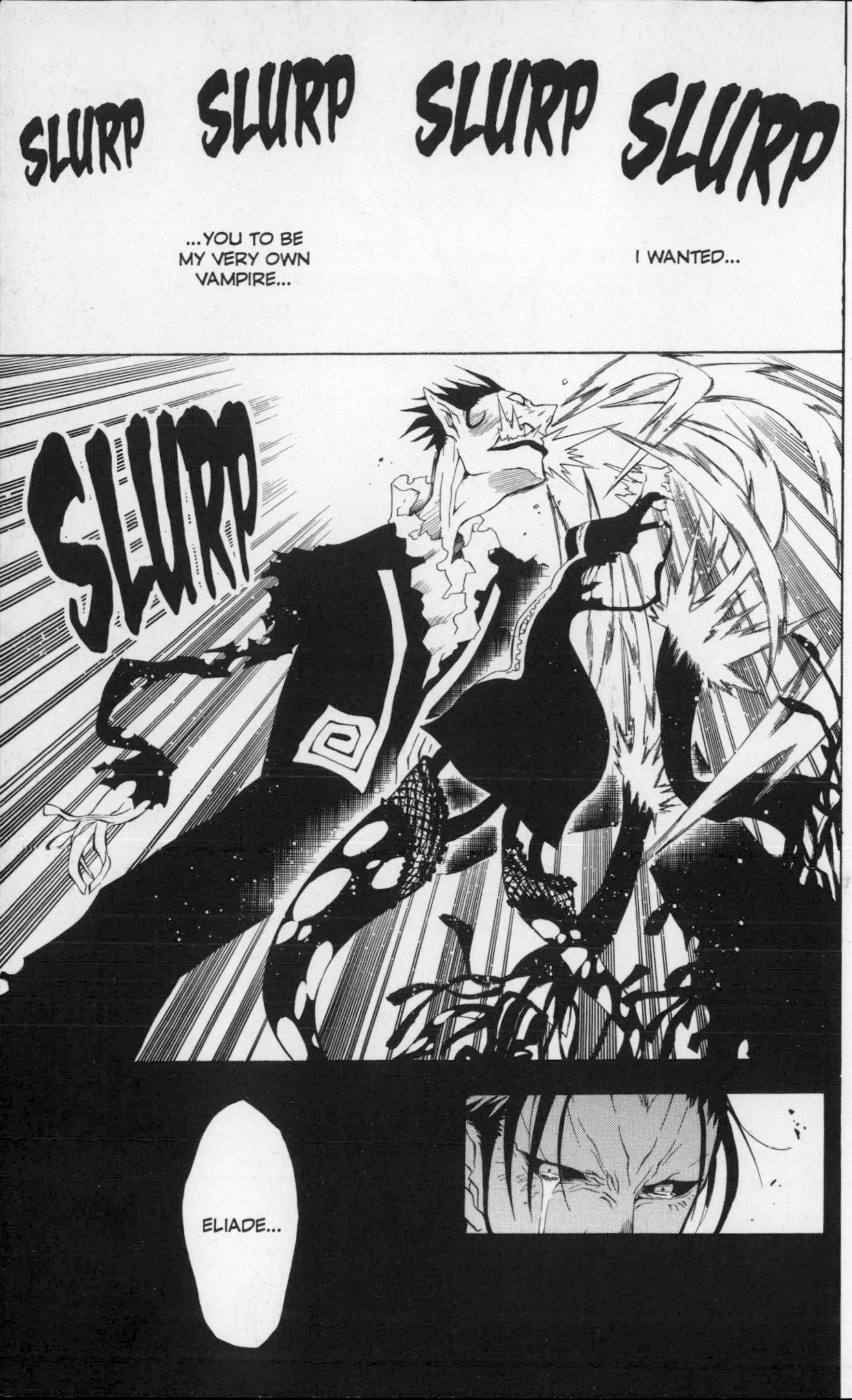
SLURP
SLURP
SLURP
SLURP
I WANTED...
...YOU TO BE MY VERY OWN VAMPIRE...
SLURP
ELIADE...

KOMUI'S DISCUSSION ROOM VOL. 3

Q. WHY DOES KOMUI REFER TO HIMSELF AS SCIENCE SECTION CHIEF?

A. HMM...THAT'S PROBABLY BECAUSE HE USED TO BE IN THE SCIENCE SECTION BEFORE BEING APPOINTED CHIEF. AND EVEN NOW, HE STILL DOES WORK FOR THE SCIENCE SECTION, SO HE DECIDED TO ADOPT THAT TITLE...OR SO I'M TOLD. I MEAN, HE IS IMPORTANT, BUT DOES HE HAVE TO FLAUNT IT? BY THE WAY, I'M THE SECTION LEADER OF THE SCIENCE SECTION, SO I'M SUPPOSED TO BE IN CHARGE. BUT GETTING A POSITION OF IMPORTANCE JUST MEANS MORE WORK. (SIGH) WELL, AS A SCIENTIST, I HAVE TO ADMIT THAT IT'S REALLY GREAT TO WORK HERE. IF ONLY WE DIDN'T HAVE TO DEAL WITH THAT SELFISH CHIEF...

Q. WHAT KIND OF WORK DO SECTION LEADER REEVER AND THE OTHERS USUALLY DO?

A. MAINLY WE ANALYZE THE DATA COLLECTED BY THE SURVEY SECTION FROM ALL OVER THE WORLD, AND DEVELOP WEAPONRY AND EQUIPMENT. THE SCIENCE SECTION HAS NUMEROUS SPECIALISTS AND RESEARCHERS ASSIGNED TO VARIOUS DEPARTMENTS. THERE'S PHYSICS, ASTRONOMY, BIOLOGY, ARCHEOLOGY, GEOLOGY, LINGUISTICS, ANTHROPOLOGY, PSYCHOLOGY, CHEMISTRY, MATHEMATICS, MINERALOGY, MECHANICAL ENGINEERING...THE LIST GOES ON AD NAUSEUM. IT MAY LOOK LIKE WE'RE ALL OVER THE PLACE, BUT THE BOTTOM LINE IS THAT WE'RE ALL STRIVING TO FIND OUT ALL WE CAN ABOUT INNOCENCE. EVERY SCIENTIST THAT COMES HERE IS OBSESSED WITH IT. HOWEVER DIFFICULT THE WORKPLACE MAY BE, THE CHANCE TO DISCOVER SOMETHING NEW KEEPS US GOING. (DISTANT STARE) BY THE WAY, MY AREAS OF EXPERTISE ARE CHEMISTRY, MATHEMATICS, AND LINGUISTICS.

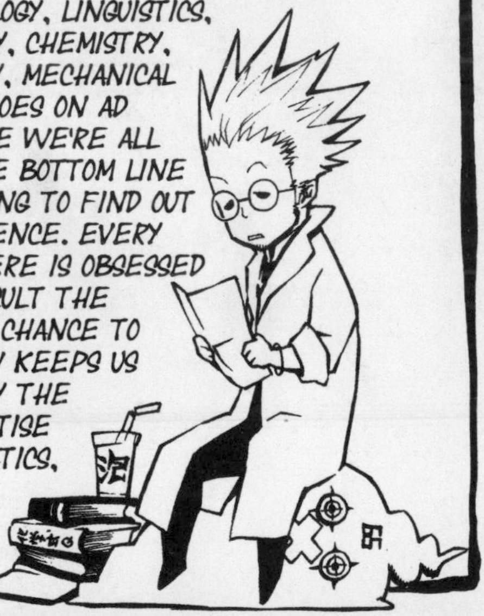

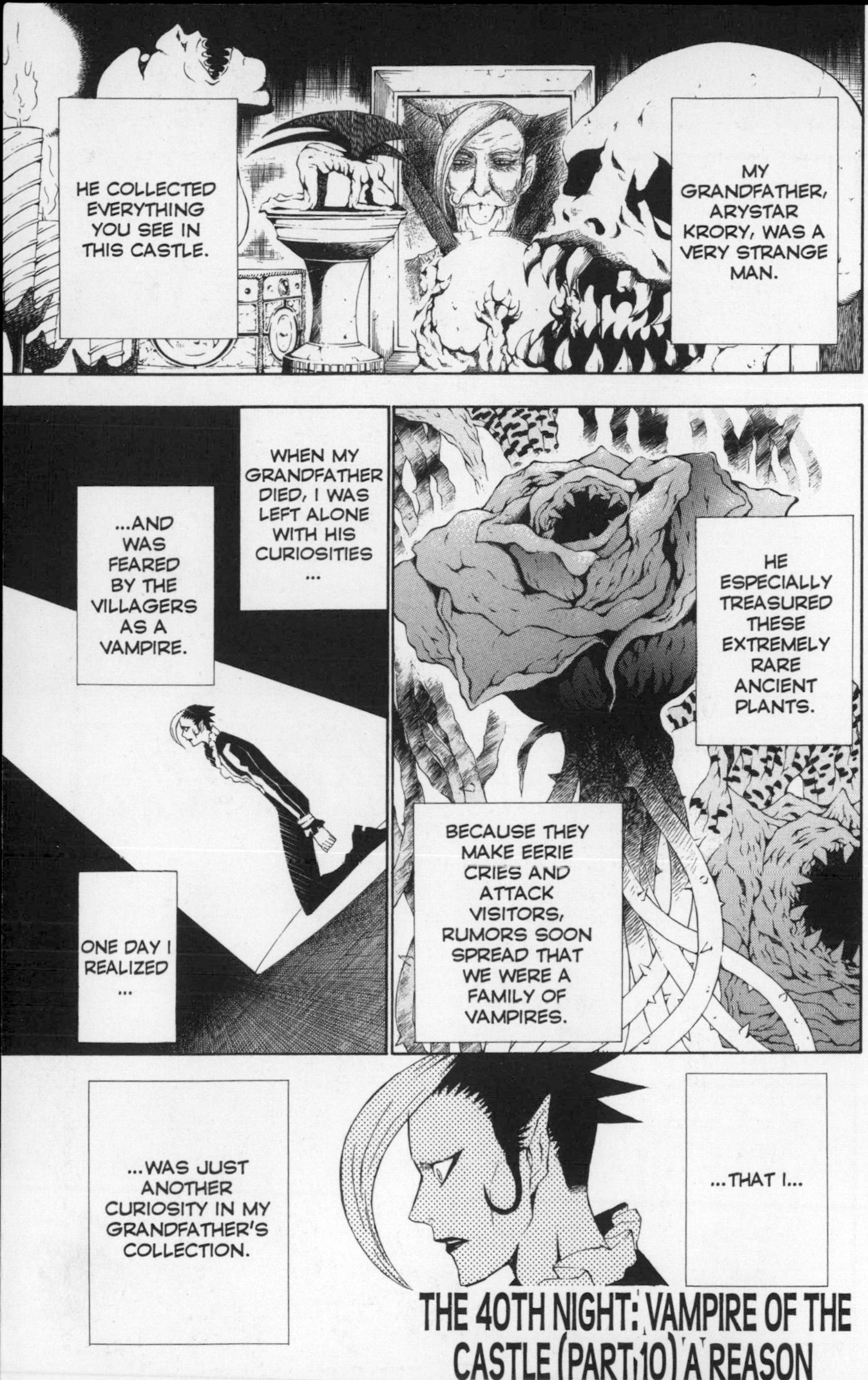
MY GRANDFATHER, ARYSTAR KRORY, WAS A VERY STRANGE MAN.
HE COLLECTED EVERYTHING YOU SEE IN THIS CASTLE.
HE ESPECIALLY TREASURED THESE EXTREMELY RARE ANCIENT PLANTS.
BECAUSE THEY MAKE EERIE CRIES AND ATTACK VISITORS, RUMORS SOON SPREAD THAT WE WERE A FAMILY OF VAMPIRES.
WHEN MY GRANDFATHER DIED, I WAS LEFT ALONE WITH HIS CURIOSITIES ...
...AND WAS FEARED BY THE VILLAGERS AS A VAMPIRE.
ONE DAY I REALIZED ...
...THAT I...
...WAS JUST ANOTHER CURIOSITY IN MY GRANDFATHER'S COLLECTION.
THE 40TH NIGHT: VAMPIRE OF THE CASTLE (PART 10) A REASON

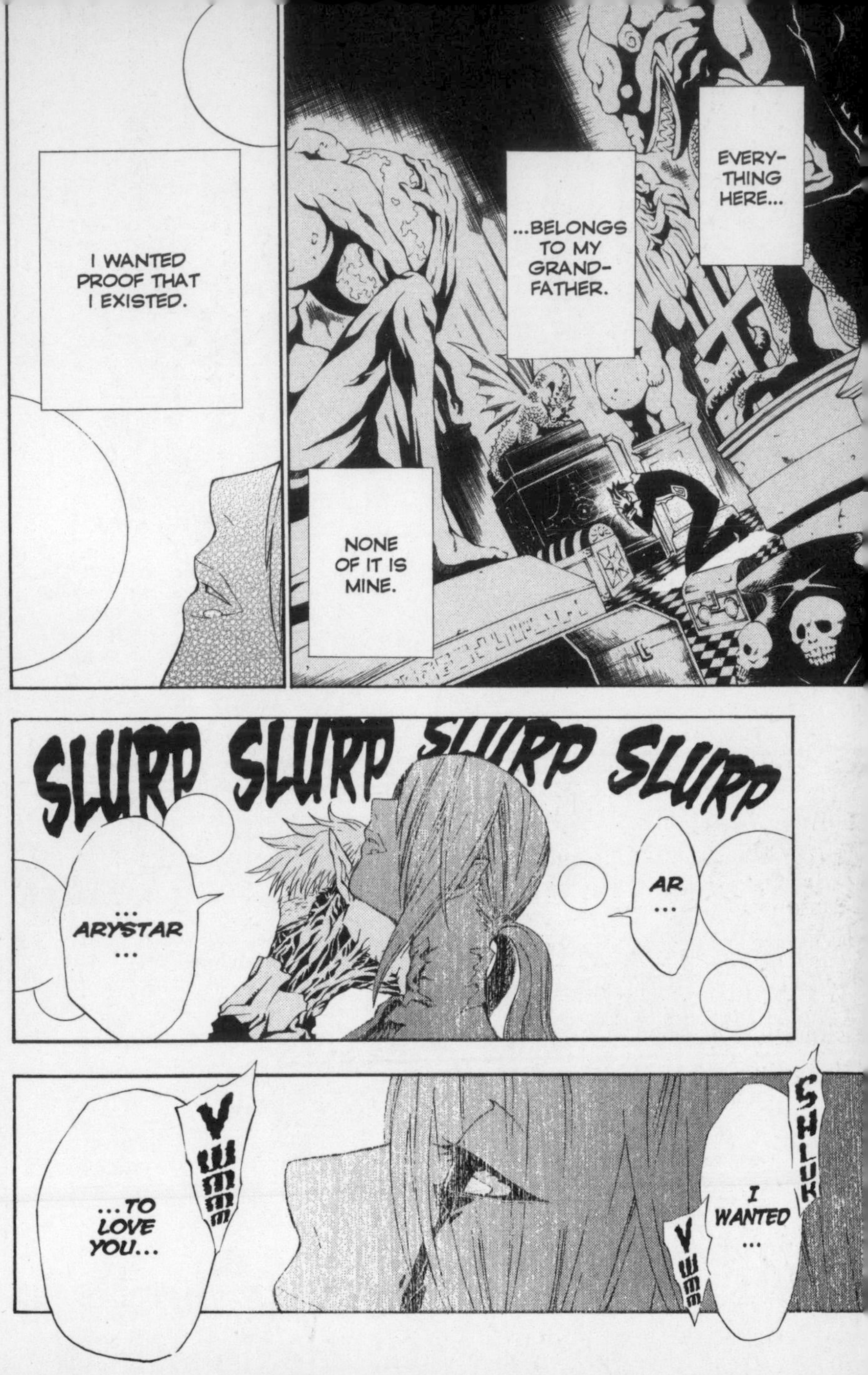
EVERY-THING HERE...
...BELONGS TO MY GRAND-FATHER.
NONE OF IT IS MINE.
I WANTED PROOF THAT I EXISTED.
SLURP SLURP SLURP SLURP
AR ...
... ARYSTAR ...
SHLUK
I WANTED ...
VWMM
VWMMM
...TO LOVE YOU...

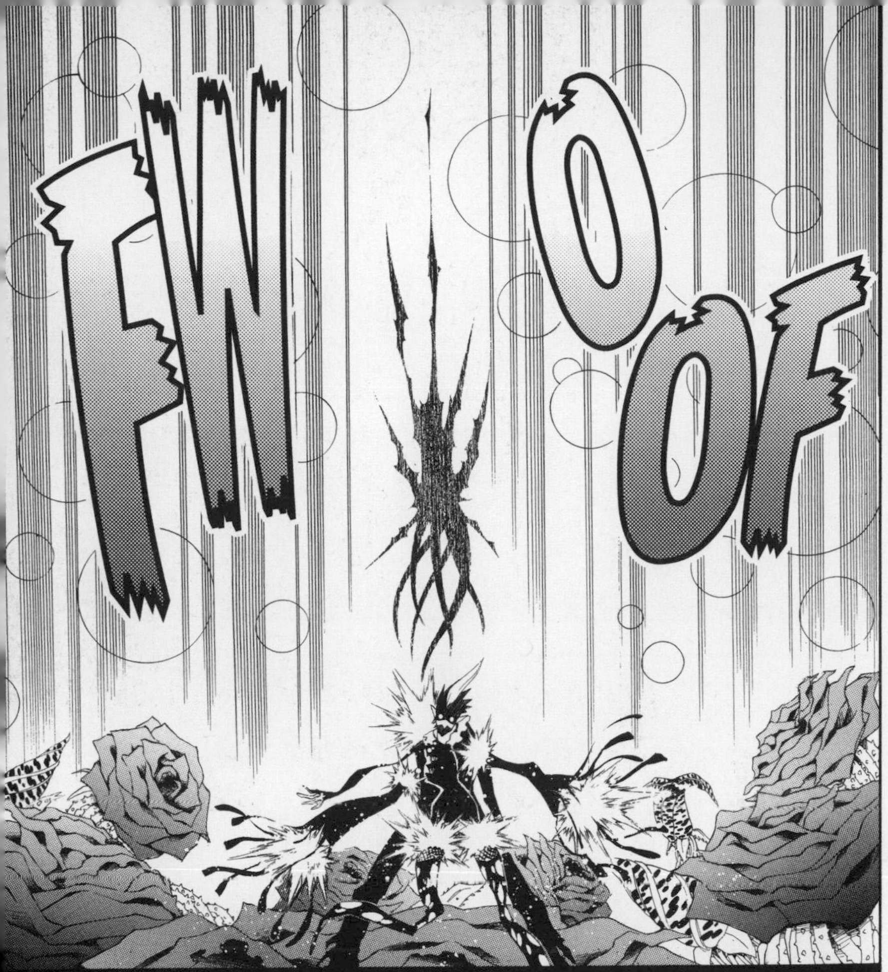
FWOOF

THE 40TH NIGHT: VAMPIRE OF THE CASTLE (PART 10) A REASON

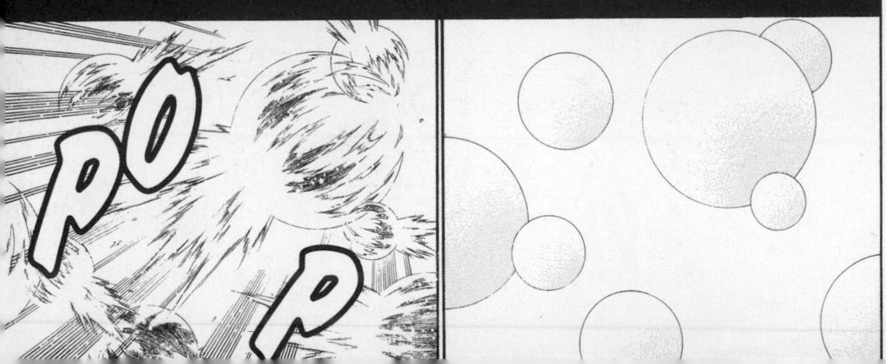
POP

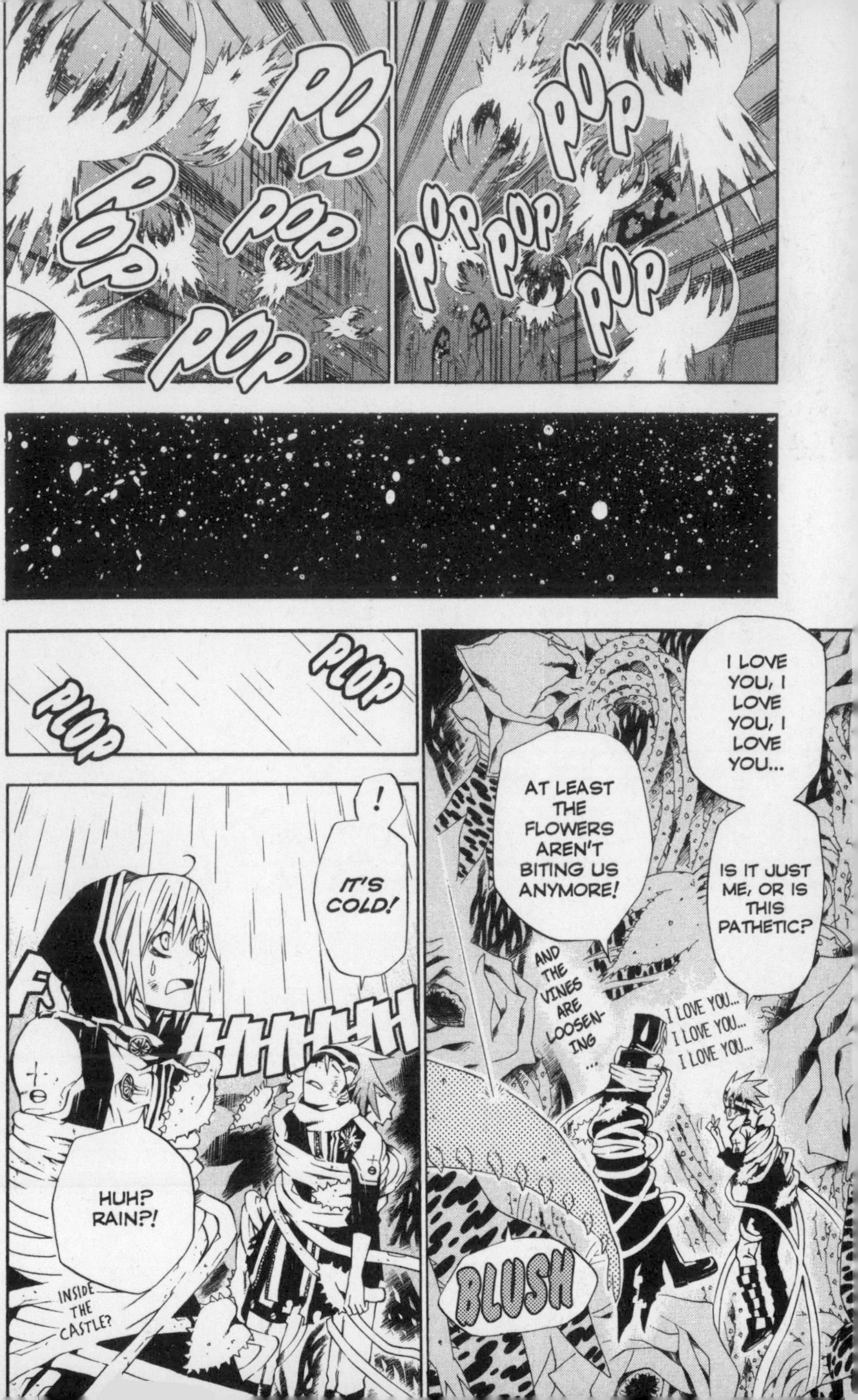
POP
POP POP
POP
POP
POP
POP
POP
I LOVE YOU, I LOVE YOU, I LOVE YOU...
IS IT JUST ME, OR IS THIS PATHETIC?
AT LEAST THE FLOWERS AREN'T BITING US ANYMORE!
AND THE VINES ARE LOOSEN-ING...
I LOVE YOU... I LOVE YOU... I LOVE YOU...
BLUSH
PLOP
PLOP
!
IT'S COLD!
HUH? RAIN?!
INSIDE THE CASTLE?

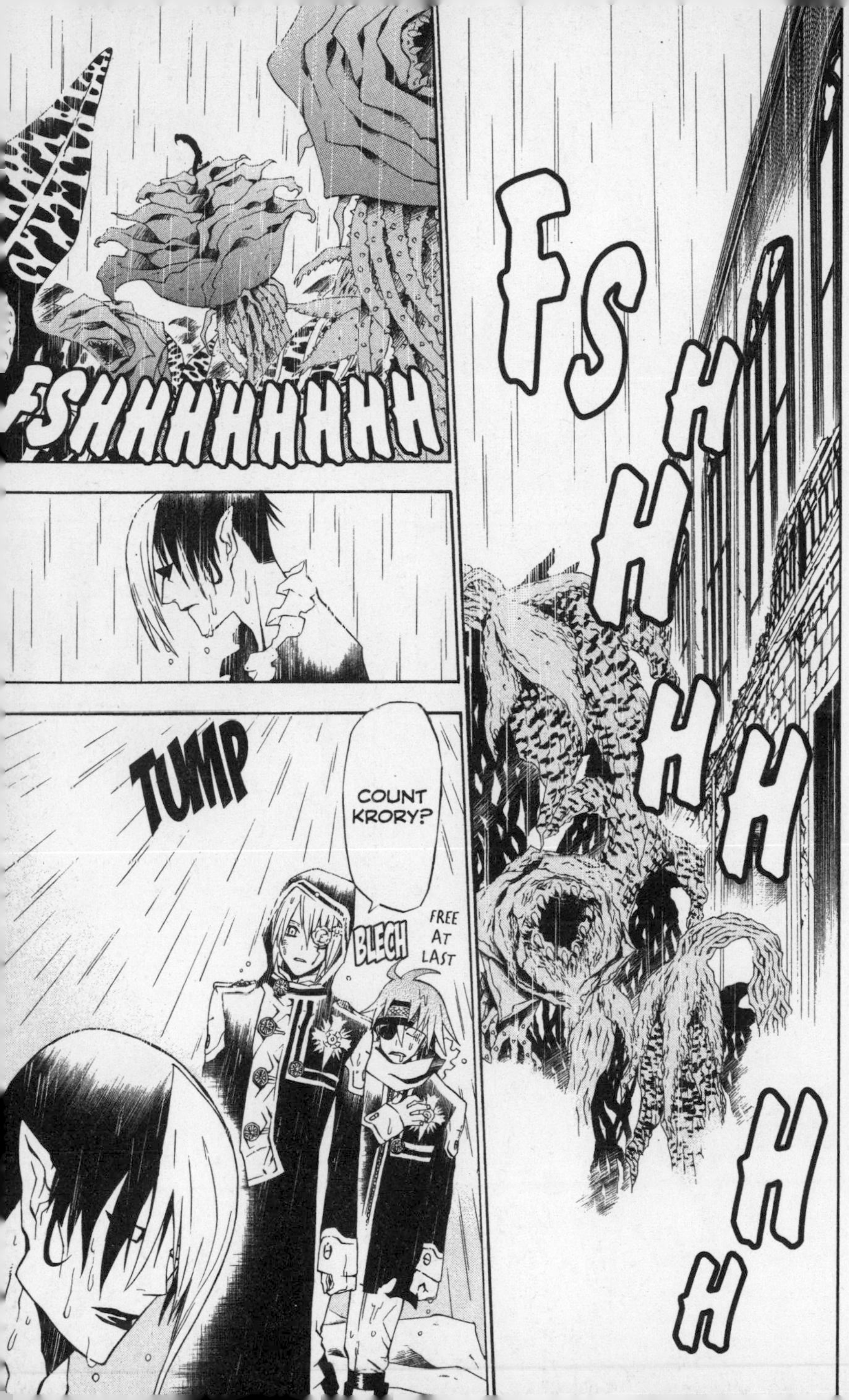
FSHHHHHHHH
FSHHHHHHHHH
TUMP
COUNT KRORY?
BLECH
FREE AT LAST

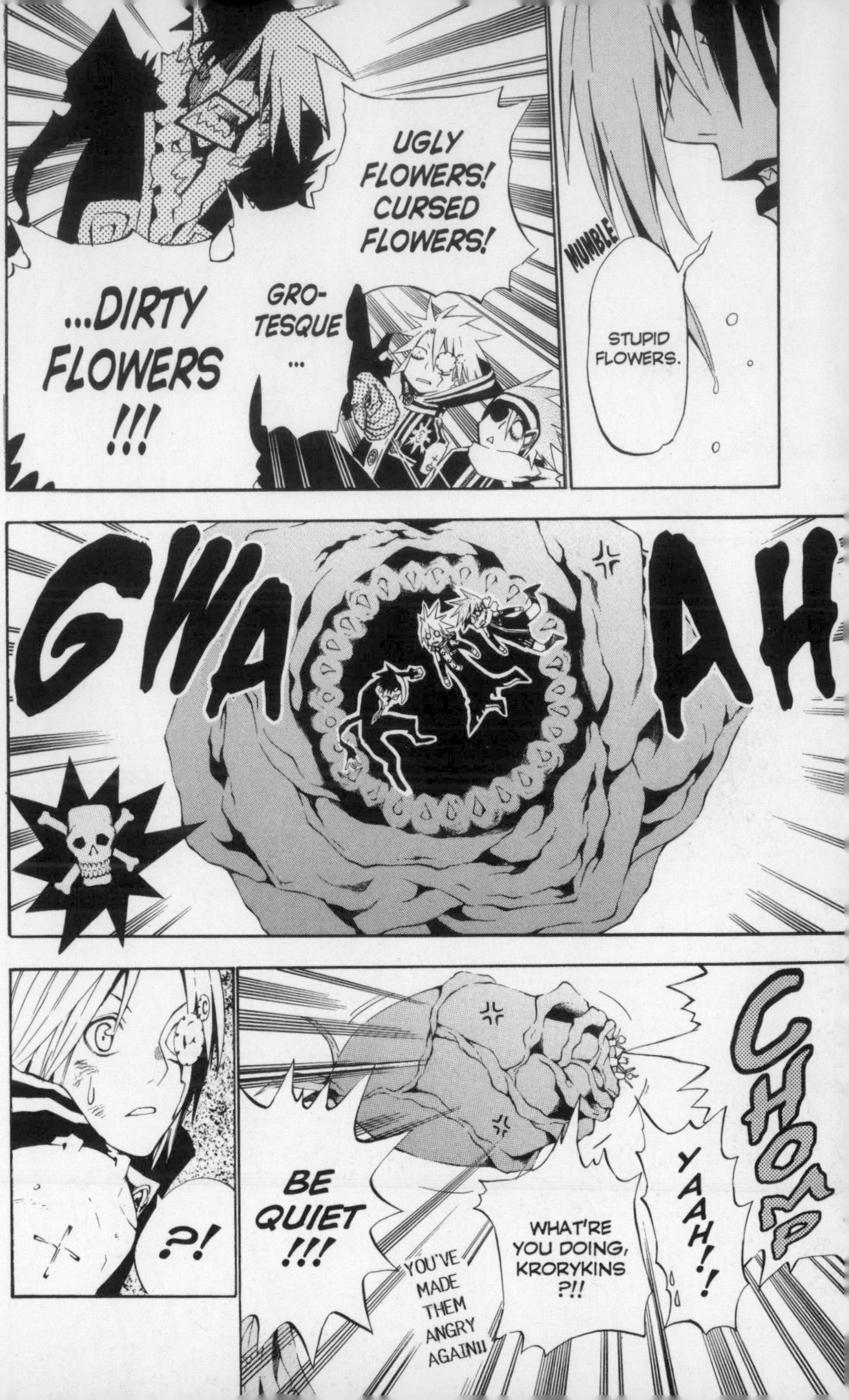
MUMBLE
STUPID FLOWERS.
UGLY FLOWERS! CURSED FLOWERS!
GRO-TESQUE ...
...DIRTY FLOWERS !!!
GWAAH
CHOMP
YAAH!!
WHAT'RE YOU DOING, KRORYKINS ?!!
YOU'VE MADE THEM ANGRY AGAIN!!
BE QUIET !!!
?!

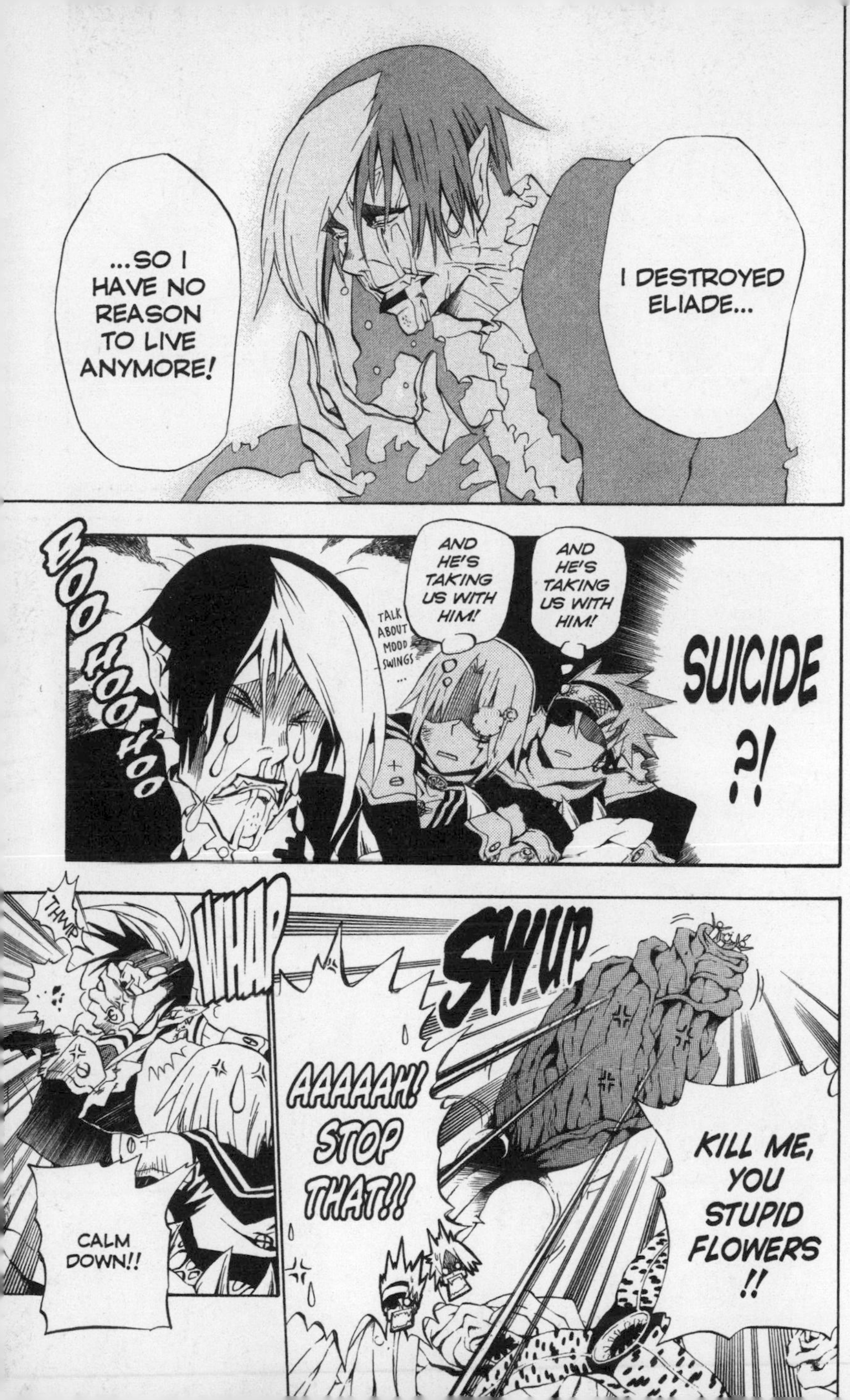
I DESTROYED ELIADE...
...SO I HAVE NO REASON TO LIVE ANYMORE!
SUICIDE ?!
AND HE'S TAKING US WITH HIM!
AND HE'S TAKING US WITH HIM!
TALK ABOUT MOOD SWINGS...
MOO HOO HOO HOO
SWUP
KILL ME, YOU STUPID FLOWERS !!
AAAAAH! STOP THAT!!
THWIP
WHAP
CALM DOWN!!

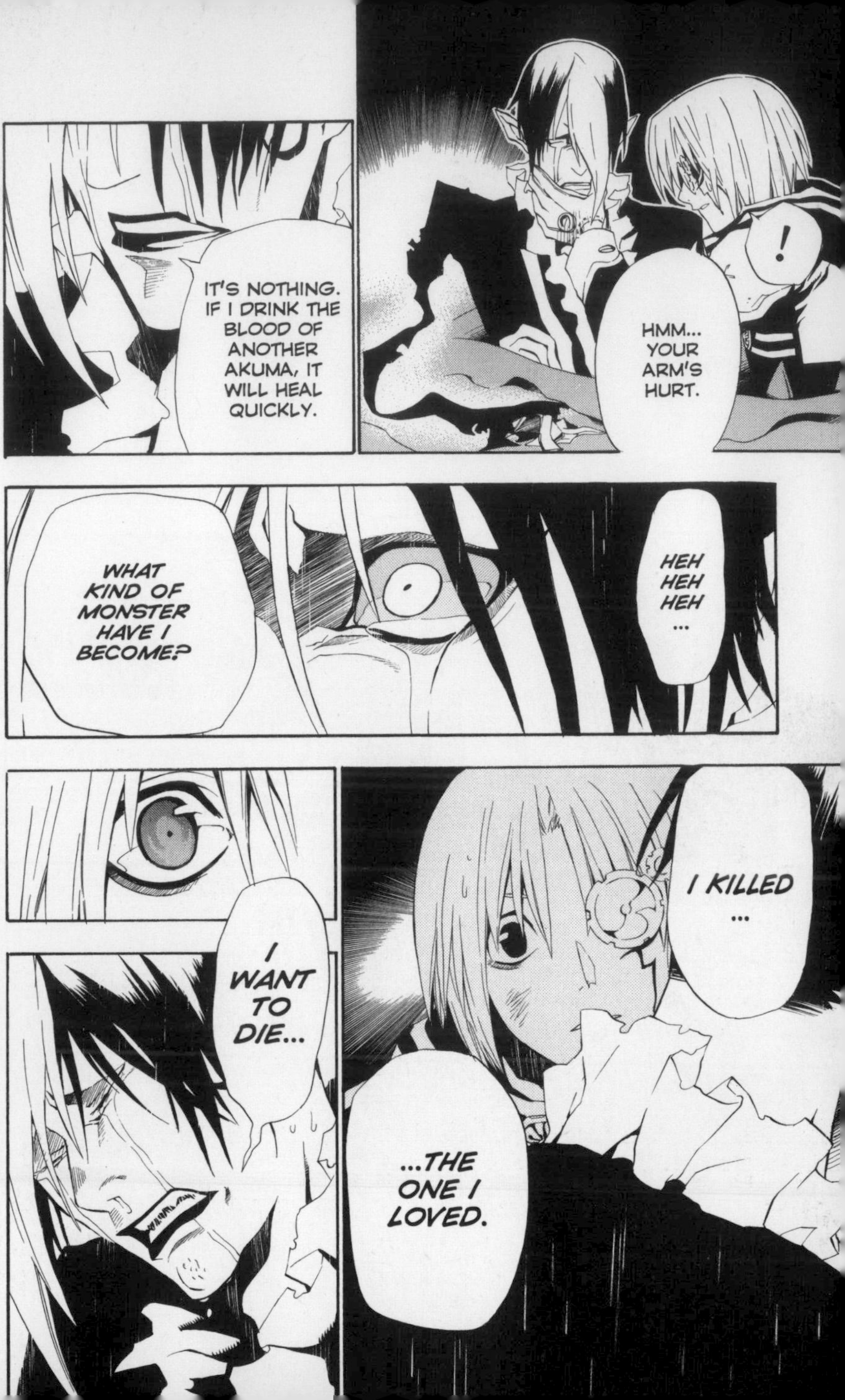
!
HMM... YOUR ARM'S HURT.
IT'S NOTHING. IF I DRINK THE BLOOD OF ANOTHER AKUMA, IT WILL HEAL QUICKLY.
HEH HEH HEH ...
WHAT KIND OF MONSTER HAVE I BECOME?
I KILLED ...
...THE ONE I LOVED.
I WANT TO DIE...

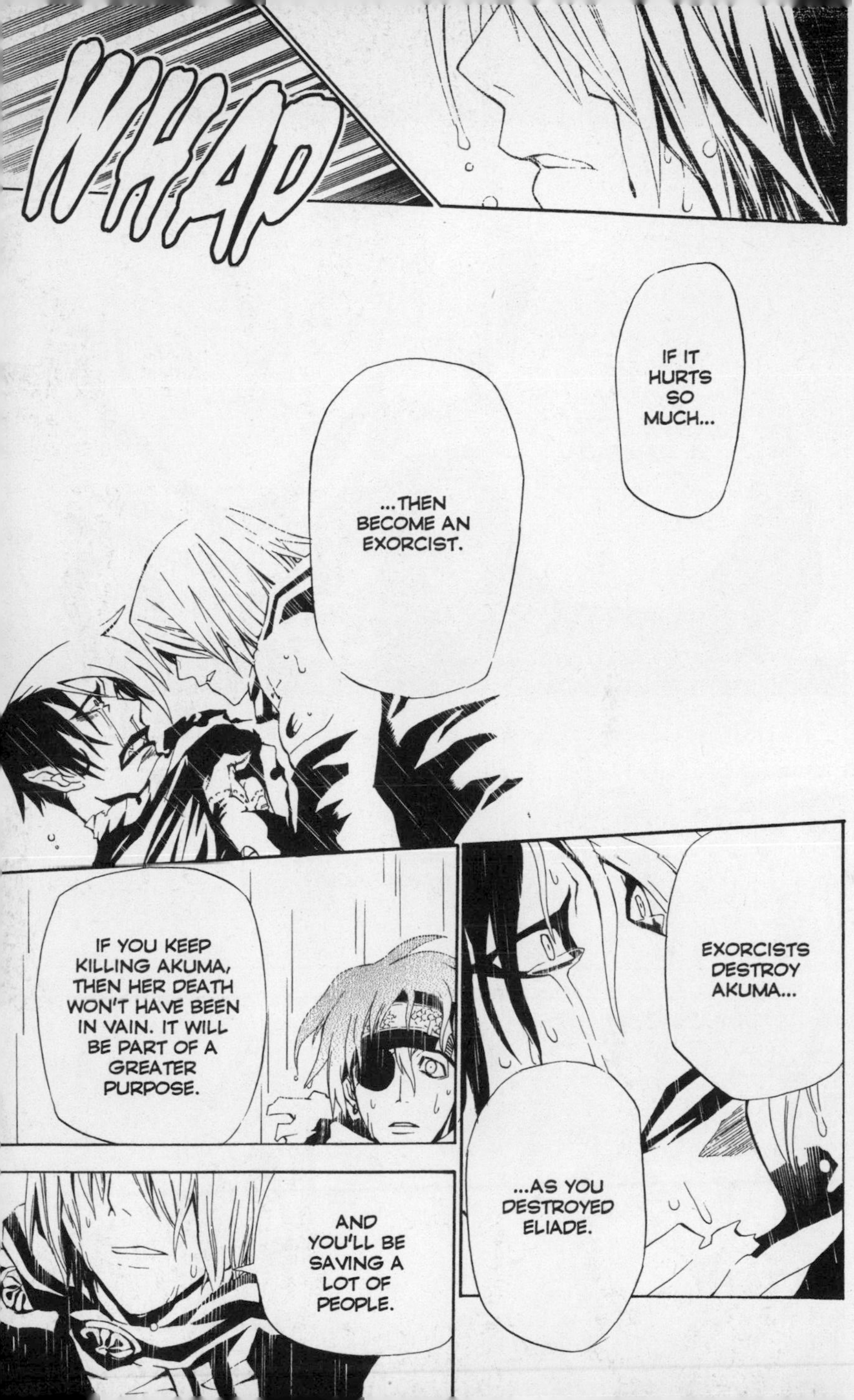
WHAP
IF IT HURTS SO MUCH...
...THEN BECOME AN EXORCIST.
EXORCISTS DESTROY AKUMA...
...AS YOU DESTROYED ELIADE.
IF YOU KEEP KILLING AKUMA, THEN HER DEATH WON'T HAVE BEEN IN VAIN. IT WILL BE PART OF A GREATER PURPOSE.
AND YOU'LL BE SAVING A LOT OF PEOPLE.

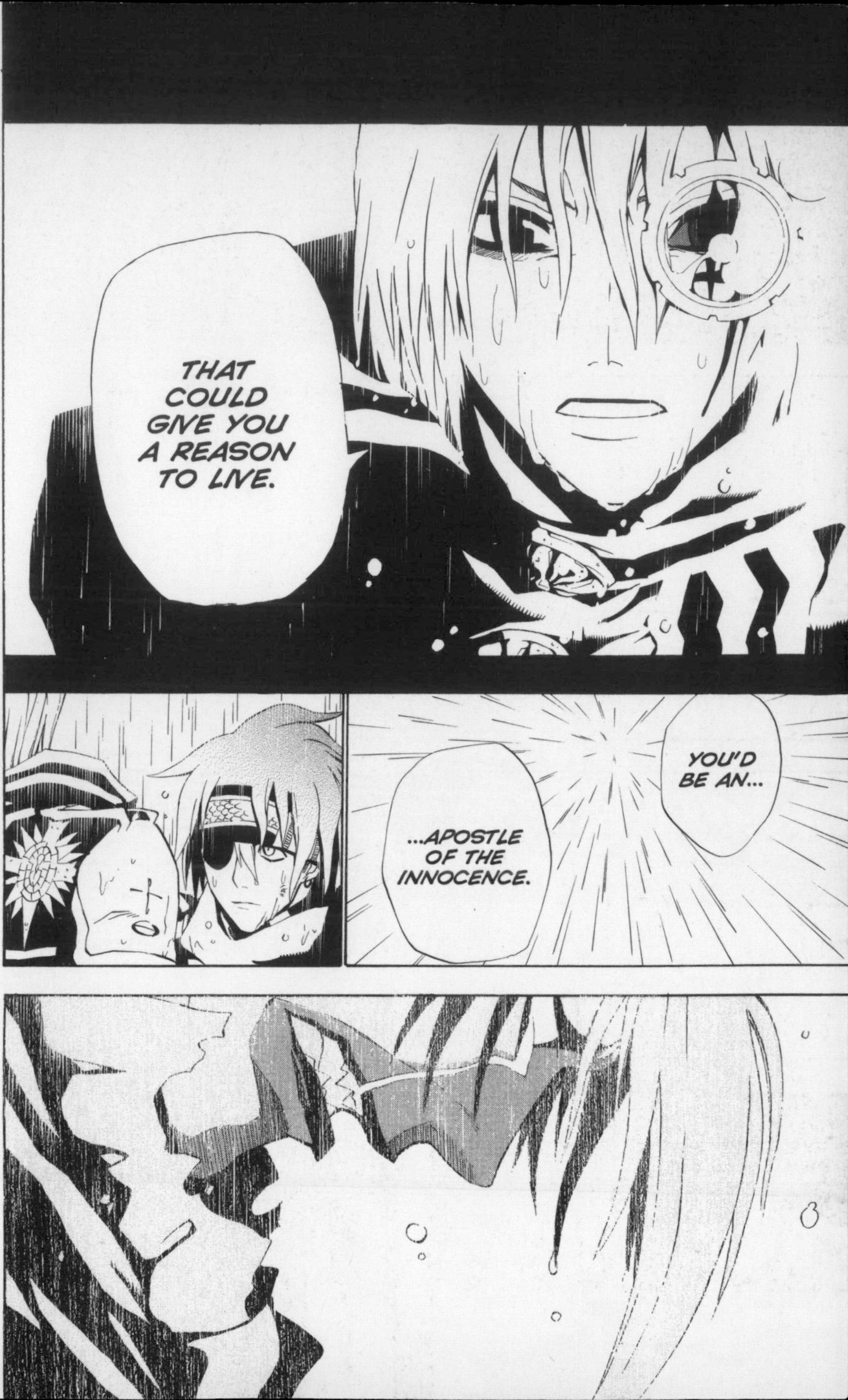
THAT COULD GIVE YOU A REASON TO LIVE.
YOU'D BE AN...
...APOSTLE OF THE INNOCENCE.

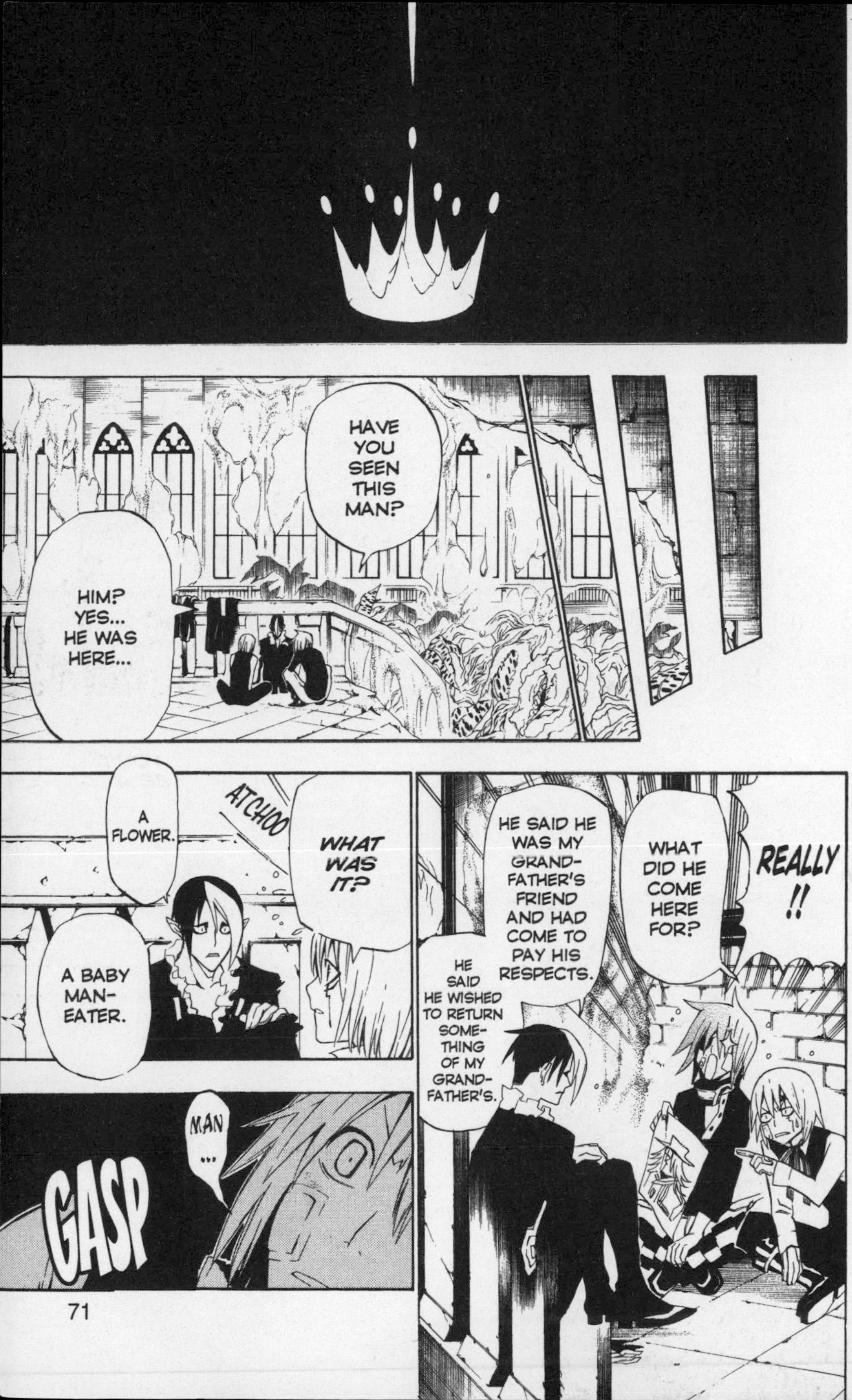
HAVE YOU SEEN THIS MAN?
HIM? YES... HE WAS HERE...
REALLY!!
WHAT DID HE COME HERE FOR?
HE SAID HE WAS MY GRAND-FATHER'S FRIEND AND HAD COME TO PAY HIS RESPECTS.
HE SAID HE WISHED TO RETURN SOME-THING OF MY GRAND-FATHER'S.
WHAT WAS IT?
ATCHOO
A FLOWER.
A BABY MAN-EATER.
MAN...
GASP

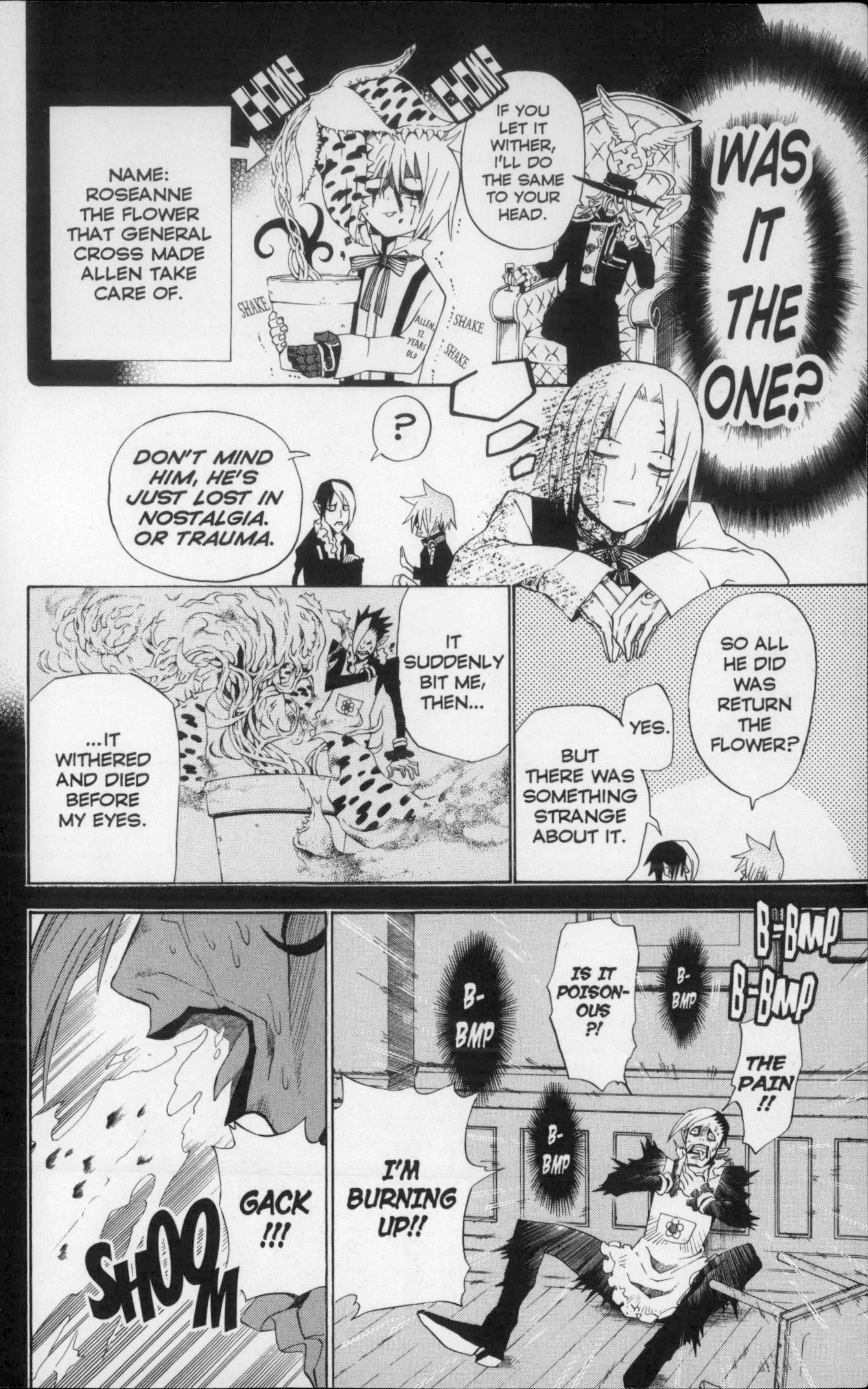
WAS IT THE ONE?
IF YOU LET IT WITHER, I'LL DO THE SAME TO YOUR HEAD.
SHAKE
SHAKE
SHAKE
ALLEN, 12 YEARS OLD
NAME: ROSEANNE THE FLOWER THAT GENERAL CROSS MADE ALLEN TAKE CARE OF.
?
DON'T MIND HIM, HE'S JUST LOST IN NOSTALGIA. OR TRAUMA.
SO ALL HE DID WAS RETURN THE FLOWER?
YES.
BUT THERE WAS SOMETHING STRANGE ABOUT IT.
IT SUDDENLY BIT ME, THEN...
...IT WITHERED AND DIED BEFORE MY EYES.
B-BMP
B-BMP
THE PAIN!!
B-BMP
IS IT POISON-OUS?!
B-BMP
B-BMP
I'M BURNING UP!!
GACK!!!
SHOOM

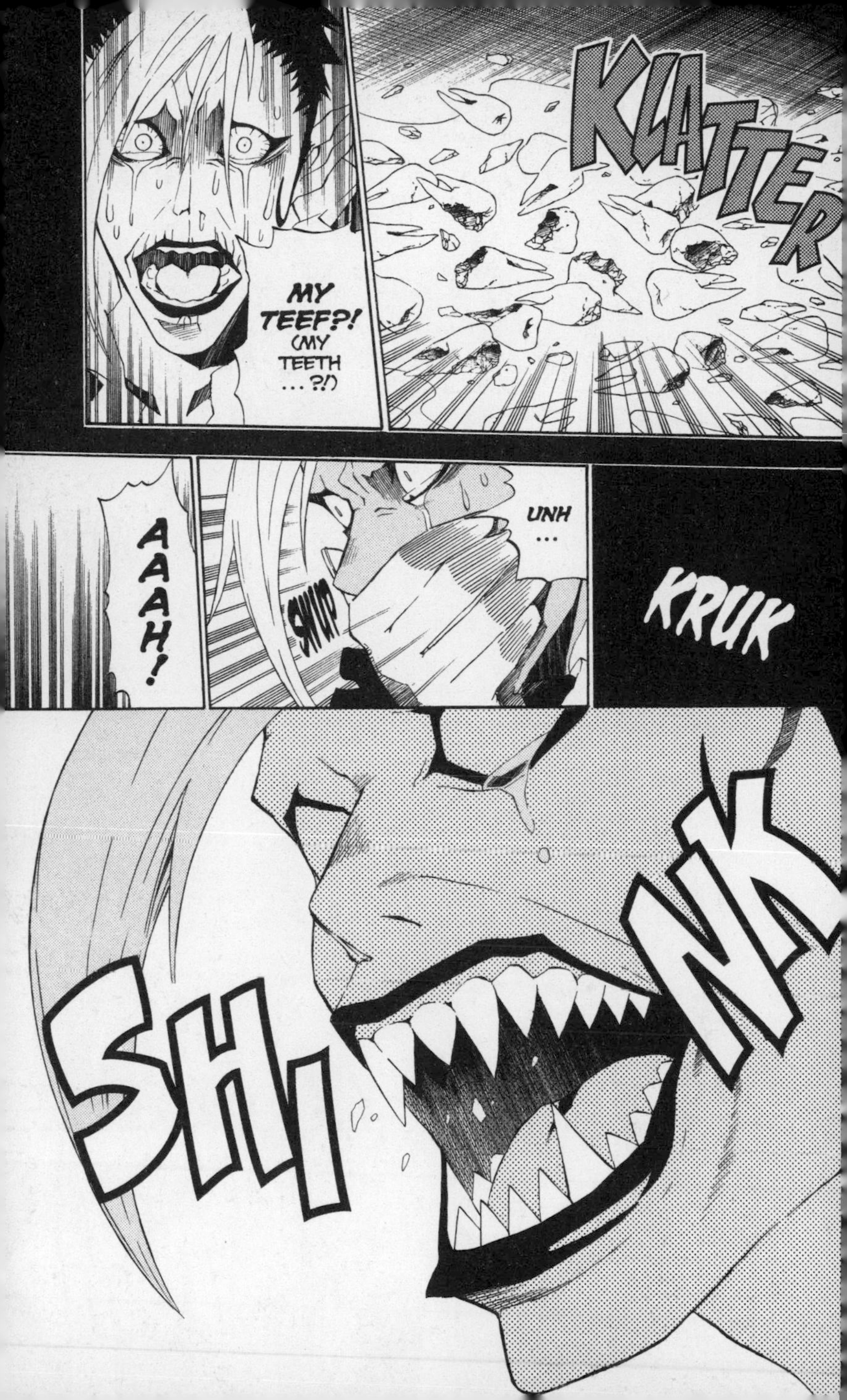
KLATTER
MY TEEF?! (MY TEETH ...?!)
KRUK
UNH ...
AAAAH!
SHINK

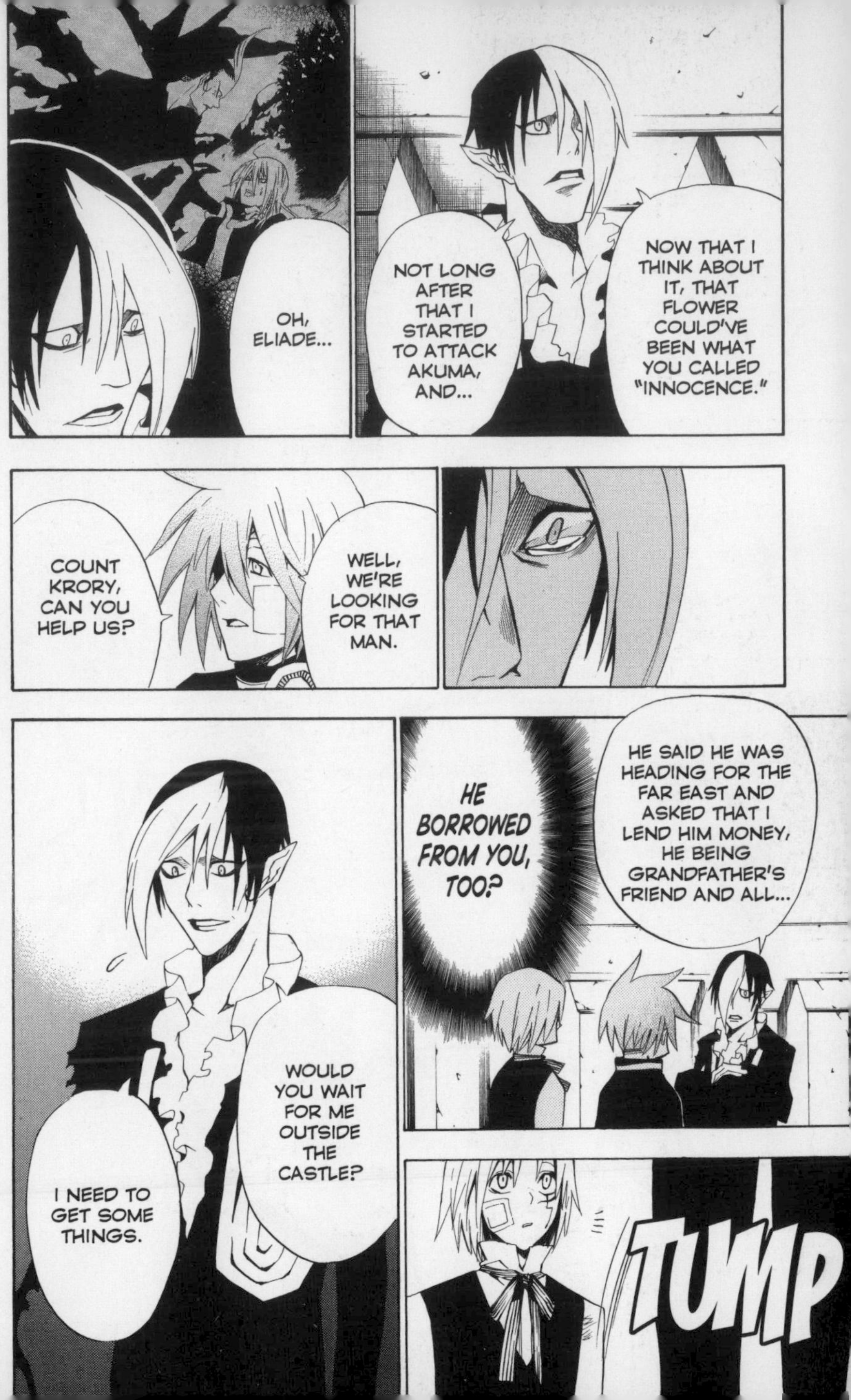
NOW THAT I THINK ABOUT IT, THAT FLOWER COULD'VE BEEN WHAT YOU CALLED "INNOCENCE."
NOT LONG AFTER THAT I STARTED TO ATTACK AKUMA, AND...
OH, ELIADE...
WELL, WE'RE LOOKING FOR THAT MAN.
COUNT KRORY, CAN YOU HELP US?
HE SAID HE WAS HEADING FOR THE FAR EAST AND ASKED THAT I LEND HIM MONEY, HE BEING GRANDFATHER'S FRIEND AND ALL...
HE BORROWED FROM YOU, TOO?
TUMP
WOULD YOU WAIT FOR ME OUTSIDE THE CASTLE?
I NEED TO GET SOME THINGS.

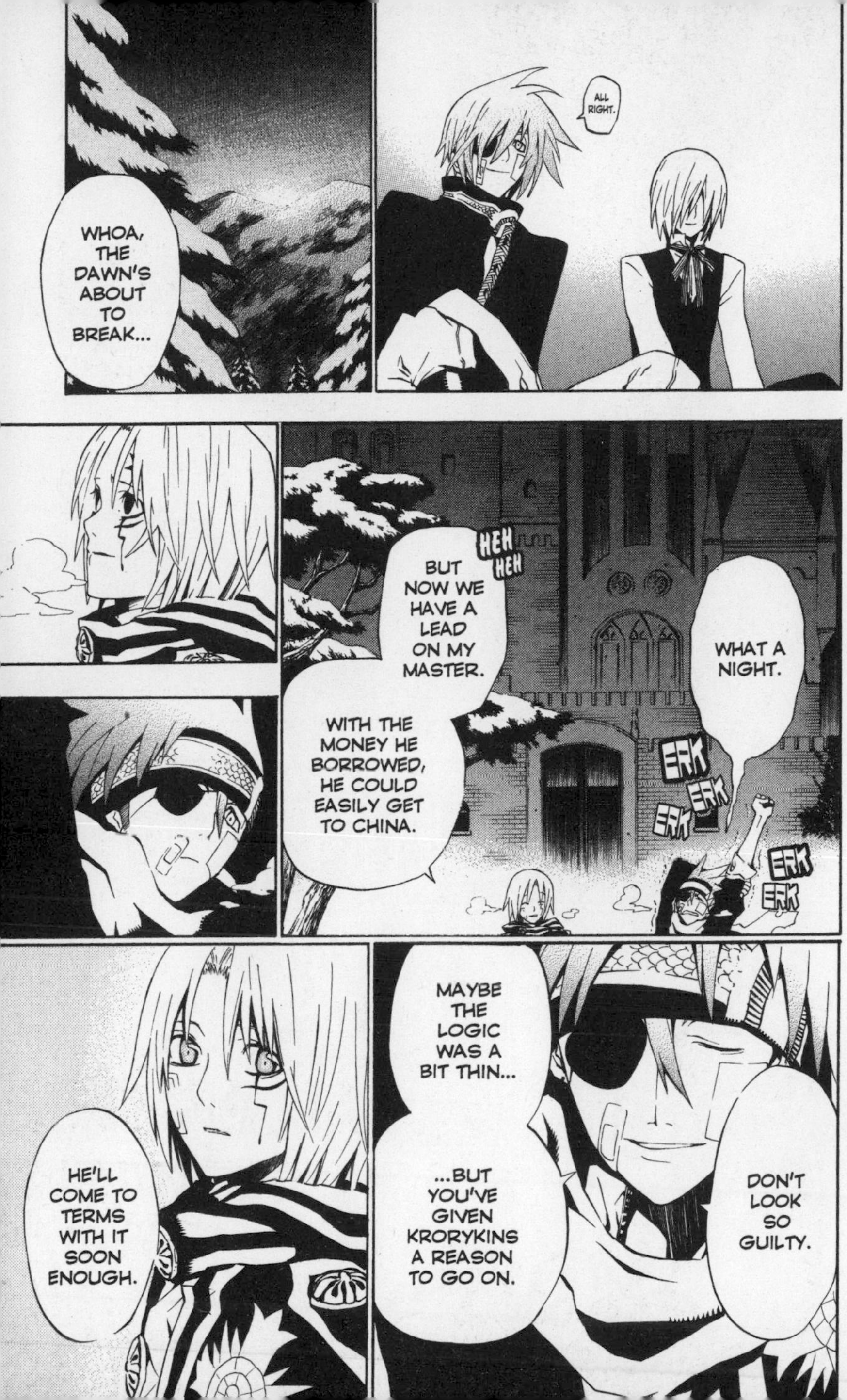
ALL RIGHT.
WHOA, THE DAWN'S ABOUT TO BREAK...
WHAT A NIGHT.
ERK
ERK
ERK
ERK
ERK
HEH HEH
BUT NOW WE HAVE A LEAD ON MY MASTER.
WITH THE MONEY HE BORROWED, HE COULD EASILY GET TO CHINA.
DON'T LOOK SO GUILTY.
MAYBE THE LOGIC WAS A BIT THIN...
...BUT YOU'VE GIVEN KRORYKINS A REASON TO GO ON.
HE'LL COME TO TERMS WITH IT SOON ENOUGH.

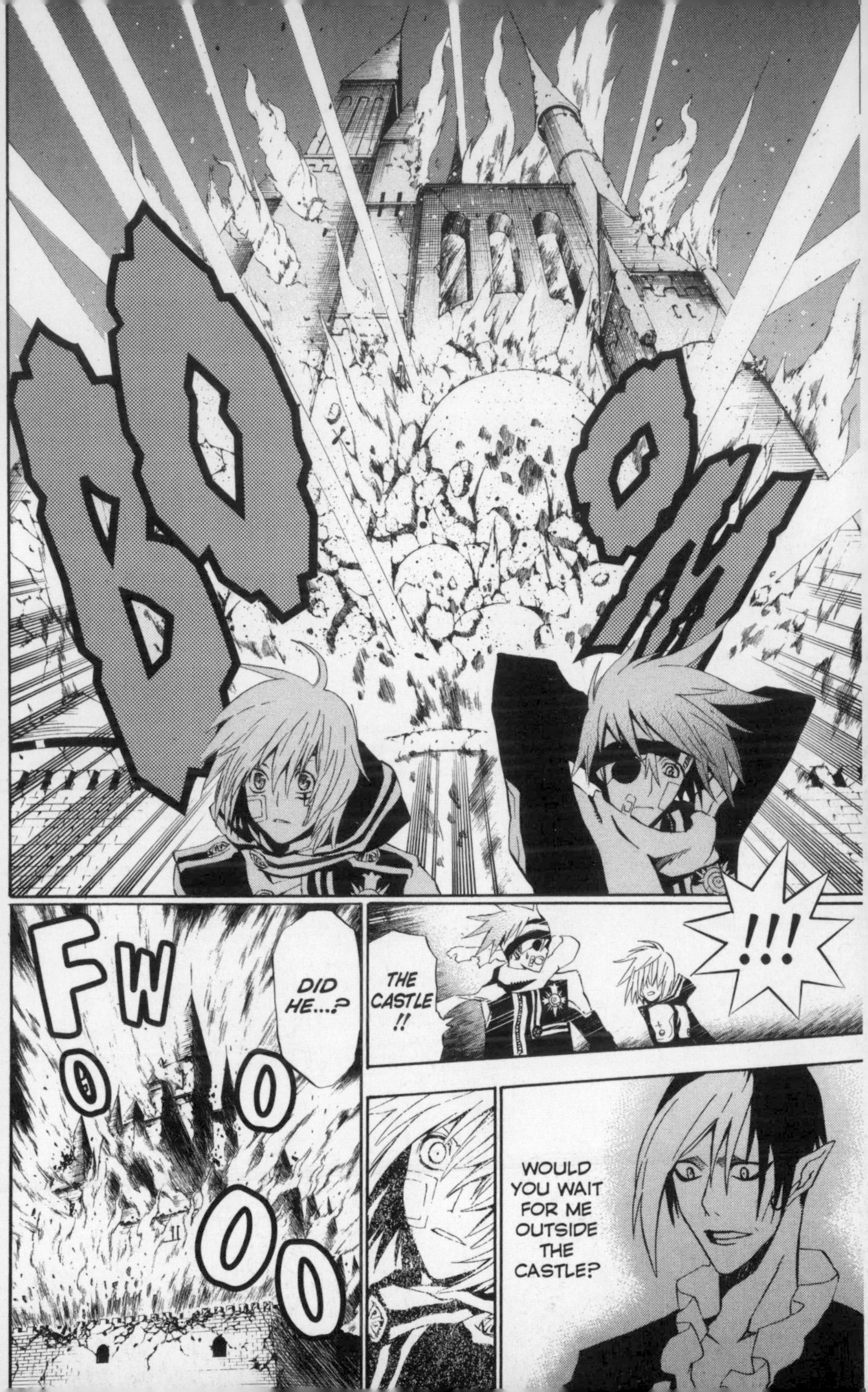
BOOM
!!!
THE CASTLE !!
WOULD YOU WAIT FOR ME OUTSIDE THE CASTLE?
FWOOOO
DID HE...?

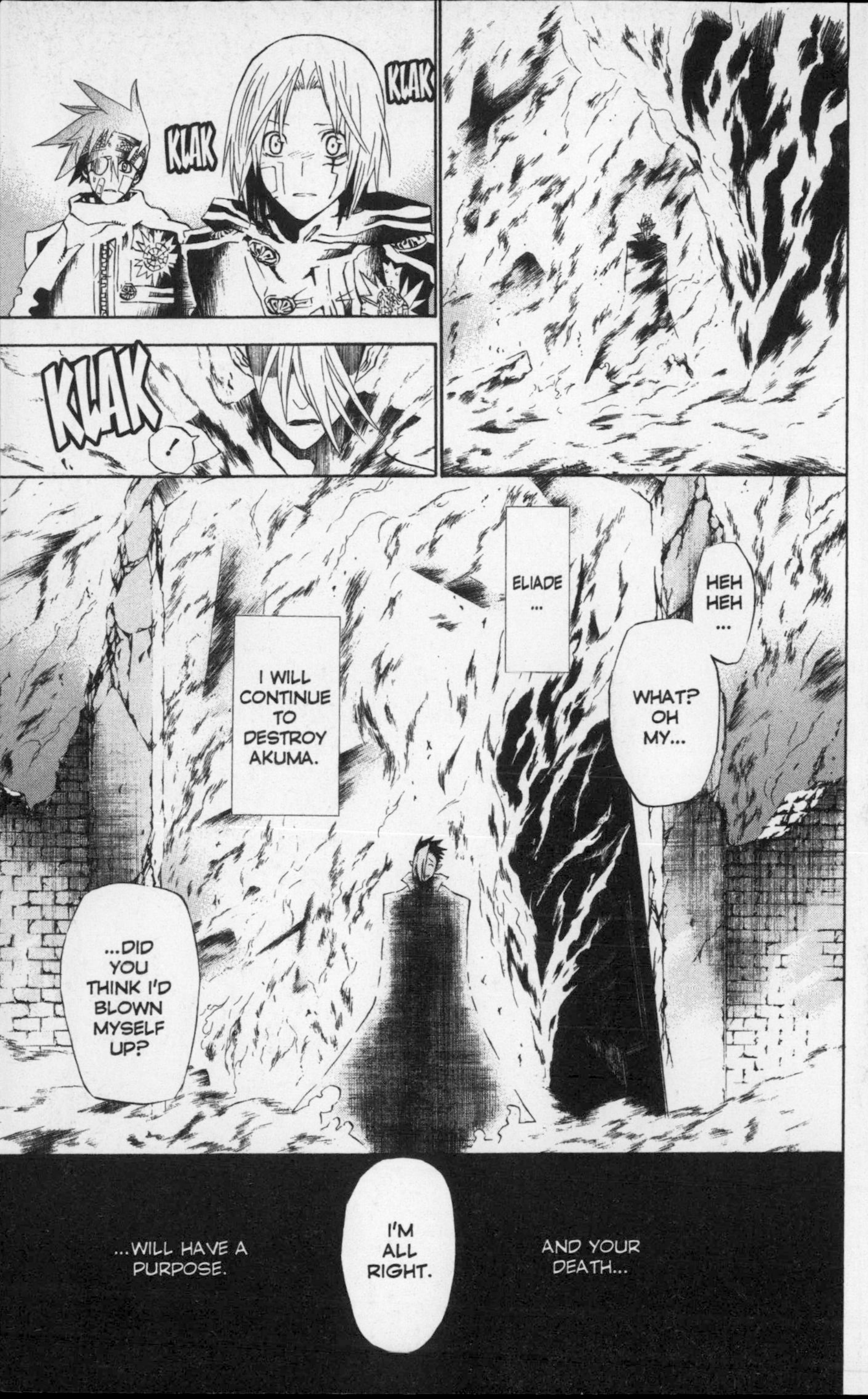
KLAK
KLAK
KLAK
!
HEH HEH ...
WHAT? OH MY...
ELIADE ...
I WILL CONTINUE TO DESTROY AKUMA.
...DID YOU THINK I'D BLOWN MYSELF UP?
AND YOUR DEATH...
I'M ALL RIGHT.
...WILL HAVE A PURPOSE.

KOMUI'S DISCUSSION ROOM VOL. 4

Q. WHEN DID KATSURA FIRST WANT TO BECOME A MANGA ARTIST?

A. I HEAR HE SERIOUSLY STARTED TO THINK ABOUT IT
WHEN HE WAS 21. UNTIL THEN, HE WAS MORE OR LESS
A HERMIT WHO SAT AROUND DRAWING MANGA AT HOME.

Q. HOW DID KATSURA GET TO BE A MANGA ARTIST?

A. HE SAID, "A FRIEND AT MY PART-TIME JOB SUGGESTED
THAT I TRY IT AND SO DID MY TWIN SISTER, WHO USED TO
CRITICIZE MY ARTWORK WHEN WE WERE KIDS. BECAUSE OF
THOSE TWO, ONE DAY I FOUND MYSELF WALKING INTO
SHUEISHA WITH MY HANDS SHAKING."

Q. DO YOU USE A MAPPING NIB WHEN YOU DRAW YOUR CHARACTERS?

A. I UNDERSTAND THAT THE AUTHOR NORMALLY USES A G NIB
AND A MAPPING NIB FOR DETAILED WORK.
BUT THE ONLY PLACE I USE A MAPPING
NIB IS ON MY BEARD.

Q. DOES THE AUTHOR HAVE A SIGNIFICANT
OTHER?

A. YES, HIS CAT "KORO."

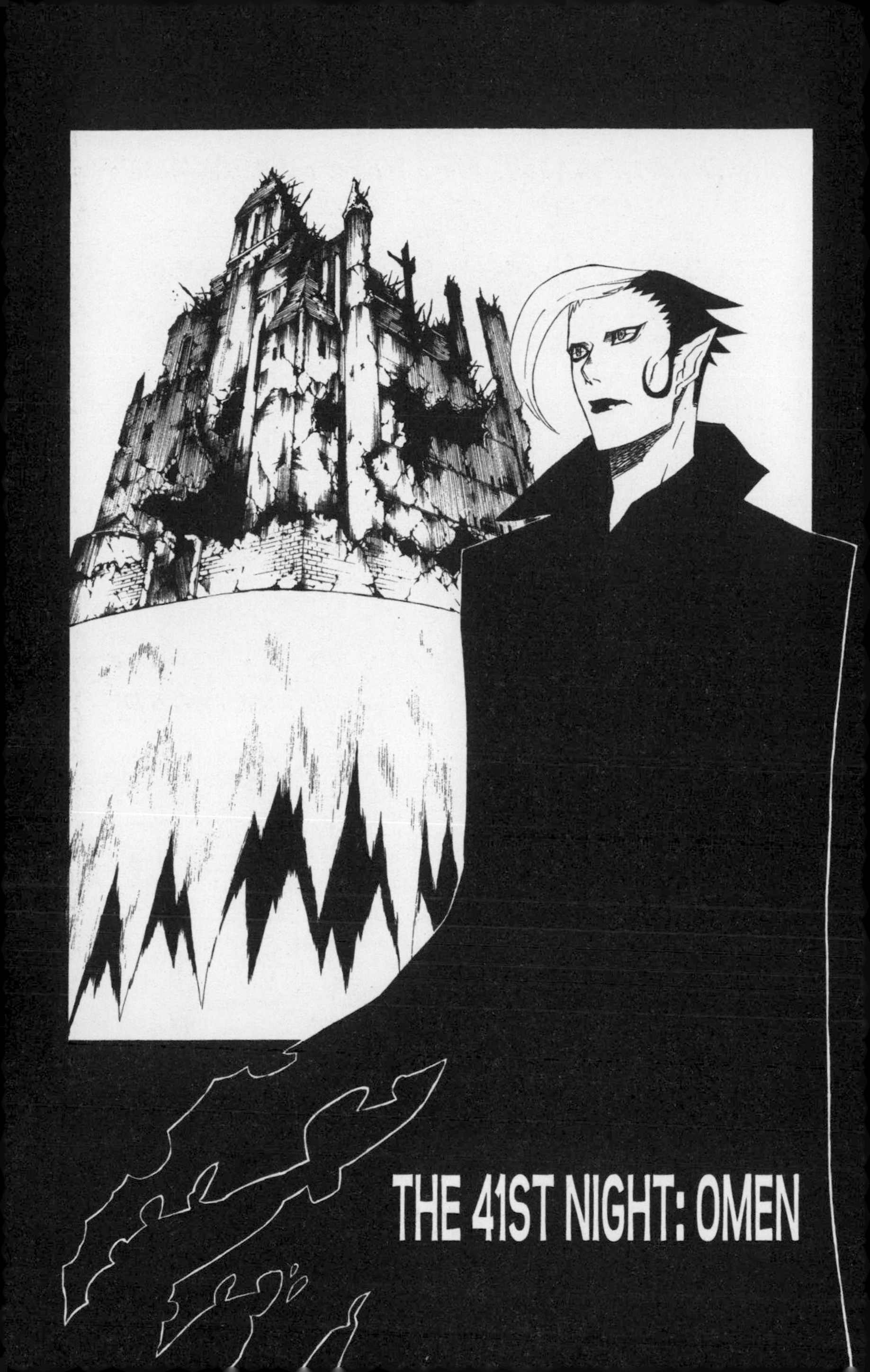
THE 41ST NIGHT: OMEN

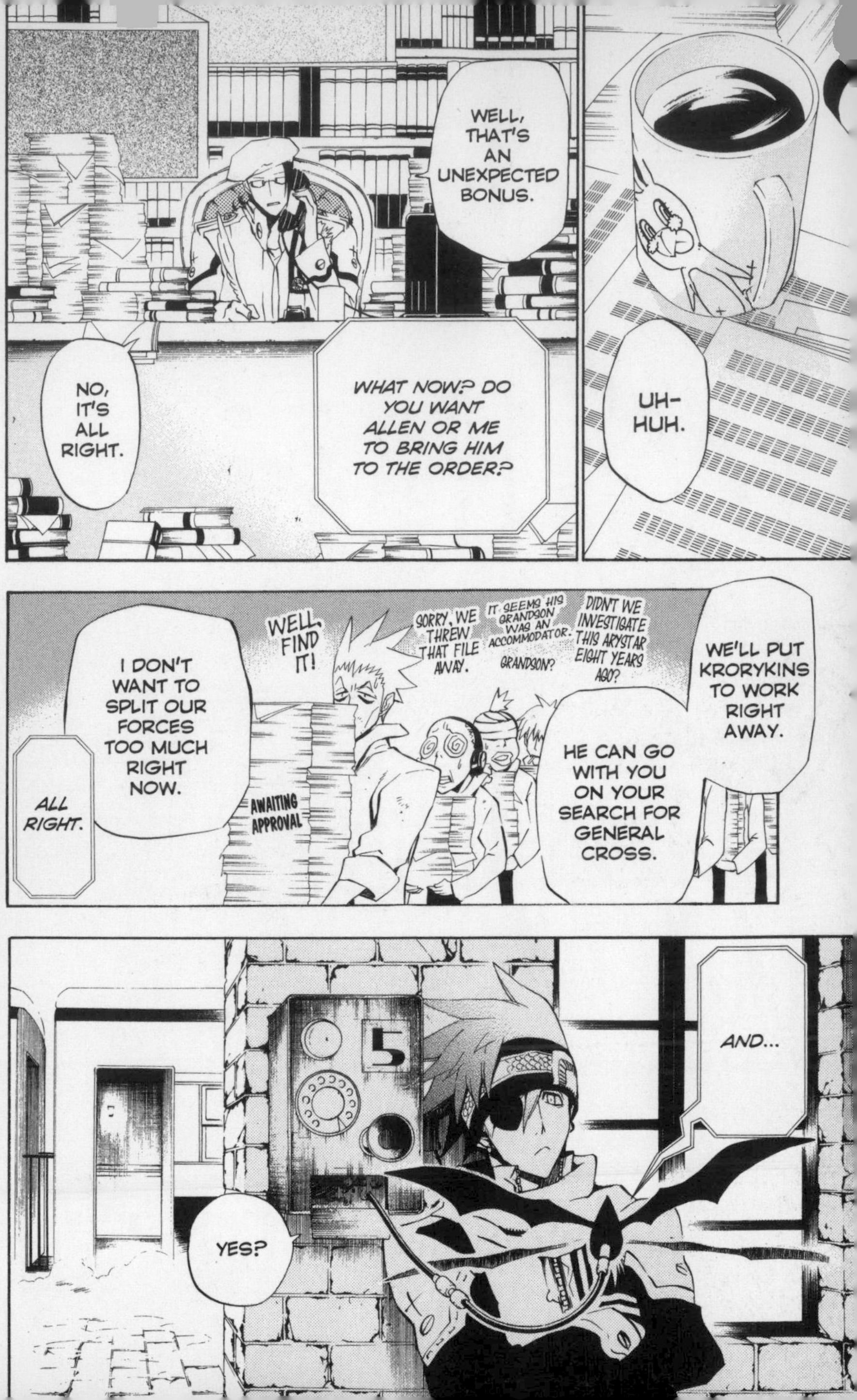
UH-HUH.
WELL, THAT'S AN UNEXPECTED BONUS.
WHAT NOW? DO YOU WANT ALLEN OR ME TO BRING HIM TO THE ORDER?
NO, IT'S ALL RIGHT.
WE'LL PUT KRORYKINS TO WORK RIGHT AWAY.
HE CAN GO WITH YOU ON YOUR SEARCH FOR GENERAL CROSS.
DIDN'T WE INVESTIGATE THIS ARYSTAR EIGHT YEARS AGO?
IT SEEMS HIS GRANDSON WAS AN ACCOMMODATOR.
GRANDSON?
SORRY, WE THREW THAT FILE AWAY.
WELL, FIND IT!
AWAITING APPROVAL
I DON'T WANT TO SPLIT OUR FORCES TOO MUCH RIGHT NOW.
ALL RIGHT.
AND...
5
YES?

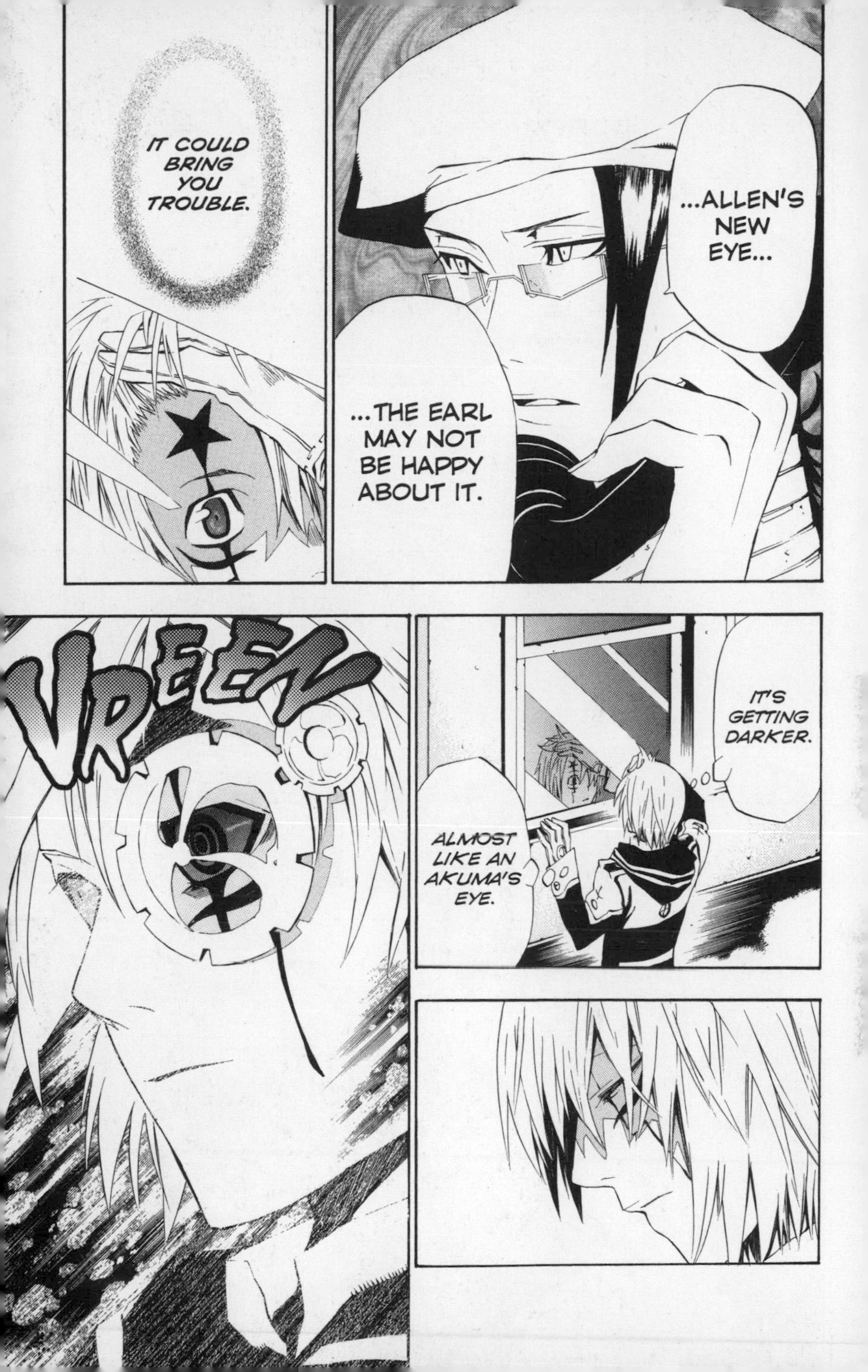
...ALLEN'S NEW EYE...
...THE EARL MAY NOT BE HAPPY ABOUT IT.
IT COULD BRING YOU TROUBLE.
IT'S GETTING DARKER.
ALMOST LIKE AN AKUMA'S EYE.
VREEN

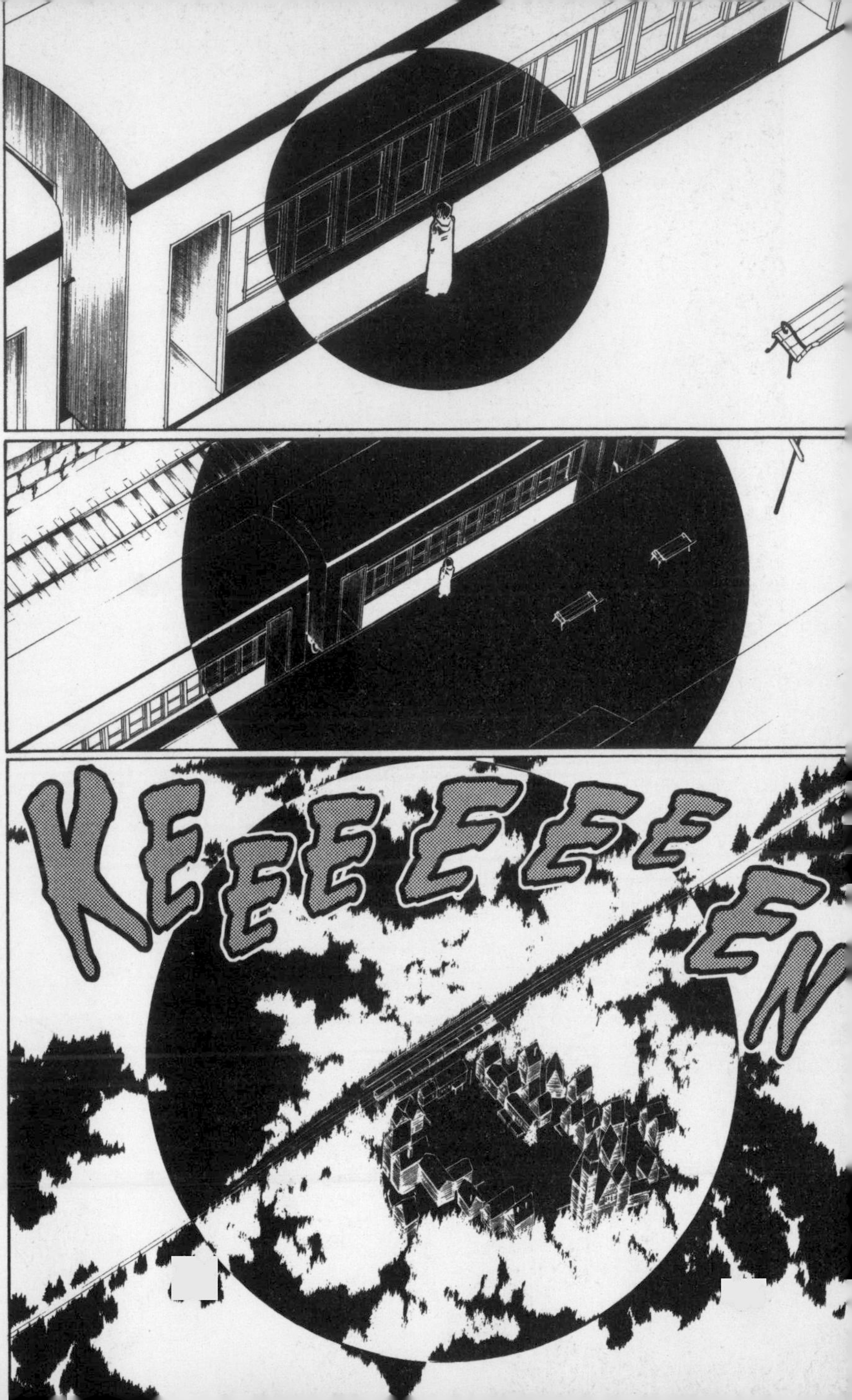
KEEEEEEEN

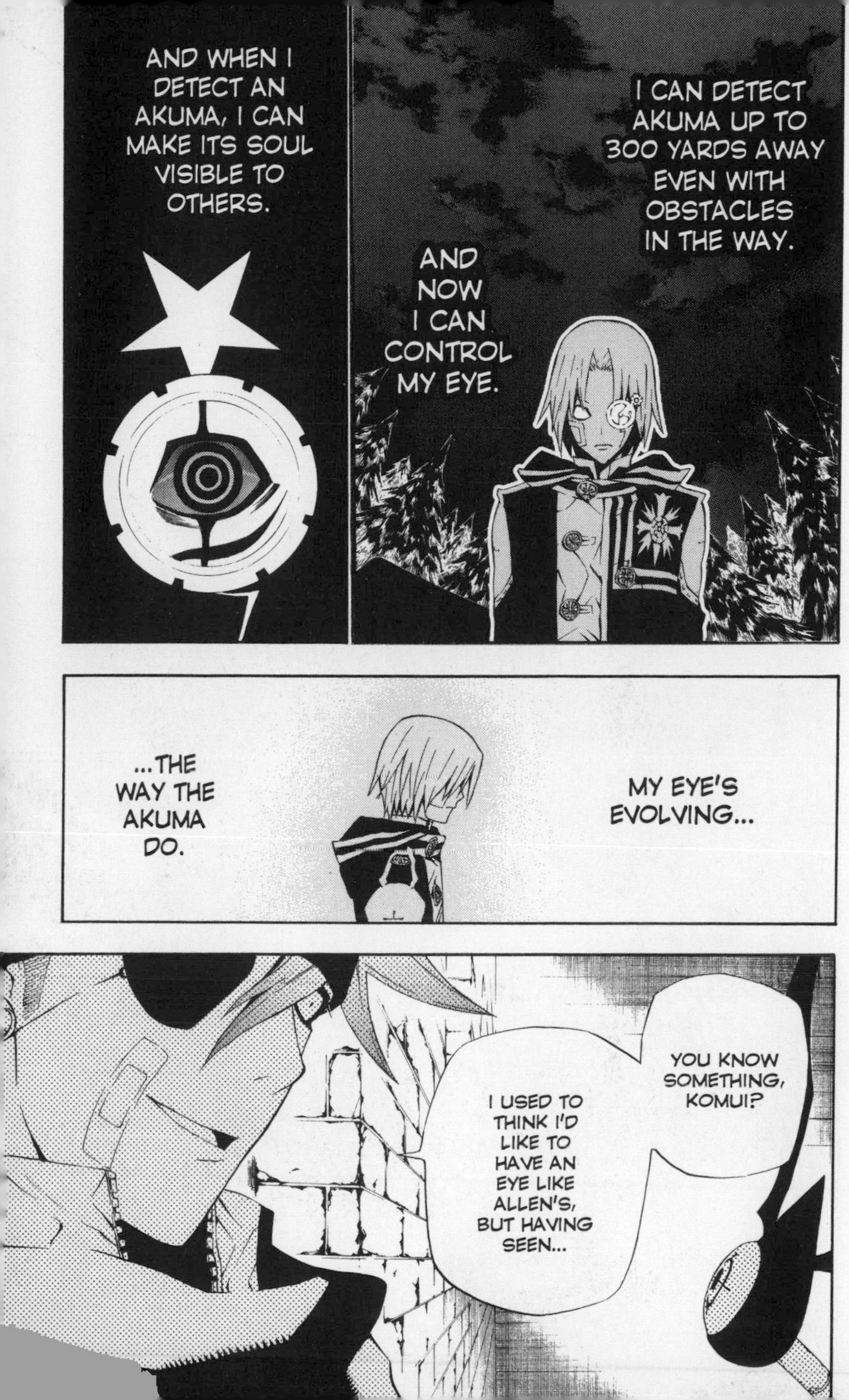
I CAN DETECT AKUMA UP TO 300 YARDS AWAY EVEN WITH OBSTACLES IN THE WAY.
AND NOW I CAN CONTROL MY EYE.
AND WHEN I DETECT AN AKUMA, I CAN MAKE ITS SOUL VISIBLE TO OTHERS.
MY EYE'S EVOLVING...
...THE WAY THE AKUMA DO.
YOU KNOW SOMETHING, KOMUI?
I USED TO THINK I'D LIKE TO HAVE AN EYE LIKE ALLEN'S, BUT HAVING SEEN...

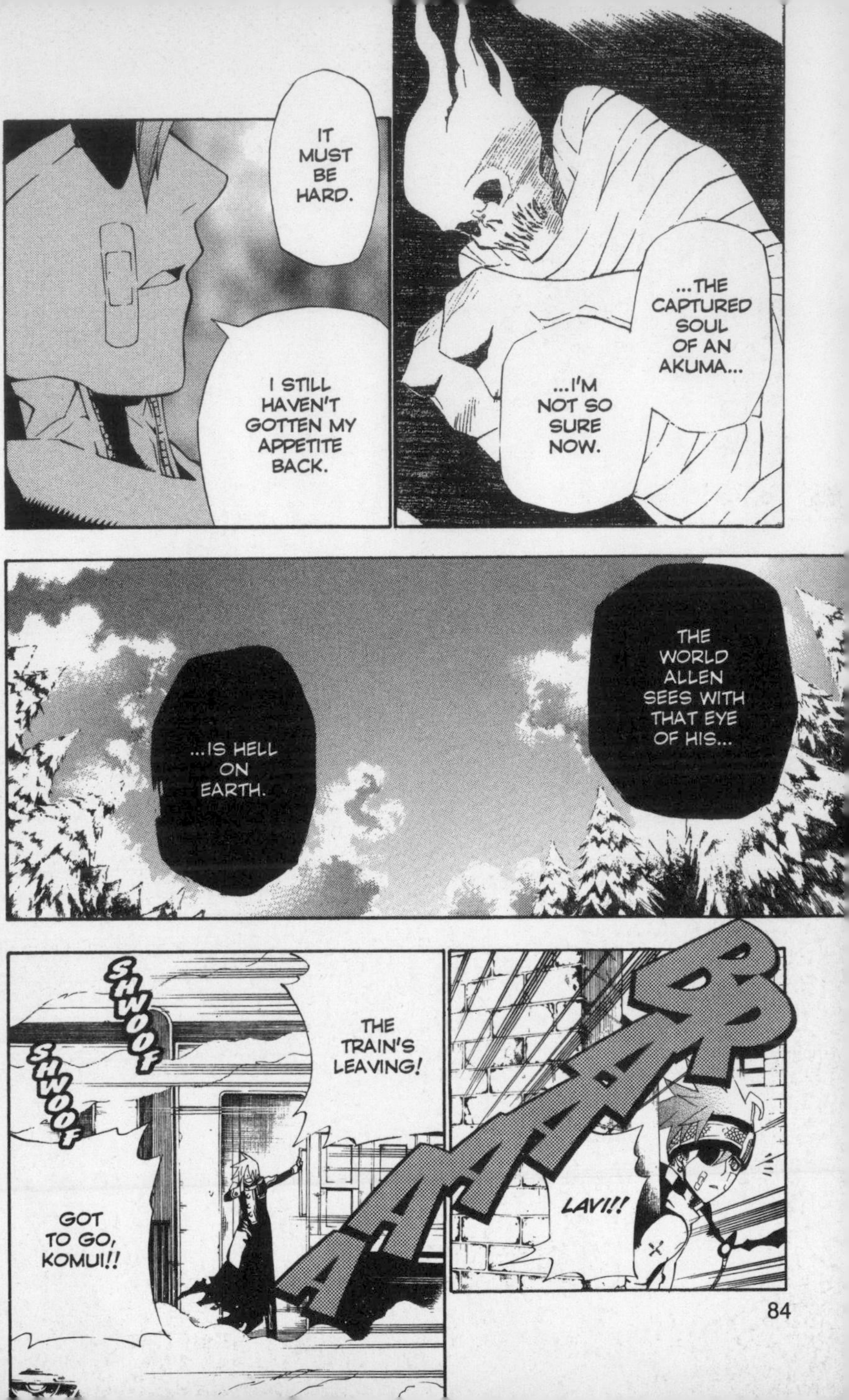
...THE CAPTURED SOUL OF AN AKUMA...
...I'M NOT SO SURE NOW.
IT MUST BE HARD.
I STILL HAVEN'T GOTTEN MY APPETITE BACK.
THE WORLD ALLEN SEES WITH THAT EYE OF HIS...
...IS HELL ON EARTH.
LAVI!!
SHWOOF
SHWOOF
THE TRAIN'S LEAVING!
GOT TO GO, KOMUI!!

READ THIS WAY

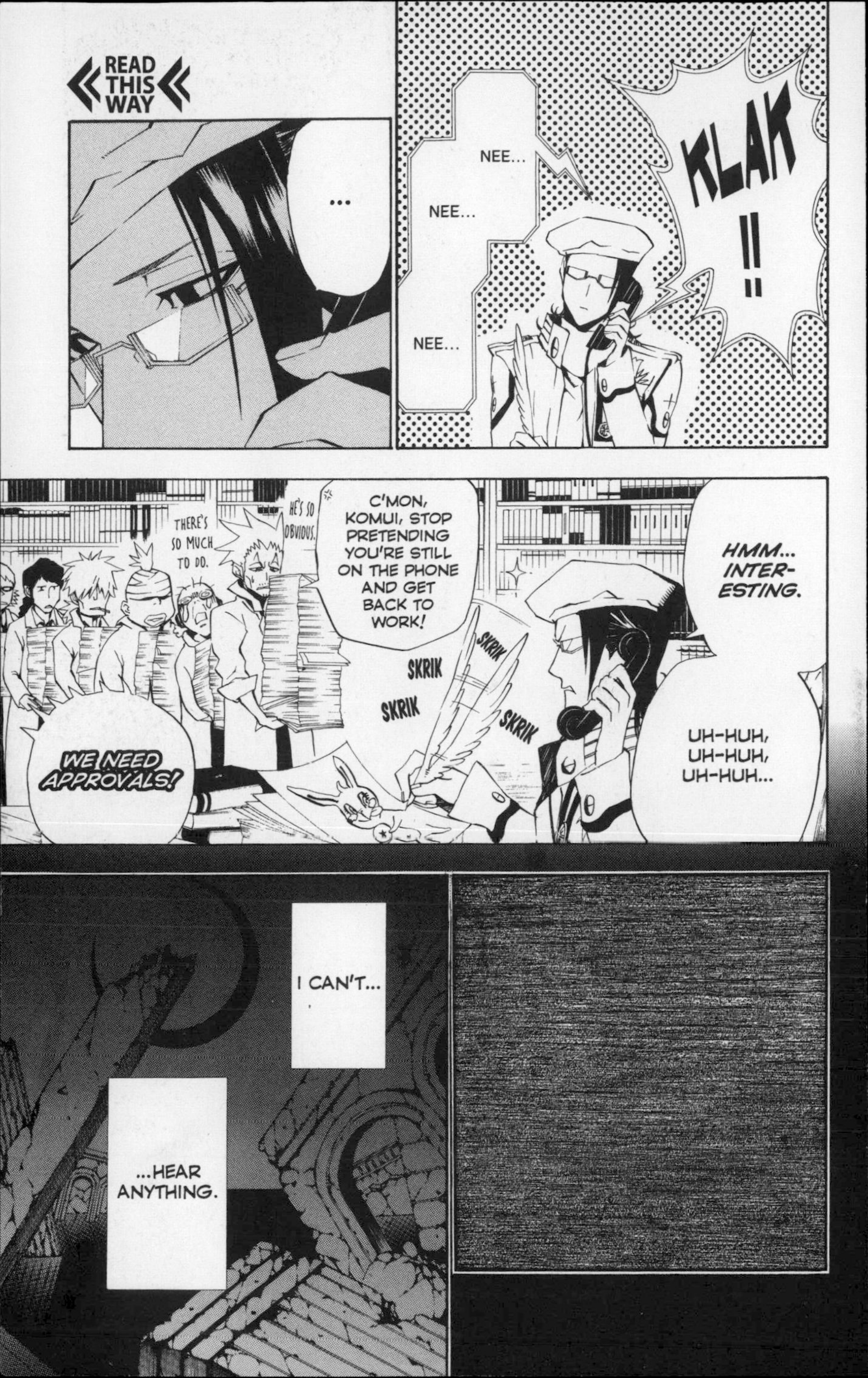
KLAK !!
NEE...
NEE...
NEE...
...
HMM... INTER-ESTING.
UH-HUH, UH-HUH, UH-HUH...
C'MON, KOMUI, STOP PRETENDING YOU'RE STILL ON THE PHONE AND GET BACK TO WORK!
HE'S SO OBVIOUS.
THERE'S SO MUCH TO DO.
SKRIK
SKRIK
SKRIK
SKRIK
WE NEED APPROVALS!
I CAN'T...
...HEAR ANYTHING.

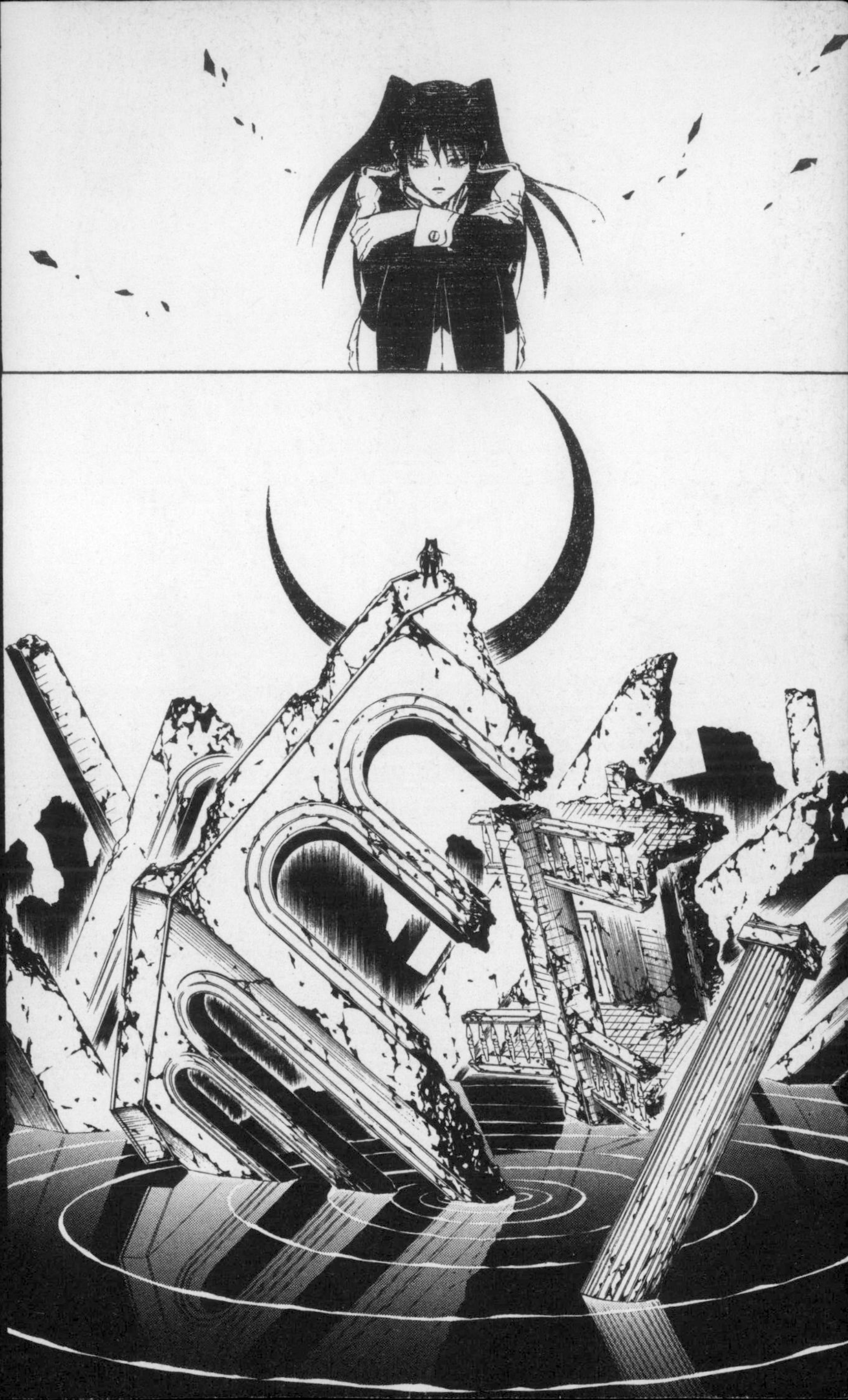

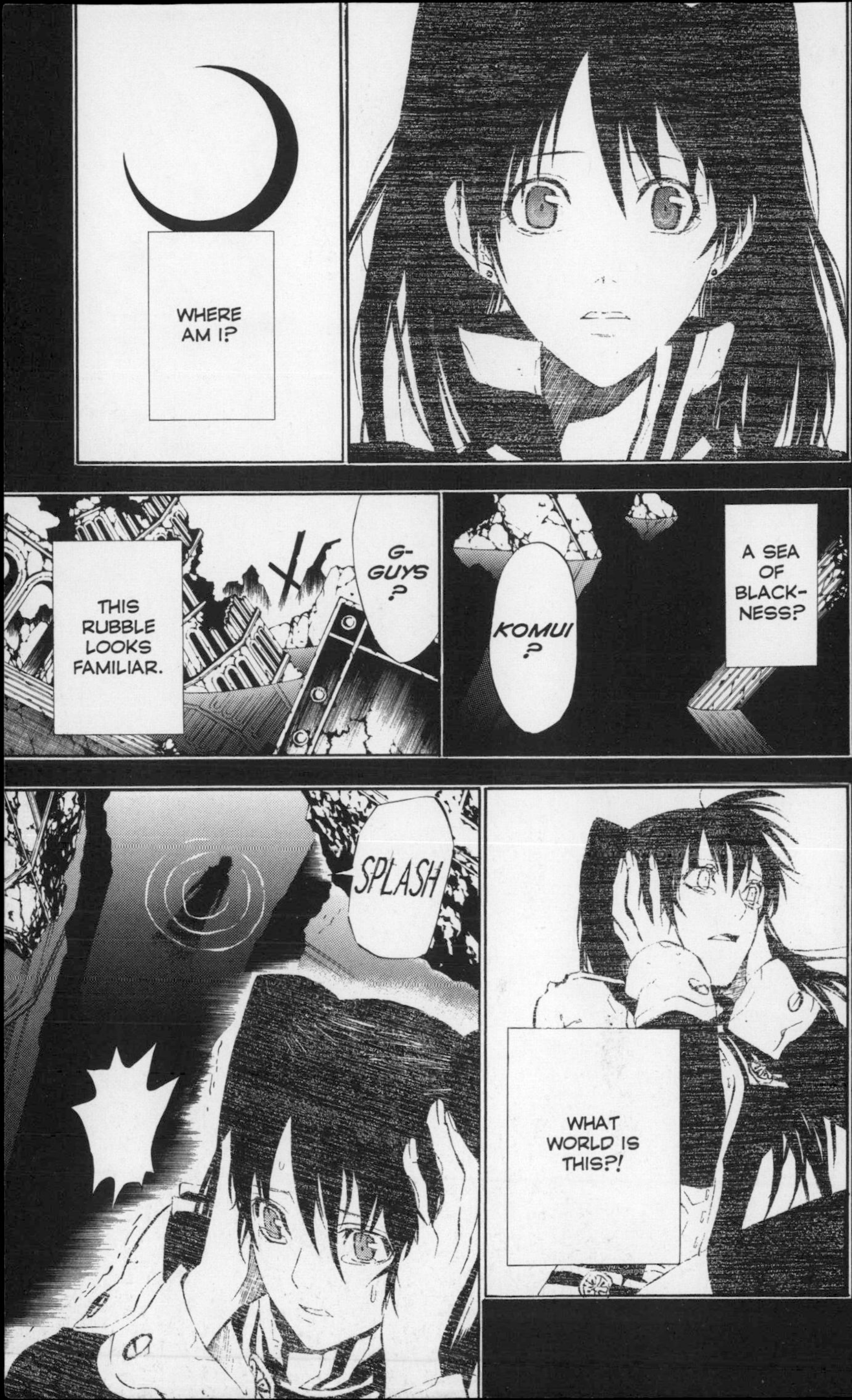
WHERE AM I?
A SEA OF BLACKNESS?
KOMUI?
G-GUYS?
THIS RUBBLE LOOKS FAMILIAR.
WHAT WORLD IS THIS?!
SPLASH

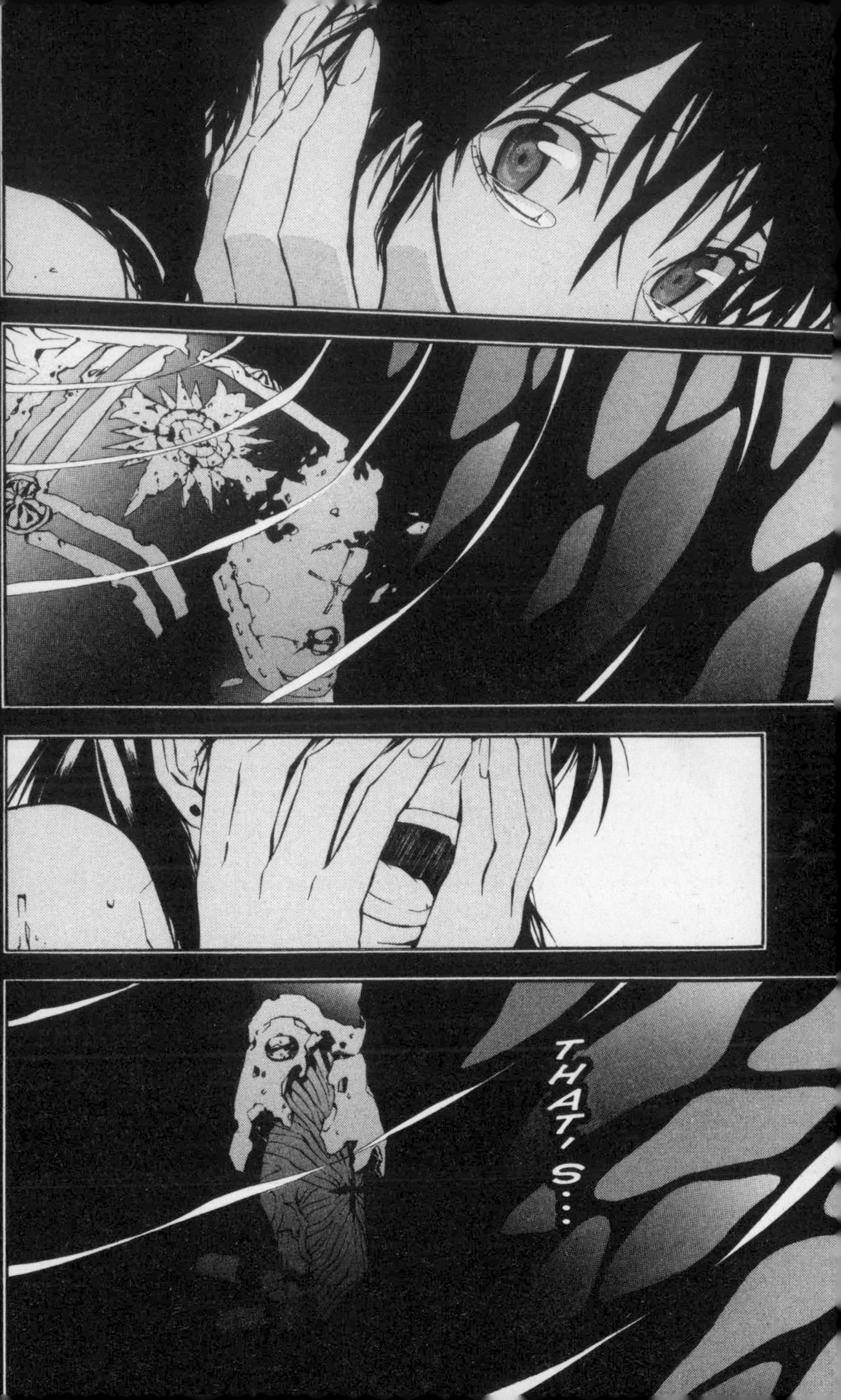
THAT'S...

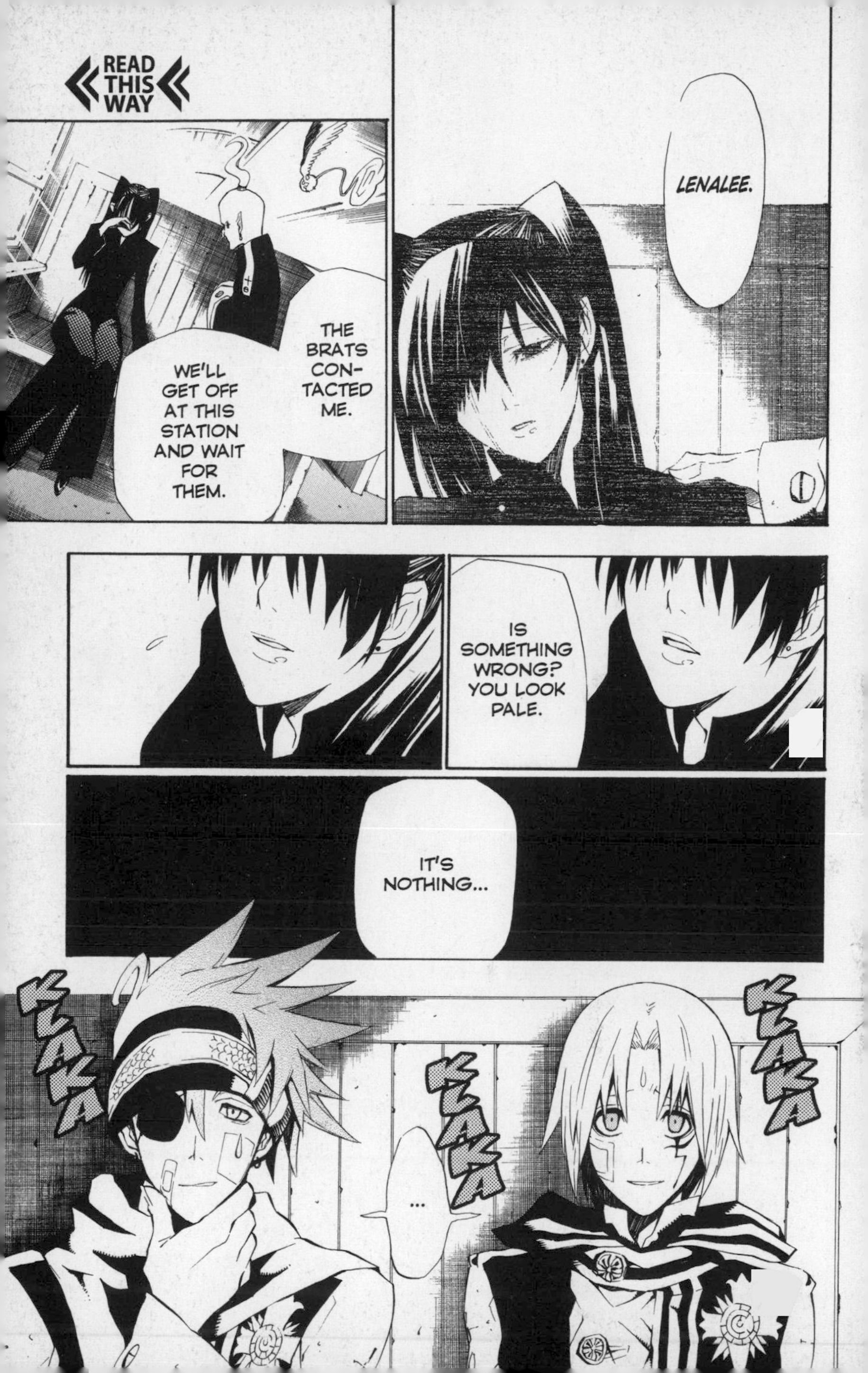
READ THIS WAY
LENALEE.
THE BRATS CONTACTED ME.
WE'LL GET OFF AT THIS STATION AND WAIT FOR THEM.
IS SOMETHING WRONG? YOU LOOK PALE.
IT'S NOTHING...
KLAKA
KLAKA
...
KLAKA

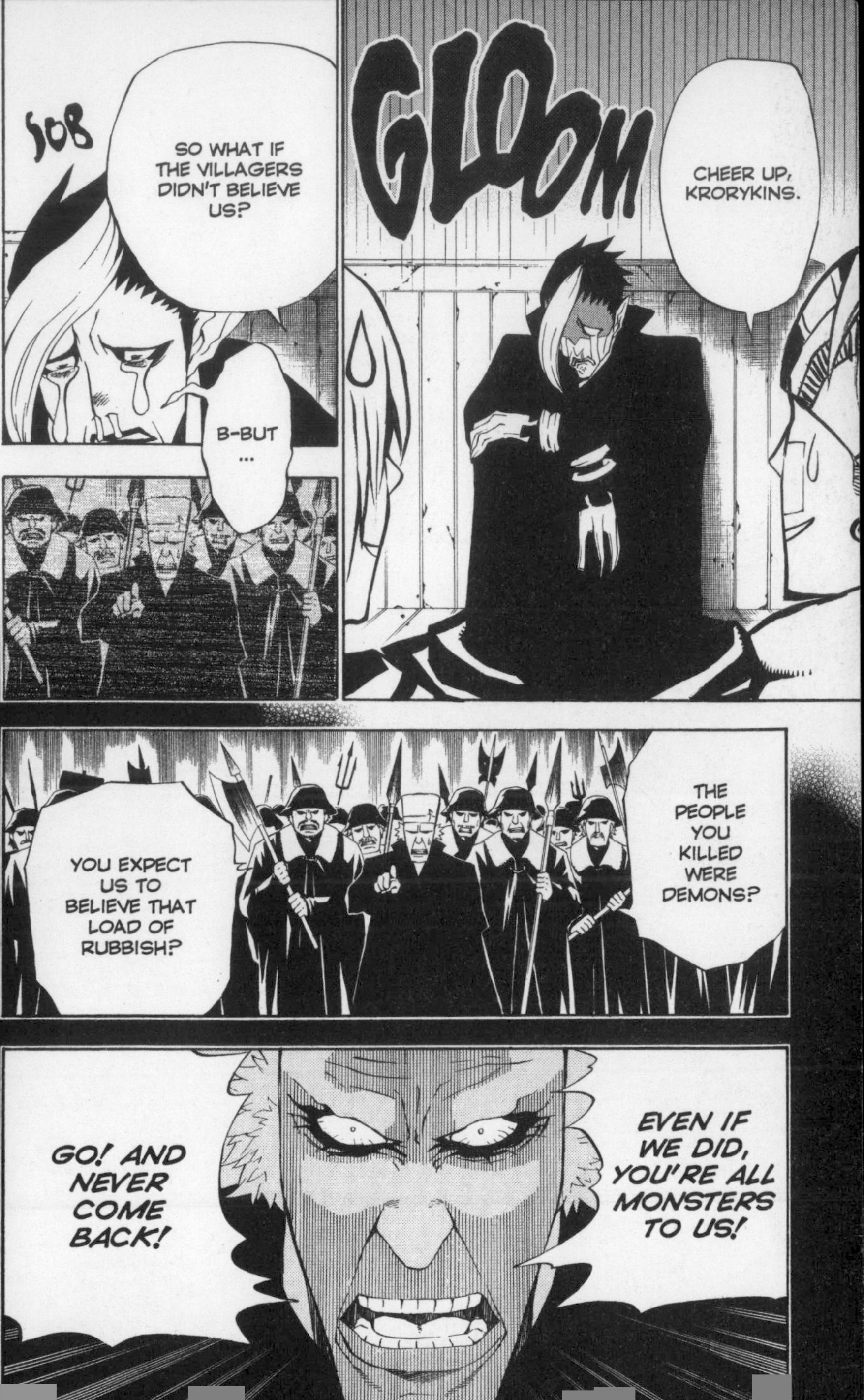
GLOOM
CHEER UP, KRORYKINS.
SOB
SO WHAT IF THE VILLAGERS DIDN'T BELIEVE US?
B-BUT ...
THE PEOPLE YOU KILLED WERE DEMONS?
YOU EXPECT US TO BELIEVE THAT LOAD OF RUBBISH?
EVEN IF WE DID, YOU'RE ALL MONSTERS TO US!
GO! AND NEVER COME BACK!

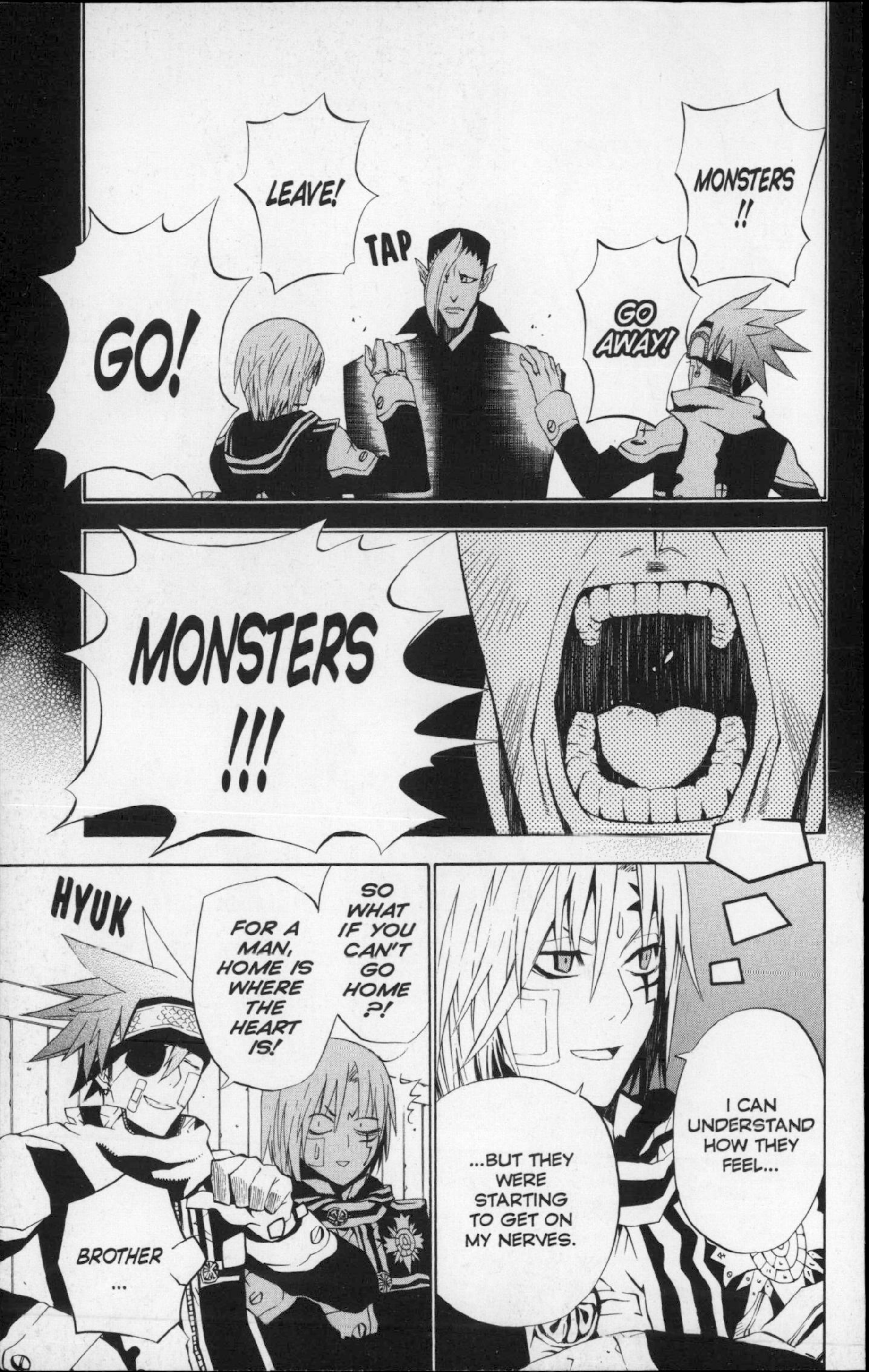
MONSTERS !!
GO AWAY!
TAP
LEAVE!
GO!
MONSTERS !!!
I CAN UNDERSTAND HOW THEY FEEL...
...BUT THEY WERE STARTING TO GET ON MY NERVES.
SO WHAT IF YOU CAN'T GO HOME ?!
FOR A MAN, HOME IS WHERE THE HEART IS!
HYUK
BROTHER ...

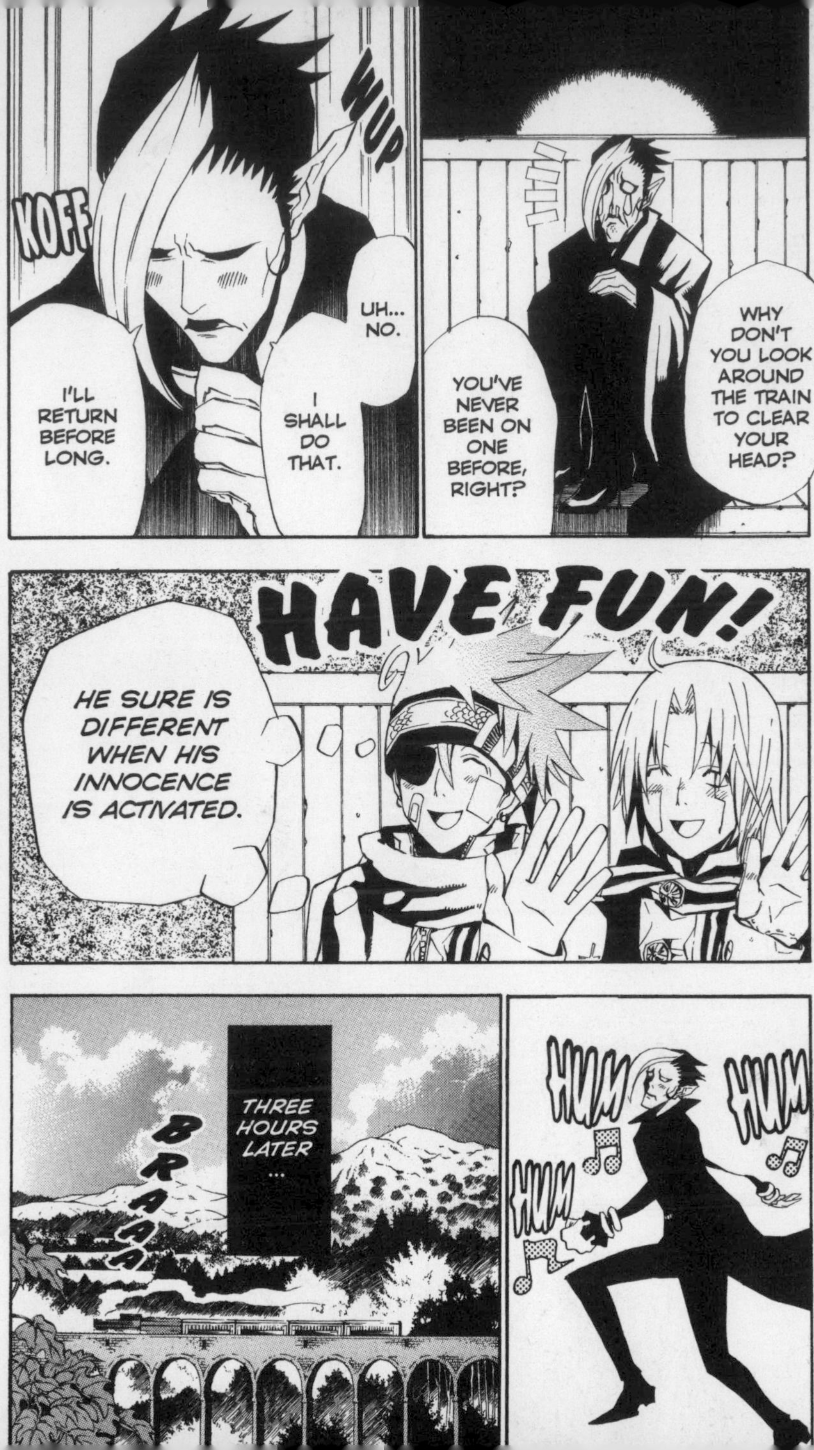
WHY DON'T YOU LOOK AROUND THE TRAIN TO CLEAR YOUR HEAD?
YOU'VE NEVER BEEN ON ONE BEFORE, RIGHT?
WUP
UH... NO.
KOFF
I SHALL DO THAT.
I'LL RETURN BEFORE LONG.
HAVE FUN!
HE SURE IS DIFFERENT WHEN HIS INNOCENCE IS ACTIVATED.
HUM
HUM
HUM
THREE HOURS LATER...
BRAAAA

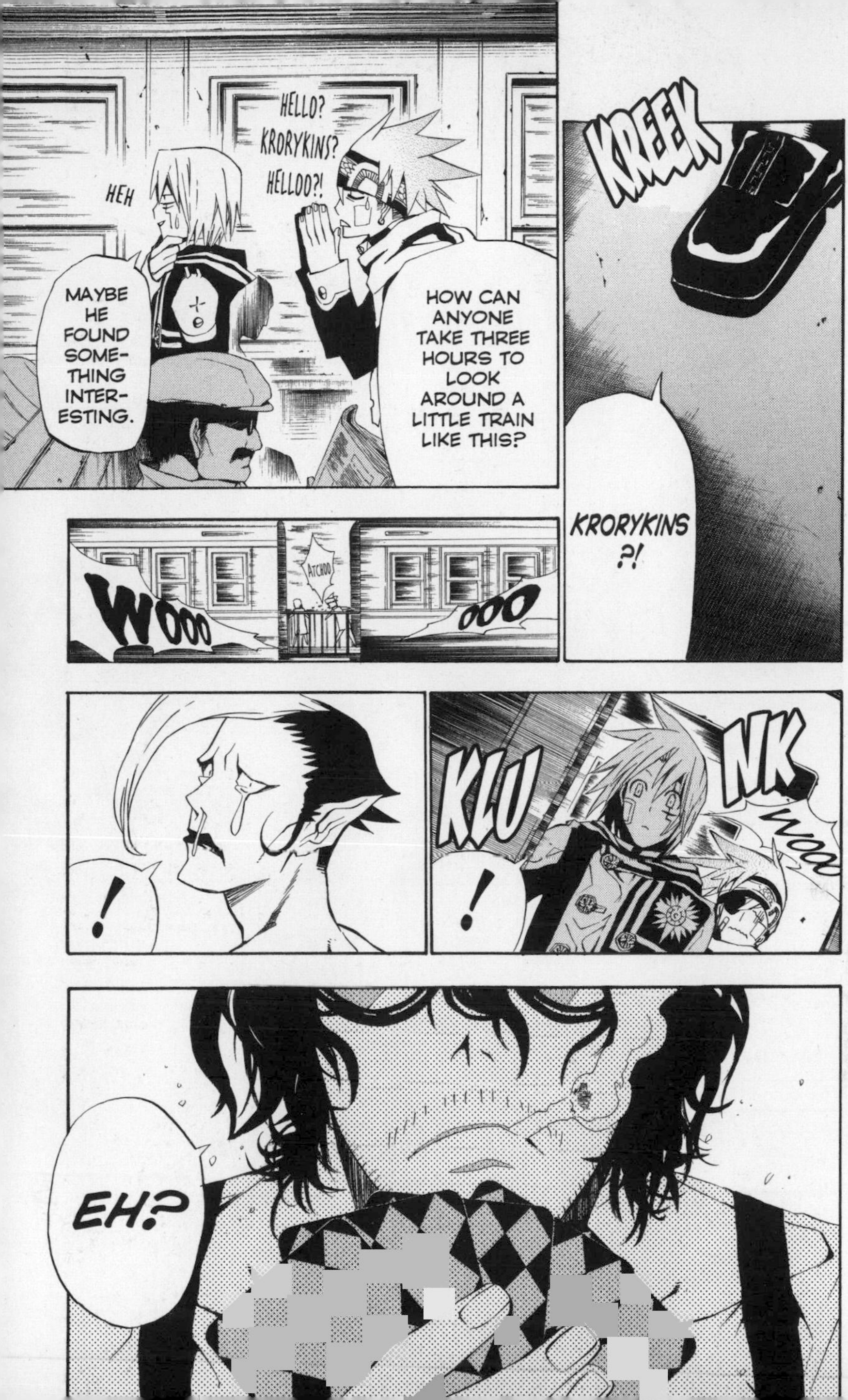
KREEK
KRORYKINS ?!
HELLO? KRORYKINS? HELLOO?!
HEH
HOW CAN ANYONE TAKE THREE HOURS TO LOOK AROUND A LITTLE TRAIN LIKE THIS?
MAYBE HE FOUND SOME-THING INTER-ESTING.
ATCHOO
WOOO OOO
KLU NK
WOOO
!
!
EH?

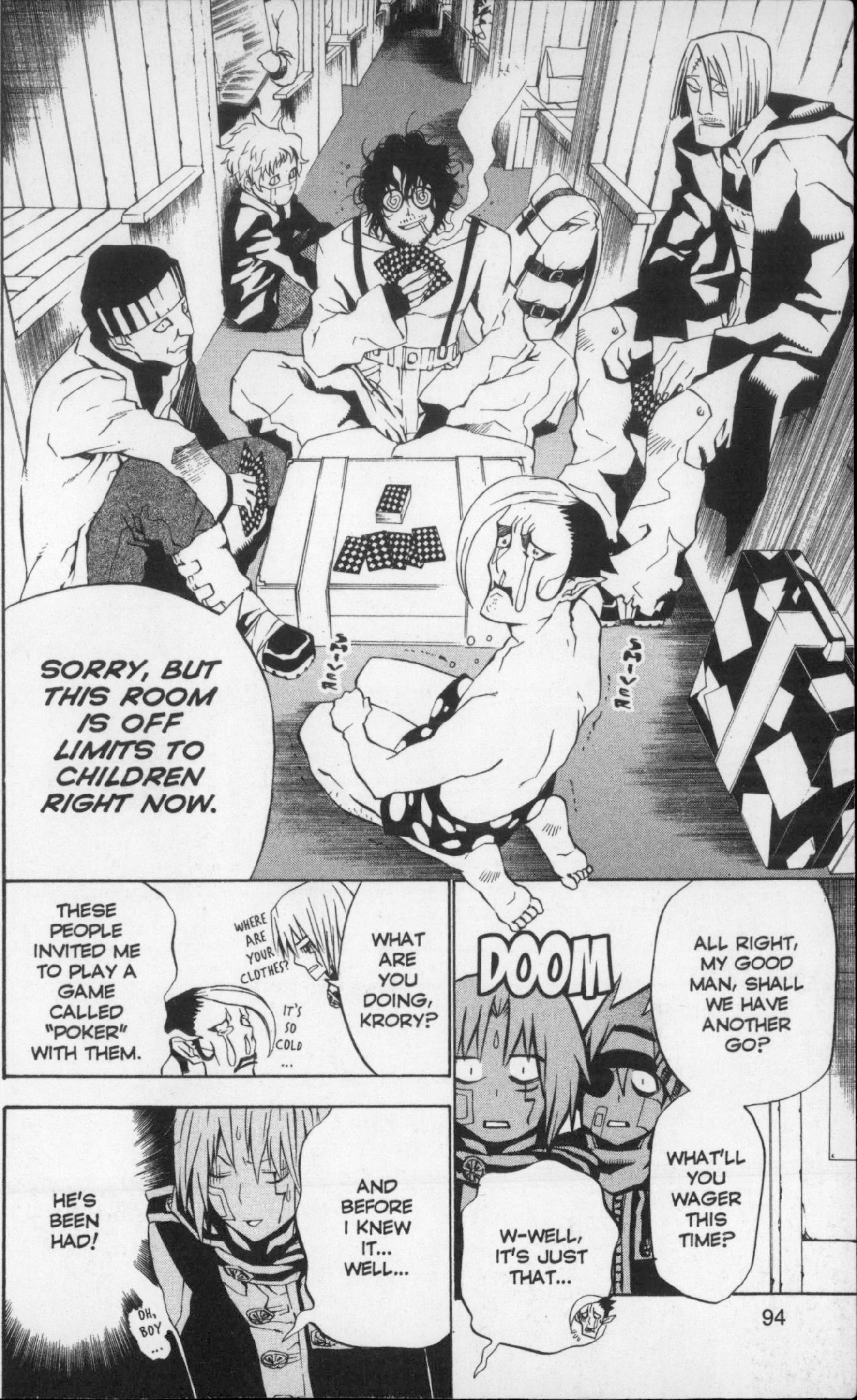
SORRY, BUT THIS ROOM IS OFF LIMITS TO CHILDREN RIGHT NOW.
SHIVER
SHIVER
DOOM
ALL RIGHT, MY GOOD MAN, SHALL WE HAVE ANOTHER GO?
WHAT'LL YOU WAGER THIS TIME?
W-WELL, IT'S JUST THAT...
WHAT ARE YOU DOING, KRORY?
WHERE ARE YOUR CLOTHES?
THESE PEOPLE INVITED ME TO PLAY A GAME CALLED "POKER" WITH THEM.
IT'S SO COLD...
AND BEFORE I KNEW IT... WELL...
HE'S BEEN HAD!
OH, BOY...

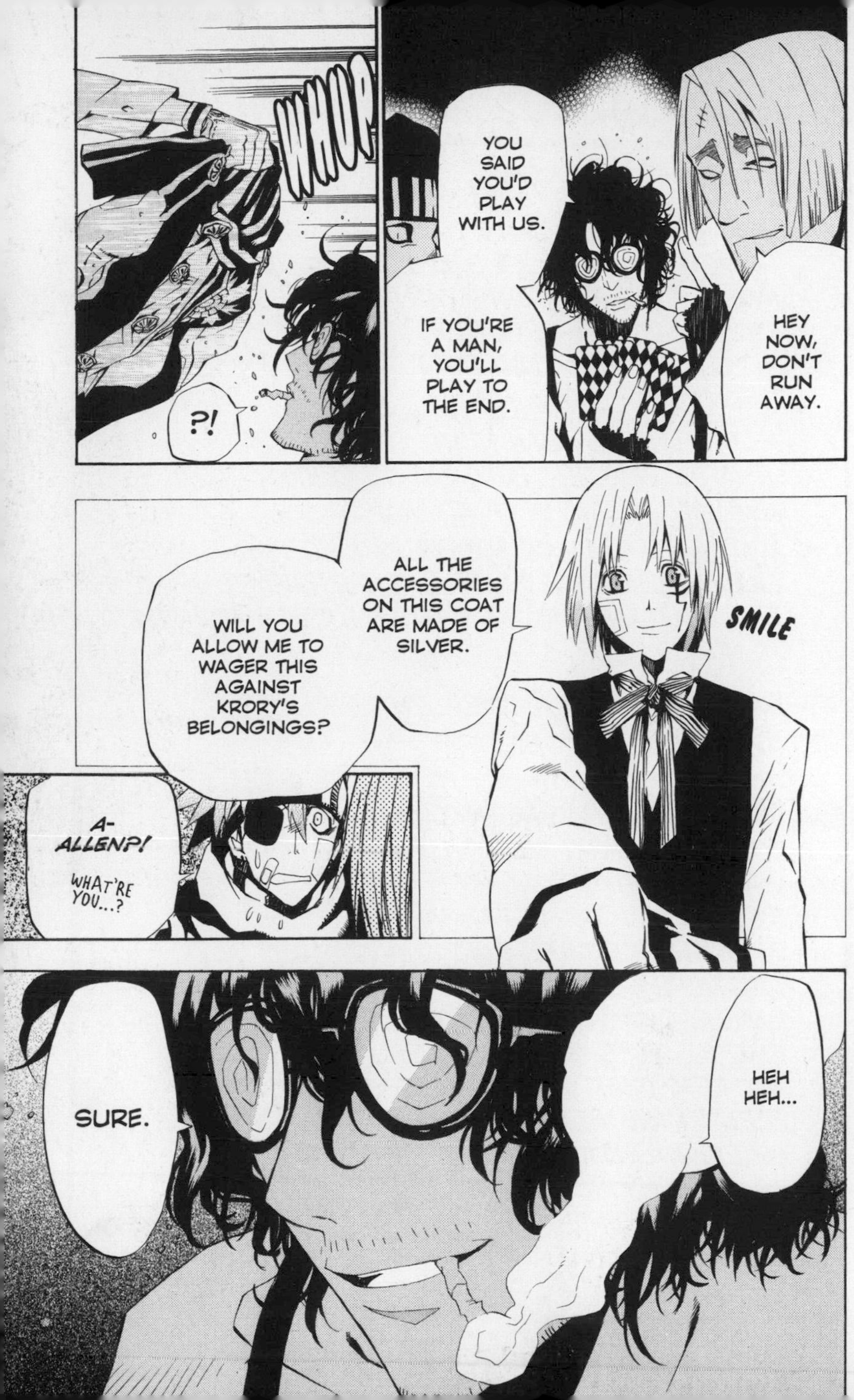
HEY NOW, DON'T RUN AWAY.
YOU SAID YOU'D PLAY WITH US.
IF YOU'RE A MAN, YOU'LL PLAY TO THE END.
WHOP
?!
SMILE
ALL THE ACCESSORIES ON THIS COAT ARE MADE OF SILVER.
WILL YOU ALLOW ME TO WAGER THIS AGAINST KRORY'S BELONGINGS?
A- ALLEN?!
WHAT'RE YOU...?
HEH HEH...
SURE.

KOMUI'S DISCUSSION ROOM VOL. 5

Q. IS THERE ANYTHING THAT ALLEN CAN'T EAT?

A. SOMETHING ALLEN CAN'T EAT, EH? WELL, COME TO THINK OF IT, LENALEE OFFERED HIM SOMETHING SWEET THAT SHE DIDN'T WANT TO FINISH AND, SURPRISINGLY, HE DECLINED. I THINK IT WAS CHOCOLATE CAKE. COULD IT BE THAT ALLEN DOESN'T LIKE CHOCOLATE?

Q. ALLEN, ON THE 18TH NIGHT, THINKS THAT LENALEE IS "CUTE," BUT WAS HE SERIOUS? THIS QUESTION KEEPS ME UP AT NIGHT!

A. AT THAT TIME I WAS BUSY REPAIRING THE DAMAGE THAT KOMLIN CAUSED. WELL, SINCE THEY'RE ABOUT THE SAME AGE, WOULDN'T IT BE NATURAL FOR HIM TO NOTICE HER?

Q. WHAT KIND OF BOYS DOES LENALEE LIKE?

A. HMM... I HAVE NO IDEA.

Q. DOES LENALEE WEAR ANYTHING UNDER HER SKIRT (BUT OVER HER UNDERWEAR)?

A. GIVE ME A BREAK. IF I ANSWER A QUESTION LIKE THAT, WHO KNOWS WHAT CHIEF KOMUI WILL DO TO ME? [SWEAT DROP] IF YOU WANT TO FIND OUT MORE ABOUT LENALEE, ASK HEAD CHEF JERRY. THERE AREN'T MANY WOMEN IN THE ORDER, SO LENALEE SEEMS TO LIKE TALKING TO JERRY BECAUSE HE UNDER-STANDS HOW WOMEN THINK.

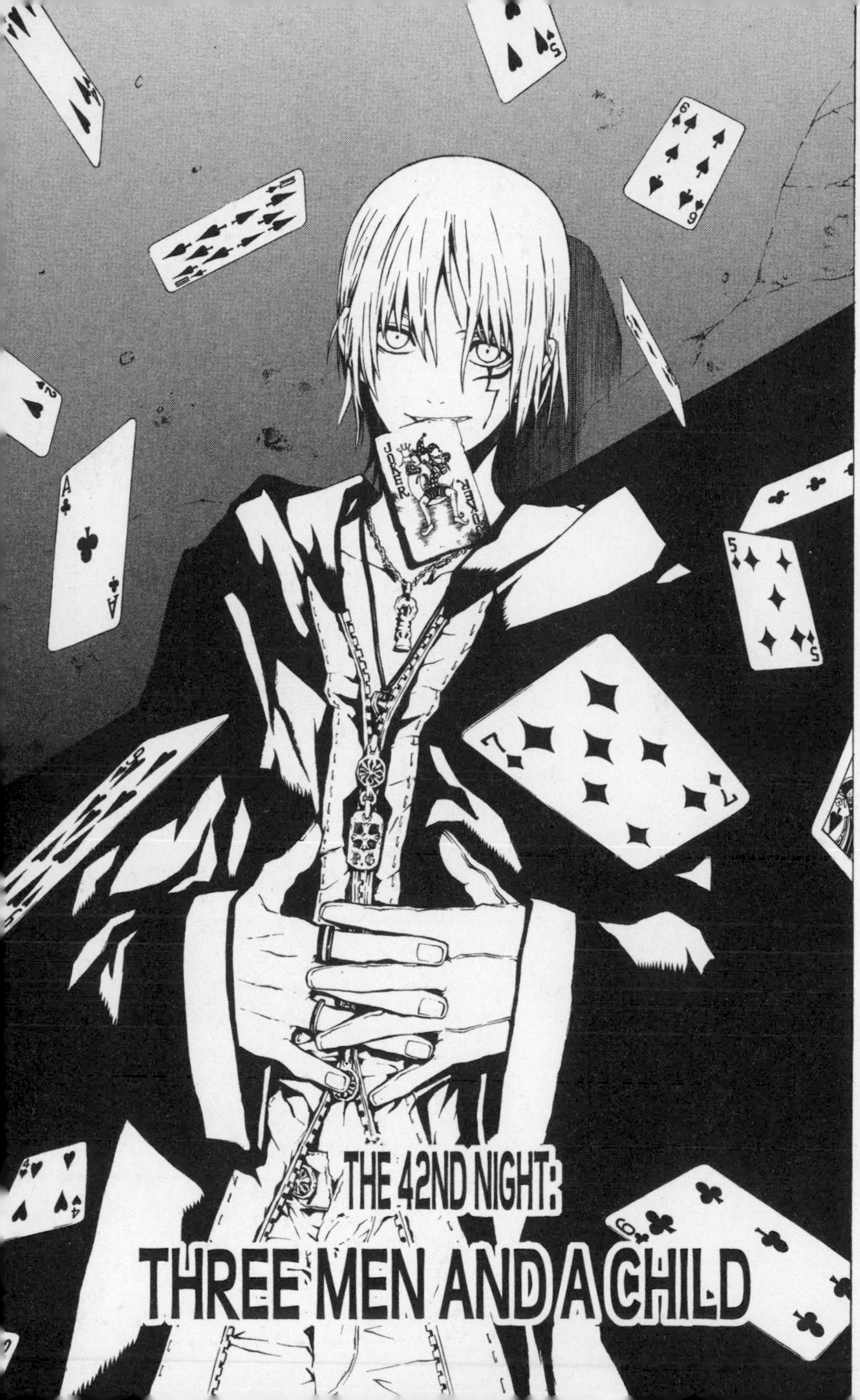
JOKER
THE 42ND NIGHT:
THREE MEN AND A CHILD

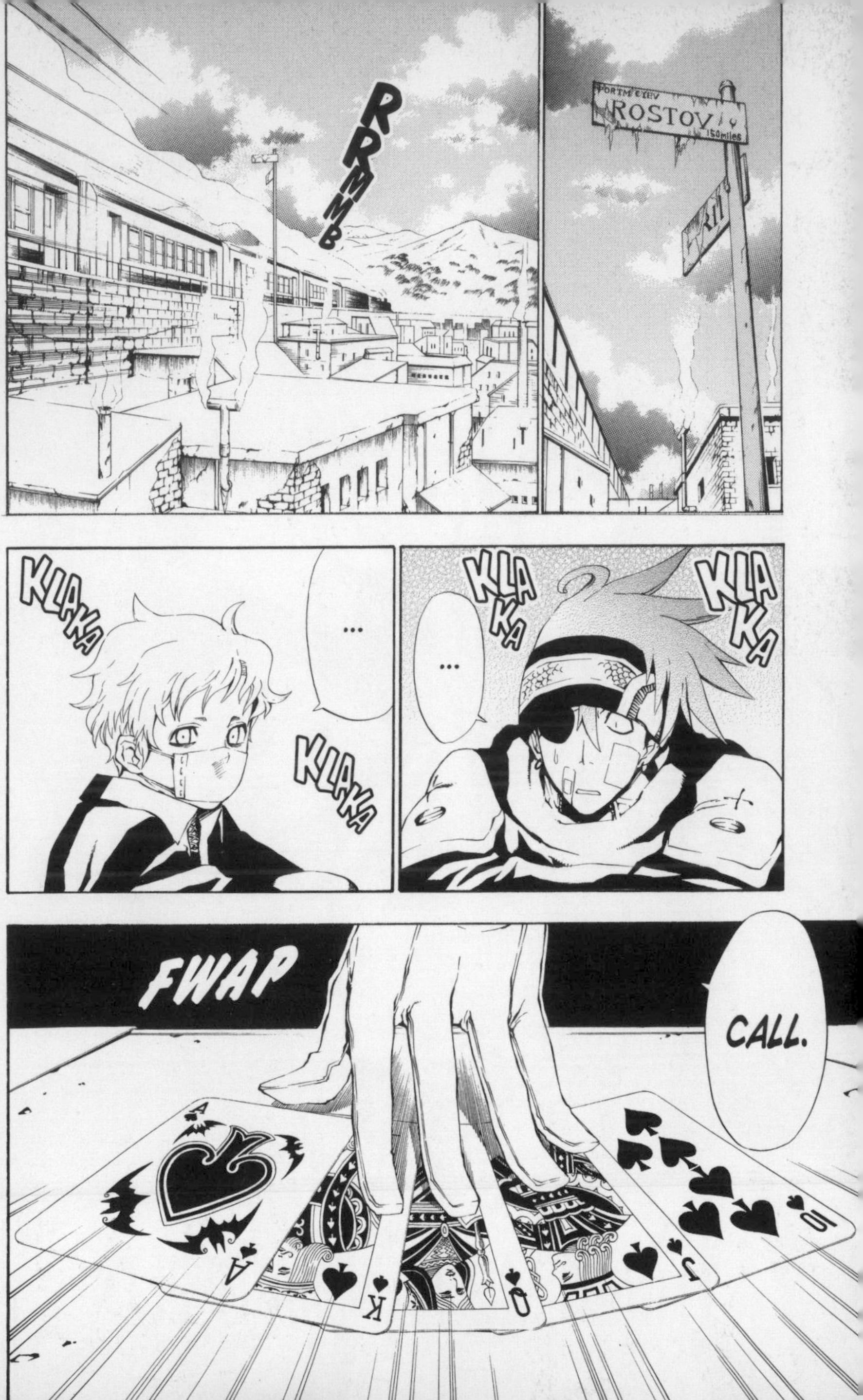
ROSTOV
150miles
RRMMB
KLAKA KA
...
KLAKA KA
KLAKA
...
KLAKA
CALL.
FWAP

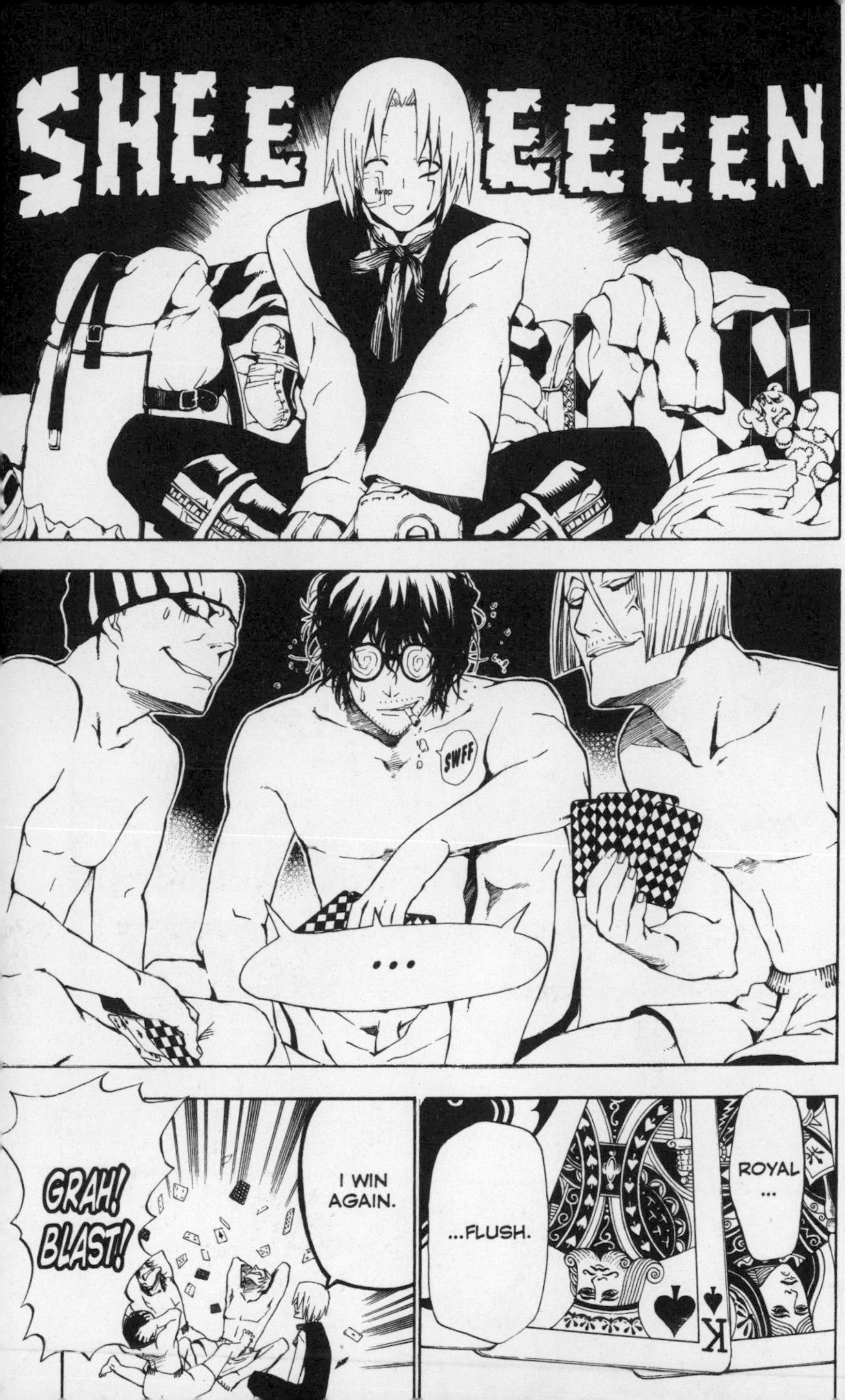
SHEE EEEEN
fwap
SWFF
...
ROYAL ...
...FLUSH.
I WIN AGAIN.
GRAH! BLAST!

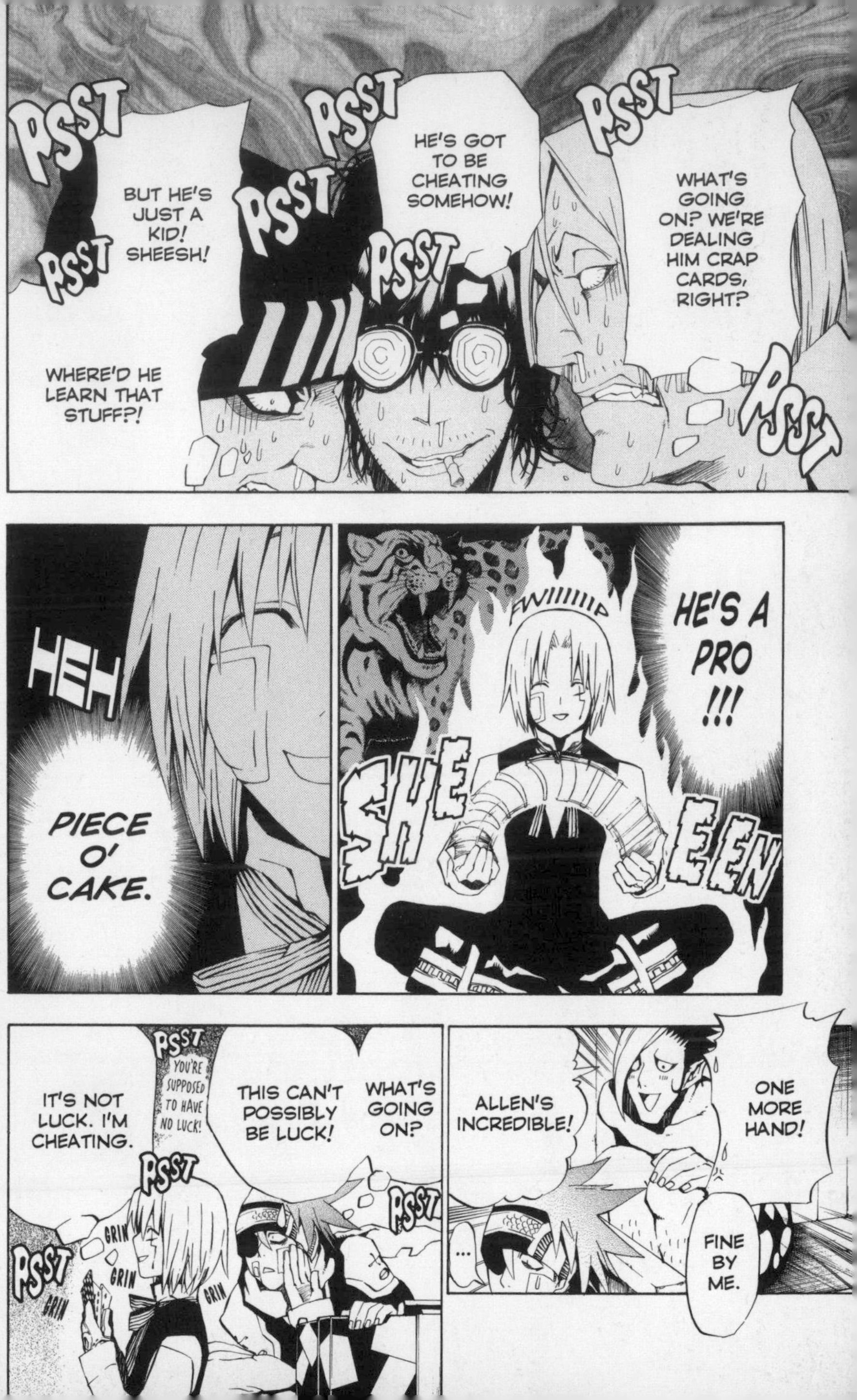
PSST
WHAT'S GOING ON? WE'RE DEALING HIM CRAP CARDS, RIGHT?
PSST
PSST
HE'S GOT TO BE CHEATING SOMEHOW!
PSST
PSST
PSST
BUT HE'S JUST A KID! SHEESH!
PSST
WHERE'D HE LEARN THAT STUFF?!
FWIIIIIIP
HE'S A PRO!!!
SHEEEN
HEH
PIECE O' CAKE.
ONE MORE HAND!
ALLEN'S INCREDIBLE!
...
FINE BY ME.
WHAT'S GOING ON?
THIS CAN'T POSSIBLY BE LUCK!
PSST
PSST
YOU'RE SUPPOSED TO HAVE NO LUCK!
IT'S NOT LUCK. I'M CHEATING.
PSST
GRIN
GRIN
GRIN
PSST
GRIN

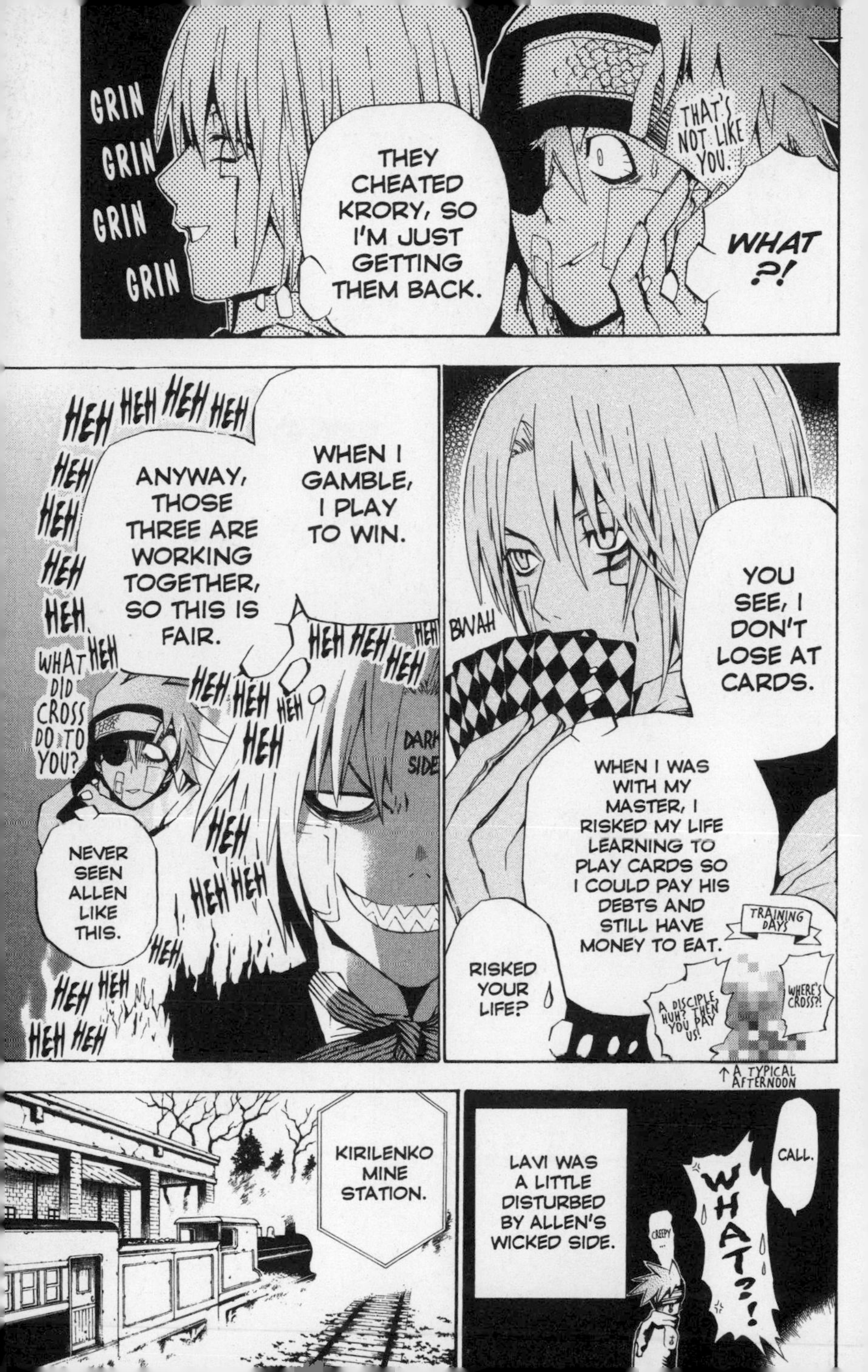
THAT'S NOT LIKE YOU.
WHAT?!
THEY CHEATED KRORY, SO I'M JUST GETTING THEM BACK.
GRIN GRIN GRIN GRIN
YOU SEE, I DON'T LOSE AT CARDS.
WHEN I WAS WITH MY MASTER, I RISKED MY LIFE LEARNING TO PLAY CARDS SO I COULD PAY HIS DEBTS AND STILL HAVE MONEY TO EAT.
TRAINING DAYS
WHERE'S CROSS?!
A DISCIPLE HUH? THEN YOU PAY US!
RISKED YOUR LIFE?
BWAH
WHEN I GAMBLE, I PLAY TO WIN.
HEH HEH HEH HEH
ANYWAY, THOSE THREE ARE WORKING TOGETHER, SO THIS IS FAIR.
HEH HEH HEH HEH HEH HEH HEH HEH HEH HEH HEH HEH HEH HEH HEH HEH HEH
DARK SIDE
HEH HEH HEH HEH HEH HEH HEH
WHAT DID CROSS DO TO YOU?
NEVER SEEN ALLEN LIKE THIS.
↑ A TYPICAL AFTERNOON
CALL.
WHAT?!
CREEPY...
LAVI WAS A LITTLE DISTURBED BY ALLEN'S WICKED SIDE.
KIRILENKO MINE STATION.

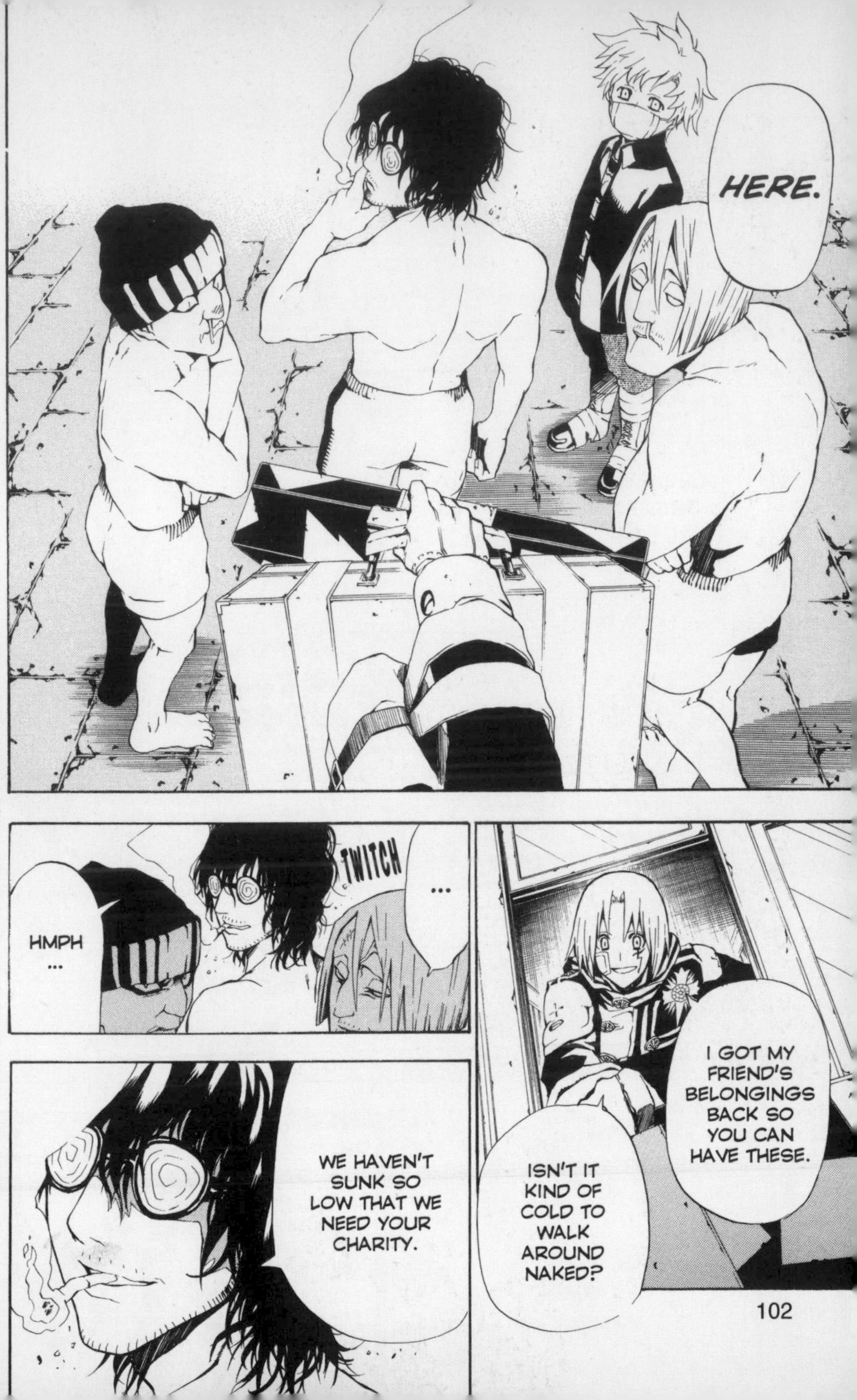
HERE.
I GOT MY FRIEND'S BELONGINGS BACK SO YOU CAN HAVE THESE.
ISN'T IT KIND OF COLD TO WALK AROUND NAKED?
...
TWITCH
HMPH ...
WE HAVEN'T SUNK SO LOW THAT WE NEED YOUR CHARITY.

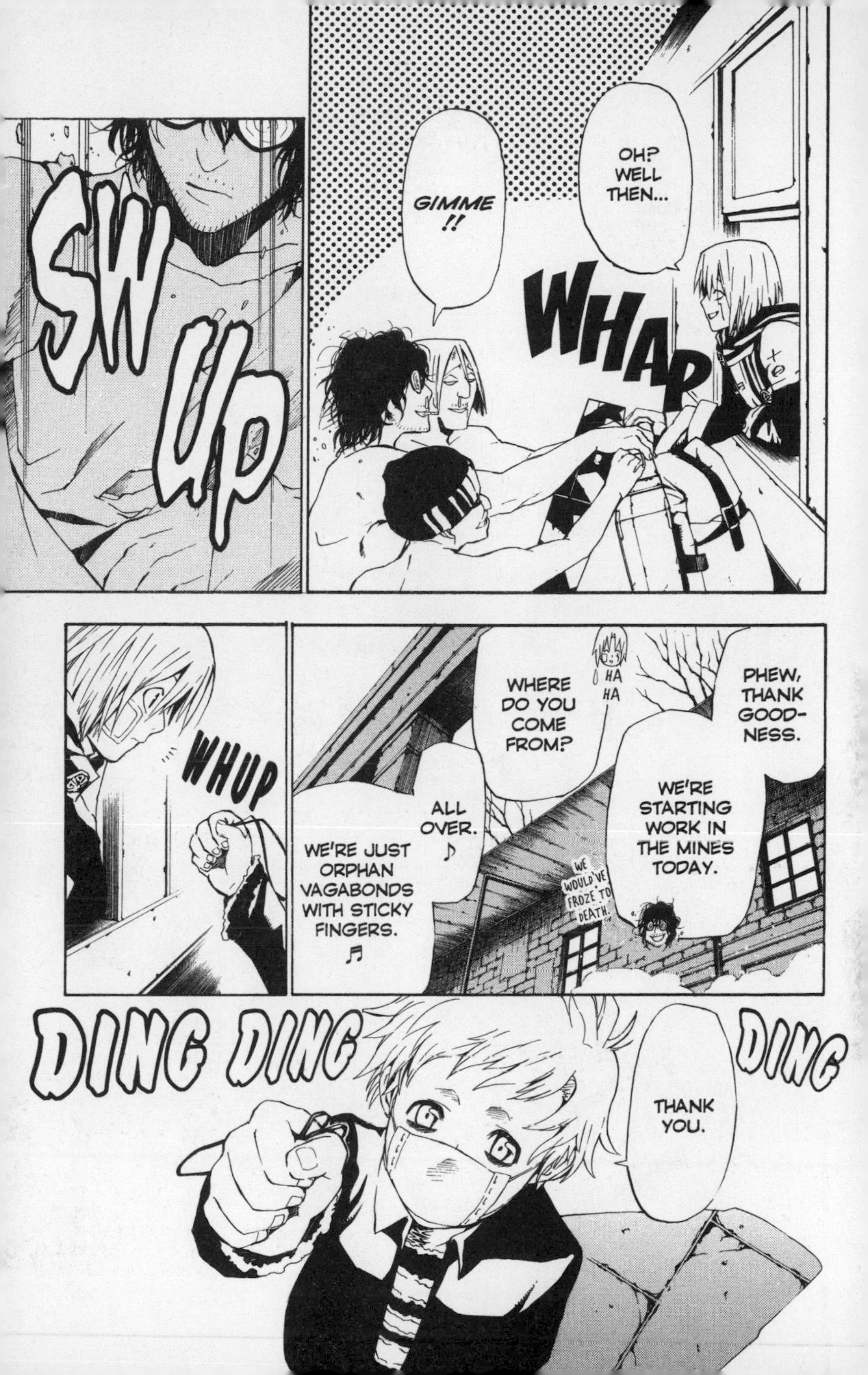
OH? WELL THEN...
GIMME !!
WHAP
SW UP
PHEW, THANK GOODNESS.
WHERE DO YOU COME FROM?
HA HA
WE'RE STARTING WORK IN THE MINES TODAY.
ALL OVER. ♪
WE WOULD'VE FROZE TO DEATH.
WE'RE JUST ORPHAN VAGABONDS WITH STICKY FINGERS. ♬
WHUP
DING
THANK YOU.
DING DING

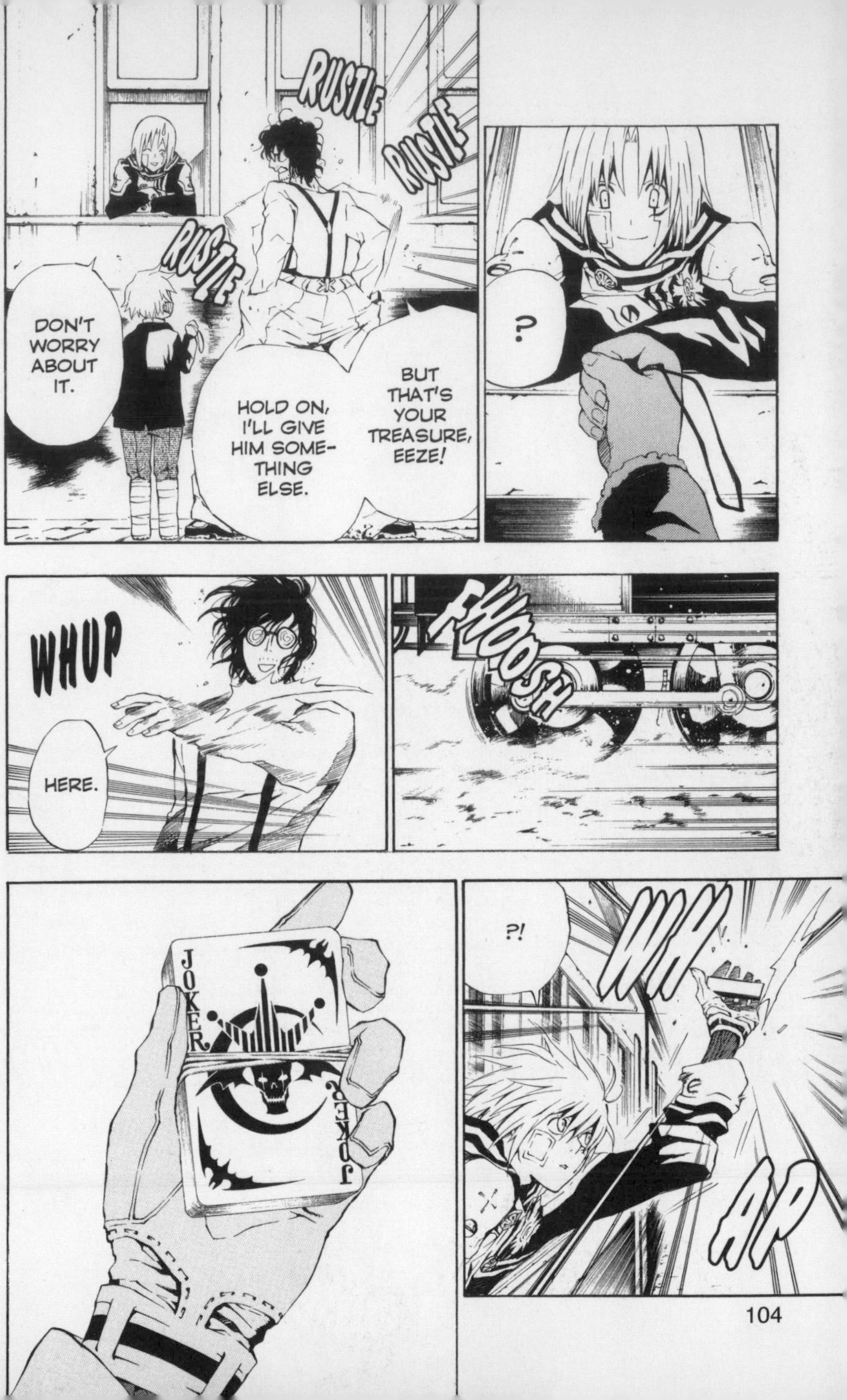
?
RUSTLE
RUSTLE
RUSTLE
BUT THAT'S YOUR TREASURE, EEZE!
DON'T WORRY ABOUT IT.
HOLD ON, I'LL GIVE HIM SOMETHING ELSE.
FWOOSH
WHUP
HERE.
?!
WHAP
JOKER
JOKER

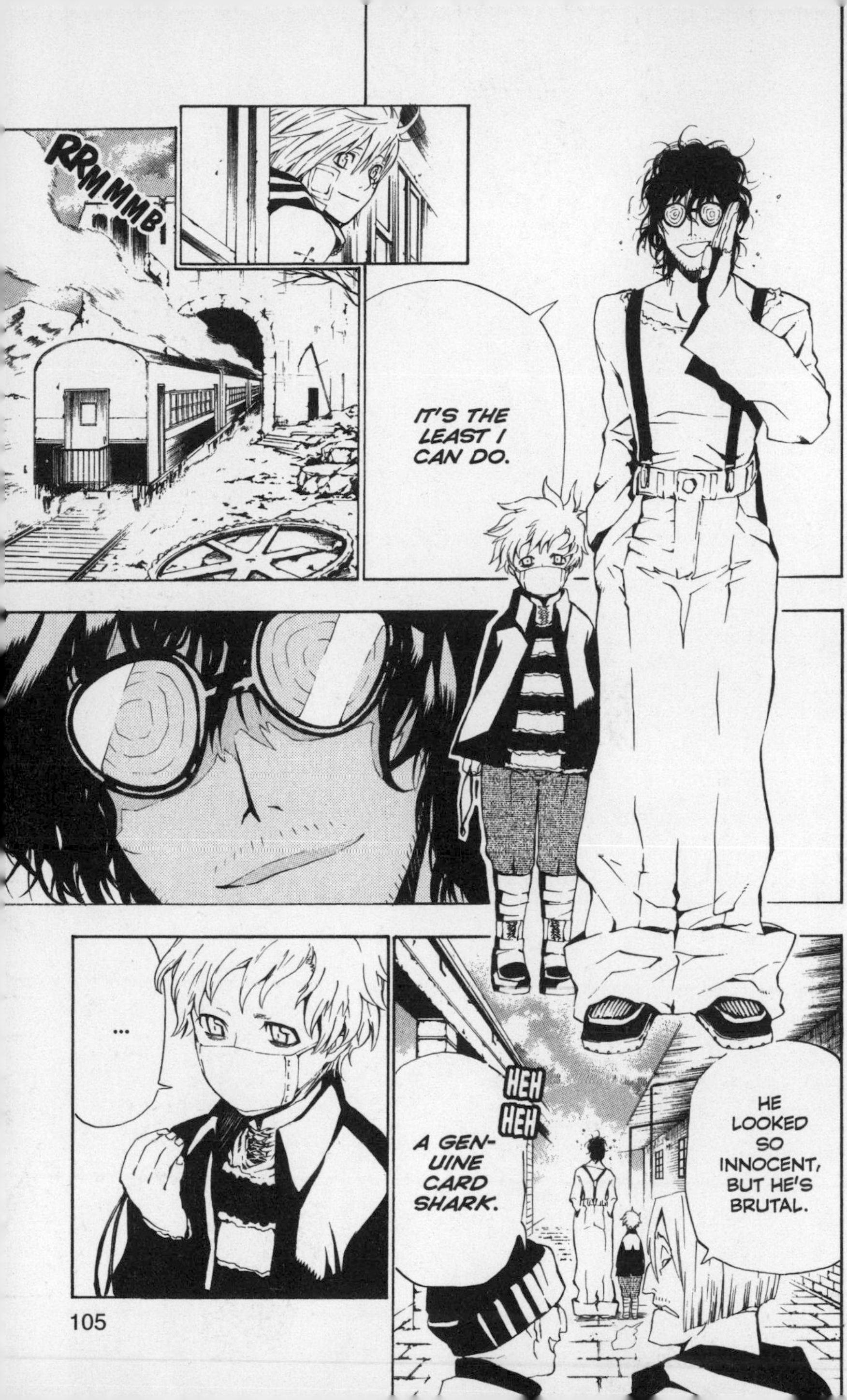
IT'S THE LEAST I CAN DO.
RRMMMB
HE LOOKED SO INNOCENT, BUT HE'S BRUTAL.
HEH HEH
A GEN-UINE CARD SHARK.
...

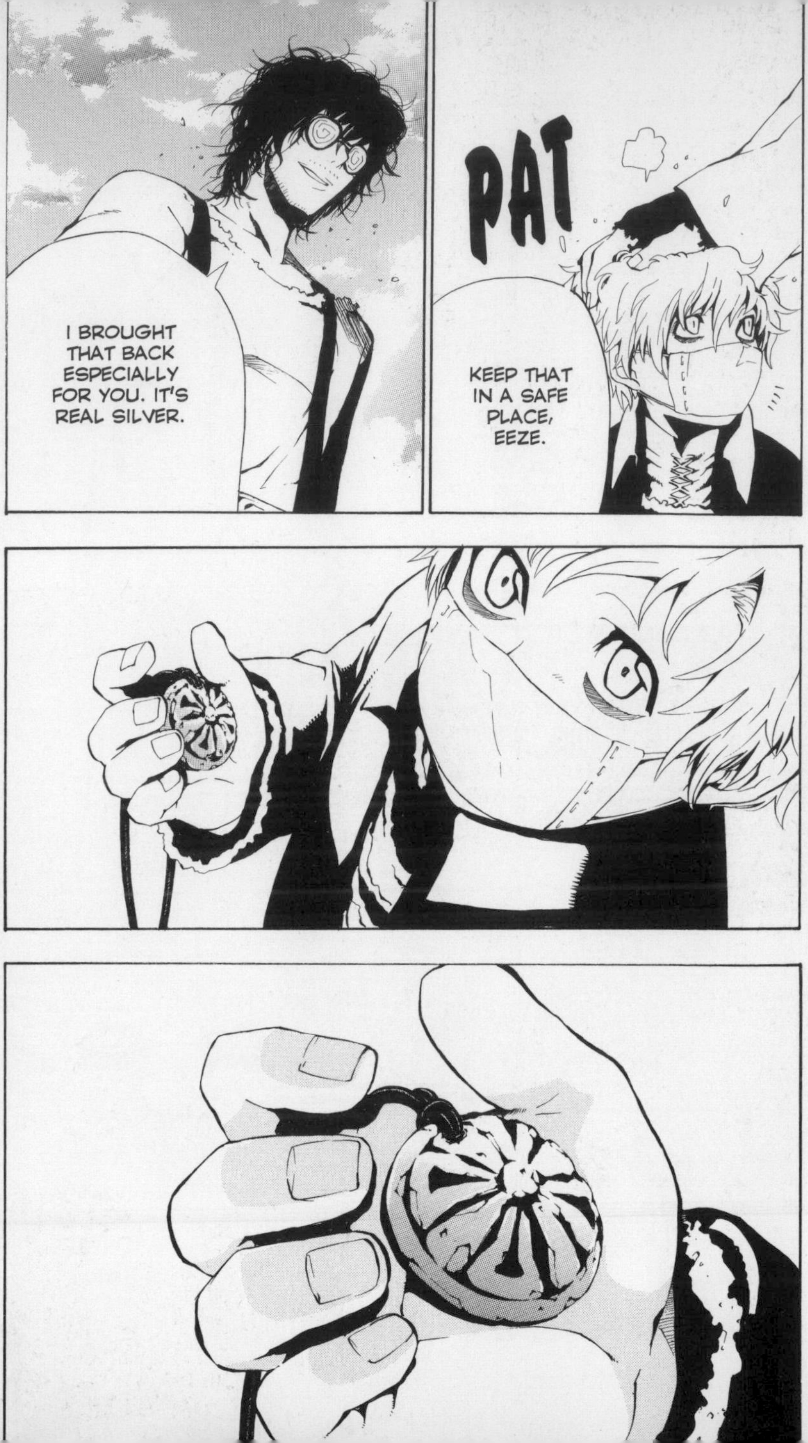
PAT
KEEP THAT IN A SAFE PLACE, EEZE.
I BROUGHT THAT BACK ESPECIALLY FOR YOU. IT'S REAL SILVER.

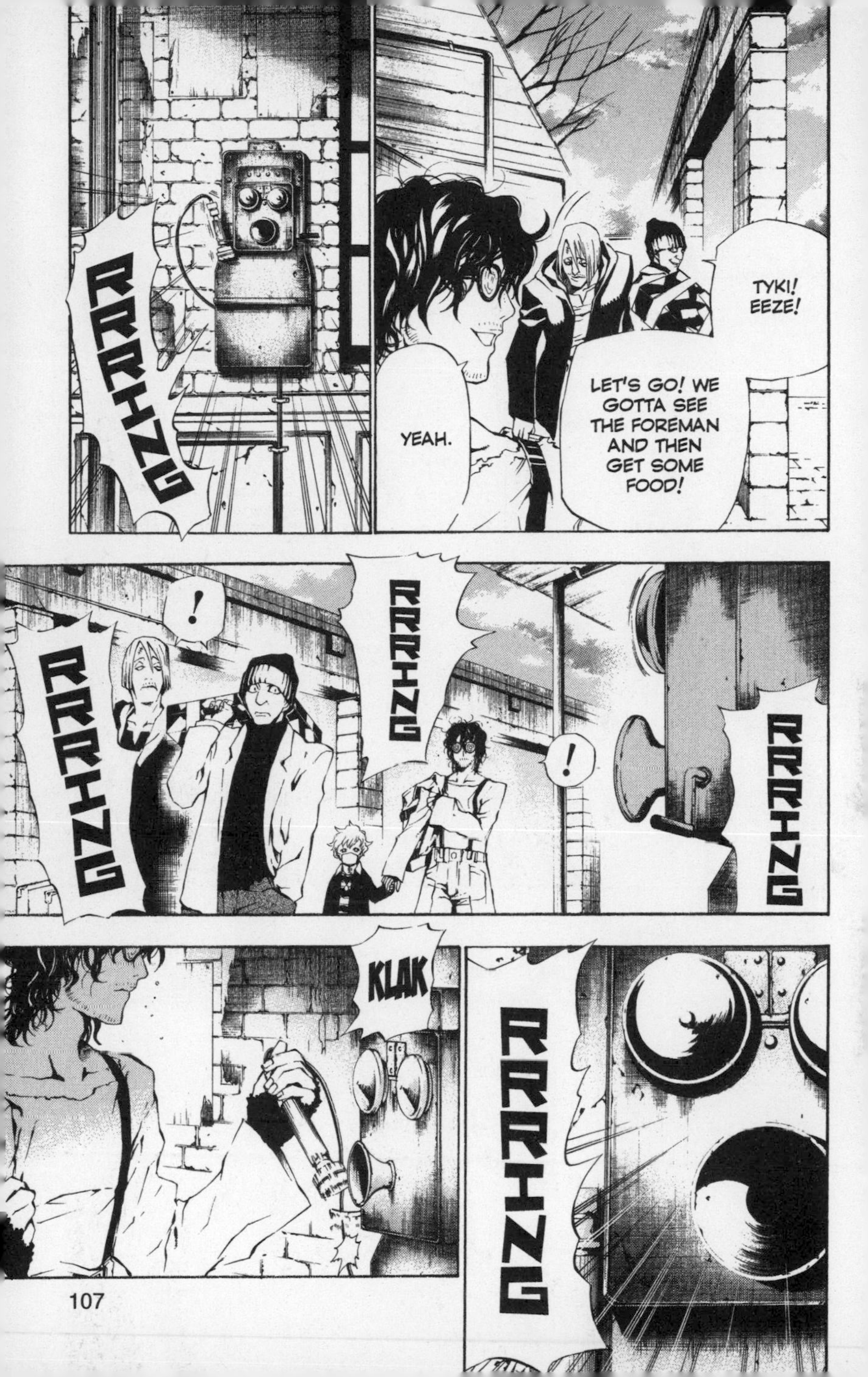
TYKI! EEZE!
LET'S GO! WE GOTTA SEE THE FOREMAN AND THEN GET SOME FOOD!
YEAH.
RRRING
RRRING
!
RRRING
!
RRRING
RRRING
KLAK

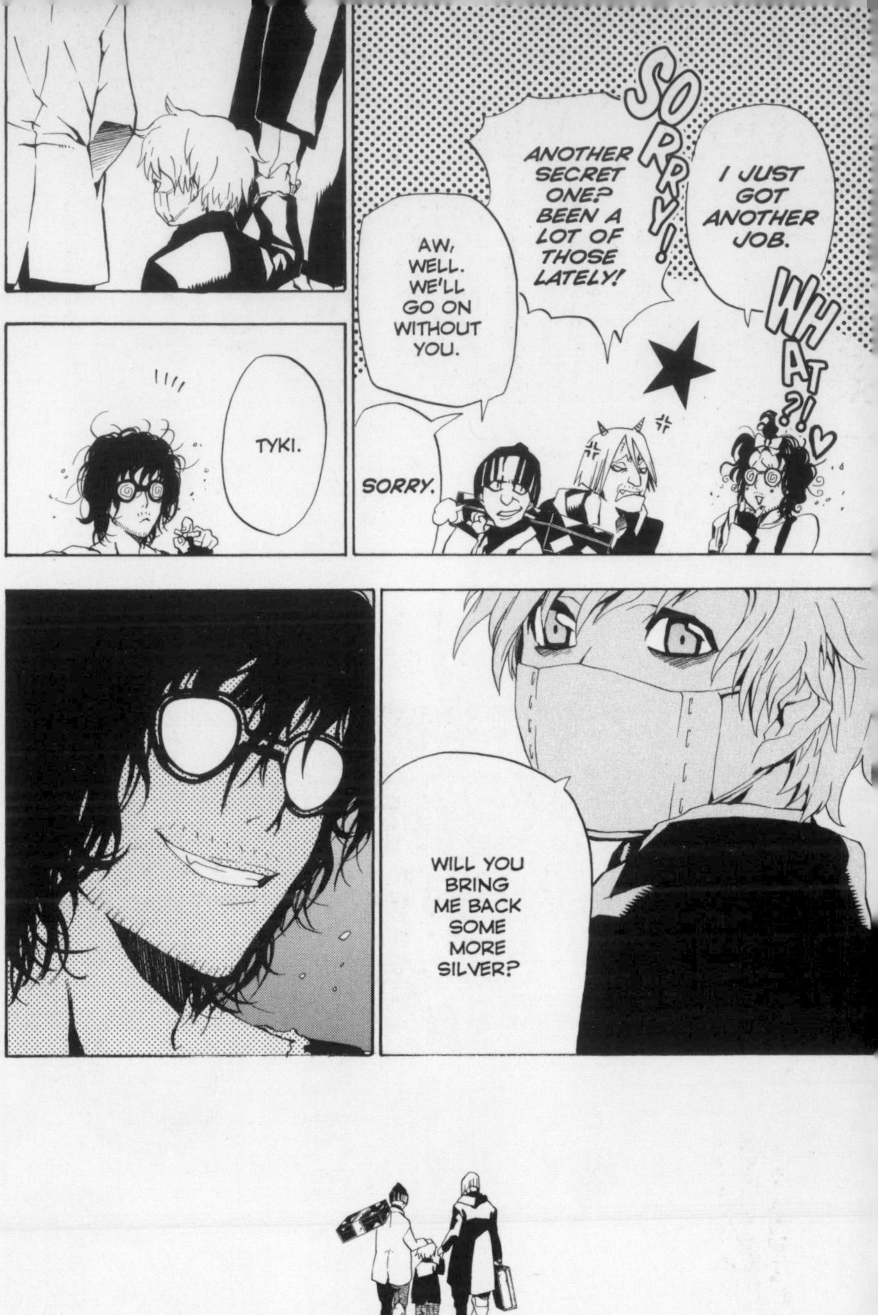
I JUST GOT ANOTHER JOB.
SORRY!
WHAT?!
ANOTHER SECRET ONE? BEEN A LOT OF THOSE LATELY!
AW, WELL. WE'LL GO ON WITHOUT YOU.
SORRY.
TYKI.
WILL YOU BRING ME BACK SOME MORE SILVER?

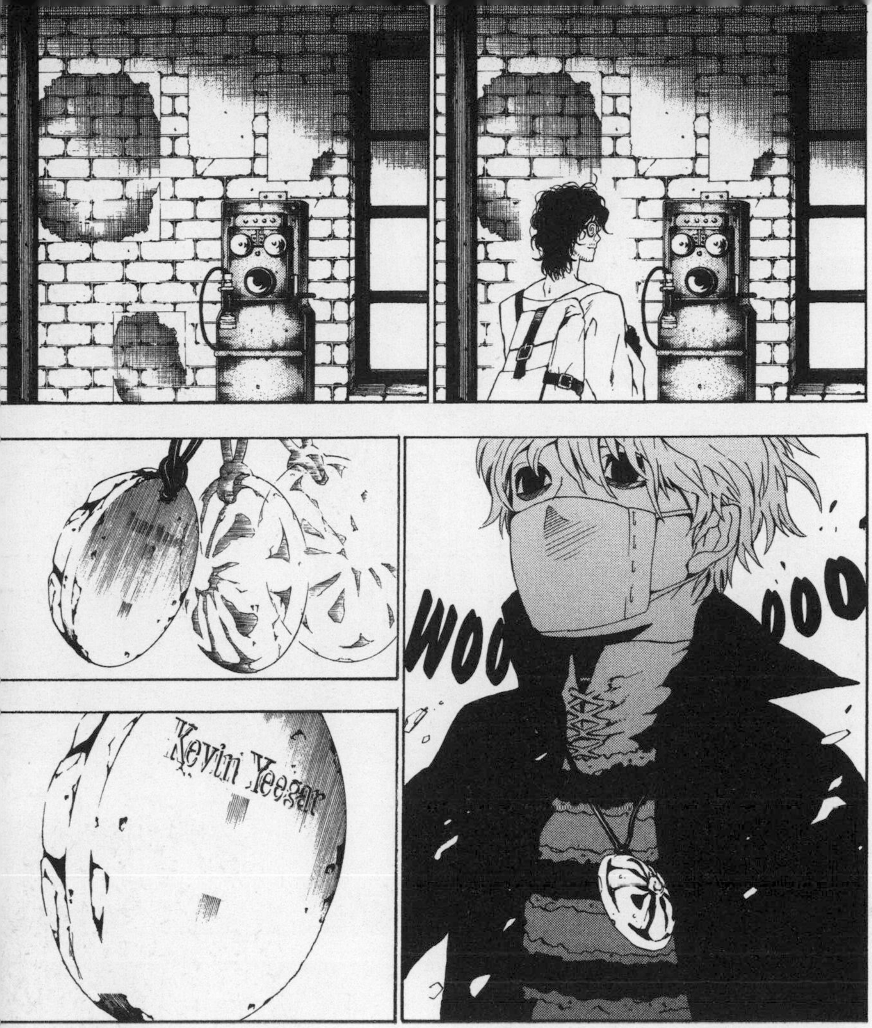
WOO OOO
Kevin Yeegar

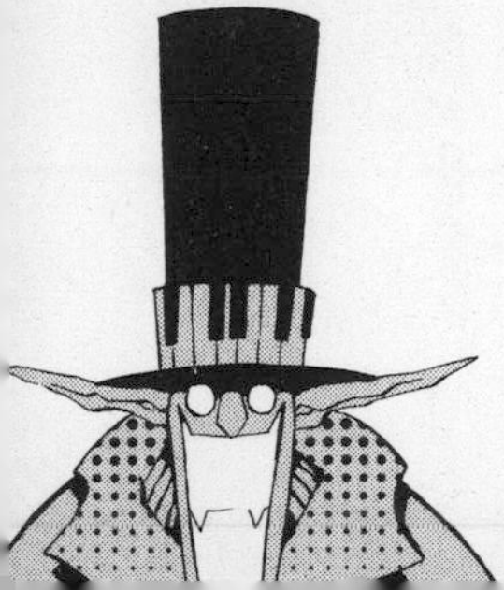

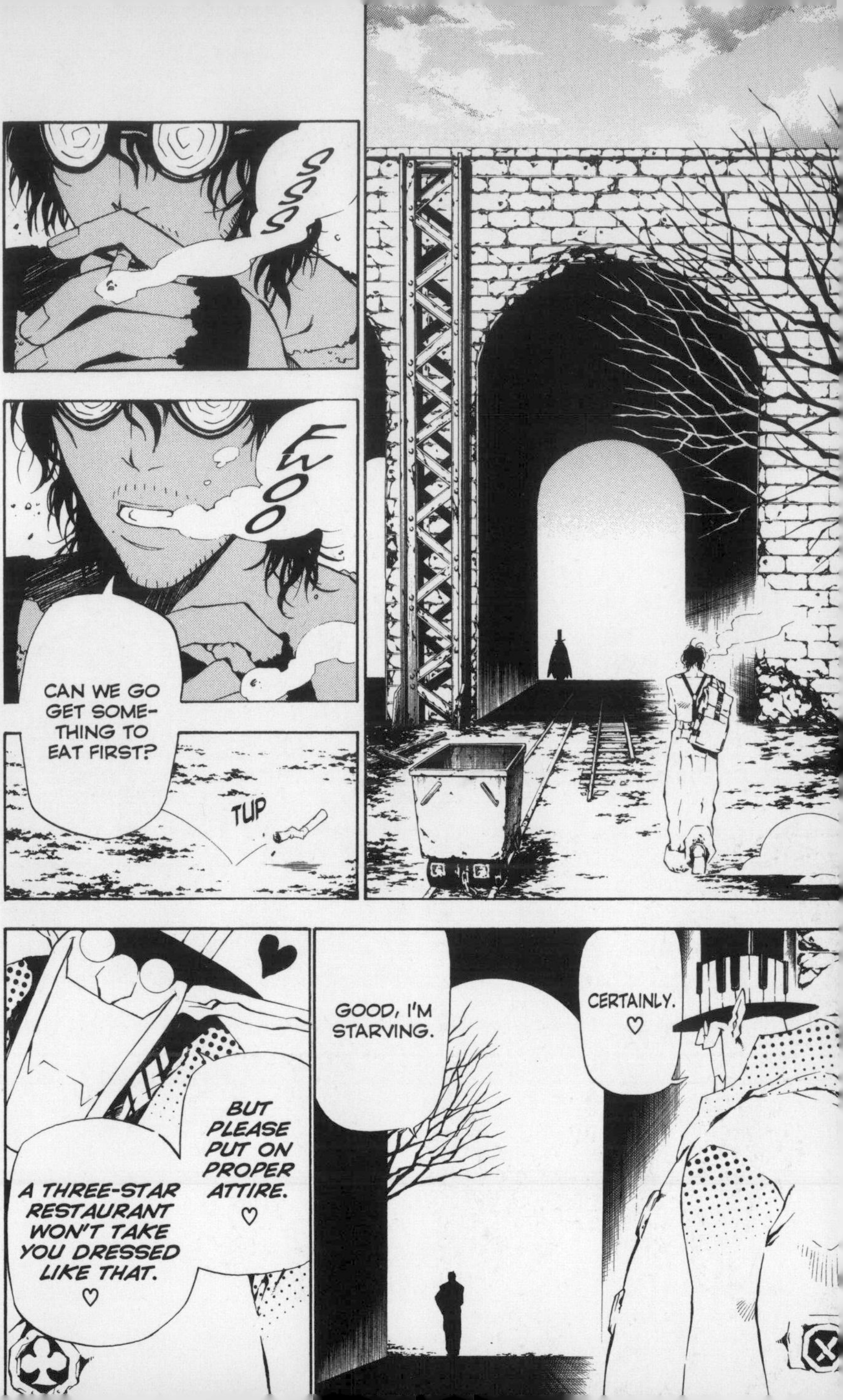
SCSS
FWOO
CAN WE GO GET SOMETHING TO EAT FIRST?
TUP
CERTAINLY. ♡
GOOD, I'M STARVING.
BUT PLEASE PUT ON PROPER ATTIRE. ♡
A THREE-STAR RESTAURANT WON'T TAKE YOU DRESSED LIKE THAT. ♡

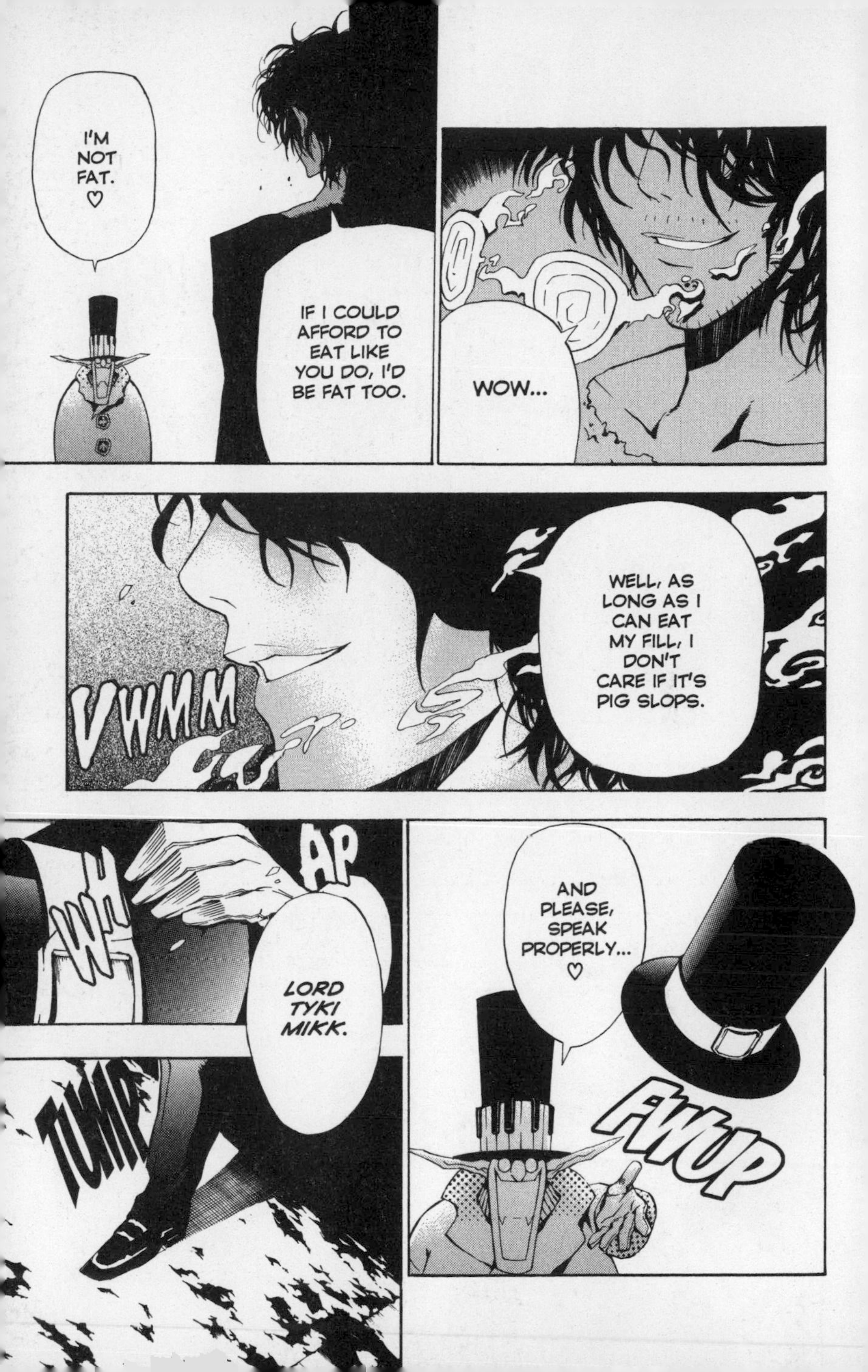
WOW...
IF I COULD AFFORD TO EAT LIKE YOU DO, I'D BE FAT TOO.
I'M NOT FAT. ♡
WELL, AS LONG AS I CAN EAT MY FILL, I DON'T CARE IF IT'S PIG SLOPS.
VWMM
AND PLEASE, SPEAK PROPERLY... ♡
FWUP
WHAP
LORD TYKI MIKK.
TUMP

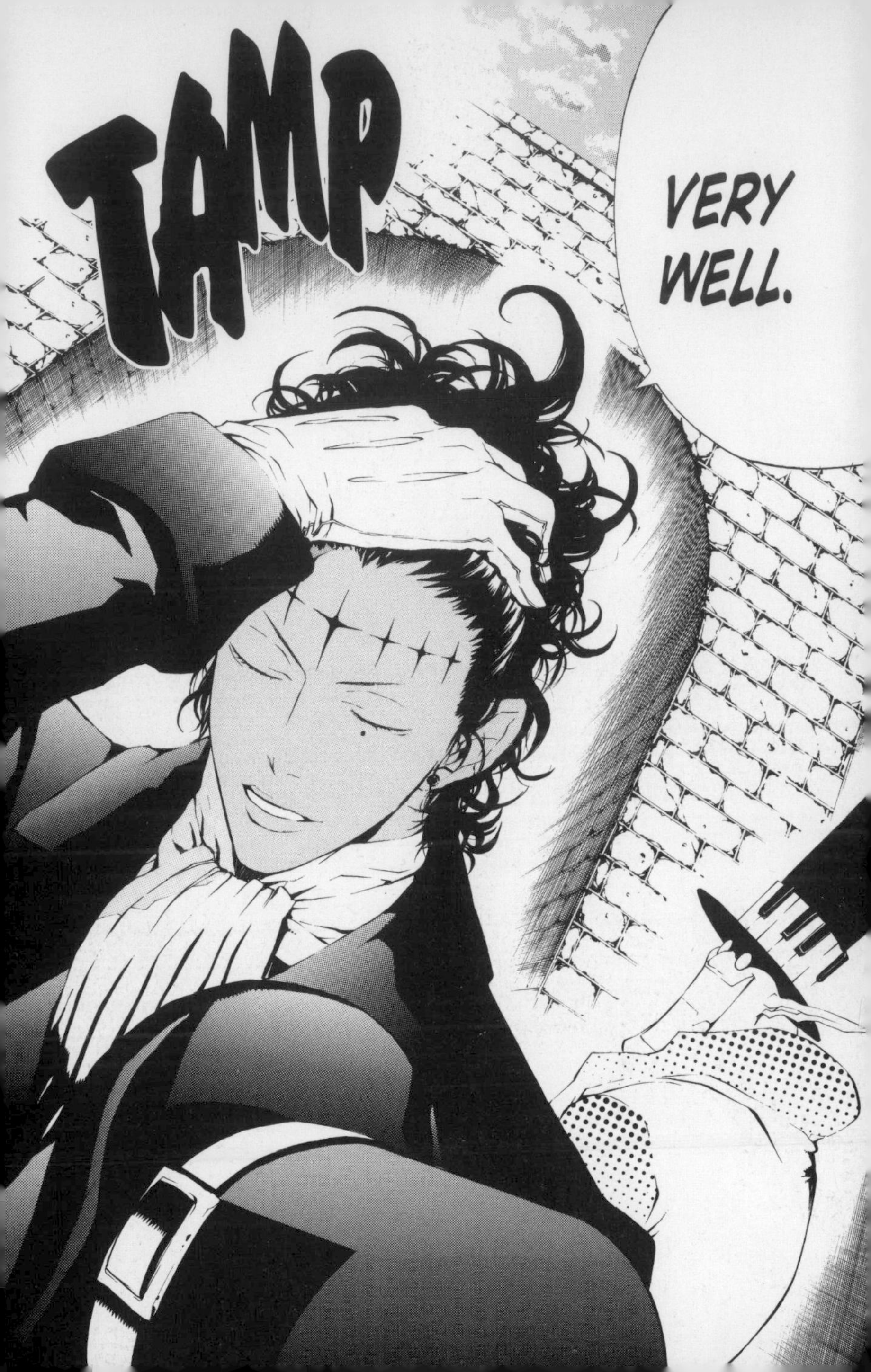
VERY WELL.
TAMP

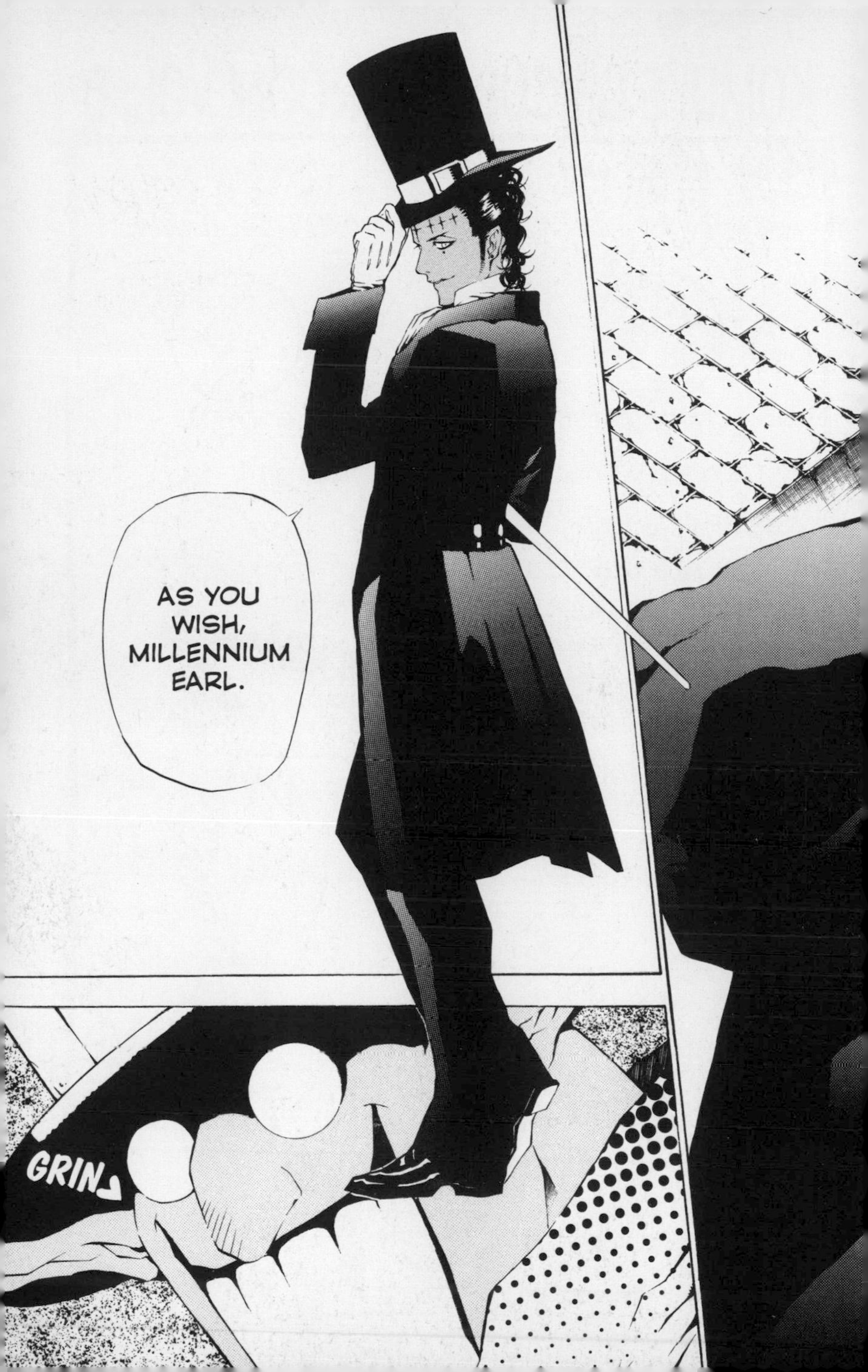
AS YOU WISH, MILLENNIUM EARL.
GRIN

KOMUI'S DISCUSSION ROOM VOL. 6

Q. CAN YOU TELL ME THE NAMES OF THE GUY WITH GLASSES, THE FAT GUY, AND THE GHOST IN THE SCIENCE SECTION?

A. GLASSES AND THE FAT GUY? OH, YOU MEAN THEM. (LAUGHS) THEY ARE...

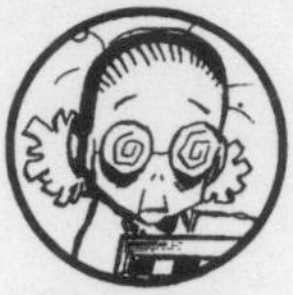

JOHNNY GILL

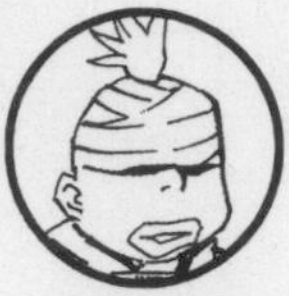

TAP DOP

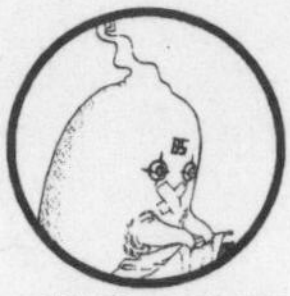

SIXTY-FIVE

THEY'RE REALLY GOOD GUYS WITH A LOT OF GUTS.

"SECTION CHIEF!!!"

(R) HUH? THAT SOUNDS LIKE JOHNNY. WHAT IS IT?

(J) W-WE FOUND CHIEF KOMUI!

(CHAIR FALLING OVER) WHAT?! CATCH HIM! I'LL COME TOO! OH, I GUESS THIS IS THE END OF THE DISCUSSION ROOM FOR THIS VOLUME. SORRY ABOUT THE COMMOTION. OH, I ALMOST FORGOT. THE DESIGNS FOR THE EARL'S TOP HAT THAT APPEAR IN THIS VOLUME WERE BASED ON THE IDEAS SENT IN BY THESE KIDS. THANKS AGAIN!

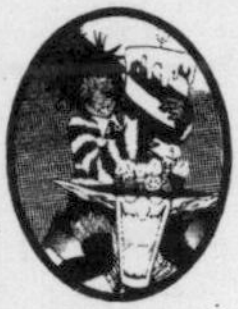

- LITTLE DEVIL JIRO OF HOKKAIDO
- HANA FROM SAITAMA PREFECTURE

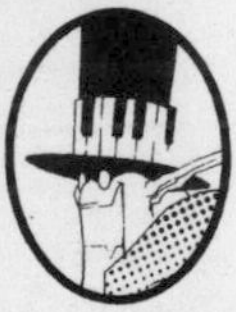

- RIO FROM AKITA PREFECTURE
- BISUKO MEITO OF MIYAZAKI PREFECTURE

LASTLY, PLEASE SEND YOUR QUESTIONS REGARDING D. GRAY-MAN TO "KOMUI'S DISCUSSION ROOM." ALL RIGHT THEN, SEE YOU NEXT TIME!

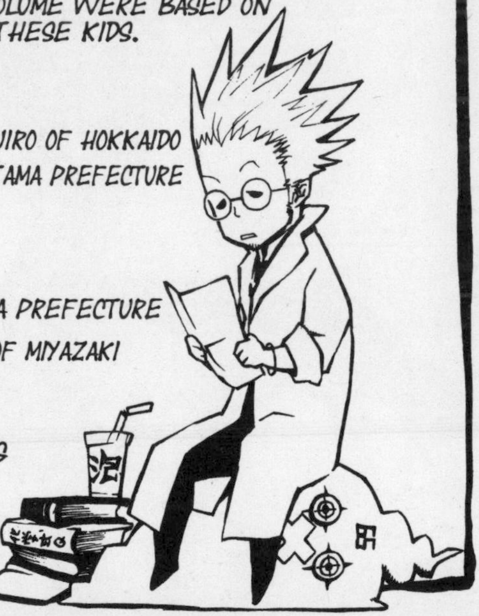

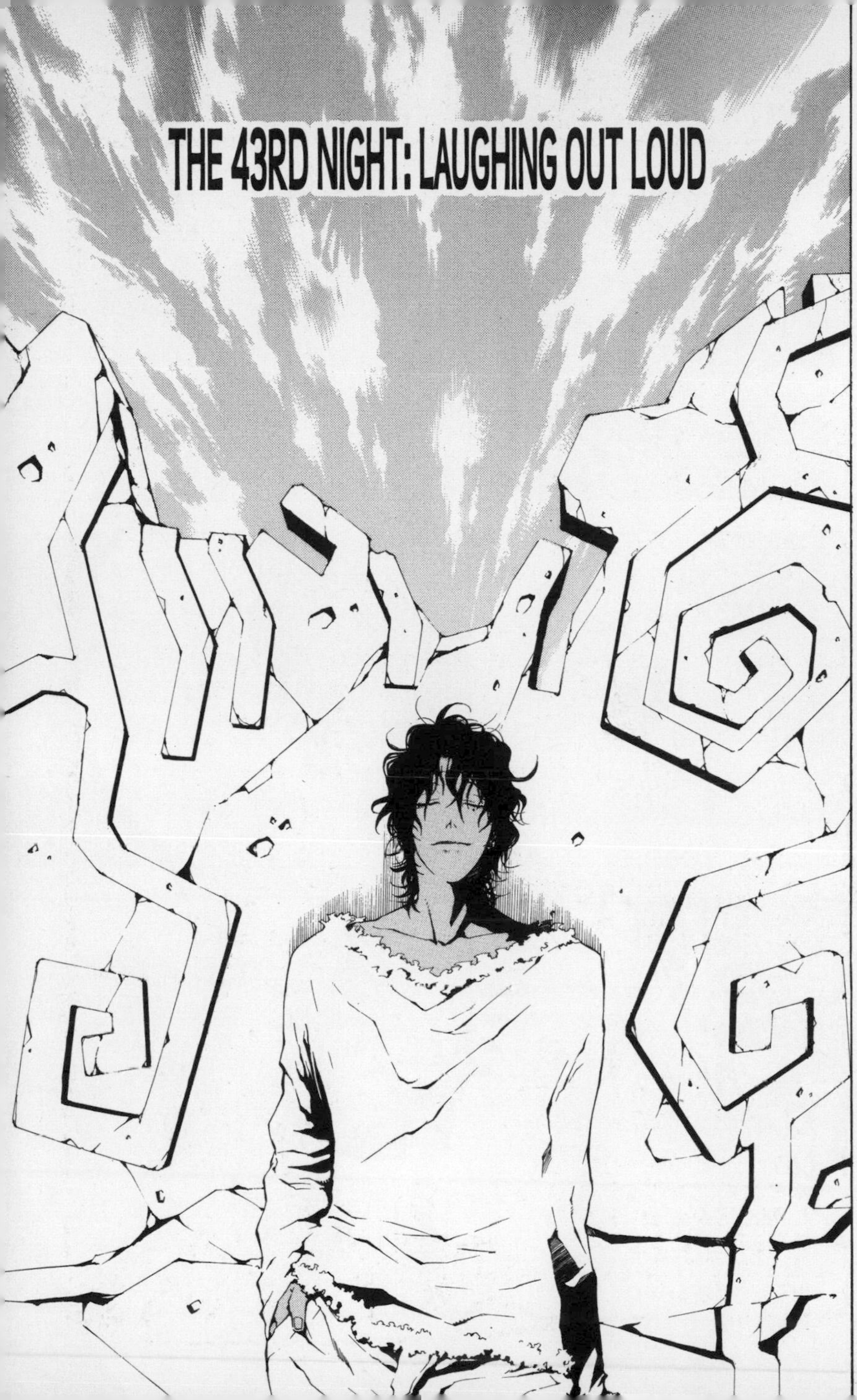
THE 43RD NIGHT: LAUGHING OUT LOUD

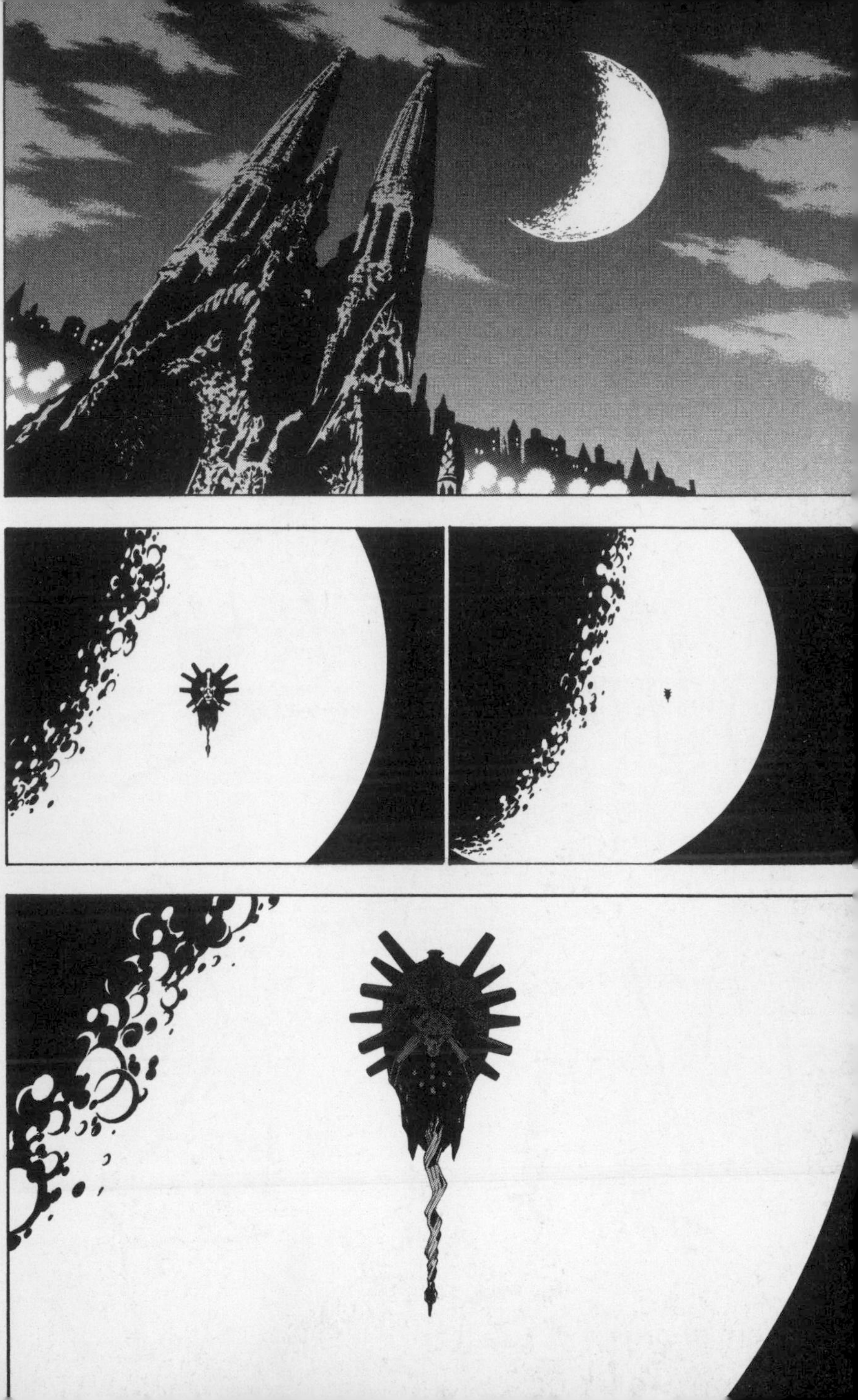

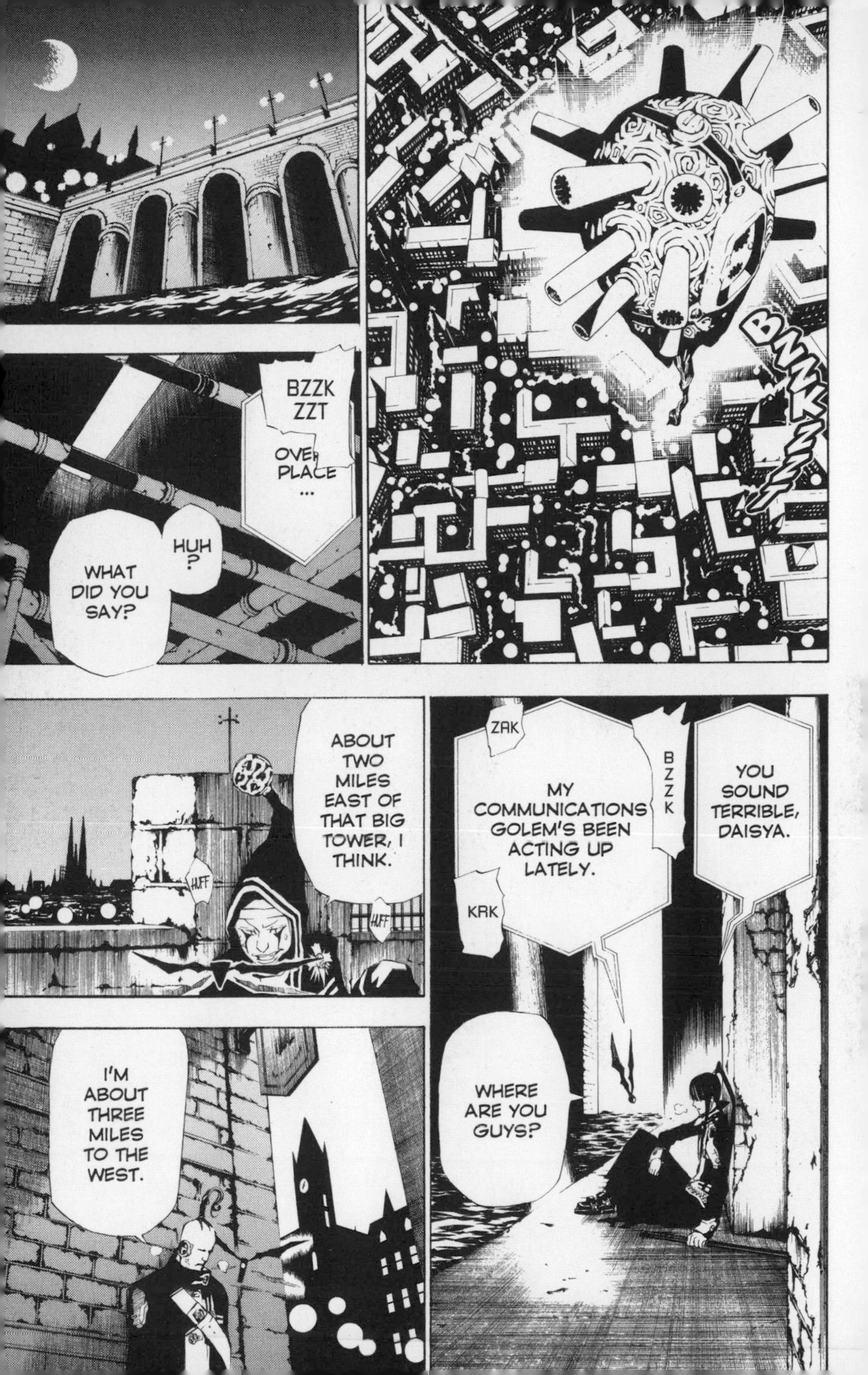
BNNKZZZT
BZZK ZZT
OVER PLACE ...
HUH?
WHAT DID YOU SAY?
YOU SOUND TERRIBLE, DAISYA.
BZZK
MY COMMUNICATIONS GOLEM'S BEEN ACTING UP LATELY.
ZAK
KRK
WHERE ARE YOU GUYS?
ABOUT TWO MILES EAST OF THAT BIG TOWER, I THINK.
HUFF
HUFF
I'M ABOUT THREE MILES TO THE WEST.

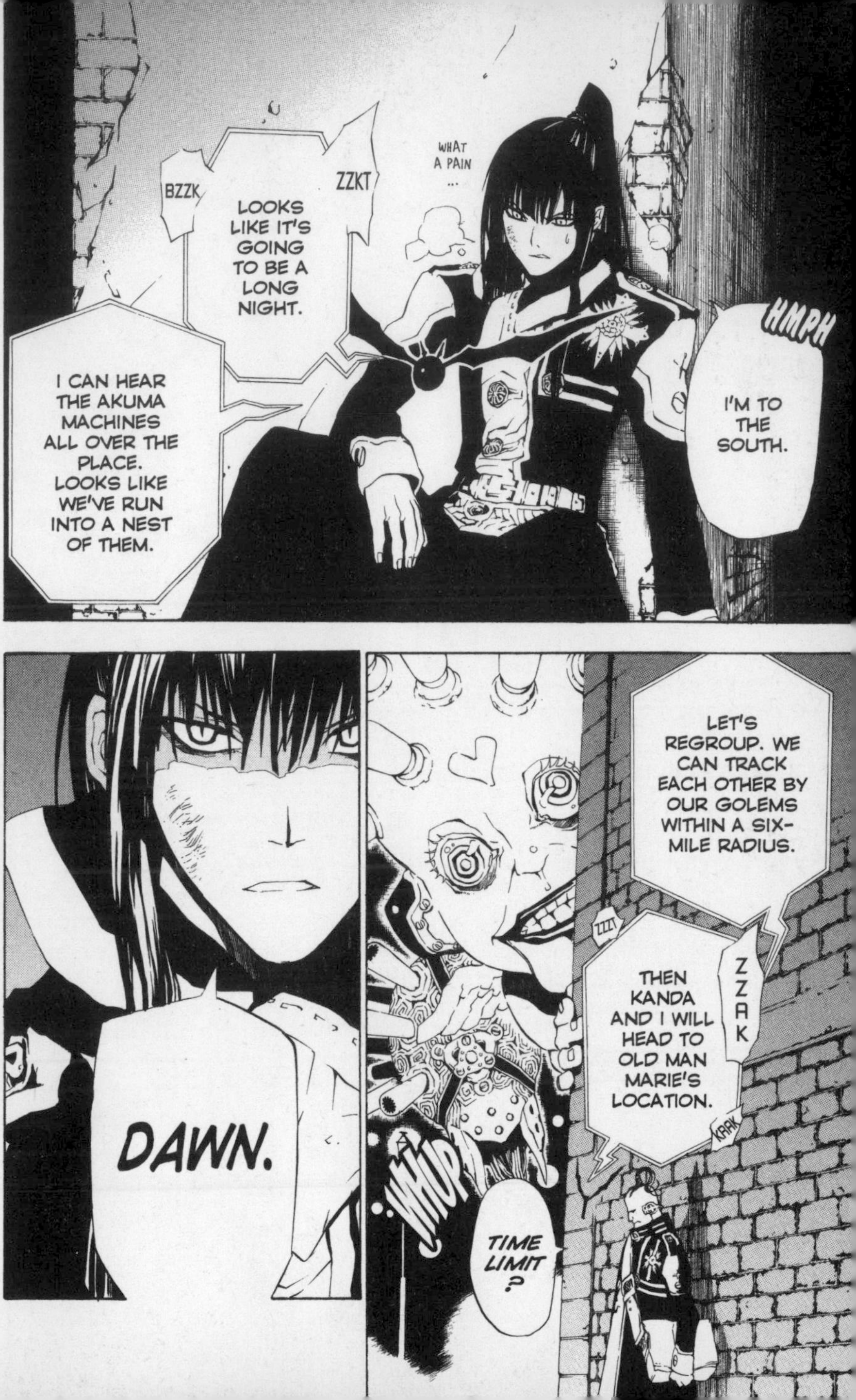
WHAT A PAIN ...
ZZKT
BZZK
LOOKS LIKE IT'S GOING TO BE A LONG NIGHT.
I CAN HEAR THE AKUMA MACHINES ALL OVER THE PLACE. LOOKS LIKE WE'VE RUN INTO A NEST OF THEM.
HMPH
I'M TO THE SOUTH.
LET'S REGROUP. WE CAN TRACK EACH OTHER BY OUR GOLEMS WITHIN A SIX-MILE RADIUS.
ZZZT
ZZAK
THEN KANDA AND I WILL HEAD TO OLD MAN MARIE'S LOCATION.
KRAK
WHOP
TIME LIMIT?
DAWN.

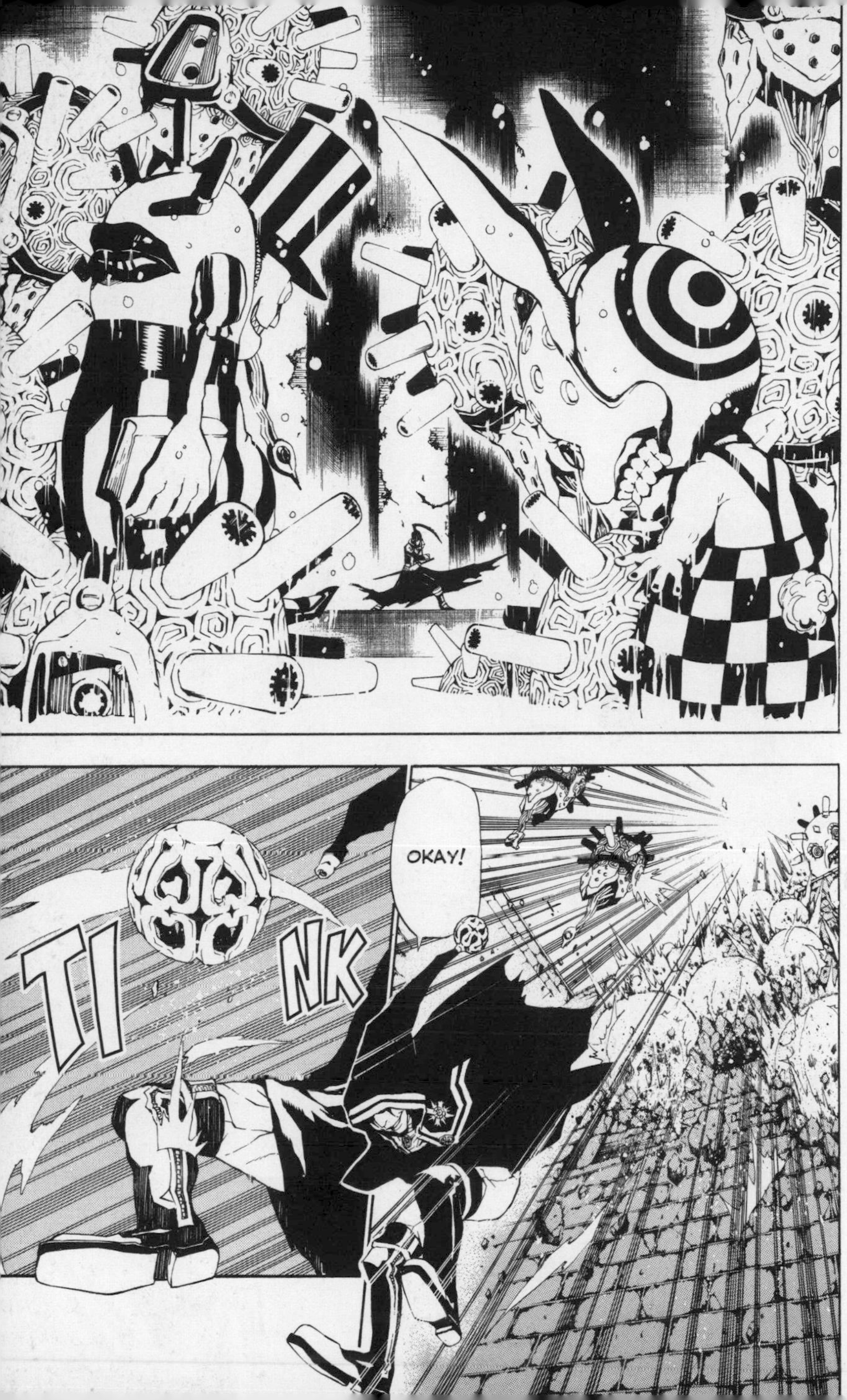
OKAY!
TI NK

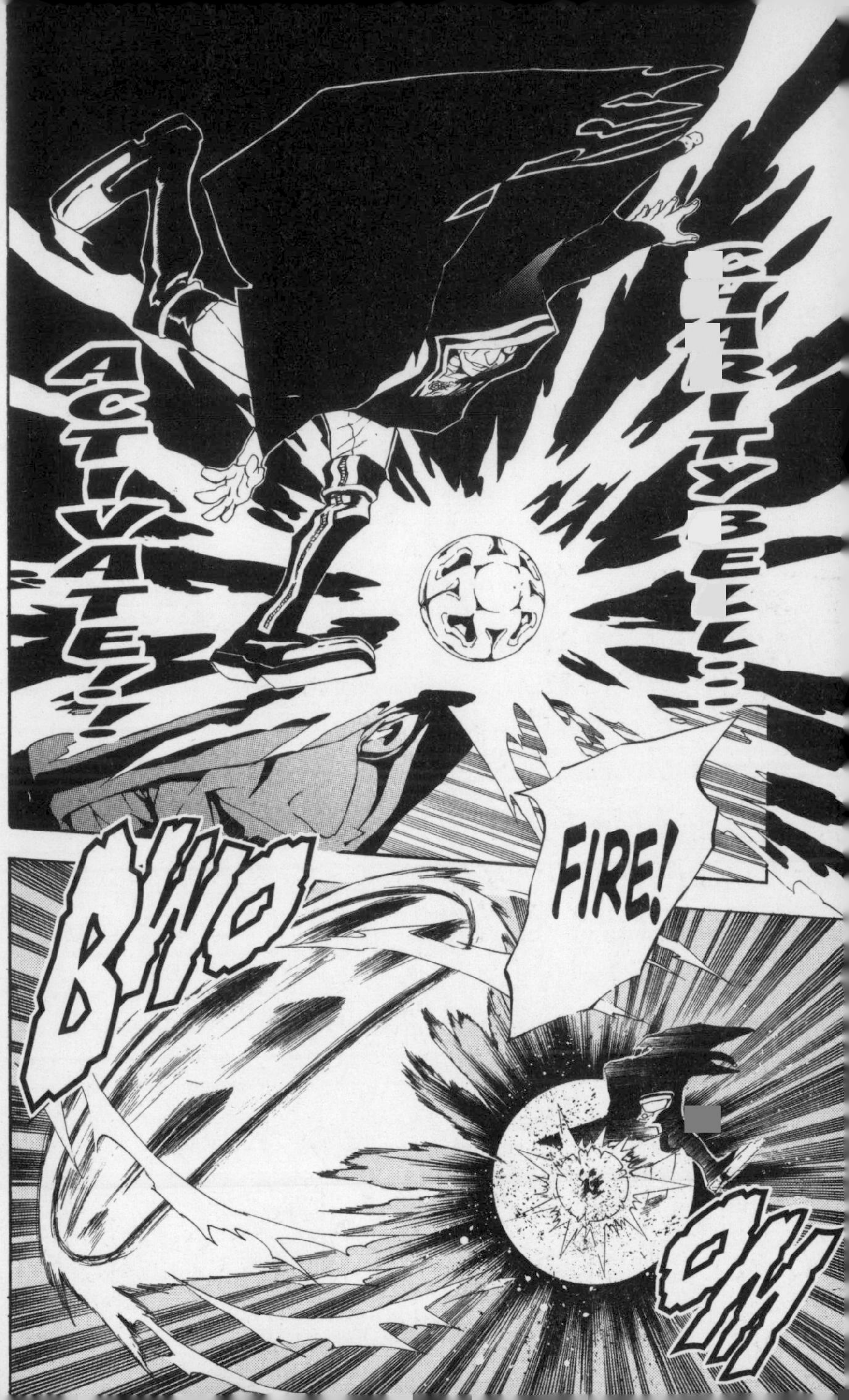
CHARITY BELL...!
ACTIVATE...!
FIRE!
BHO
OM

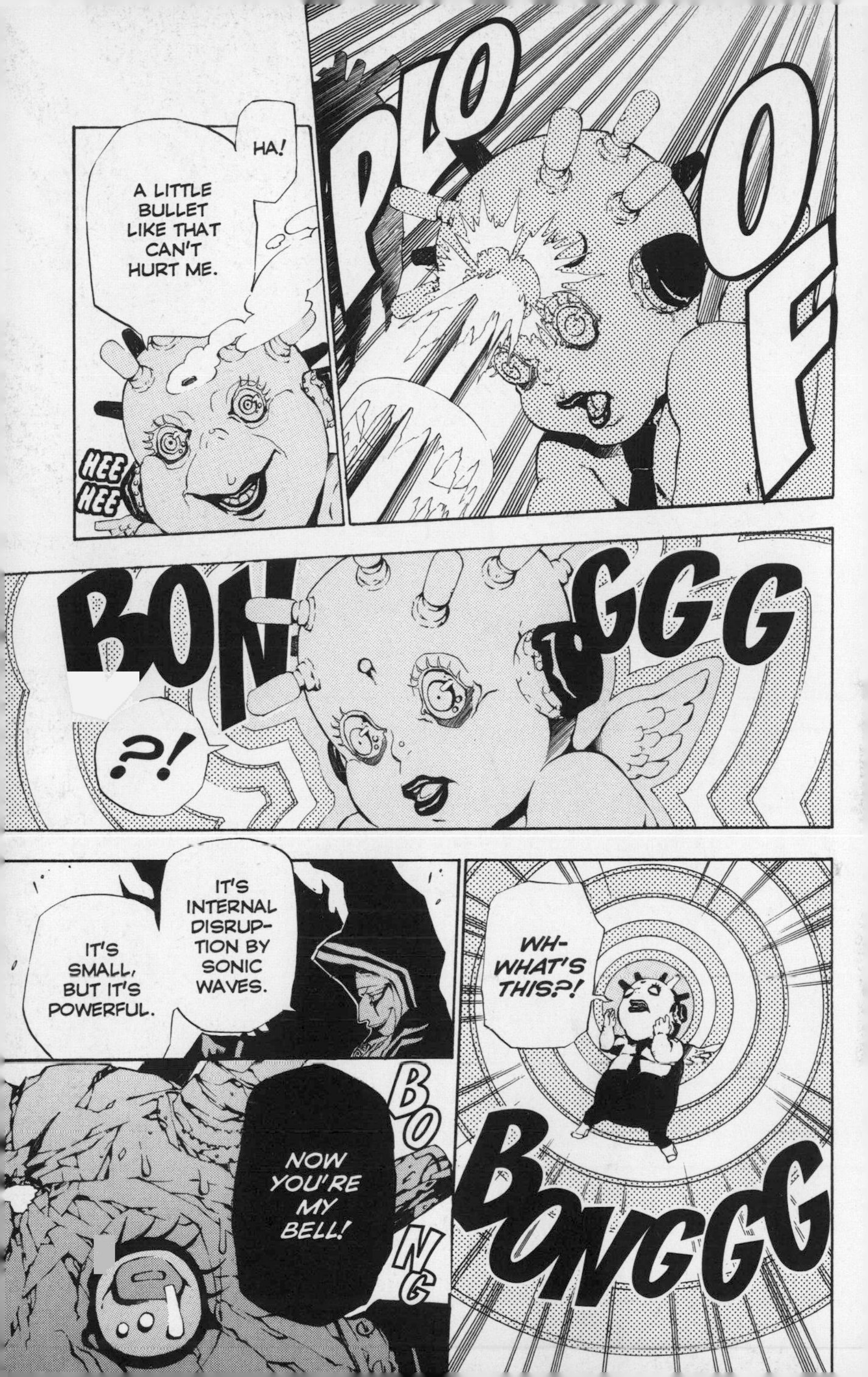
PLOOOF
HA!
A LITTLE BULLET LIKE THAT CAN'T HURT ME.
HEE HEE
BONGGGG
?!
WH-WHAT'S THIS?!
BONGGG
IT'S INTERNAL DISRUP-TION BY SONIC WAVES.
IT'S SMALL, BUT IT'S POWERFUL.
NOW YOU'RE MY BELL!
BONG

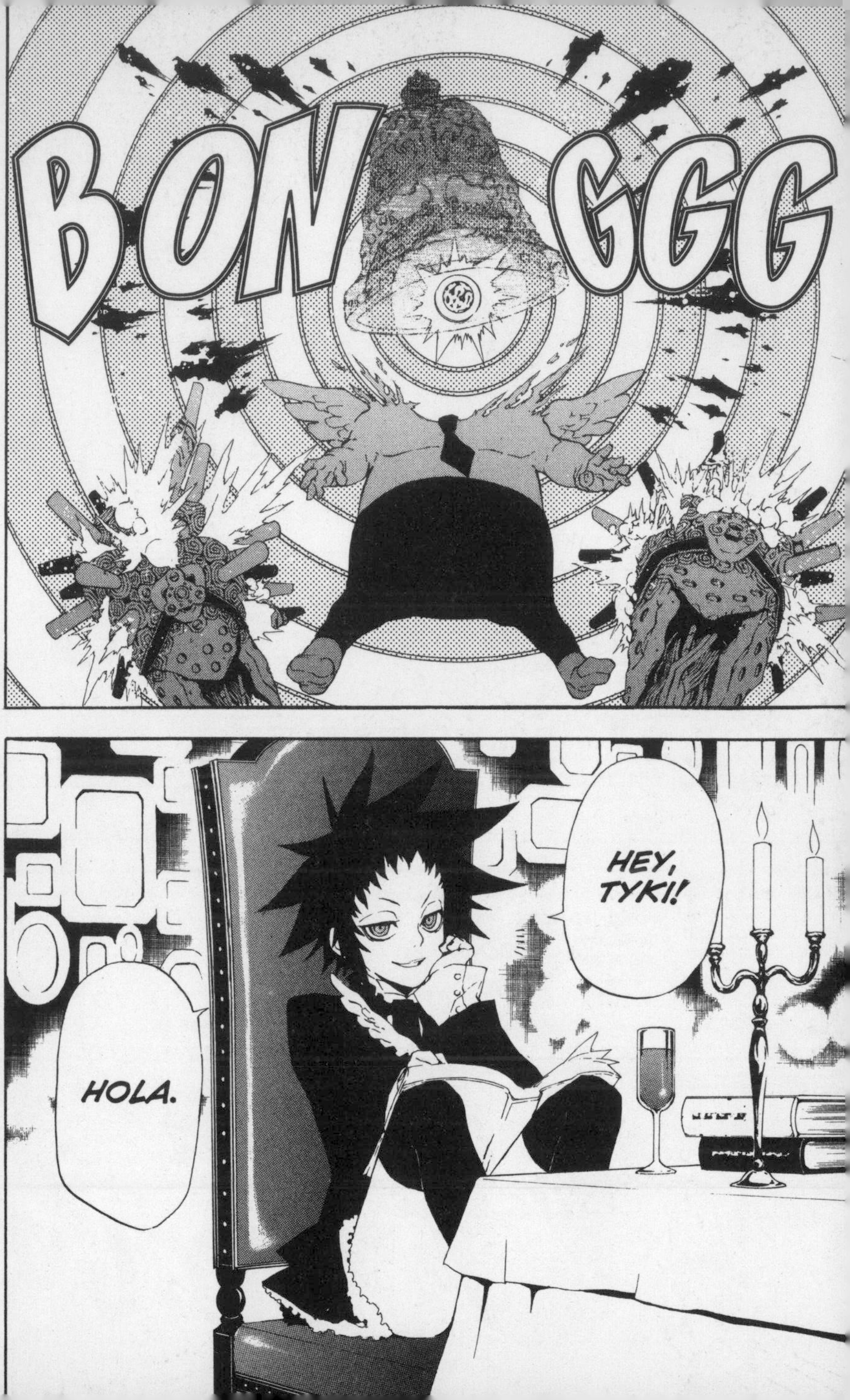
BONGGG
HEY, TYKI!
HOLA.

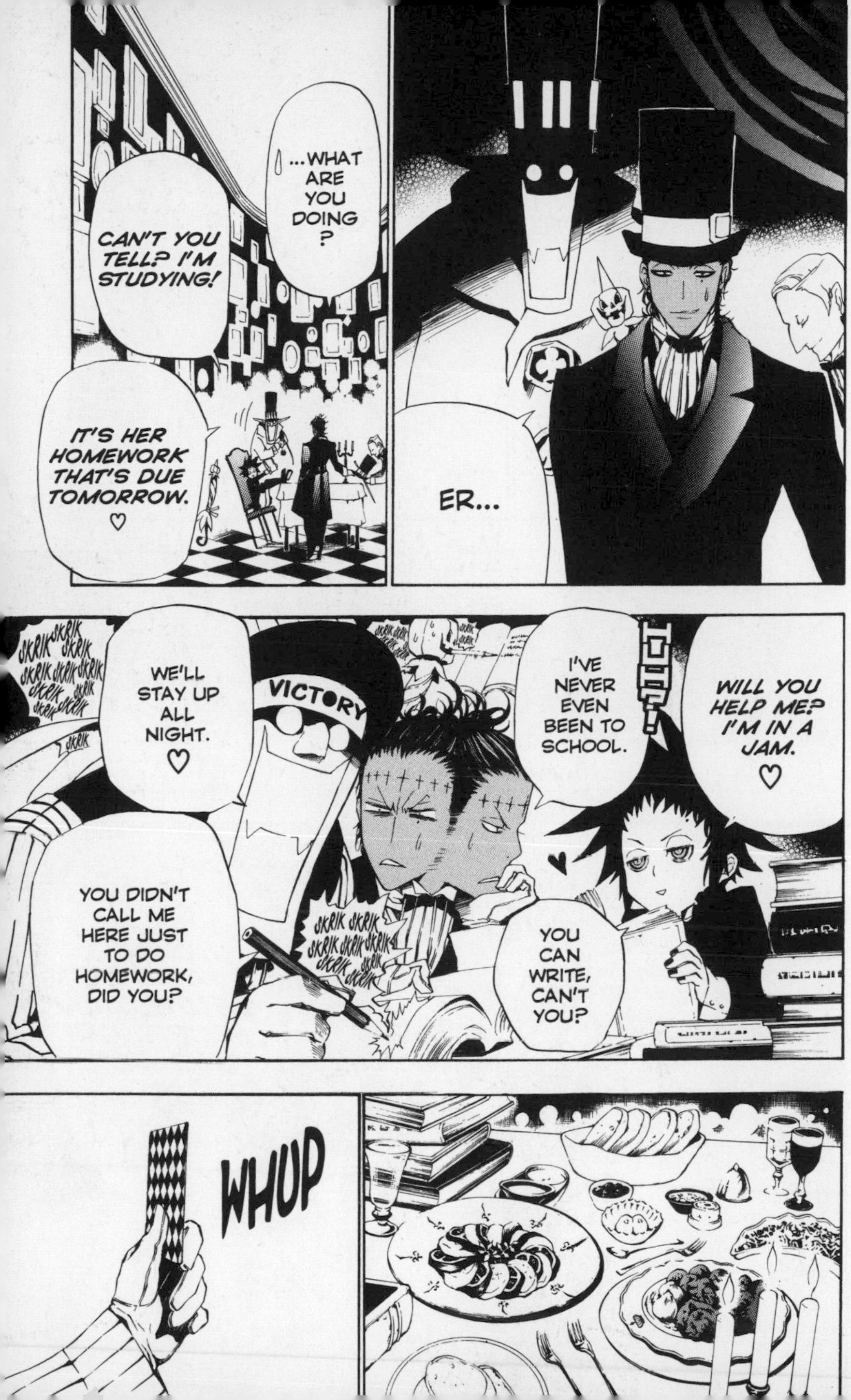
ER...
...WHAT ARE YOU DOING?
CAN'T YOU TELL? I'M STUDYING!
IT'S HER HOMEWORK THAT'S DUE TOMORROW. ♡
WILL YOU HELP ME? I'M IN A JAM. ♡
I'VE NEVER EVEN BEEN TO SCHOOL.
YOU CAN WRITE, CAN'T YOU?
SKRIK SKRIK SKRIK SKRIK SKRIK SKRIK SKRIK
WE'LL STAY UP ALL NIGHT. ♡
SKRIK SKRIK SKRIK SKRIK SKRIK SKRIK SKRIK SKRIK SKRIK SKRIK SKRIK SKRIK
VICTORY
YOU DIDN'T CALL ME HERE JUST TO DO HOMEWORK, DID YOU?
WHUP

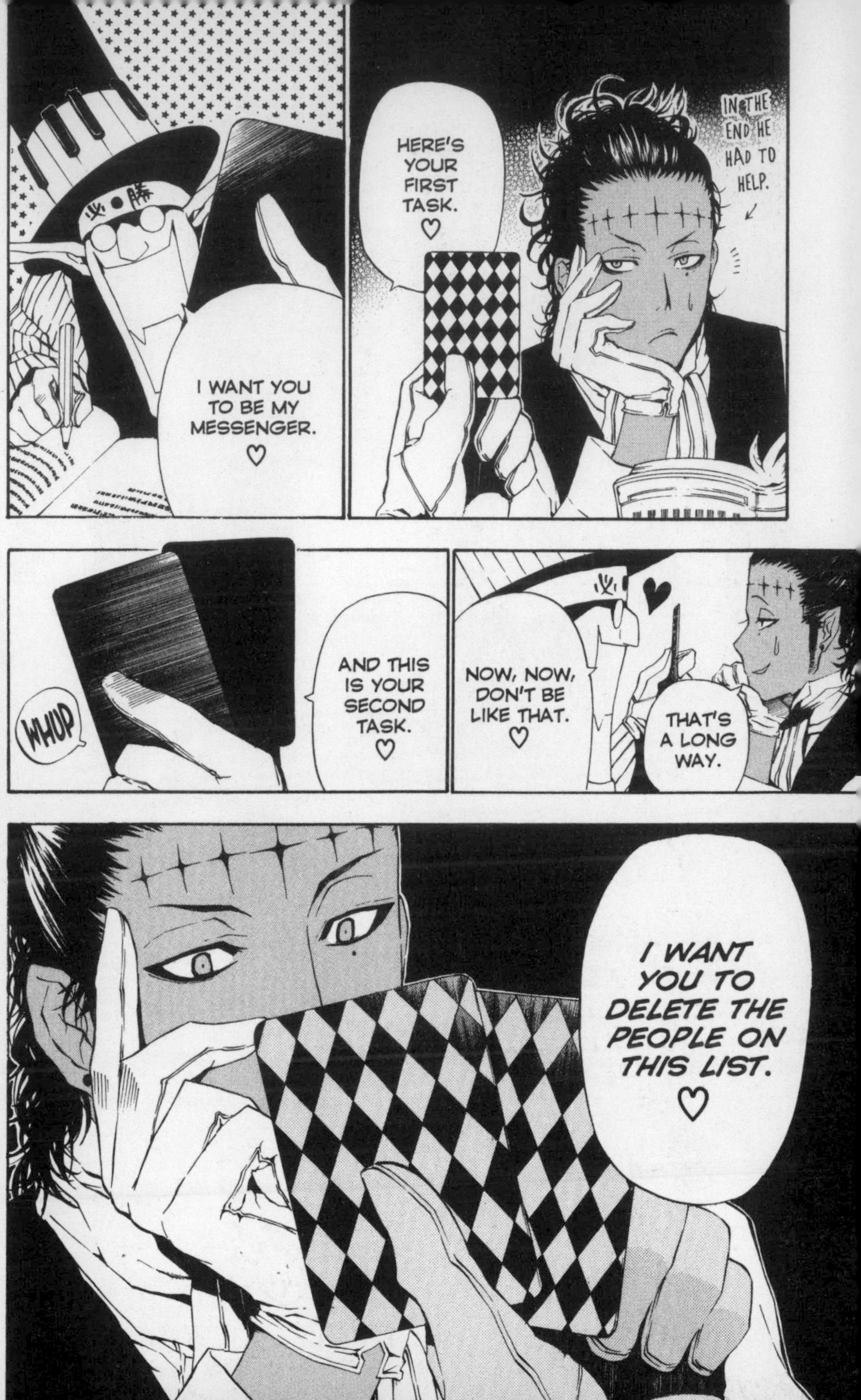
IN THE END HE HAD TO HELP.
HERE'S YOUR FIRST TASK. ♡
I WANT YOU TO BE MY MESSENGER. ♡
THAT'S A LONG WAY.
NOW, NOW, DON'T BE LIKE THAT. ♡
AND THIS IS YOUR SECOND TASK. ♡
WHUP
I WANT YOU TO DELETE THE PEOPLE ON THIS LIST. ♡

READ THIS WAY

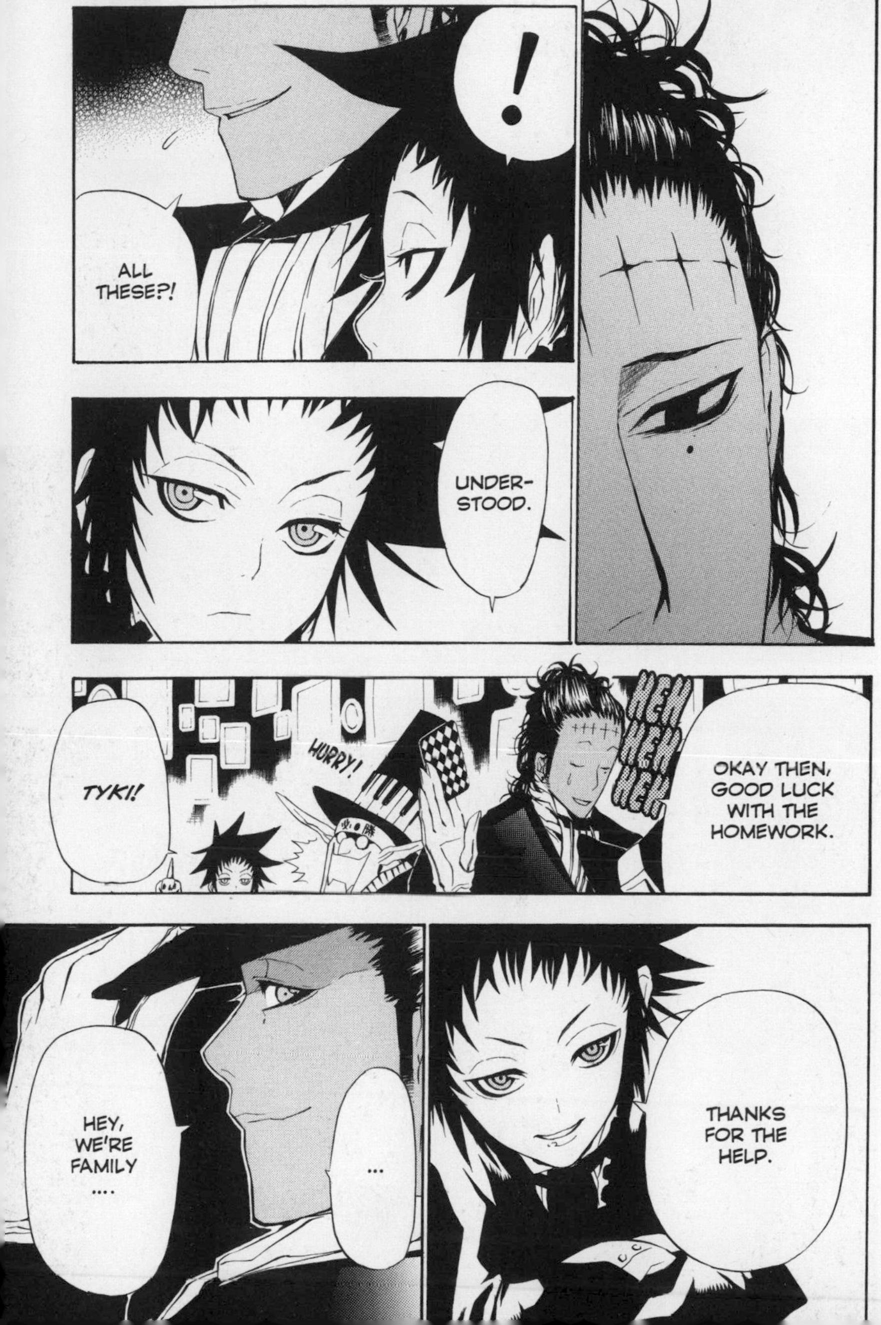
!
ALL THESE?!
UNDERSTOOD.
OKAY THEN, GOOD LUCK WITH THE HOMEWORK.
HEH HEH HEH
HURRY!
TYKI!
THANKS FOR THE HELP.
...
HEY, WE'RE FAMILY ....

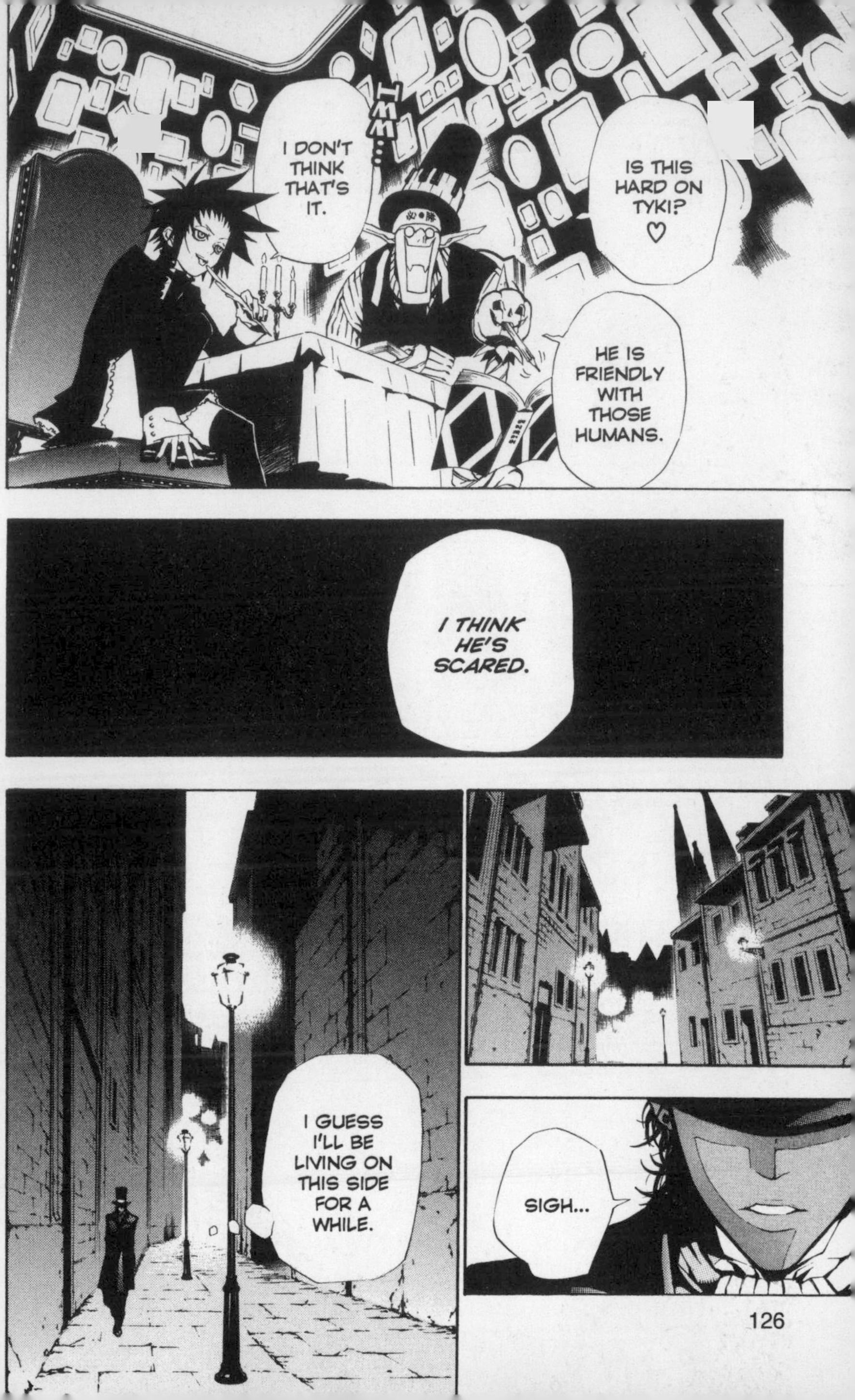
IS THIS HARD ON TYKI? ♡
HE IS FRIENDLY WITH THOSE HUMANS.
HMM...
I DON'T THINK THAT'S IT.
I THINK HE'S SCARED.
SIGH...
I GUESS I'LL BE LIVING ON THIS SIDE FOR A WHILE.

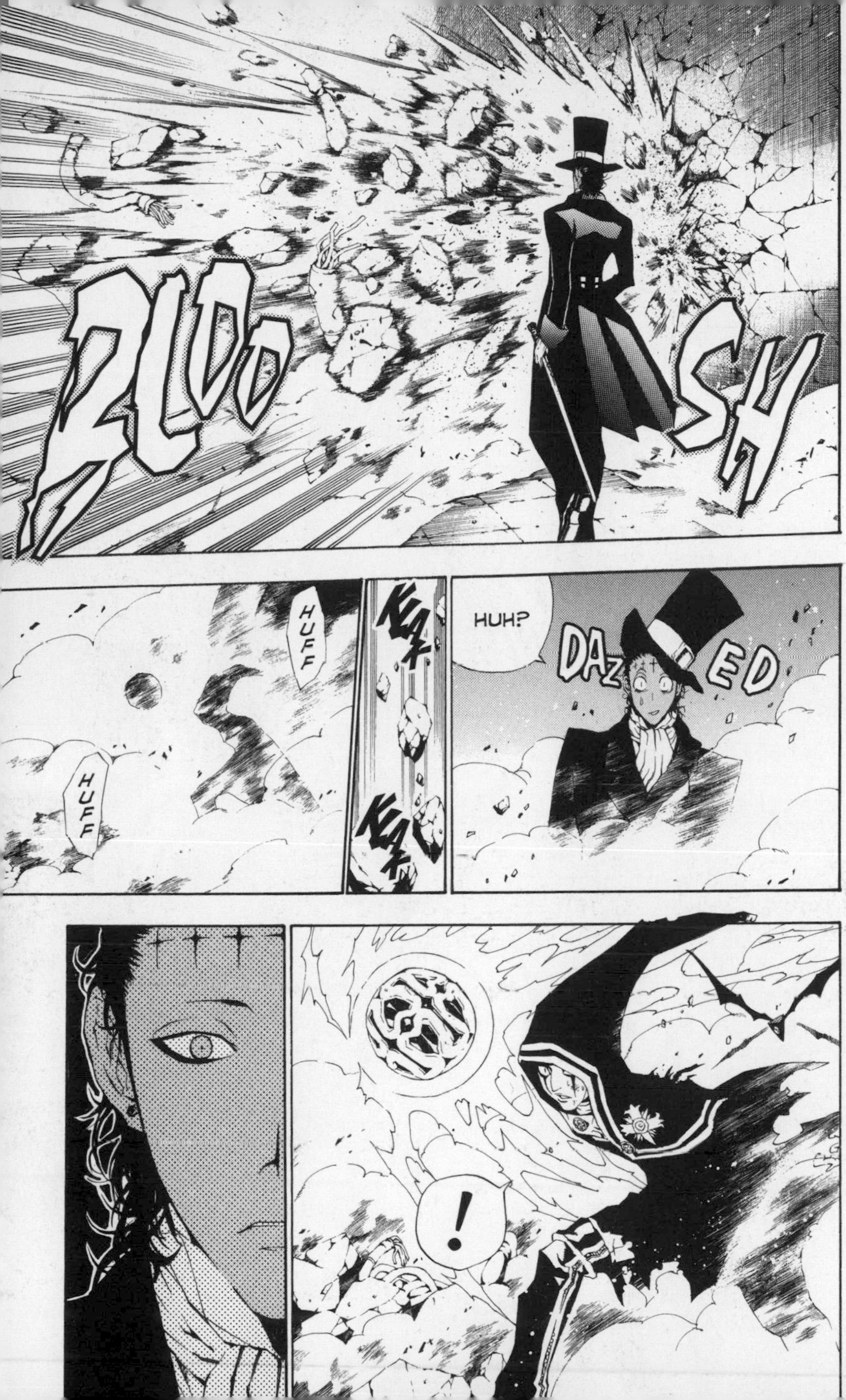
ZUOOSH
HUH?
DAZED
KLAK
KLAK
HUFF
HUFF
!

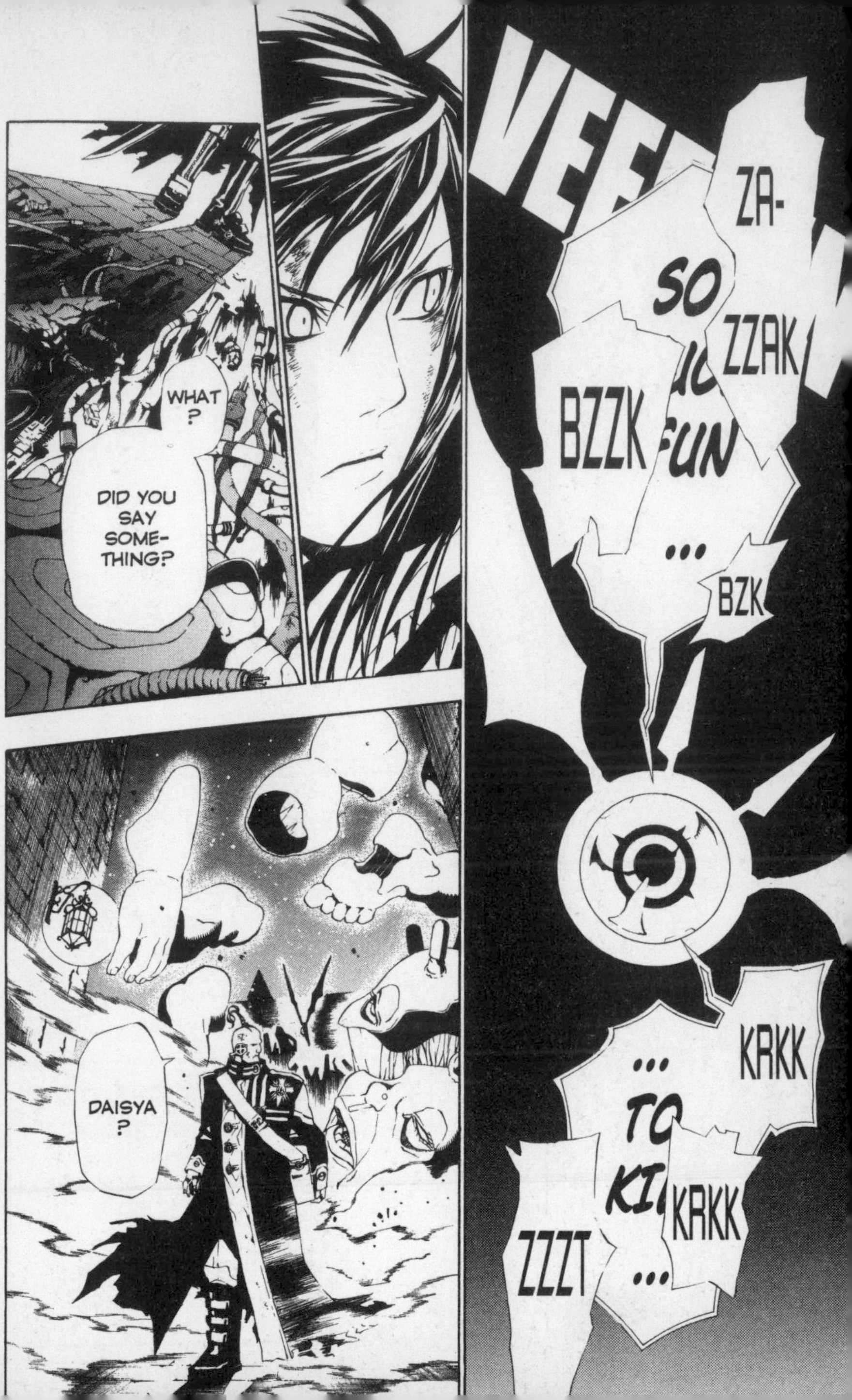
VEEE
ZA-
ZZAK
SO
FUN
...
BZZK
BZK
KRKK
...
TO
KI
...
KRKK
ZZZT
WHAT?
DID YOU SAY SOMETHING?
DAISYA?

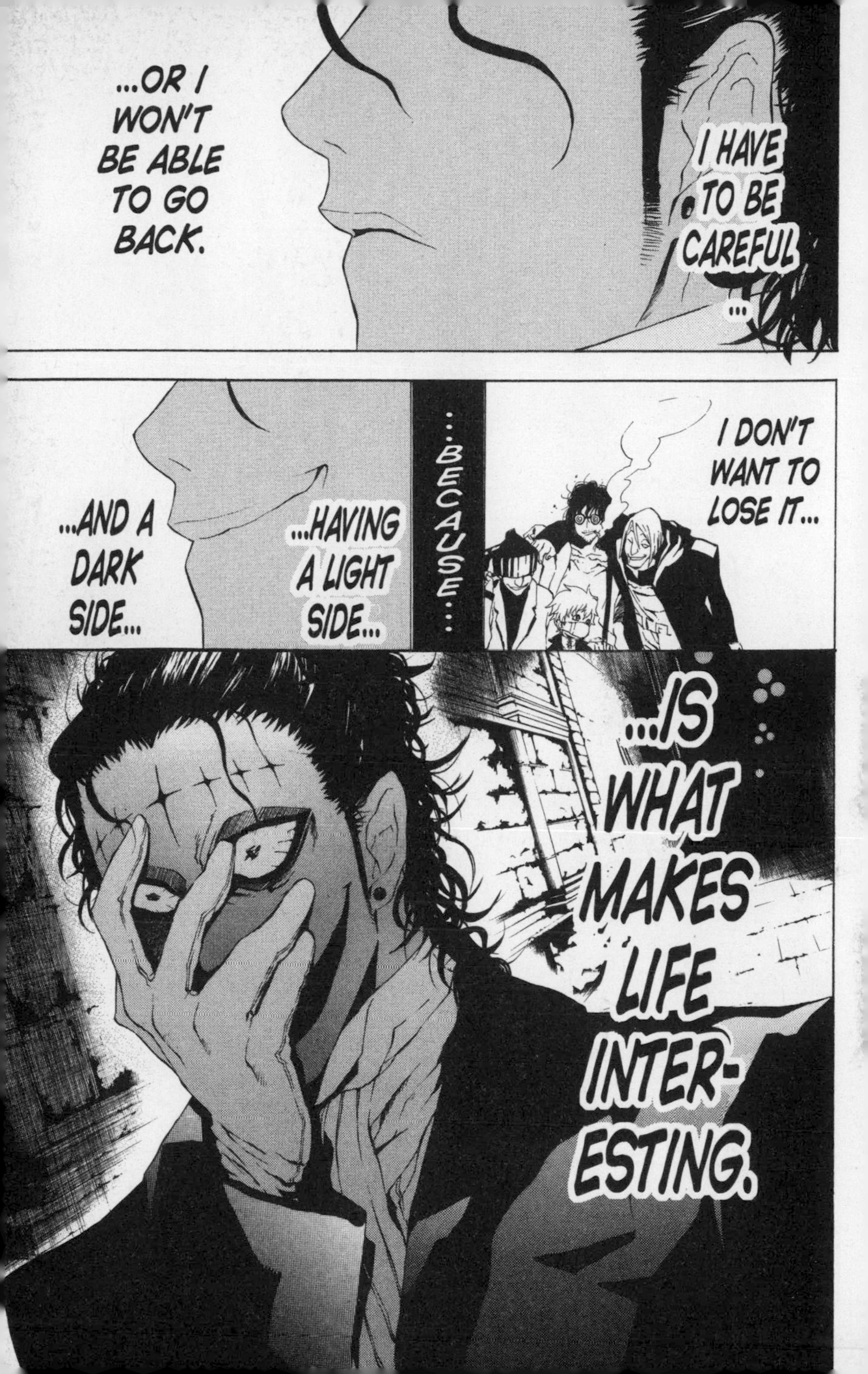
I HAVE TO BE CAREFUL...
...OR I WON'T BE ABLE TO GO BACK.
I DON'T WANT TO LOSE IT...
...BECAUSE...
...HAVING A LIGHT SIDE...
...AND A DARK SIDE...
...IS WHAT MAKES LIFE INTER-ESTING.

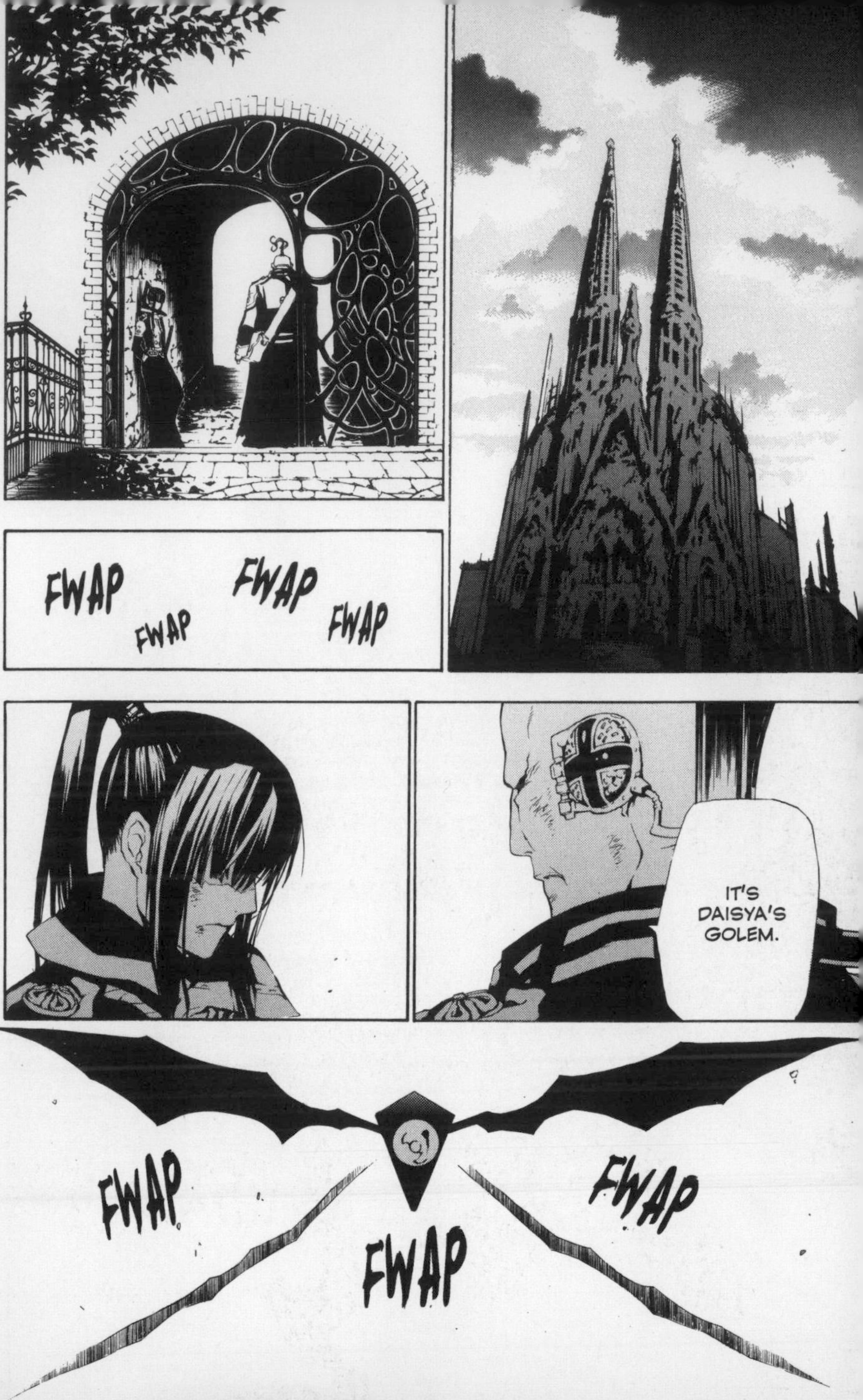
FWAP
FWAP
FWAP
FWAP
IT'S DAISYA'S GOLEM.
FWAP
FWAP
FWAP

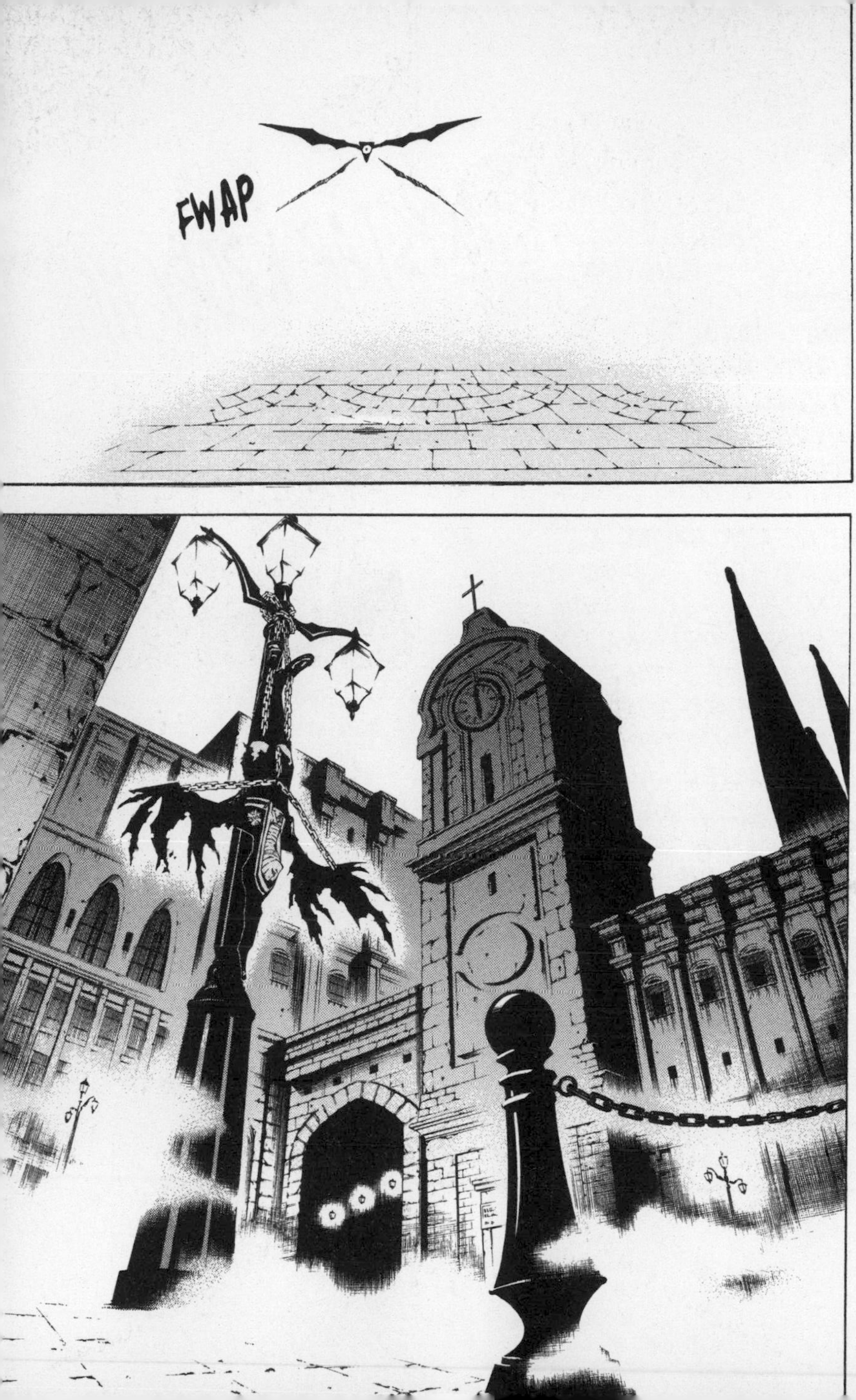
FWAP

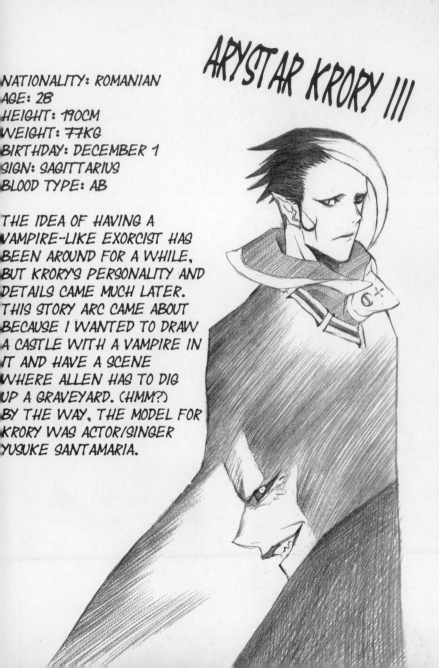

ARYSTAR KRORY III

NATIONALITY: ROMANIAN
AGE: 28
HEIGHT: 190CM
WEIGHT: 77KG
BIRTHDAY: DECEMBER 1
SIGN: SAGITTARIUS
BLOOD TYPE: AB

THE IDEA OF HAVING A VAMPIRE-LIKE EXORCIST HAS BEEN AROUND FOR A WHILE, BUT KRORY'S PERSONALITY AND DETAILS CAME MUCH LATER. THIS STORY ARC CAME ABOUT BECAUSE I WANTED TO DRAW A CASTLE WITH A VAMPIRE IN IT AND HAVE A SCENE WHERE ALLEN HAS TO DIG UP A GRAVEYARD. (HMM?) BY THE WAY, THE MODEL FOR KRORY WAS ACTOR/SINGER YUSUKE SANTAMARIA.

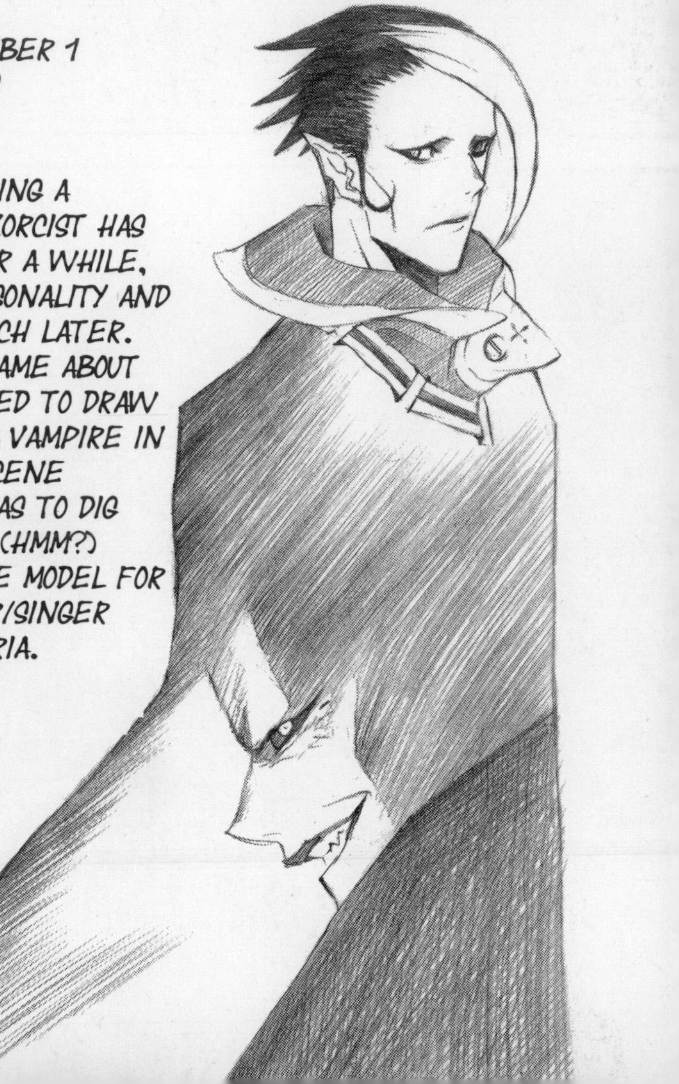

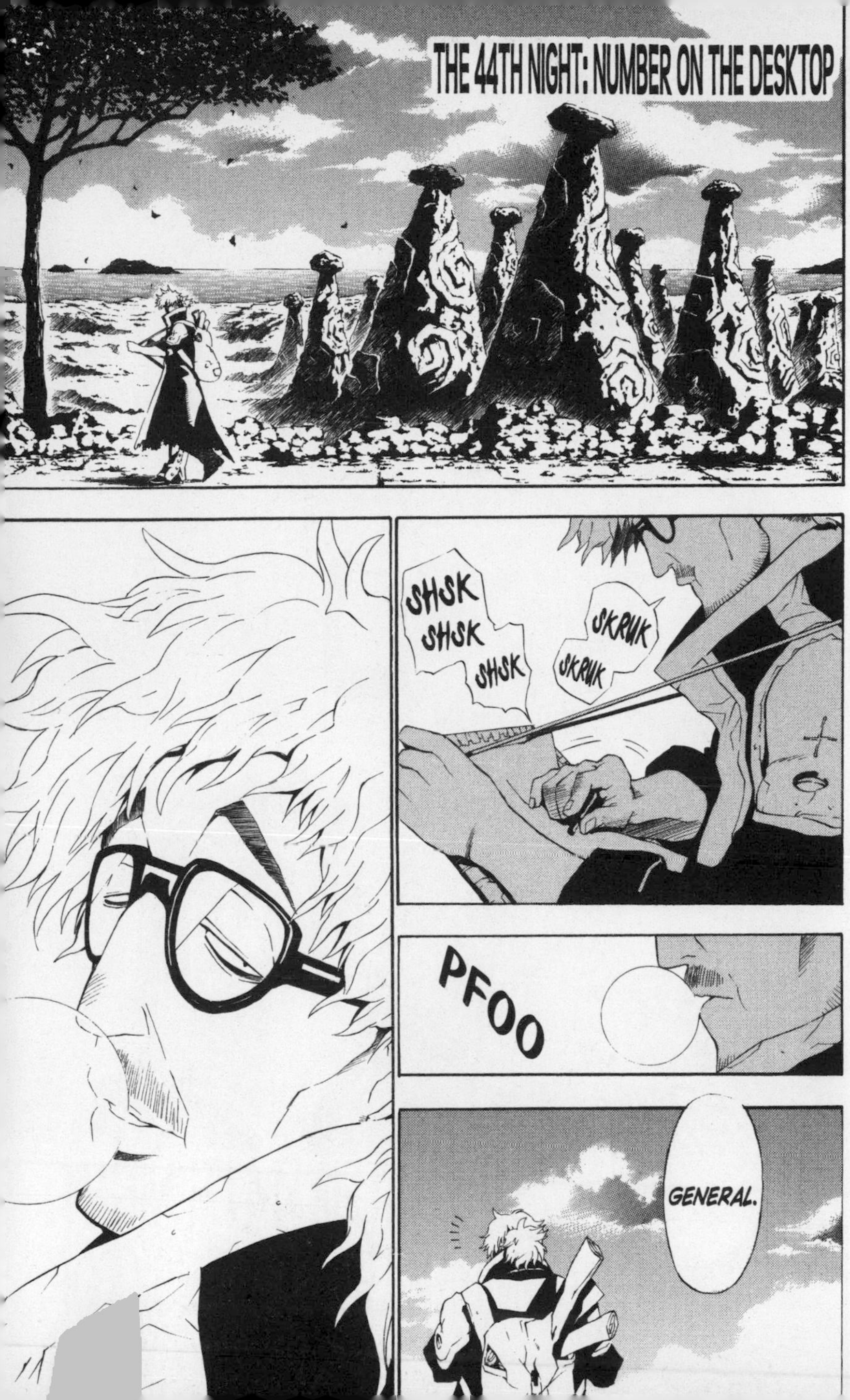
THE 44TH NIGHT: NUMBER ON THE DESKTOP
SKRUK SKRUK
SHSK SHSK SHSK
PFOO
GENERAL.

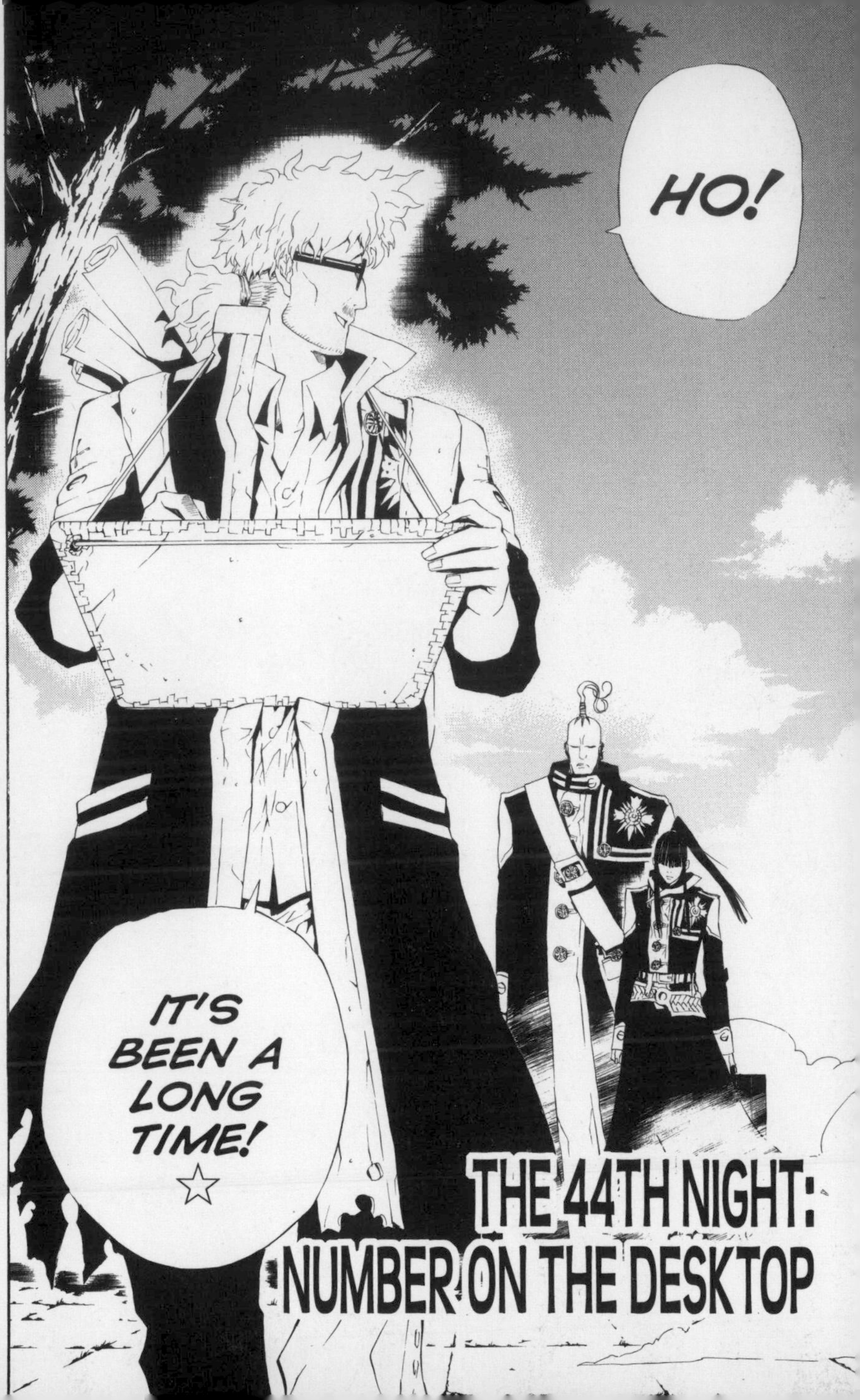
HO!
IT'S BEEN A LONG TIME! ☆
THE 44TH NIGHT: NUMBER ON THE DESKTOP

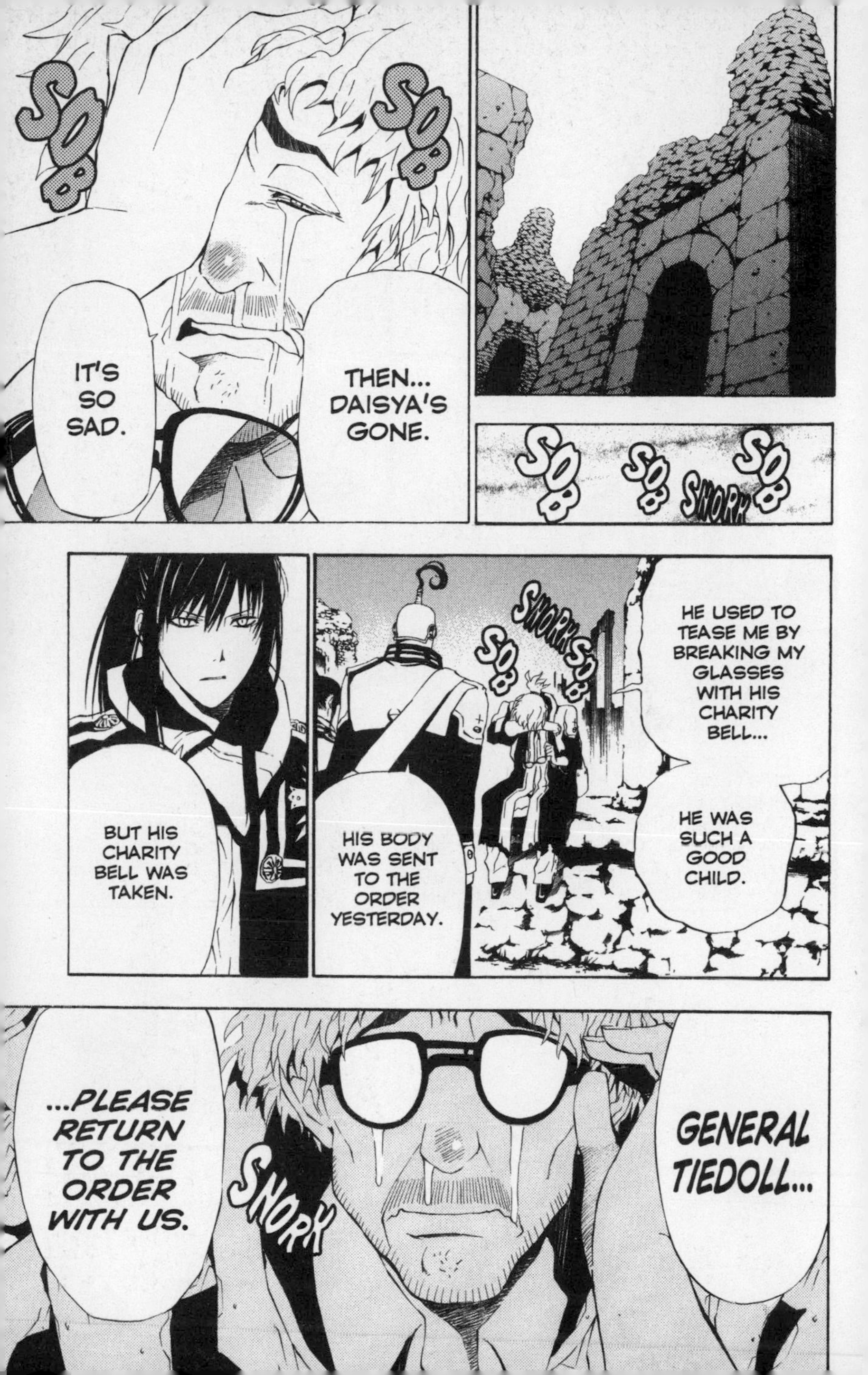
SOB SOB SNORK SOB
SOB
SOB
THEN... DAISYA'S GONE.
IT'S SO SAD.
HE USED TO TEASE ME BY BREAKING MY GLASSES WITH HIS CHARITY BELL...
HE WAS SUCH A GOOD CHILD.
SNORK SOB
SOB
HIS BODY WAS SENT TO THE ORDER YESTERDAY.
BUT HIS CHARITY BELL WAS TAKEN.
GENERAL TIEDOLL...
SNORK
...PLEASE RETURN TO THE ORDER WITH US.

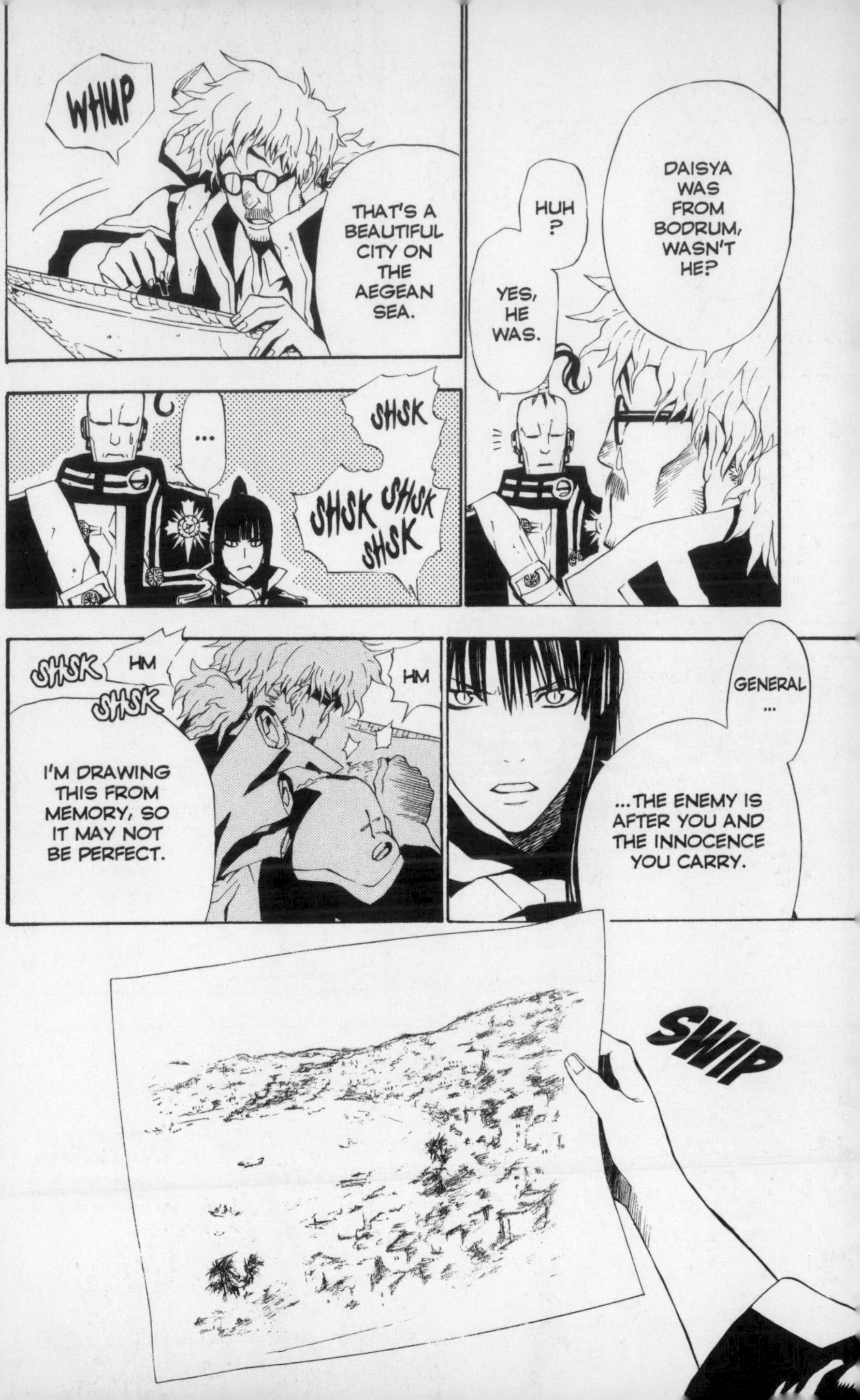
DAISYA WAS FROM BODRUM, WASN'T HE?
HUH ?
YES, HE WAS.
THAT'S A BEAUTIFUL CITY ON THE AEGEAN SEA.
WHUP
SHSK
...
SHSK SHSK SHSK
GENERAL ...
...THE ENEMY IS AFTER YOU AND THE INNOCENCE YOU CARRY.
HM
HM
SHSK
SHSK
I'M DRAWING THIS FROM MEMORY, SO IT MAY NOT BE PERFECT.
SWIP

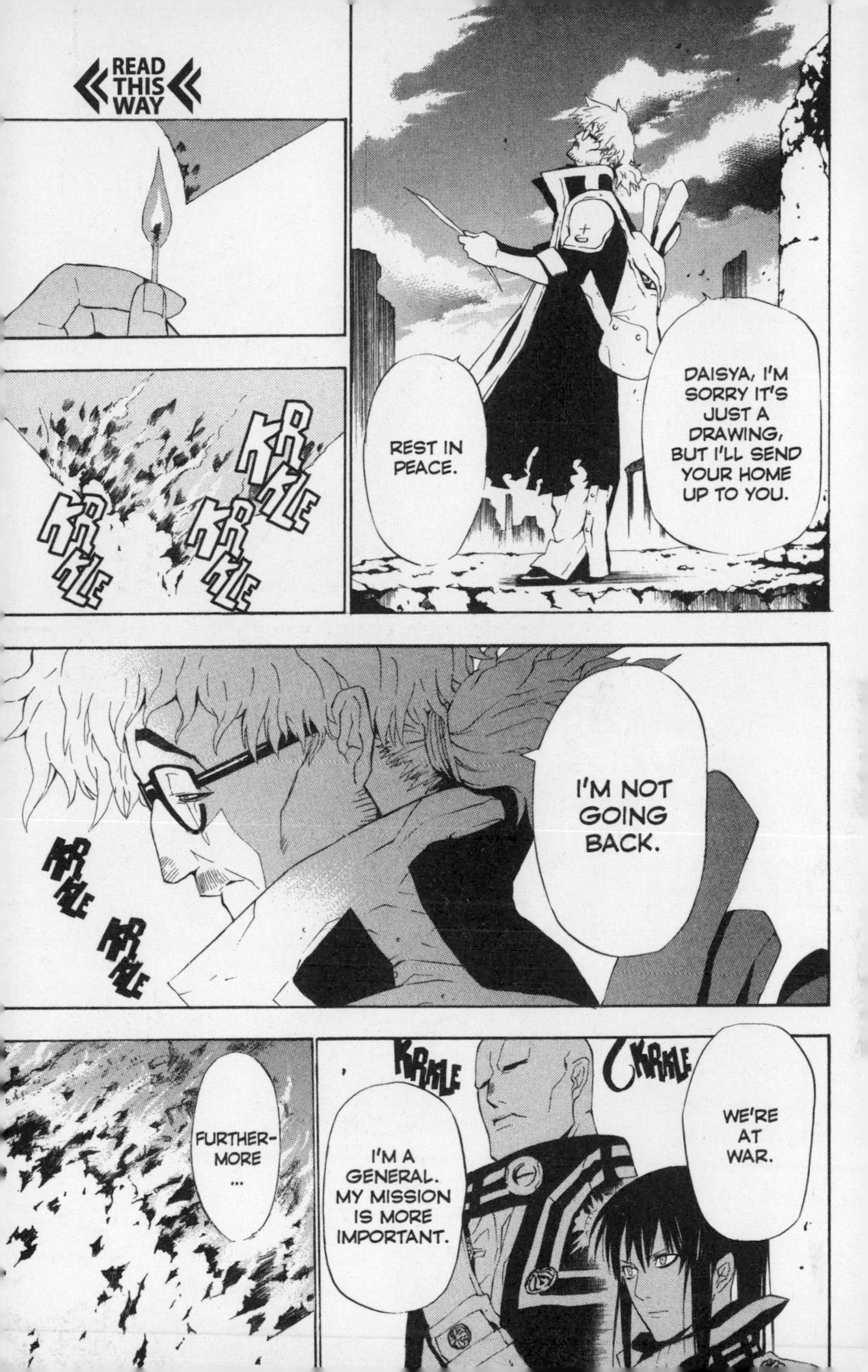

READ THIS WAY
DAISYA, I'M SORRY IT'S JUST A DRAWING, BUT I'LL SEND YOUR HOME UP TO YOU.
REST IN PEACE.
KRAKLE KRAKLE KRAKLE
I'M NOT GOING BACK.
KRAKLE KRAKLE
KRAKLE KRAKLE
WE'RE AT WAR.
I'M A GENERAL. MY MISSION IS MORE IMPORTANT.
FURTHER-MORE ...

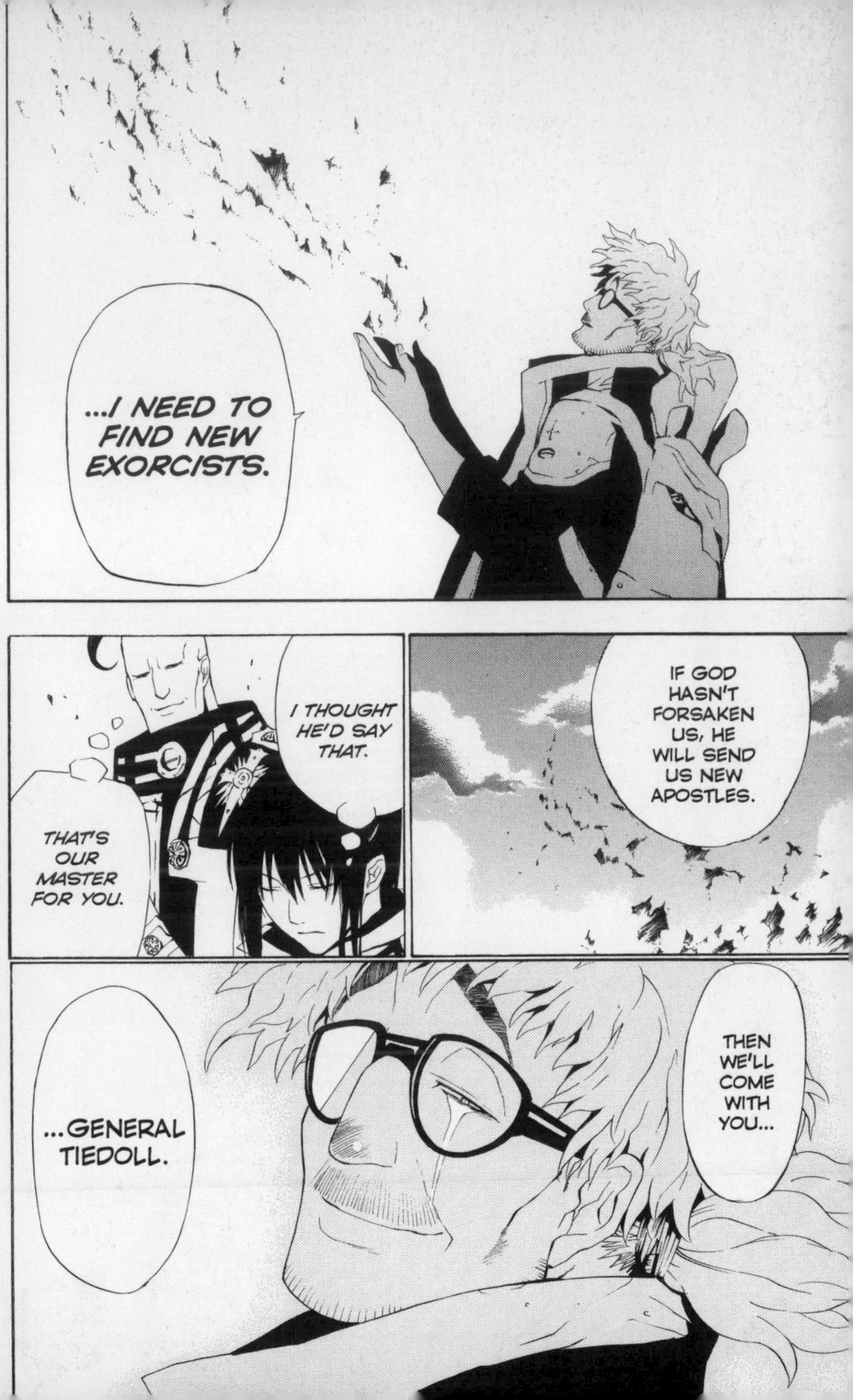
...I NEED TO FIND NEW EXORCISTS.
IF GOD HASN'T FORSAKEN US, HE WILL SEND US NEW APOSTLES.
I THOUGHT HE'D SAY THAT.
THAT'S OUR MASTER FOR YOU.
THEN WE'LL COME WITH YOU...
...GENERAL TIEDOLL.

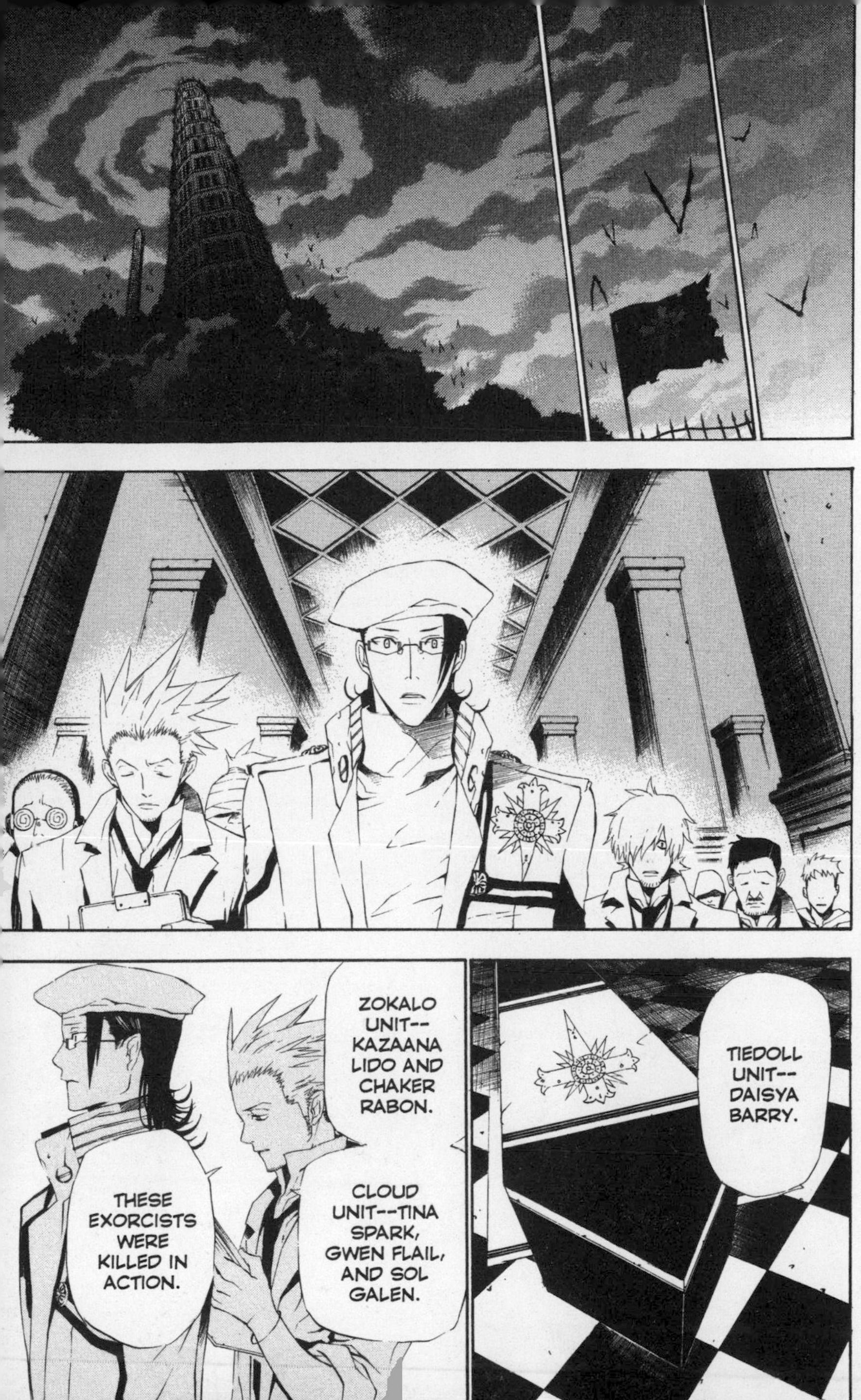
TIEDOLL UNIT--DAISYA BARRY.
ZOKALO UNIT--KAZAANA LIDO AND CHAKER RABON.
CLOUD UNIT--TINA SPARK, GWEN FLAIL, AND SOL GALEN.
THESE EXORCISTS WERE KILLED IN ACTION.

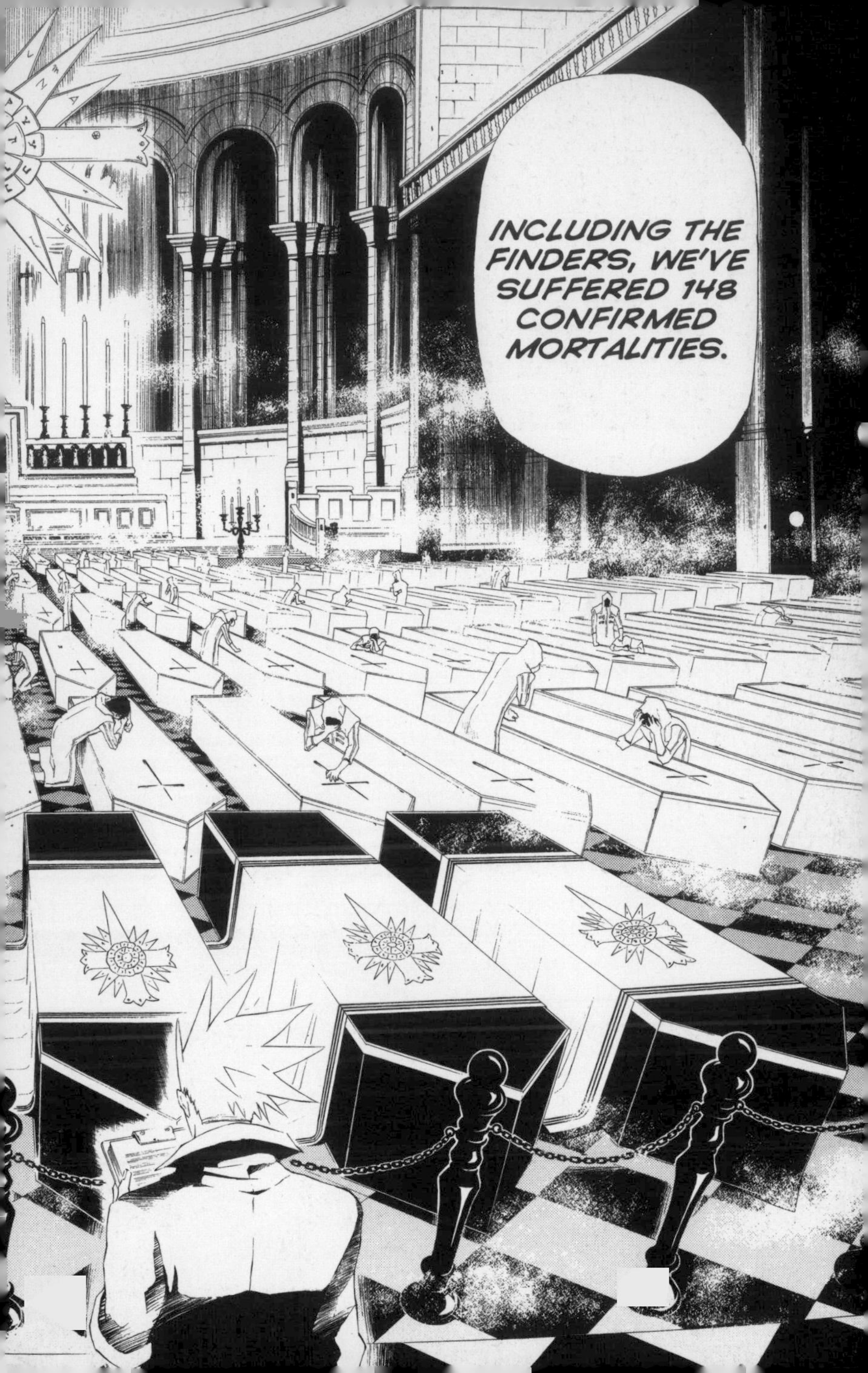
INCLUDING THE FINDERS, WE'VE SUFFERED 148 CONFIRMED MORTALITIES.

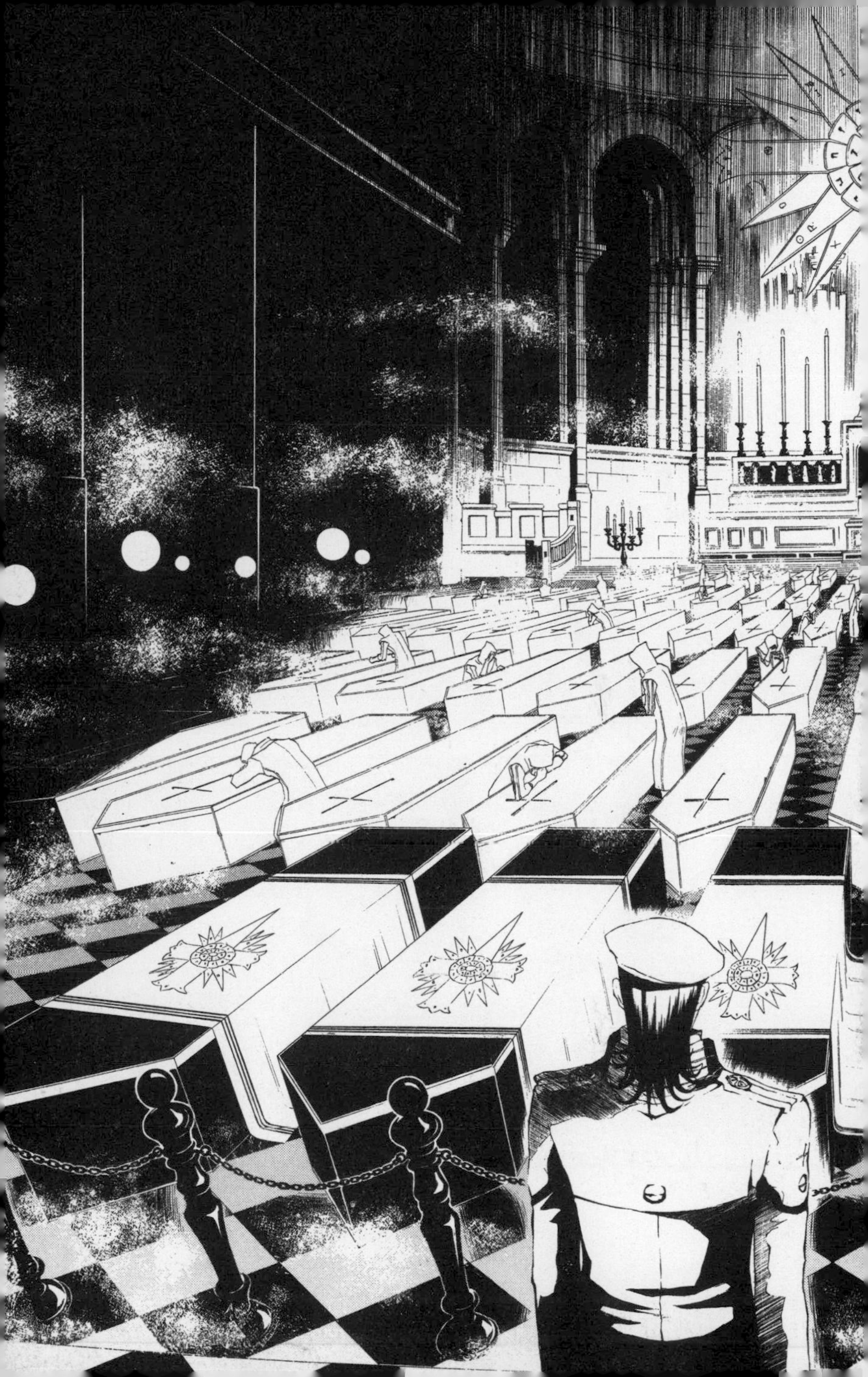

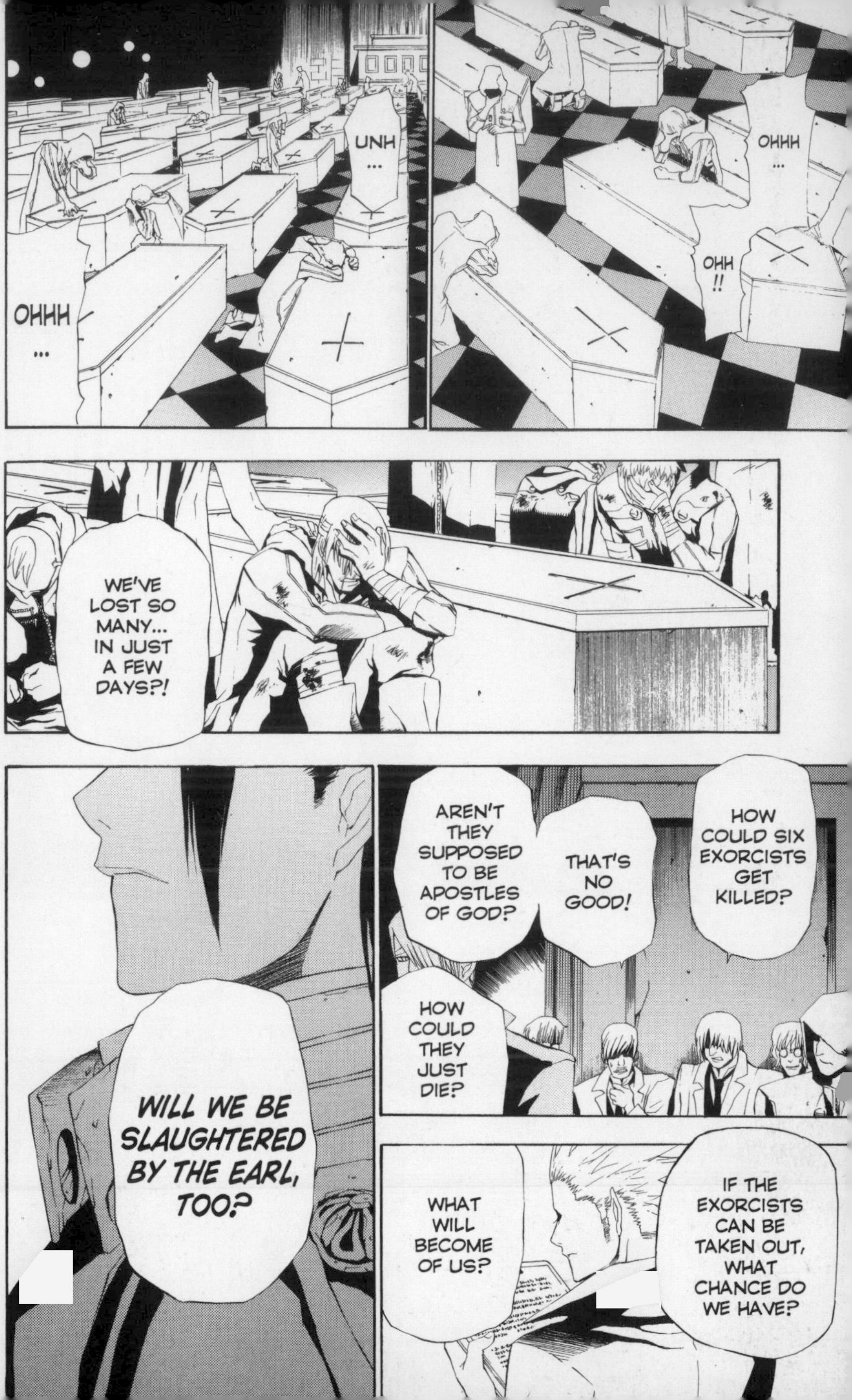
OHHH ...
OHH !!
UNH ...
OHHH ...
WE'VE LOST SO MANY... IN JUST A FEW DAYS?!
HOW COULD SIX EXORCISTS GET KILLED?
THAT'S NO GOOD!
AREN'T THEY SUPPOSED TO BE APOSTLES OF GOD?
HOW COULD THEY JUST DIE?
IF THE EXORCISTS CAN BE TAKEN OUT, WHAT CHANCE DO WE HAVE?
WHAT WILL BECOME OF US?
WILL WE BE SLAUGHTERED BY THE EARL, TOO?

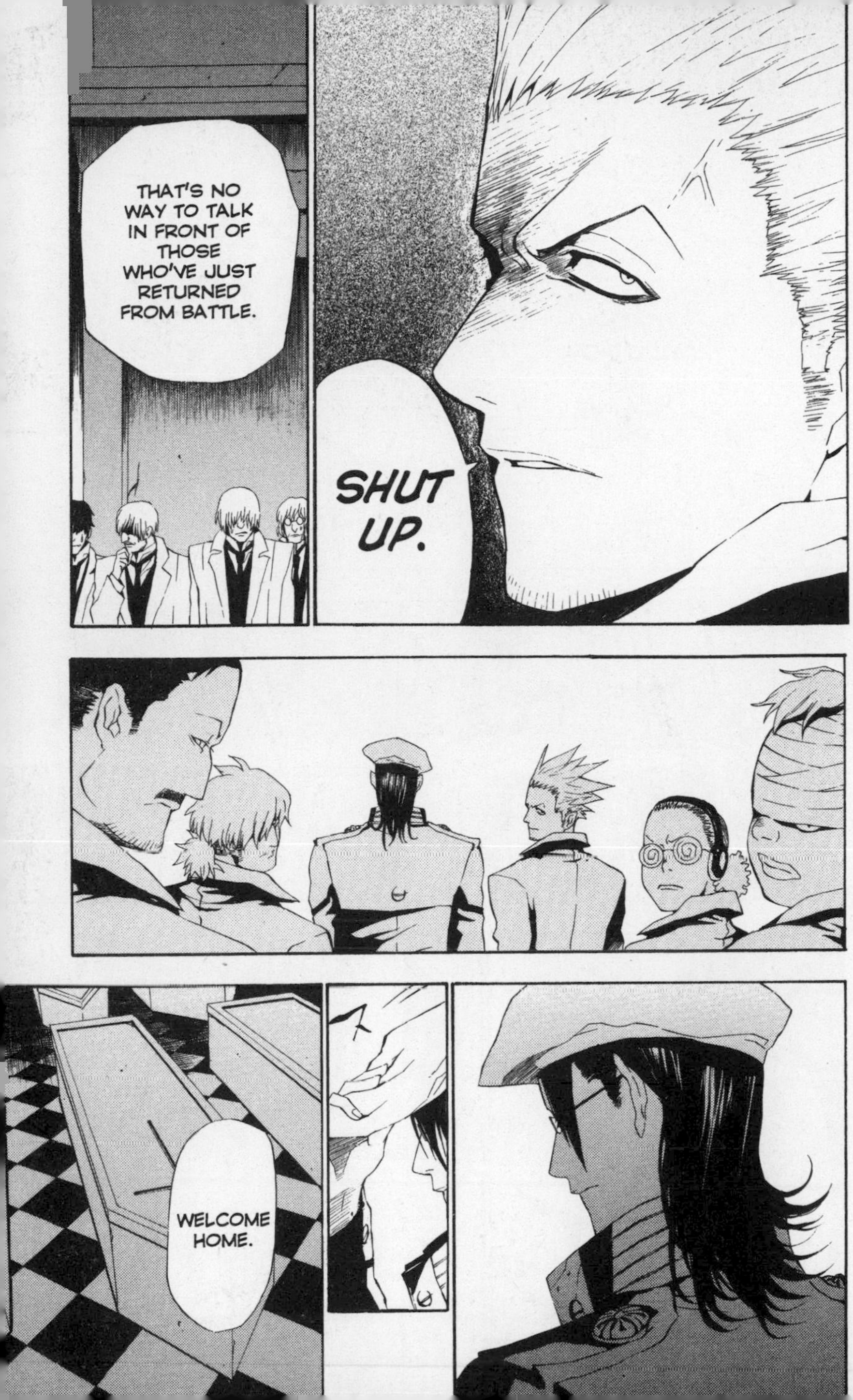
SHUT UP.
THAT'S NO WAY TO TALK IN FRONT OF THOSE WHO'VE JUST RETURNED FROM BATTLE.
WELCOME HOME.

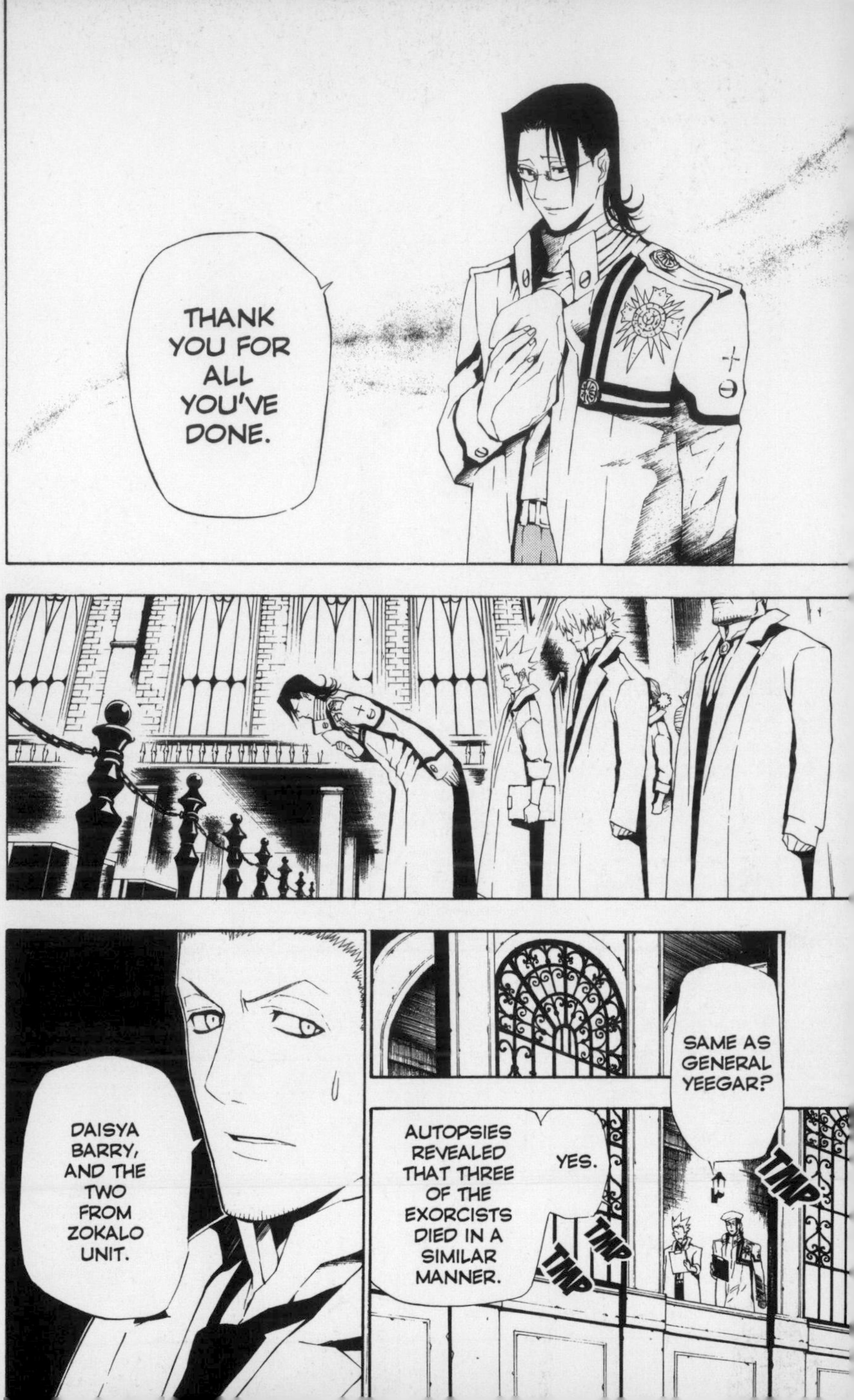
THANK YOU FOR ALL YOU'VE DONE.
SAME AS GENERAL YEEGAR?
TMP
YES.
AUTOPSIES REVEALED THAT THREE OF THE EXORCISTS DIED IN A SIMILAR MANNER.
TMP
TMP
DAISYA BARRY, AND THE TWO FROM ZOKALO UNIT.

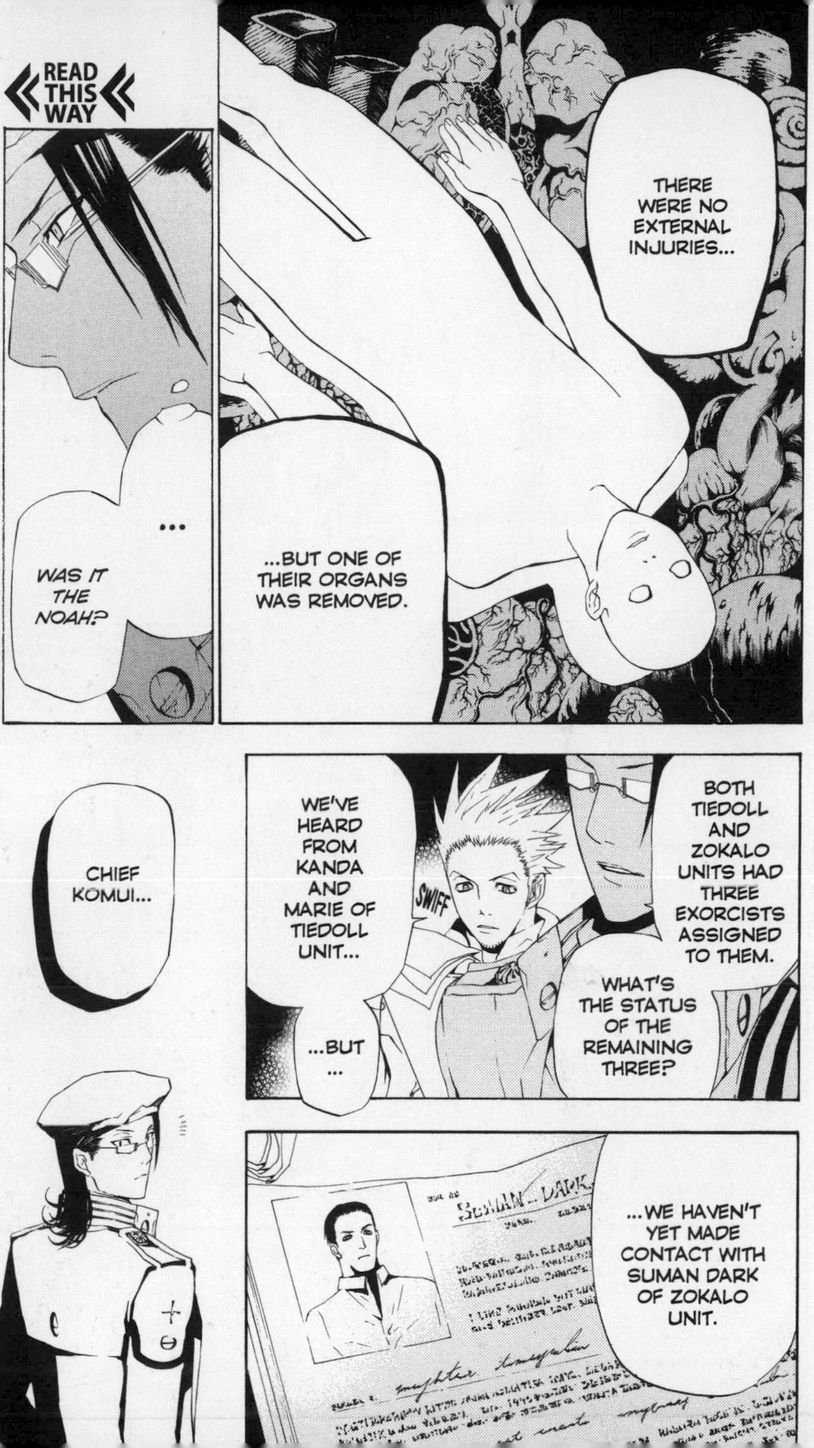
READ THIS WAY
THERE WERE NO EXTERNAL INJURIES...
...BUT ONE OF THEIR ORGANS WAS REMOVED.
...
WAS IT THE NOAH?
BOTH TIEDOLL AND ZOKALO UNITS HAD THREE EXORCISTS ASSIGNED TO THEM.
WHAT'S THE STATUS OF THE REMAINING THREE?
SWIFF
WE'VE HEARD FROM KANDA AND MARIE OF TIEDOLL UNIT...
...BUT ...
CHIEF KOMUI...
...WE HAVEN'T YET MADE CONTACT WITH SUMAN DARK OF ZOKALO UNIT.

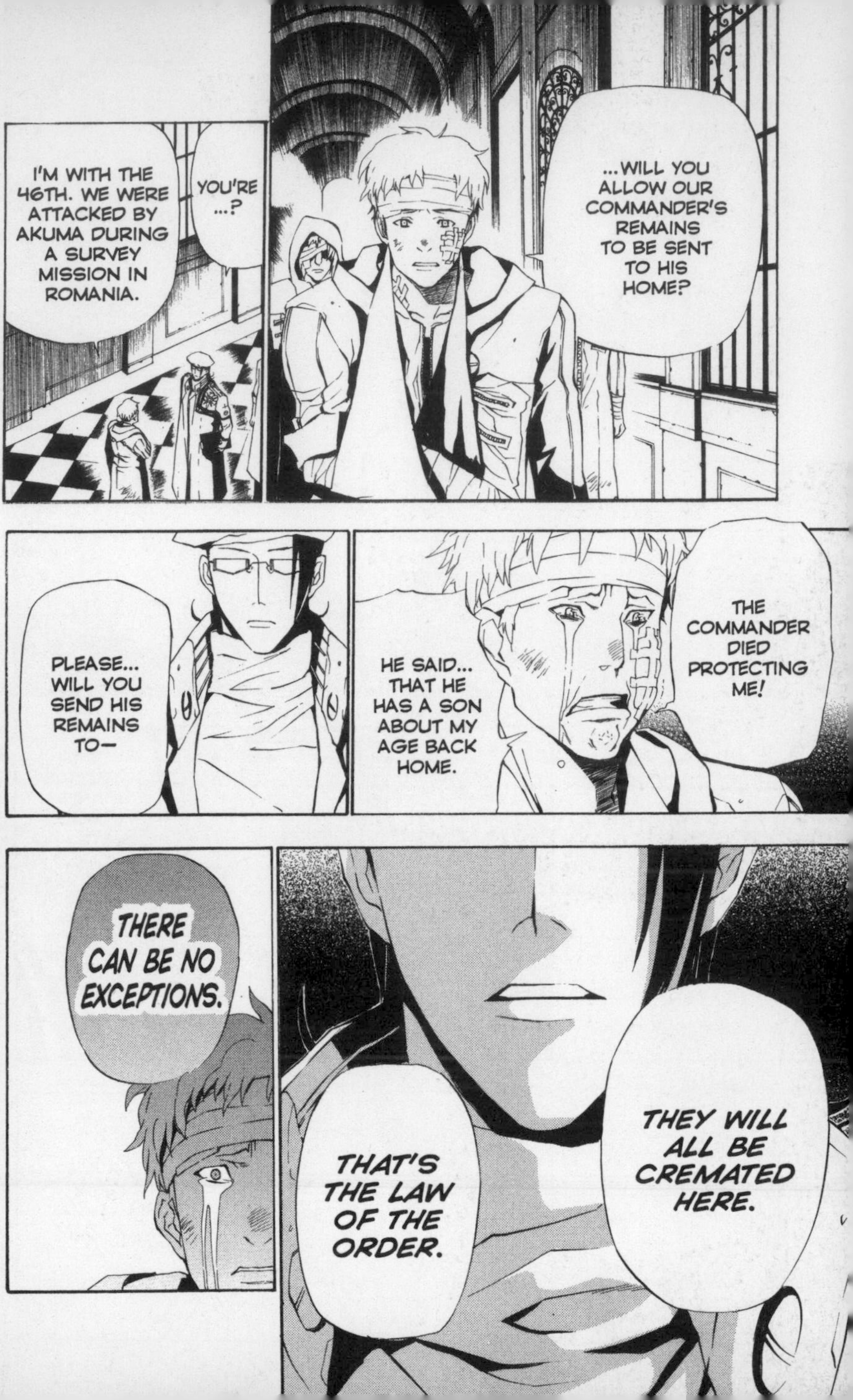
...WILL YOU ALLOW OUR COMMANDER'S REMAINS TO BE SENT TO HIS HOME?
YOU'RE ...?
I'M WITH THE 46TH. WE WERE ATTACKED BY AKUMA DURING A SURVEY MISSION IN ROMANIA.
THE COMMANDER DIED PROTECTING ME!
HE SAID... THAT HE HAS A SON ABOUT MY AGE BACK HOME.
PLEASE... WILL YOU SEND HIS REMAINS TO—
THEY WILL ALL BE CREMATED HERE.
THAT'S THE LAW OF THE ORDER.
THERE CAN BE NO EXCEPTIONS.

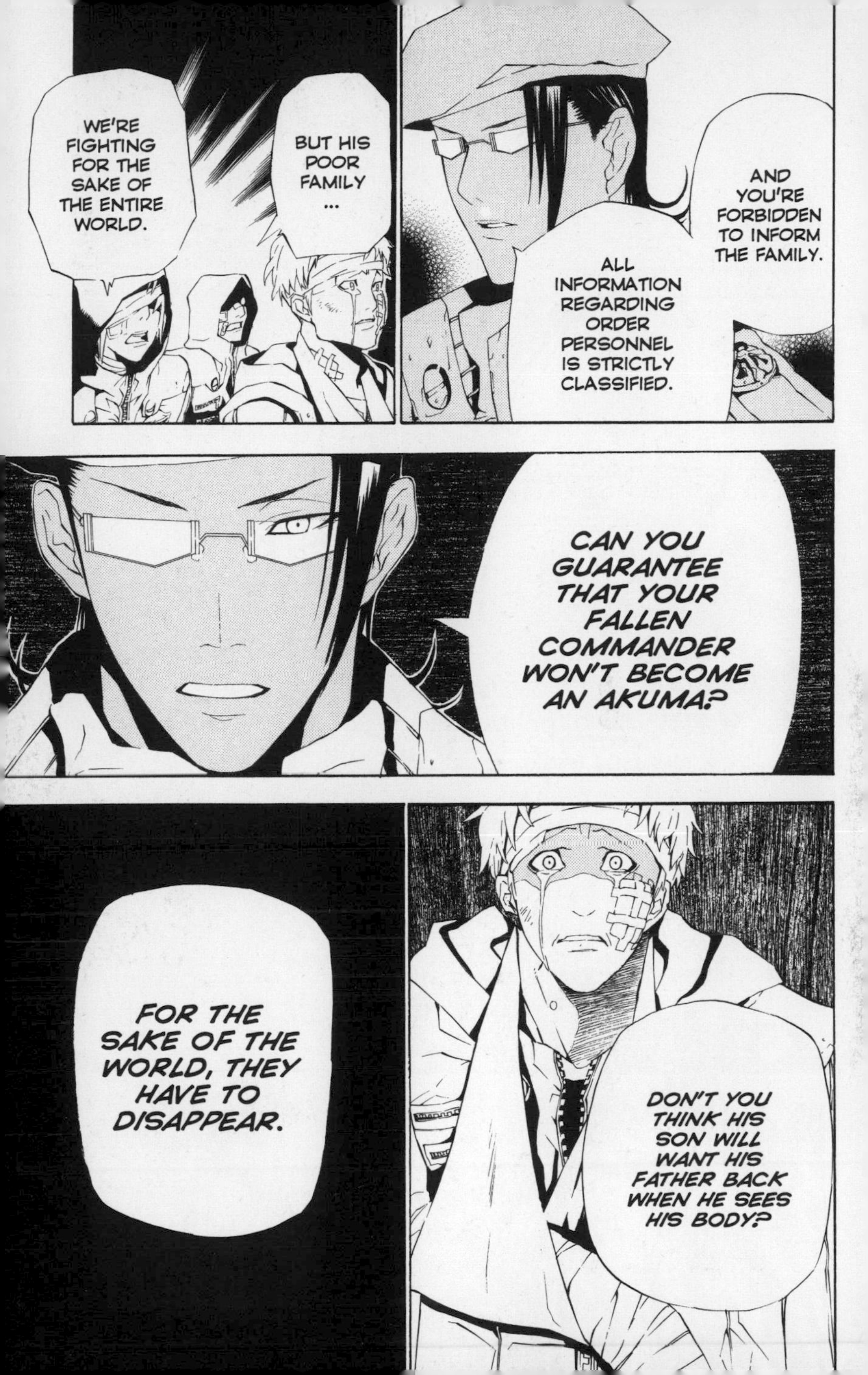
WE'RE FIGHTING FOR THE SAKE OF THE ENTIRE WORLD.
BUT HIS POOR FAMILY ...
ALL INFORMATION REGARDING ORDER PERSONNEL IS STRICTLY CLASSIFIED.
AND YOU'RE FORBIDDEN TO INFORM THE FAMILY.
CAN YOU GUARANTEE THAT YOUR FALLEN COMMANDER WON'T BECOME AN AKUMA?
FOR THE SAKE OF THE WORLD, THEY HAVE TO DISAPPEAR.
DON'T YOU THINK HIS SON WILL WANT HIS FATHER BACK WHEN HE SEES HIS BODY?

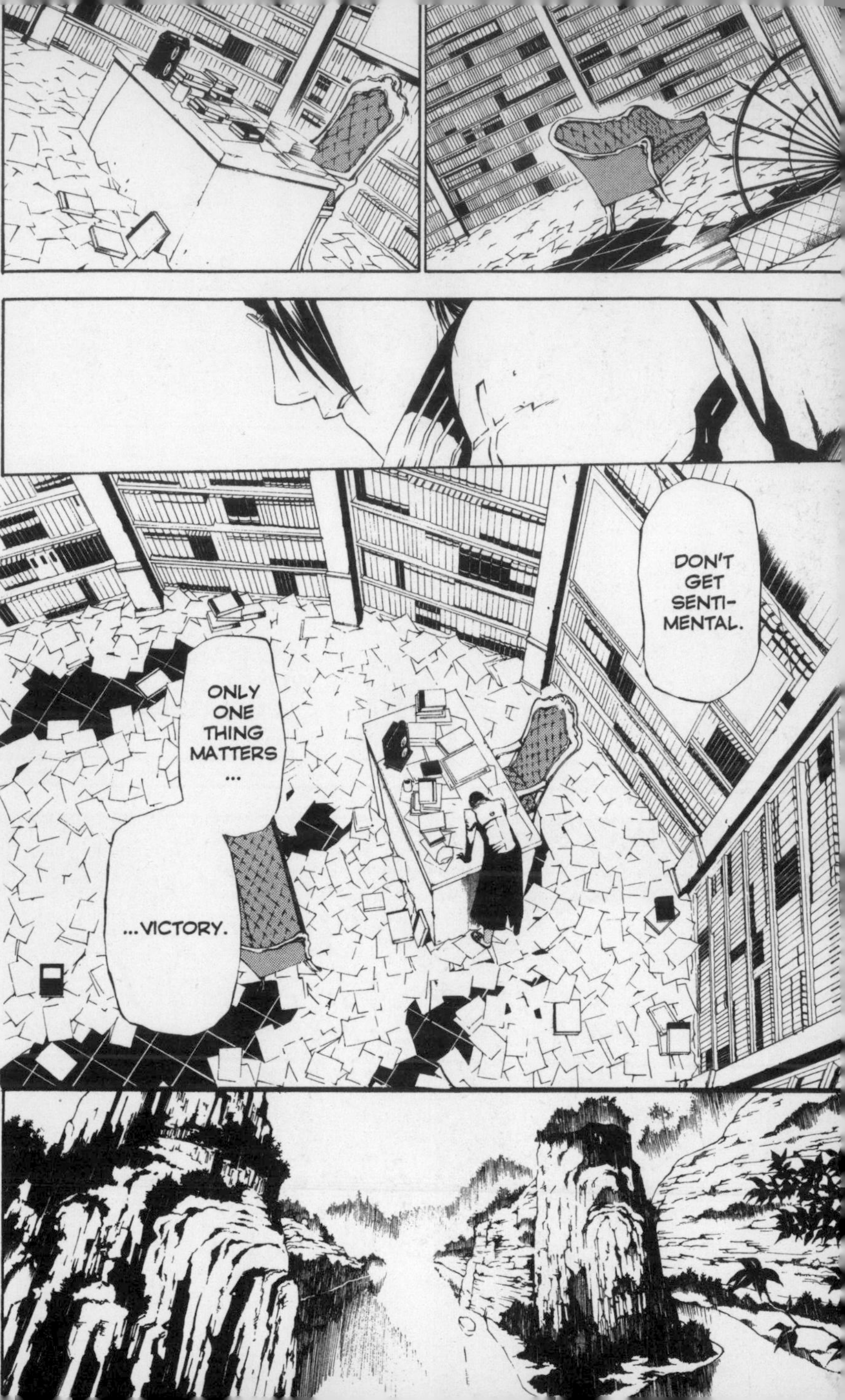
DON'T GET SENTI- MENTAL.
ONLY ONE THING MATTERS ...
...VICTORY.

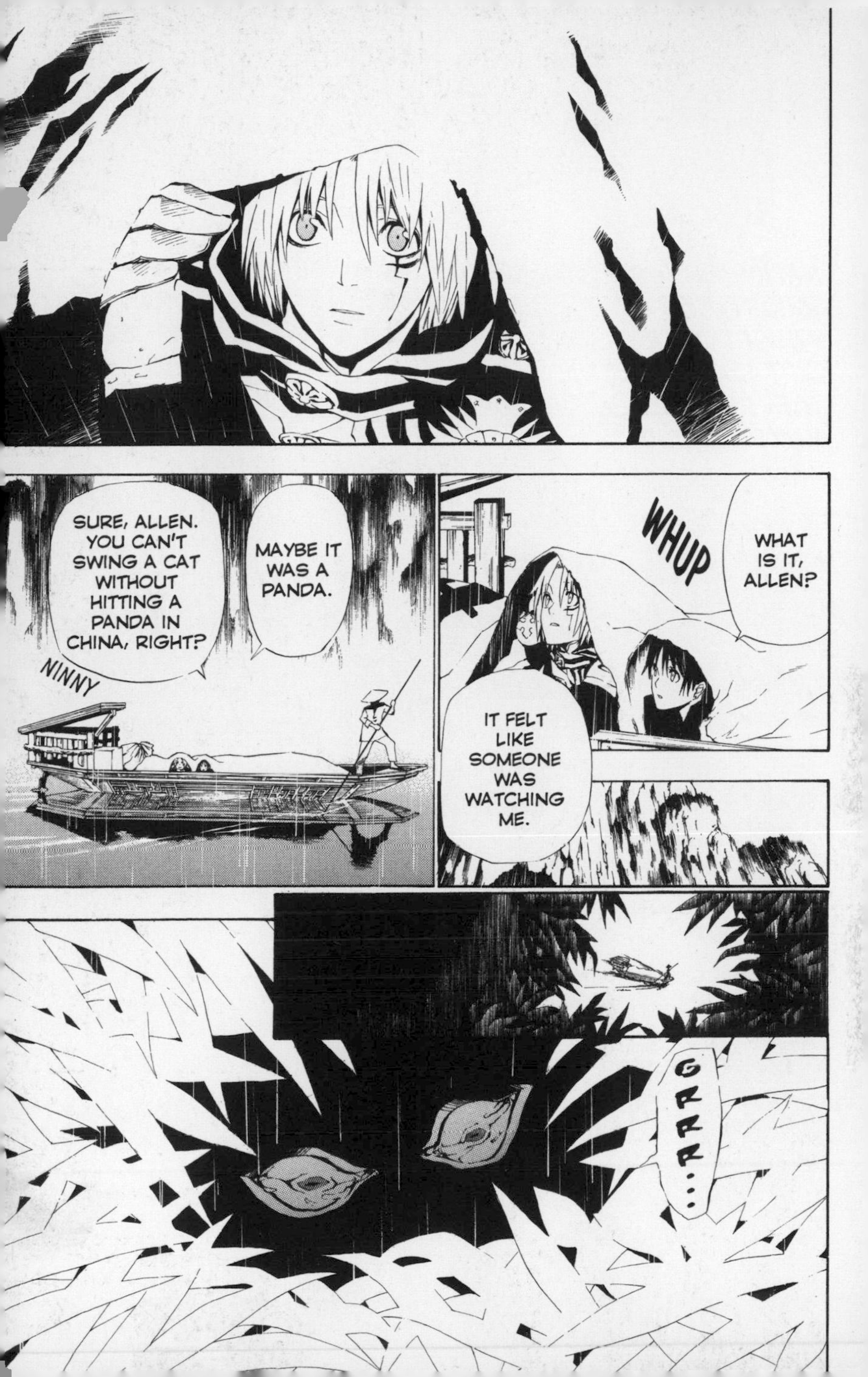
WHUP
WHAT IS IT, ALLEN?
IT FELT LIKE SOMEONE WAS WATCHING ME.
MAYBE IT WAS A PANDA.
SURE, ALLEN. YOU CAN'T SWING A CAT WITHOUT HITTING A PANDA IN CHINA, RIGHT?
NINNY
GRRR...

NATIONALITY: PORTUGUESE
HEIGHT: 188 CM
WEIGHT: 70 KG
BIRTHDAY: UNKNOWN
AGE: PROBABLY 26
BLOOD TYPE: O

HE ENJOYS LEADING A DOUBLE LIFE AS A HUMAN AND A NOAH. HE CAME ABOUT BECAUSE I WANTED TO DRAW A HANDSOME GUY LIKE BECKHAM. I REALLY ENJOY DRAWING THIS CHARACTER.

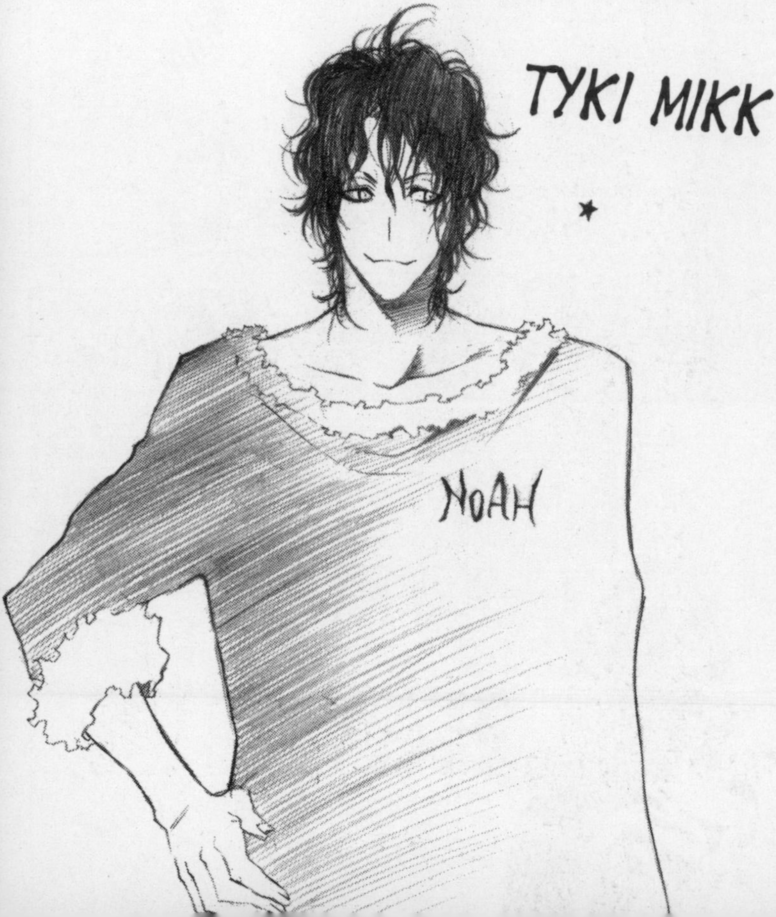
TYKI MIKK
NOAH

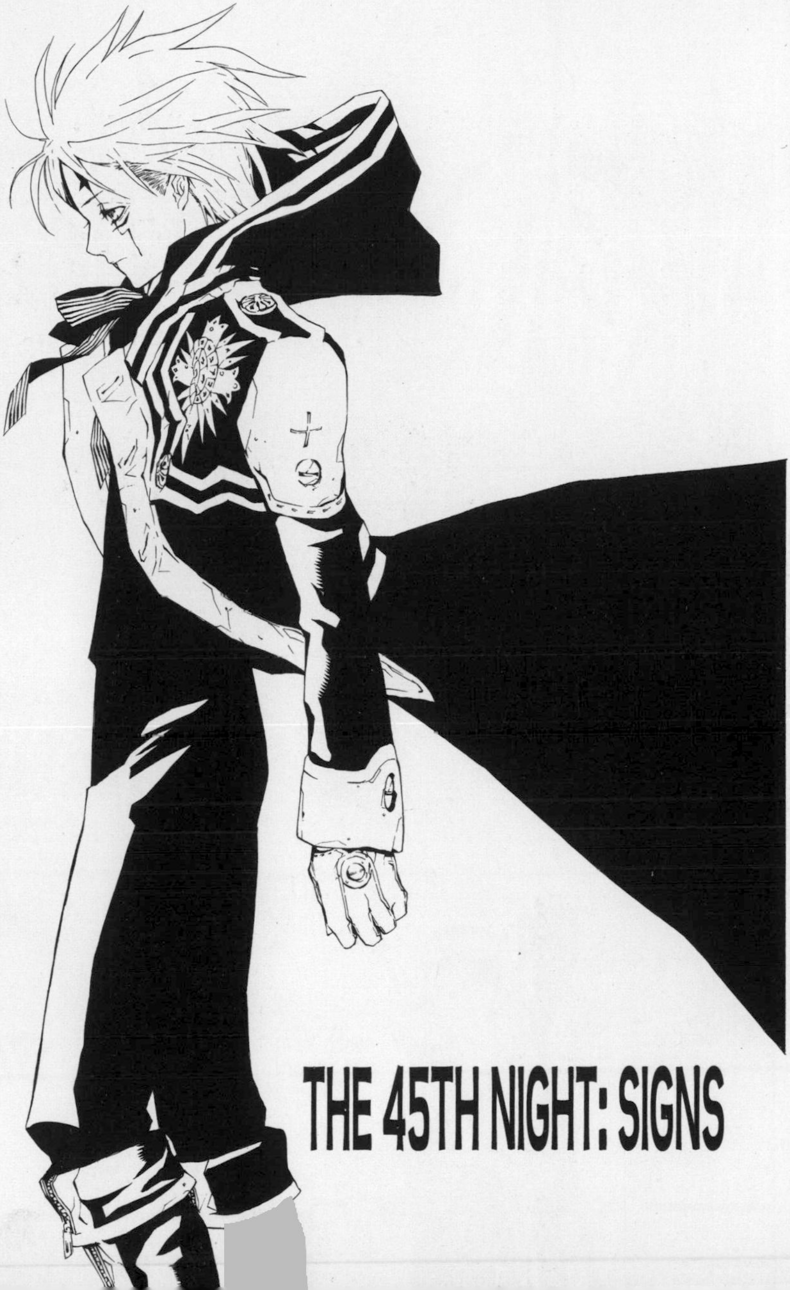

THE 45TH NIGHT: SIGNS

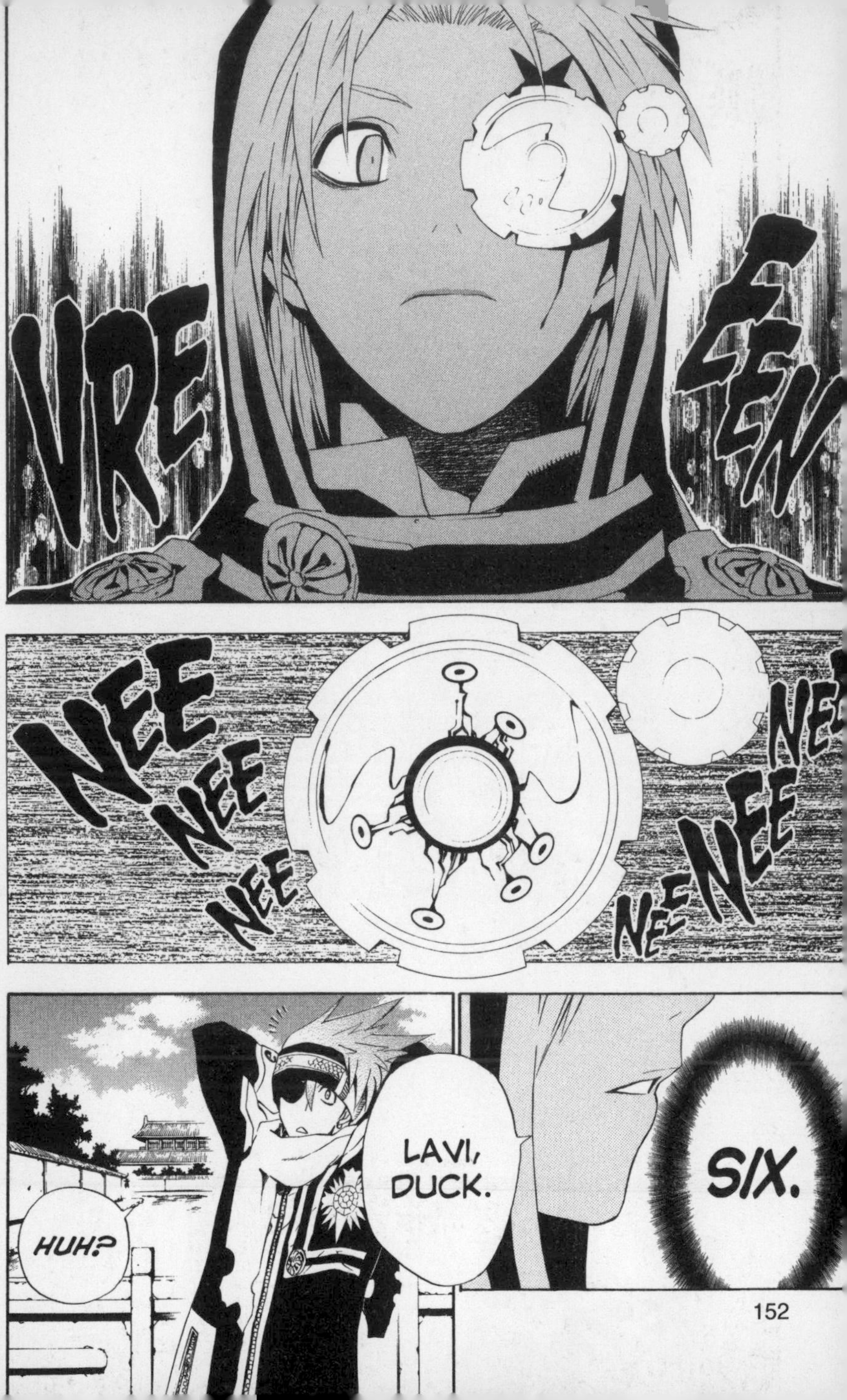
VRE
EEN
NEE NEE NEE
NEE NEE NEE NEE
SIX.
LAVI, DUCK.
HUH?

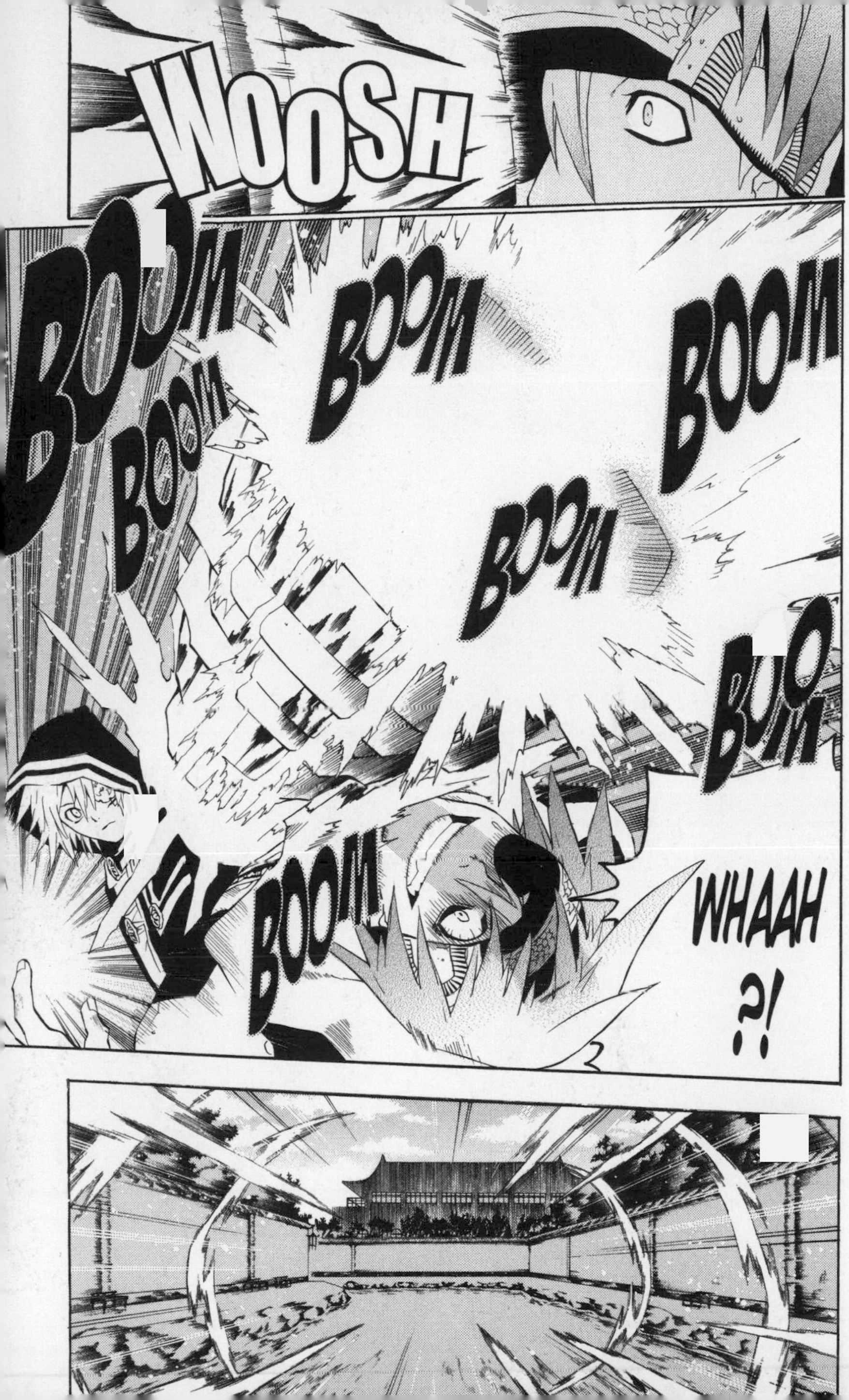
WOOSH
BOOM
BOOM
BOOM
BOOM
BOOM
BOOM
WHAAH ?!
BOOM

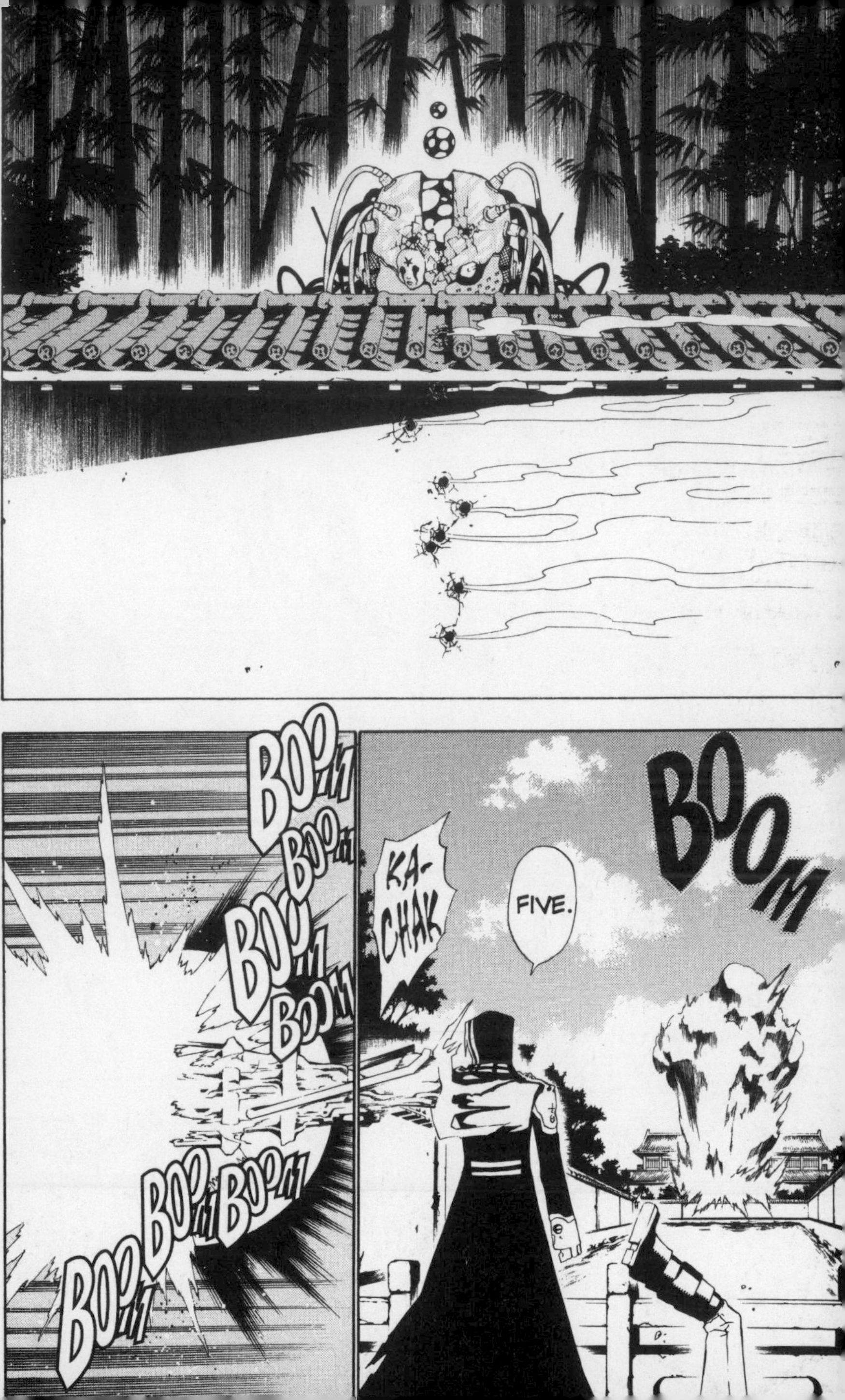
BOOOM
FIVE.
KA-CHAK
BOOM
BOOM
BOOM
BOOM
BOOM
BOOM
BOOM

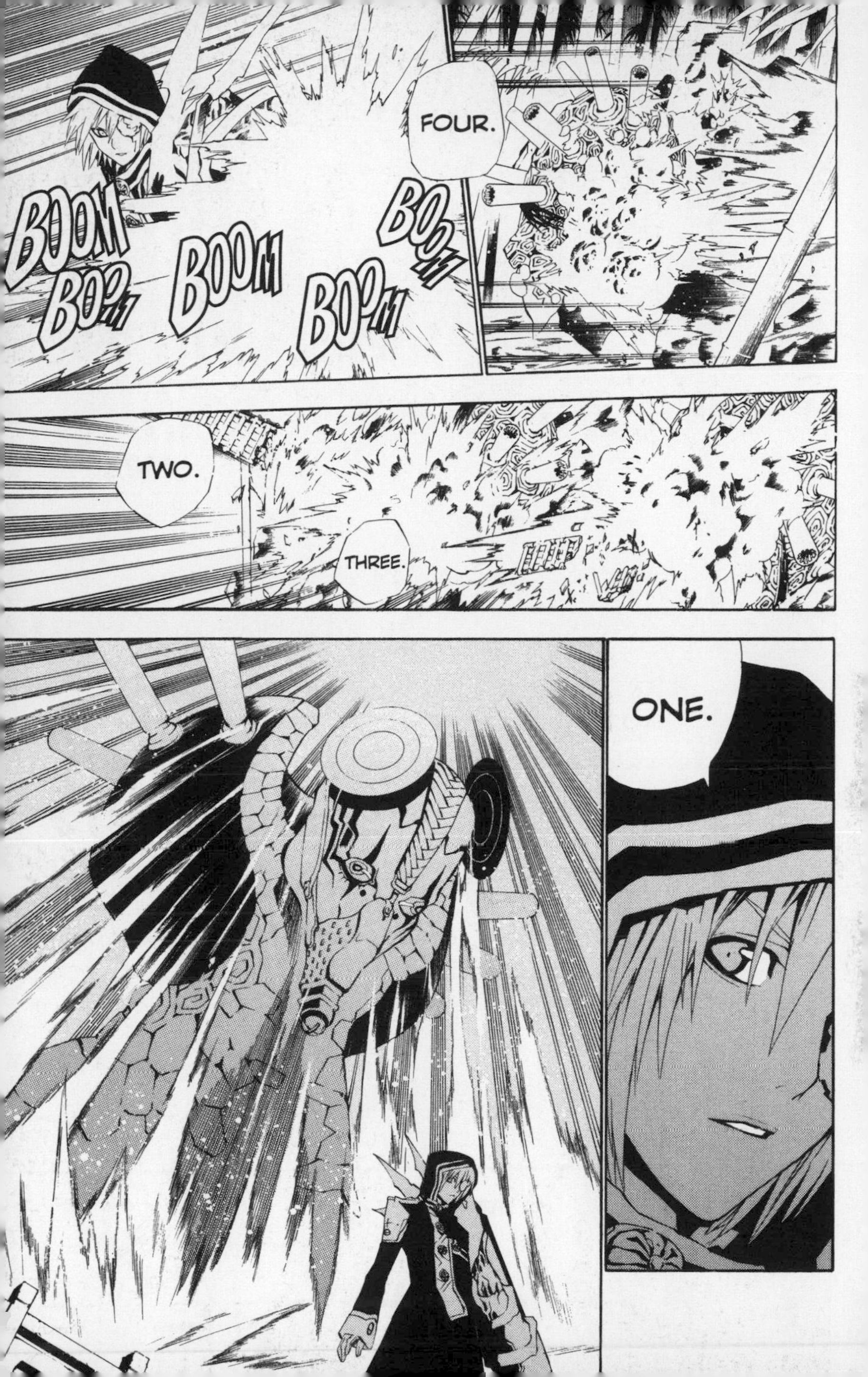
FOUR.
BOOM
BOOM
BOOM
BOOM
BOOM
THREE.
TWO.
ONE.

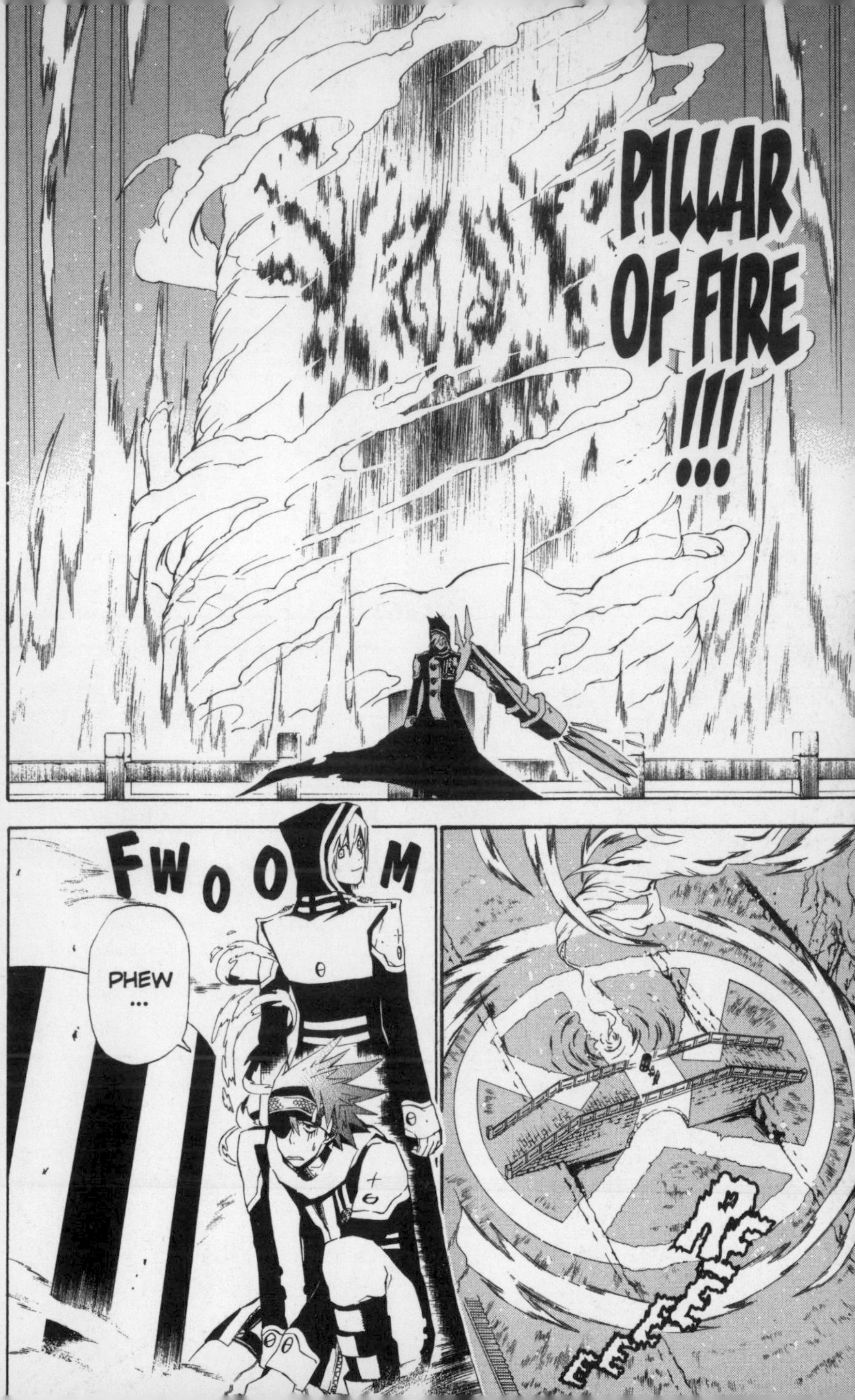
PILLAR OF FIRE!!!
FWOOM
PHEW...

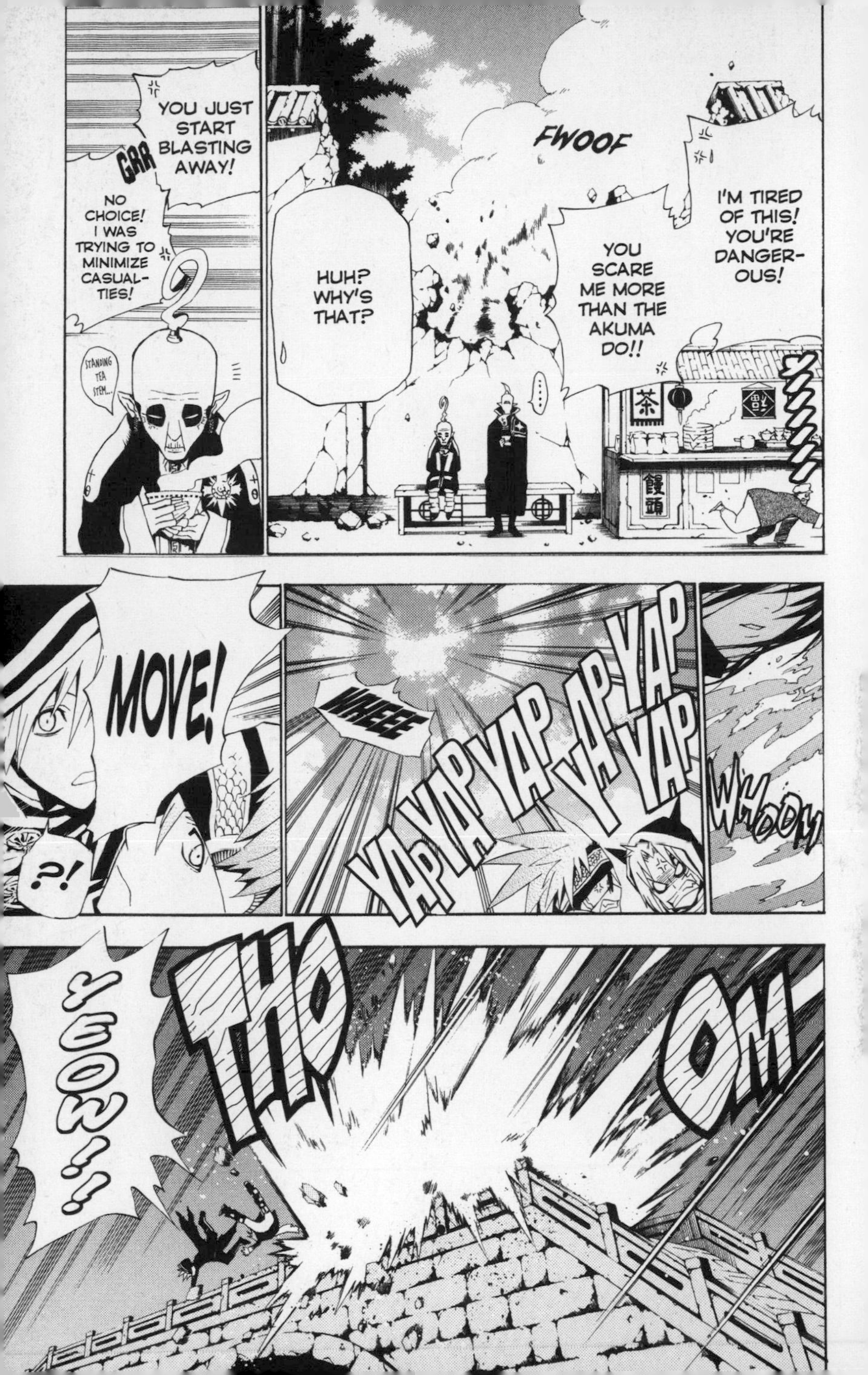
I'M TIRED OF THIS! YOU'RE DANGER-OUS!
YOU SCARE ME MORE THAN THE AKUMA DO!!
FWOOF
HUH? WHY'S THAT?
....
YOU JUST START BLASTING AWAY!
GRR
NO CHOICE! I WAS TRYING TO MINIMIZE CASUAL-TIES!
STANDING TEA STEM...
WHOOM
WHEEE
YAP YAP YAP YAP YAP YAP YAP YAP
MOVE!
?!
THOOM
YEOW!!

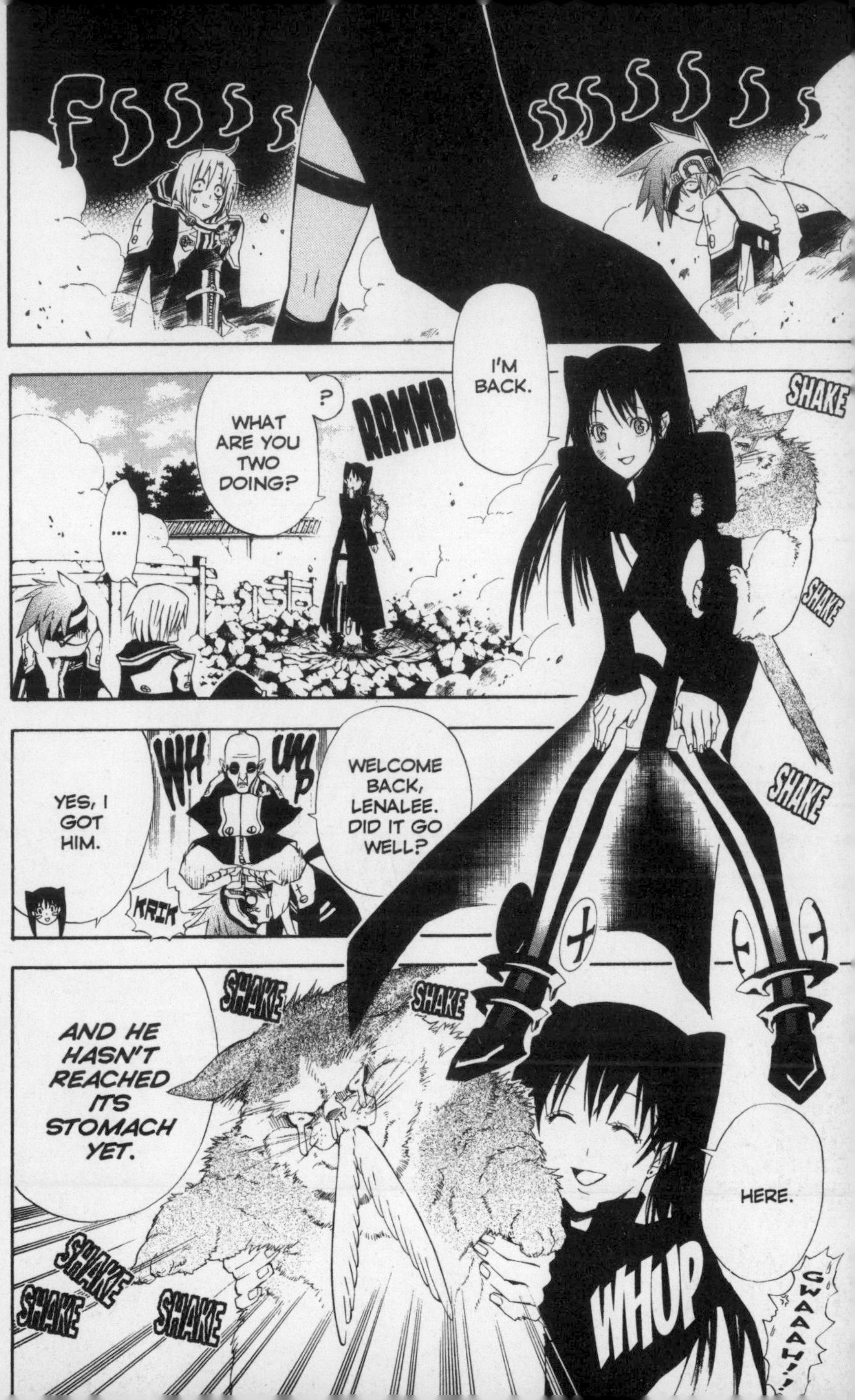
Fssss s sssssss s
I'M BACK.
SHAKE
SHAKE
SHAKE
RRMMB
?
WHAT ARE YOU TWO DOING?
...
WELCOME BACK, LENALEE. DID IT GO WELL?
WHUMP
YES, I GOT HIM.
KRIK
GWAAAAH!!
HERE.
WHUP
SHAKE
SHAKE
AND HE HASN'T REACHED ITS STOMACH YET.
SHAKE
SHAKE
SHAKE

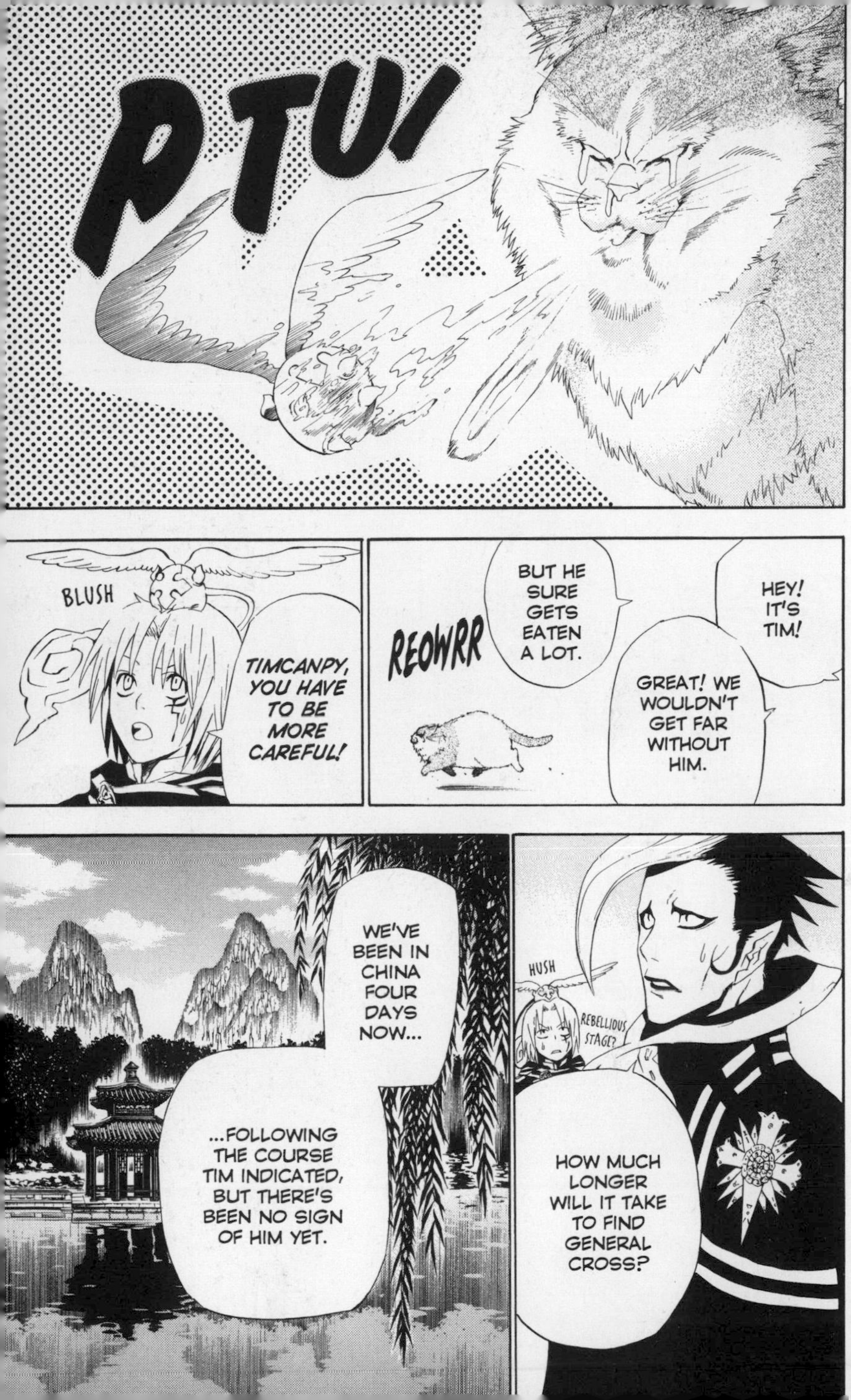
PTUI
HEY! IT'S TIM!
BUT HE SURE GETS EATEN A LOT.
GREAT! WE WOULDN'T GET FAR WITHOUT HIM.
REOWRR
BLUSH
TIMCANPY, YOU HAVE TO BE MORE CAREFUL!
HUSH
REBELLIOUS STAGE?
HOW MUCH LONGER WILL IT TAKE TO FIND GENERAL CROSS?
WE'VE BEEN IN CHINA FOUR DAYS NOW...
...FOLLOWING THE COURSE TIM INDICATED, BUT THERE'S BEEN NO SIGN OF HIM YET.

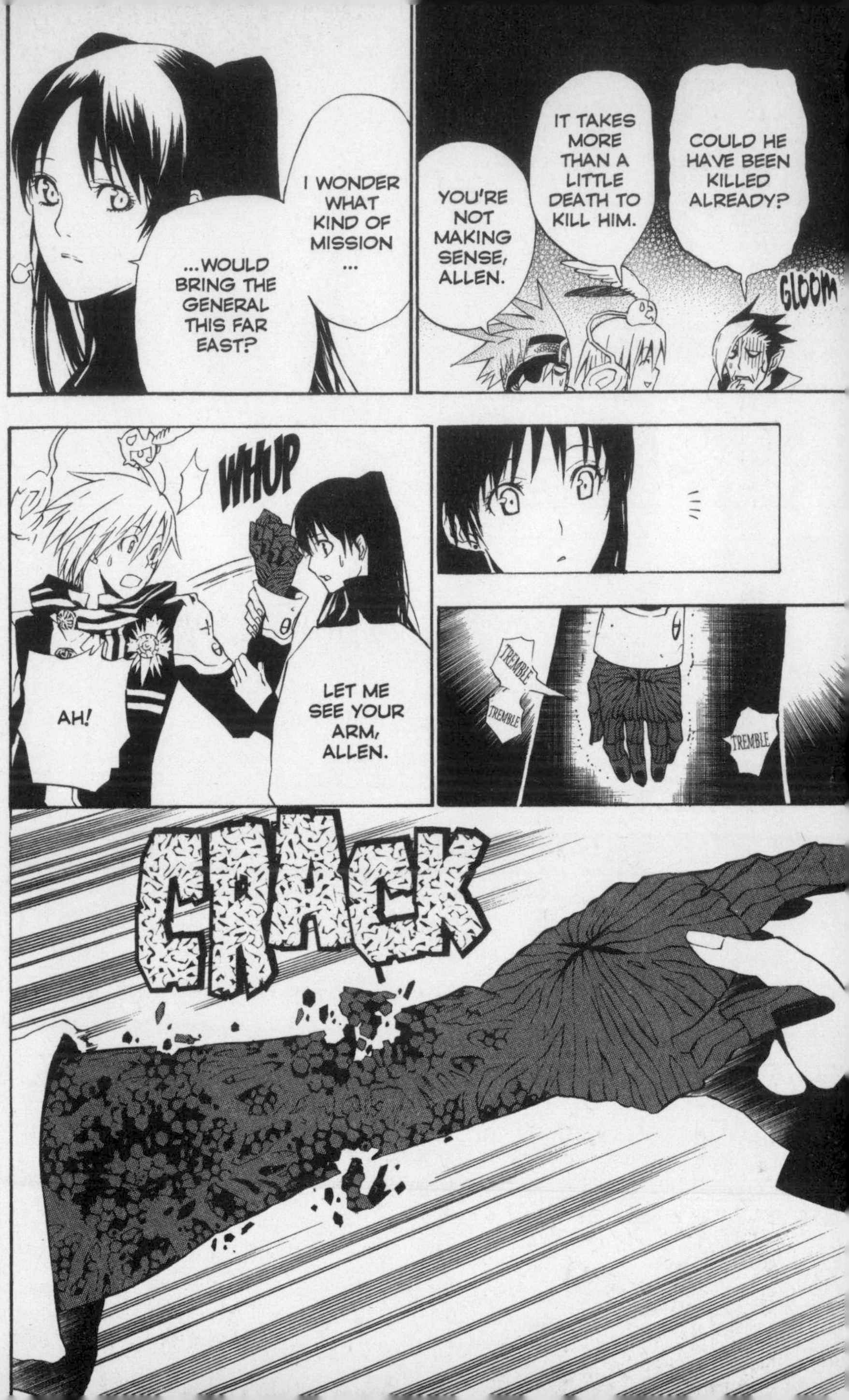
COULD HE HAVE BEEN KILLED ALREADY?
GLOOM
IT TAKES MORE THAN A LITTLE DEATH TO KILL HIM.
YOU'RE NOT MAKING SENSE, ALLEN.
I WONDER WHAT KIND OF MISSION ...
...WOULD BRING THE GENERAL THIS FAR EAST?
TREMBLE
TREMBLE
TREMBLE
WHUP
LET ME SEE YOUR ARM, ALLEN.
AH!
CRACK

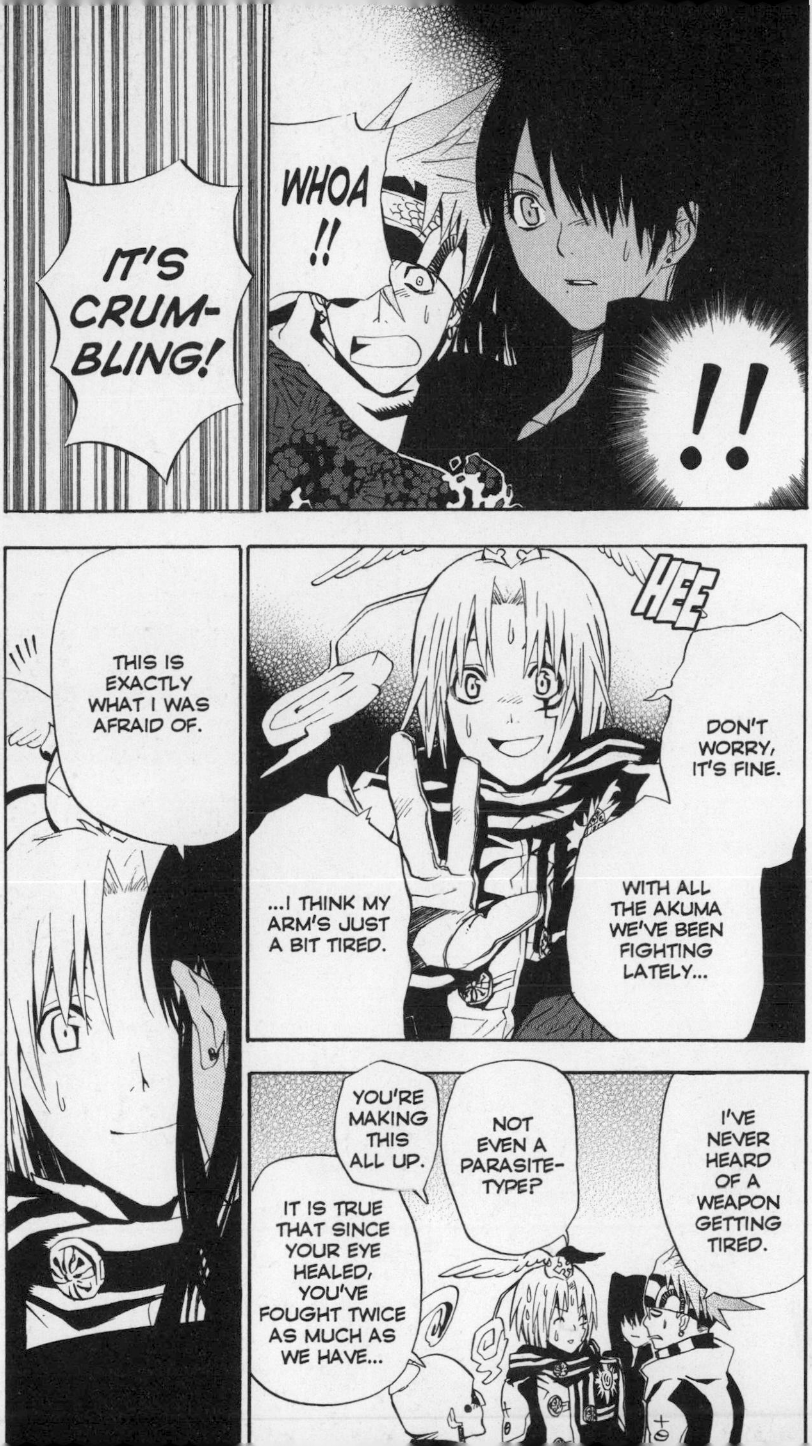
WHOA !!
!!
IT'S CRUMBLING!
HEE
DON'T WORRY, IT'S FINE.
WITH ALL THE AKUMA WE'VE BEEN FIGHTING LATELY...
...I THINK MY ARM'S JUST A BIT TIRED.
I'VE NEVER HEARD OF A WEAPON GETTING TIRED.
NOT EVEN A PARASITE-TYPE?
YOU'RE MAKING THIS ALL UP.
IT IS TRUE THAT SINCE YOUR EYE HEALED, YOU'VE FOUGHT TWICE AS MUCH AS WE HAVE...
THIS IS EXACTLY WHAT I WAS AFRAID OF.

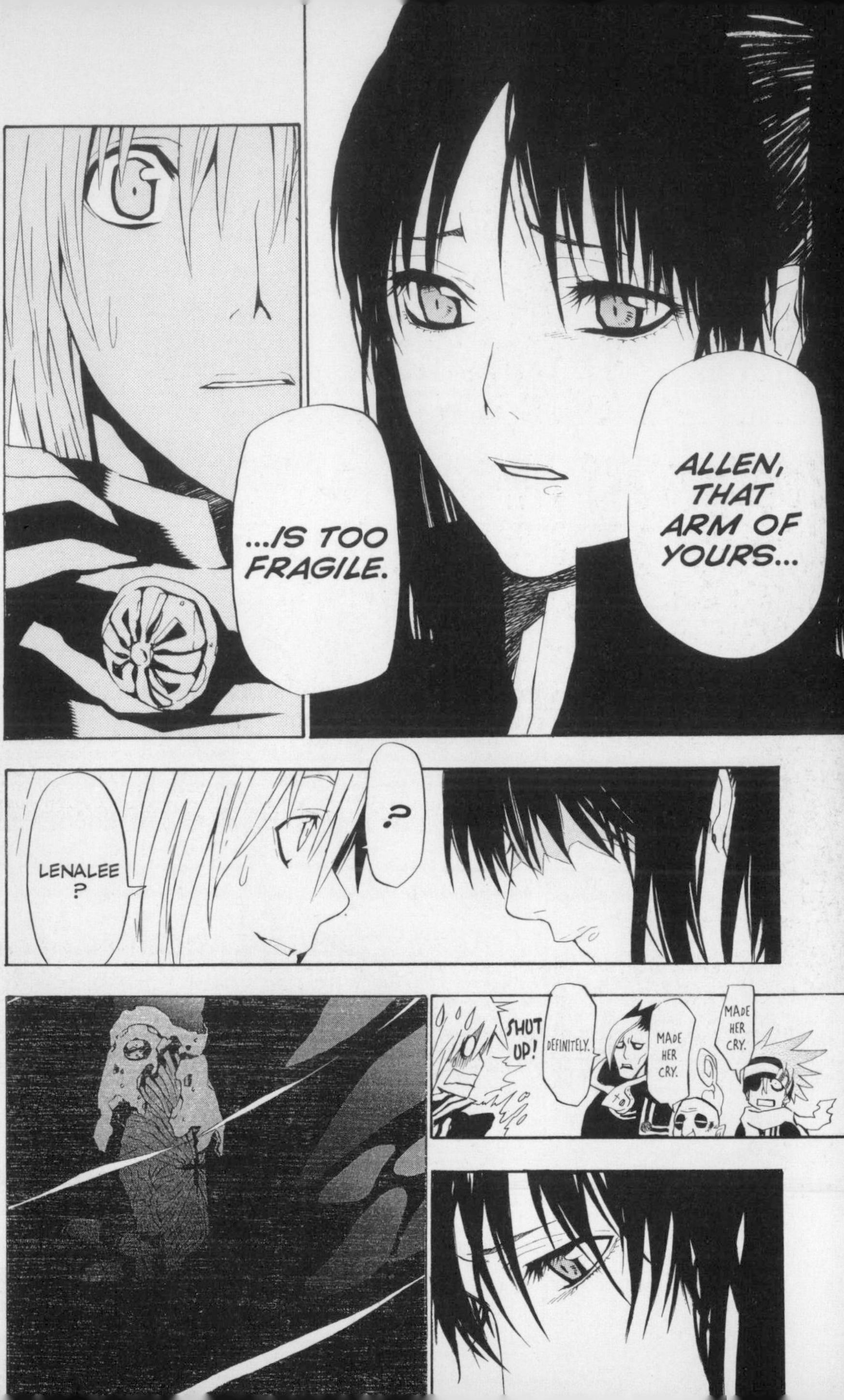
ALLEN, THAT ARM OF YOURS...
...IS TOO FRAGILE.
?
LENALEE ?
MADE HER CRY.
MADE HER CRY.
DEFINITELY.
SHUT UP!

B-BMP

WAAAAH!!

PLOOSH

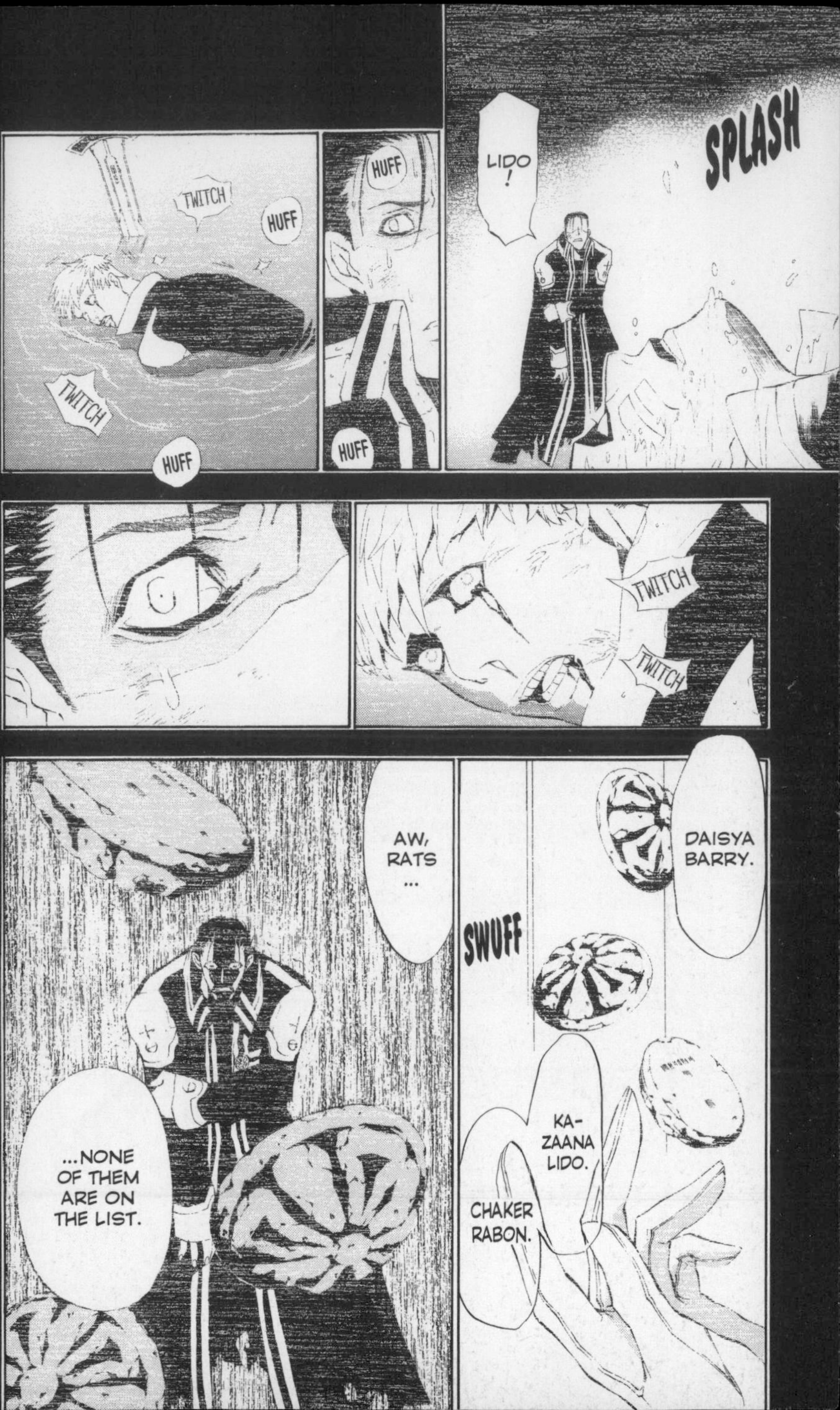
SPLASH
LIDO!
HUFF
HUFF
TWITCH
HUFF
TWITCH
HUFF
TWITCH
TWITCH
DAISYA BARRY.
SWUFF
KA-ZAANA LIDO.
CHAKER RABON.
AW, RATS...
...NONE OF THEM ARE ON THE LIST.

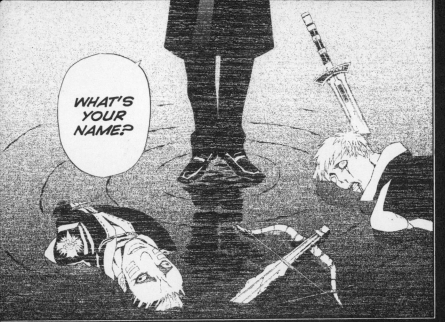

WHAT'S YOUR NAME?

PLEASE ...

HELP ME...

I DON'T

WANT...

TO

DIE...

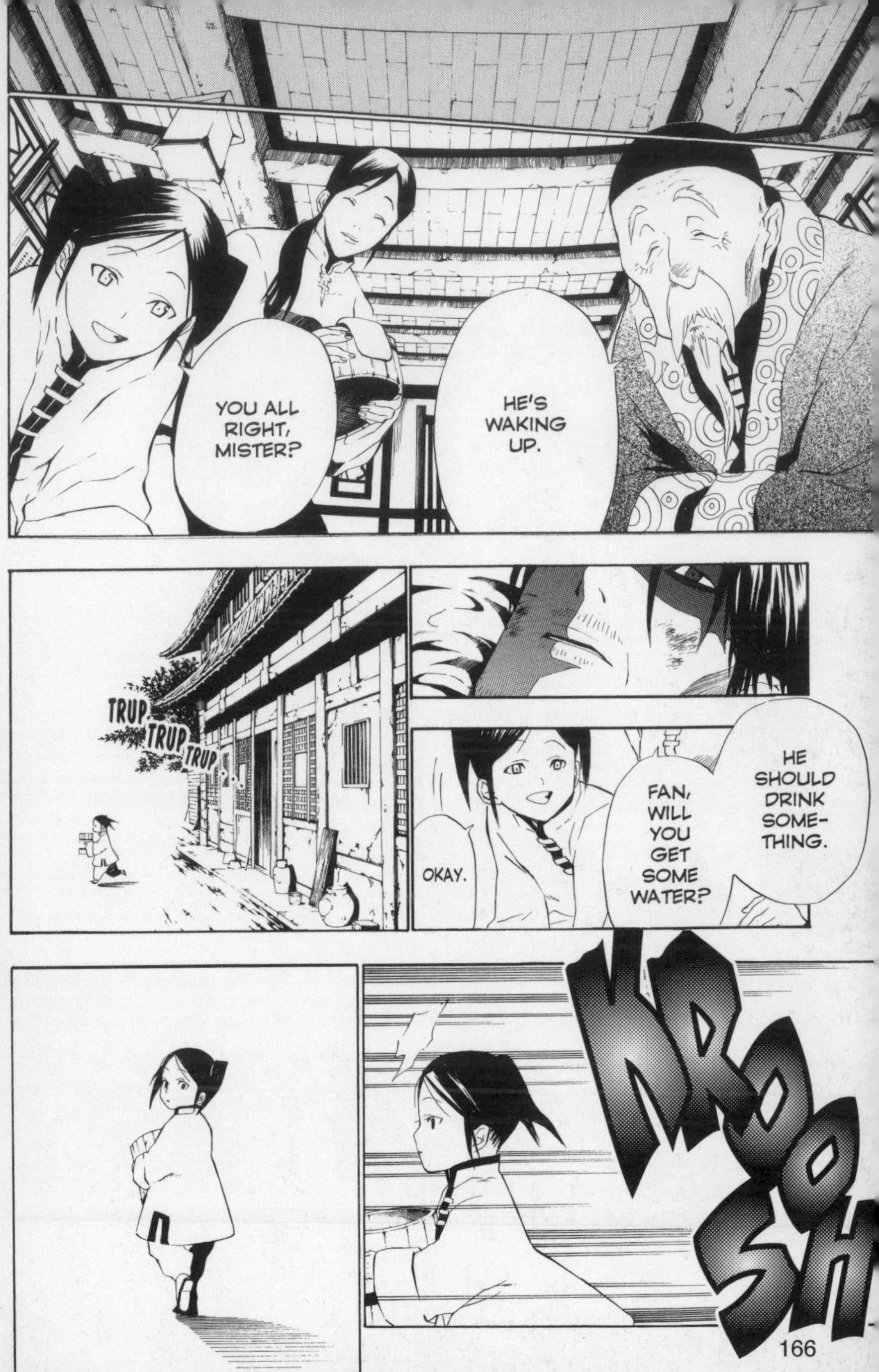
HE'S WAKING UP.
YOU ALL RIGHT, MISTER?
HE SHOULD DRINK SOME-THING.
FAN, WILL YOU GET SOME WATER?
OKAY.
TRUP TRUP TRUP
VROOSH

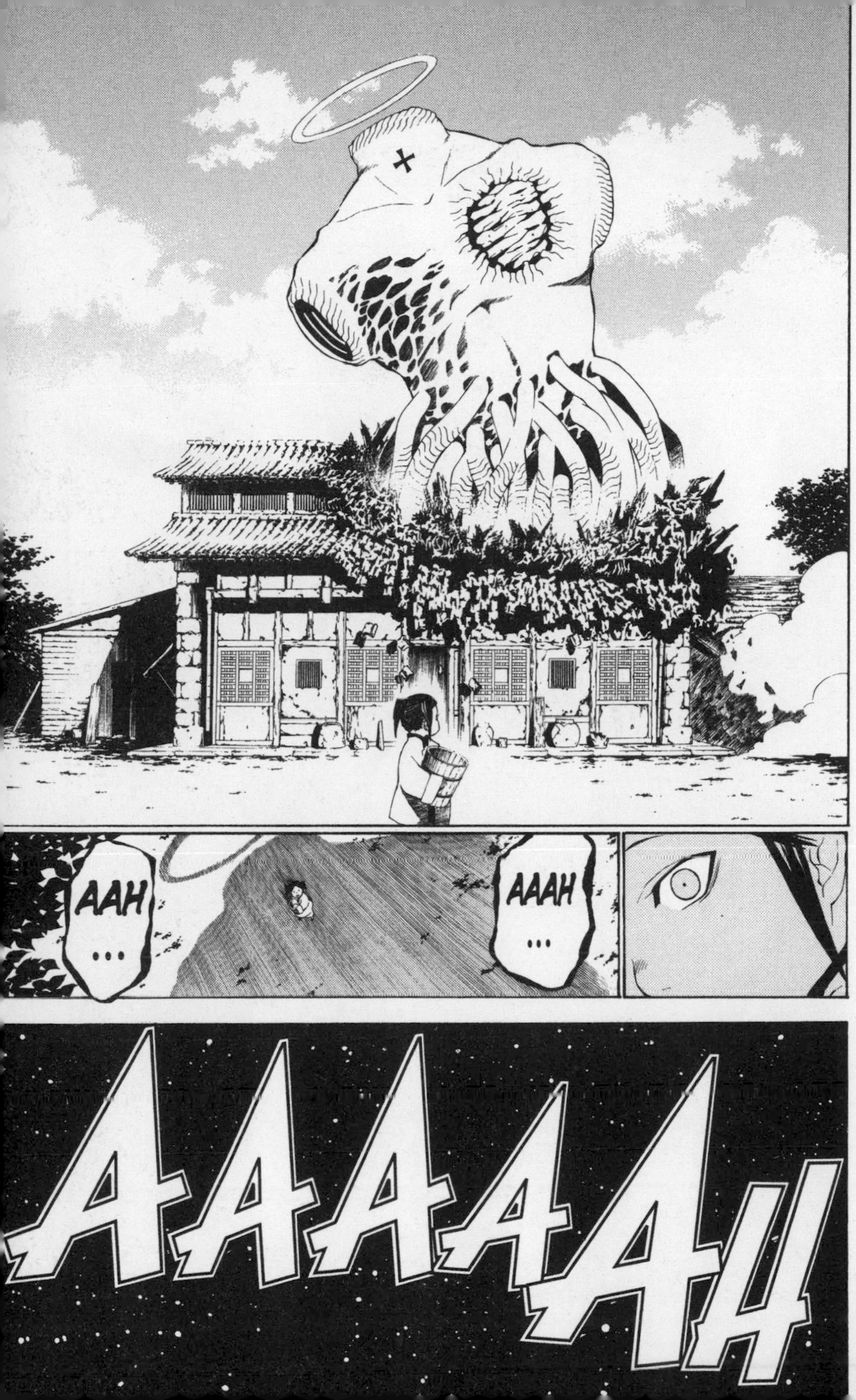
AAAH ...
AAH ...
AAAAAH

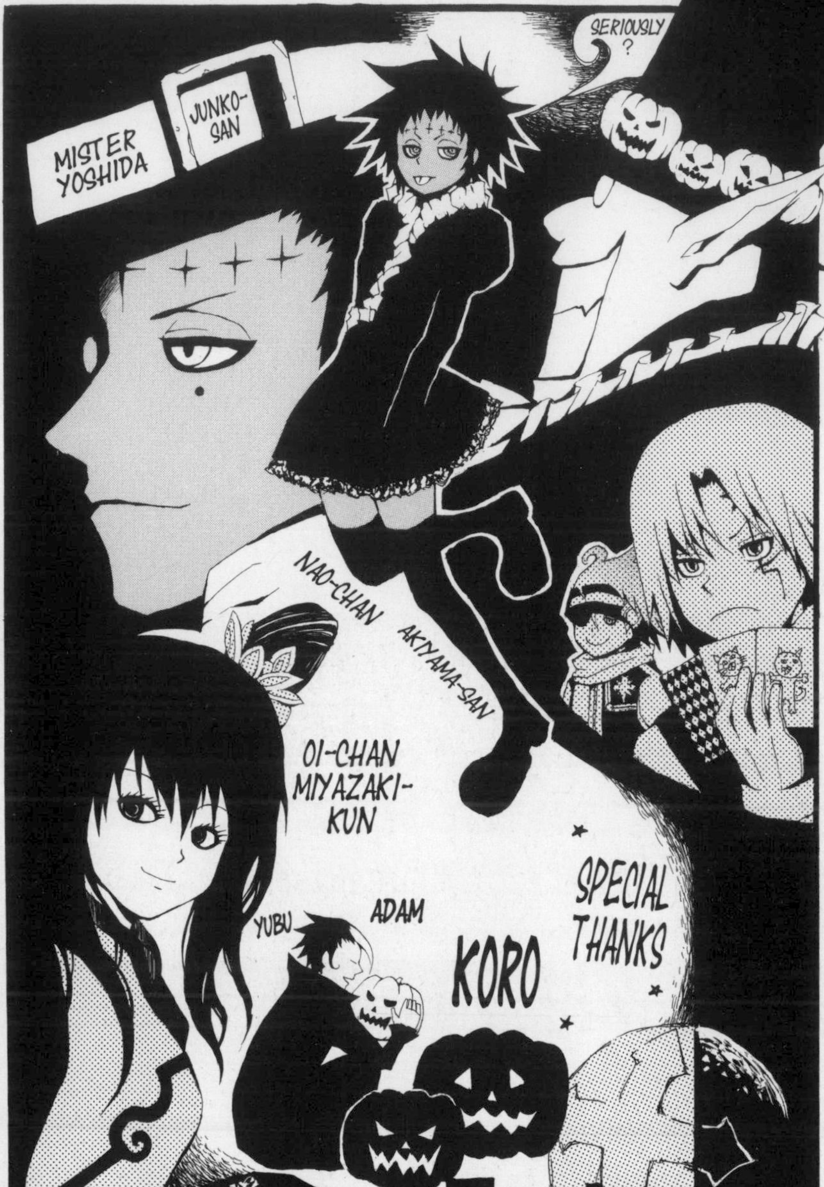
SERIOUSLY?
JUNKO-SAN
MISTER YOSHIDA
AKIYAMA-SAN
NAO-CHAN
OI-CHAN MIYAZAKI-KUN
SPECIAL THANKS
KORO
ADAM
YUBU
HEY
D.Gray-man

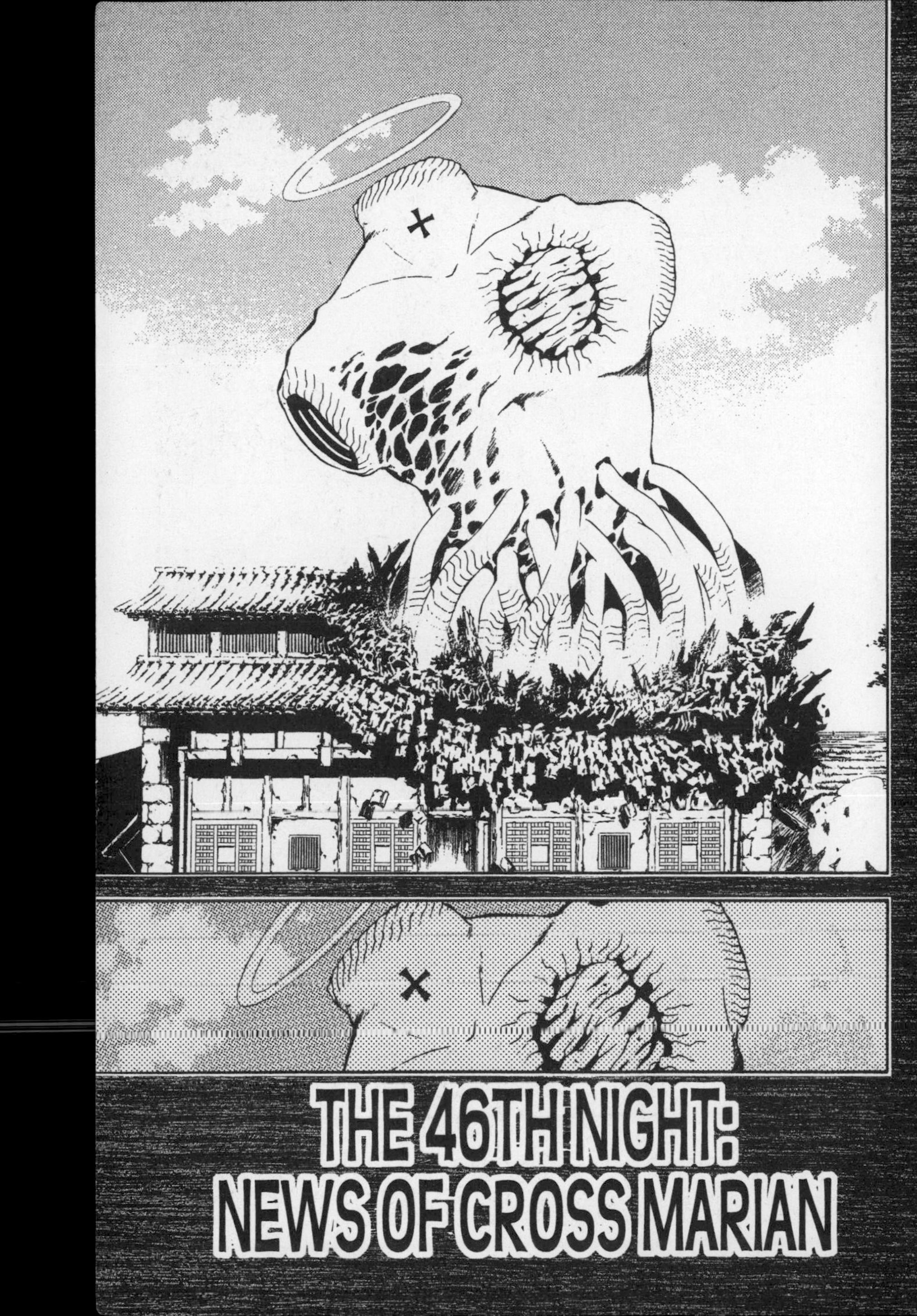

THE 46TH NIGHT: NEWS OF CROSS MARIAN

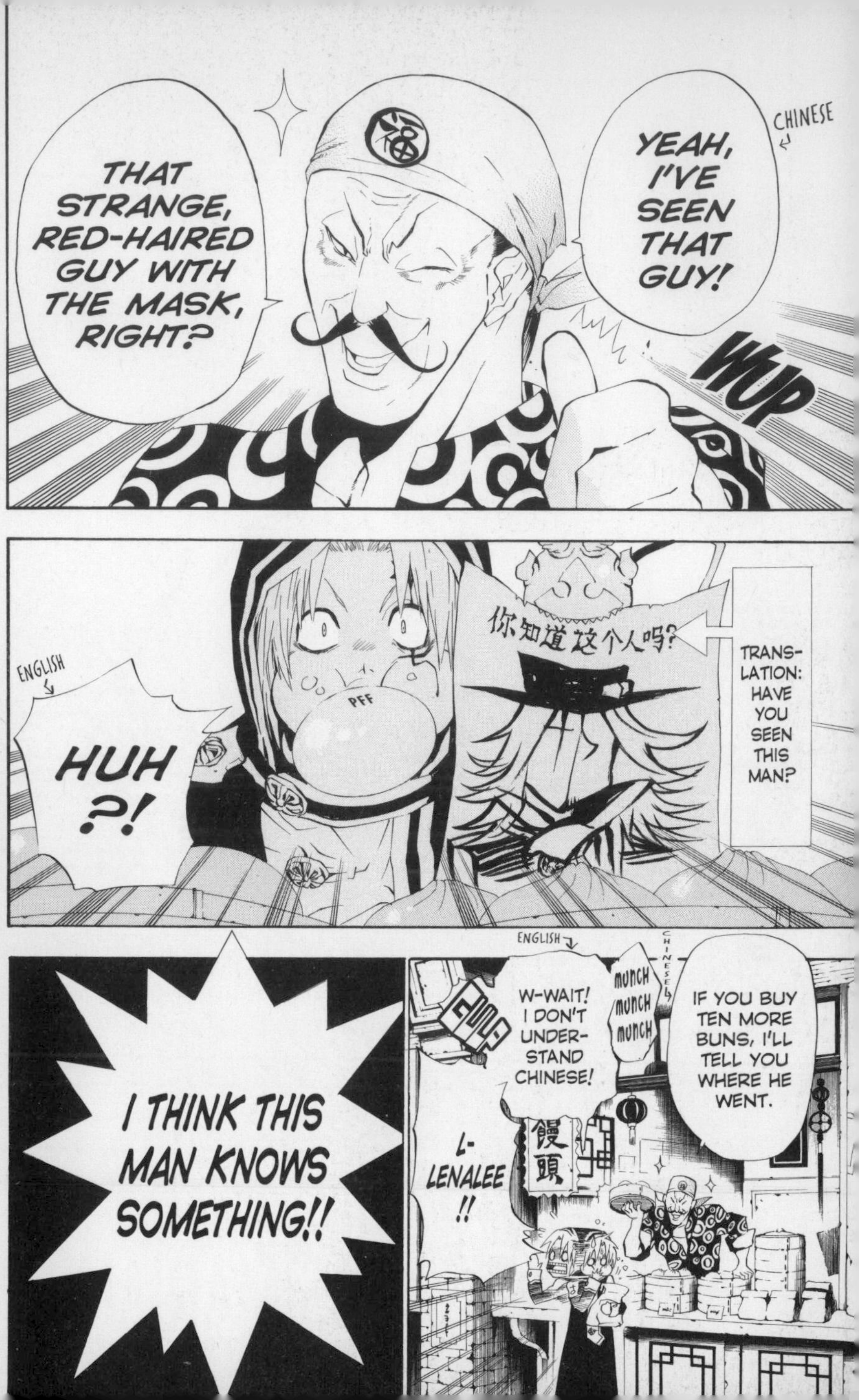
CHINESE
YEAH, I'VE SEEN THAT GUY!
THAT STRANGE, RED-HAIRED GUY WITH THE MASK, RIGHT?
WUP
TRANSLATION: HAVE YOU SEEN THIS MAN?
你知道这个人吗?
PFF
ENGLISH
HUH ?!
CHINESE
IF YOU BUY TEN MORE BUNS, I'LL TELL YOU WHERE HE WENT.
MUNCH MUNCH MUNCH
ENGLISH
W-WAIT! I DON'T UNDER-STAND CHINESE!
饅頭
L-LENALEE !!
I THINK THIS MAN KNOWS SOMETHING!!

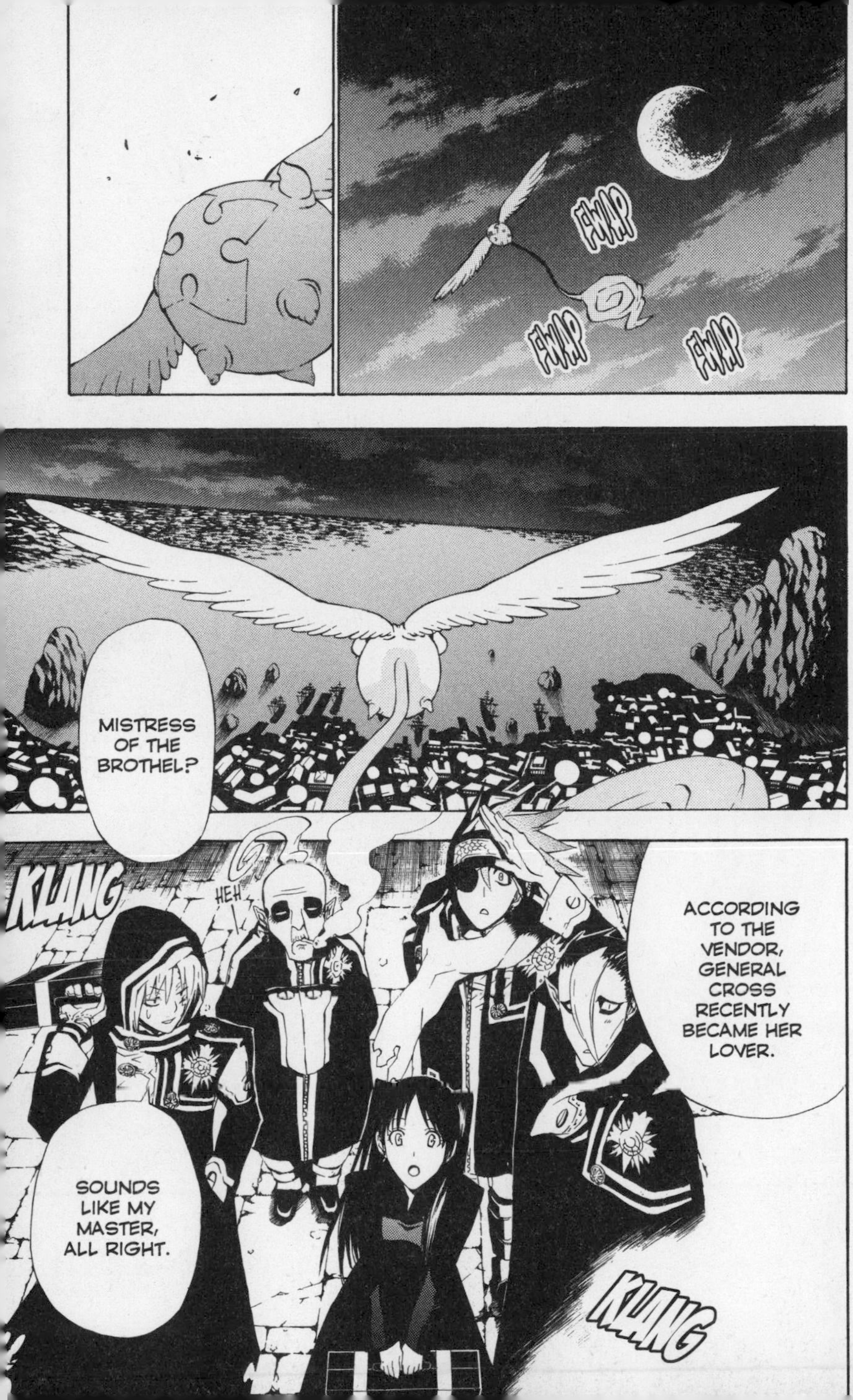
FWAP
FWAP
FWAP
MISTRESS OF THE BROTHEL?
ACCORDING TO THE VENDOR, GENERAL CROSS RECENTLY BECAME HER LOVER.
KLANG
HEH
SOUNDS LIKE MY MASTER, ALL RIGHT.
KLANG

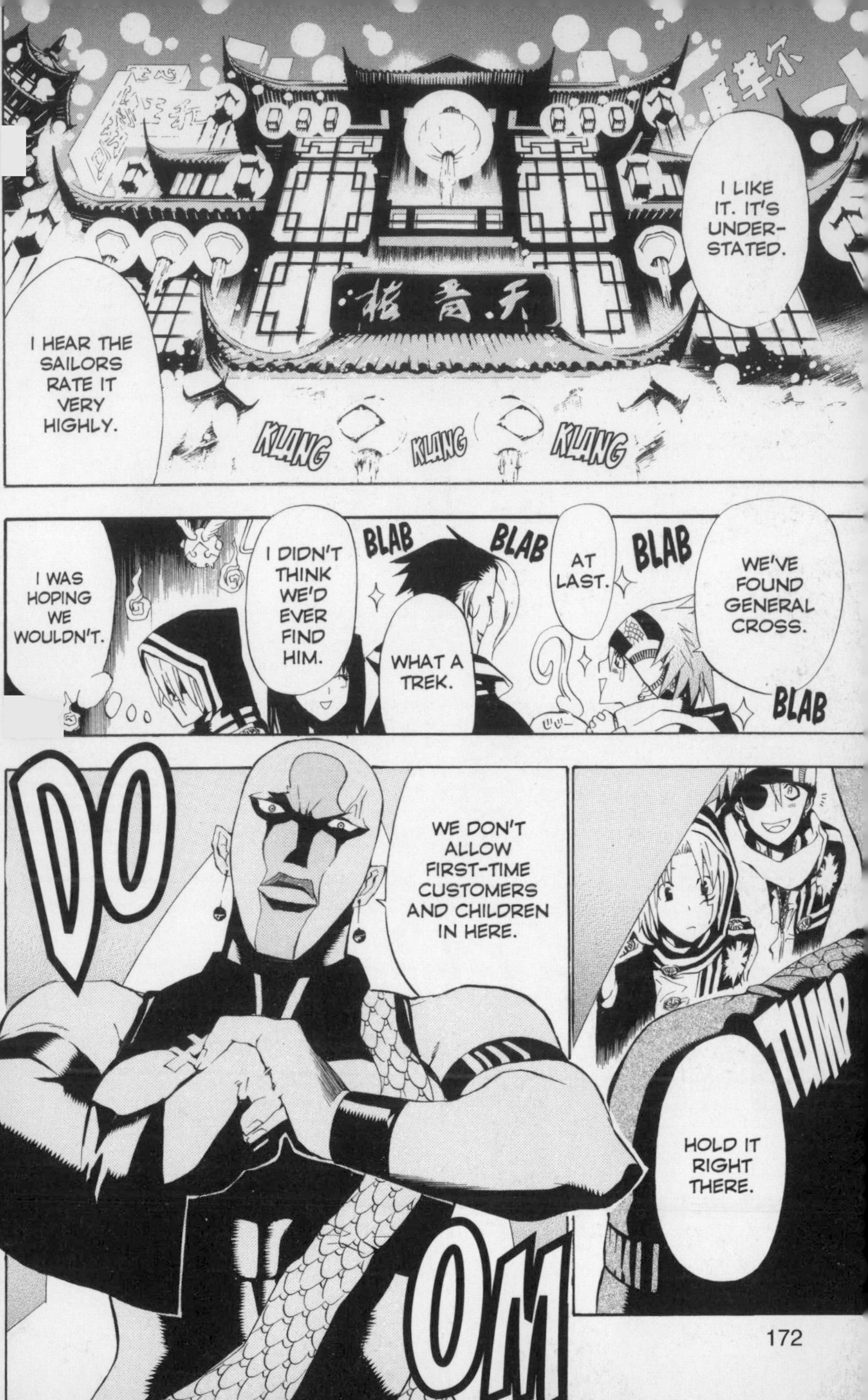
I LIKE IT. IT'S UNDER-STATED.
I HEAR THE SAILORS RATE IT VERY HIGHLY.
KLANG
KLANG
KLANG
WE'VE FOUND GENERAL CROSS.
BLAB
BLAB
AT LAST.
BLAB
WHAT A TREK.
I DIDN'T THINK WE'D EVER FIND HIM.
BLAB
I WAS HOPING WE WOULDN'T.
TUMP
HOLD IT RIGHT THERE.
DO
OM
WE DON'T ALLOW FIRST-TIME CUSTOMERS AND CHILDREN IN HERE.

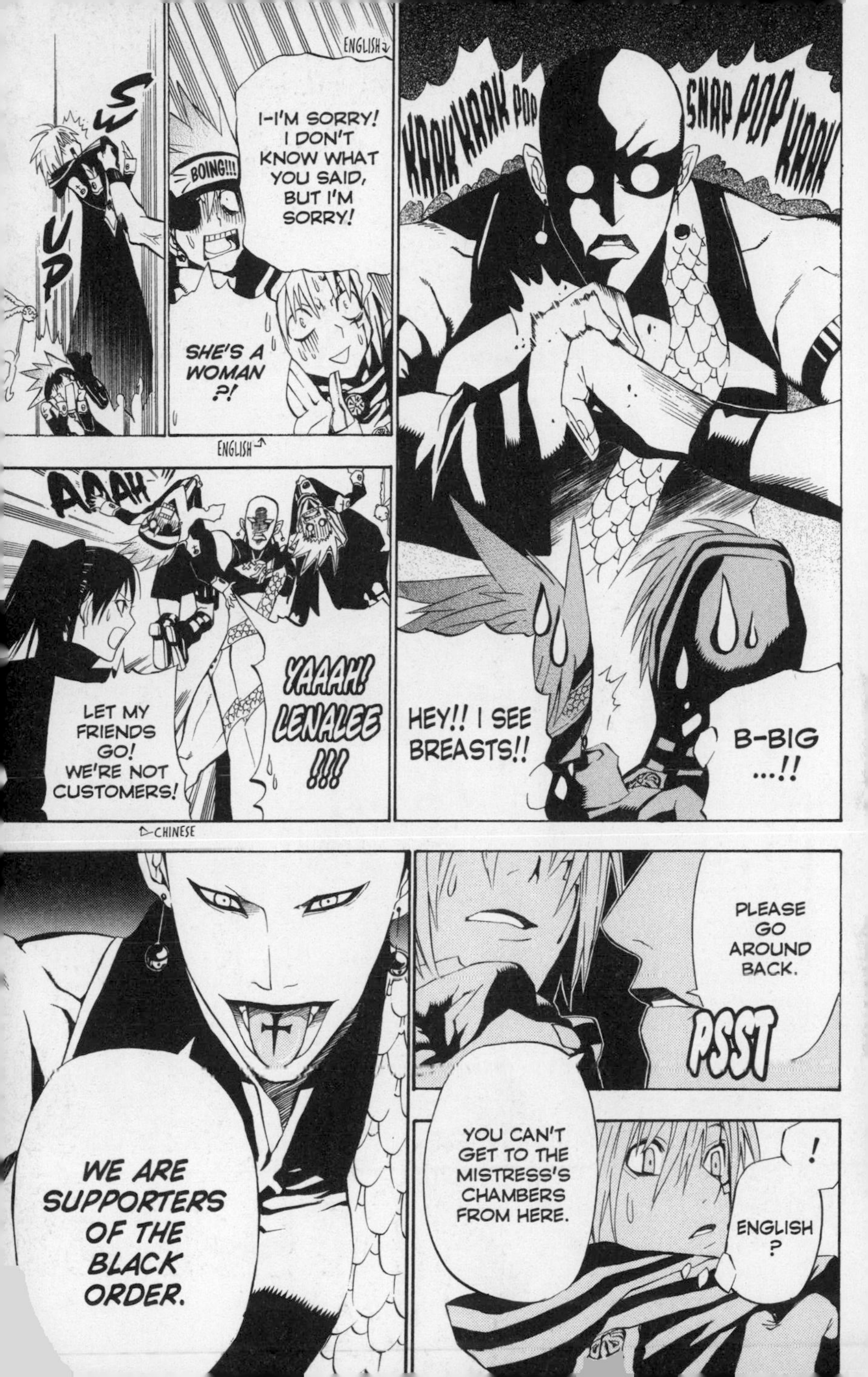KRAK KRAK POP
SNAP POP KRAK
HEY!! I SEE BREASTS!!
B-BIG ...!!
ENGLISH
I-I'M SORRY! I DON'T KNOW WHAT YOU SAID, BUT I'M SORRY!
BOING!!!
SHE'S A WOMAN ?!
ENGLISH
SWUP
AAAH
YAAAH! LENALEE !!!
LET MY FRIENDS GO! WE'RE NOT CUSTOMERS!
CHINESE
PLEASE GO AROUND BACK.
PSST
YOU CAN'T GET TO THE MISTRESS'S CHAMBERS FROM HERE.
!
ENGLISH ?
WE ARE SUPPORTERS OF THE BLACK ORDER.

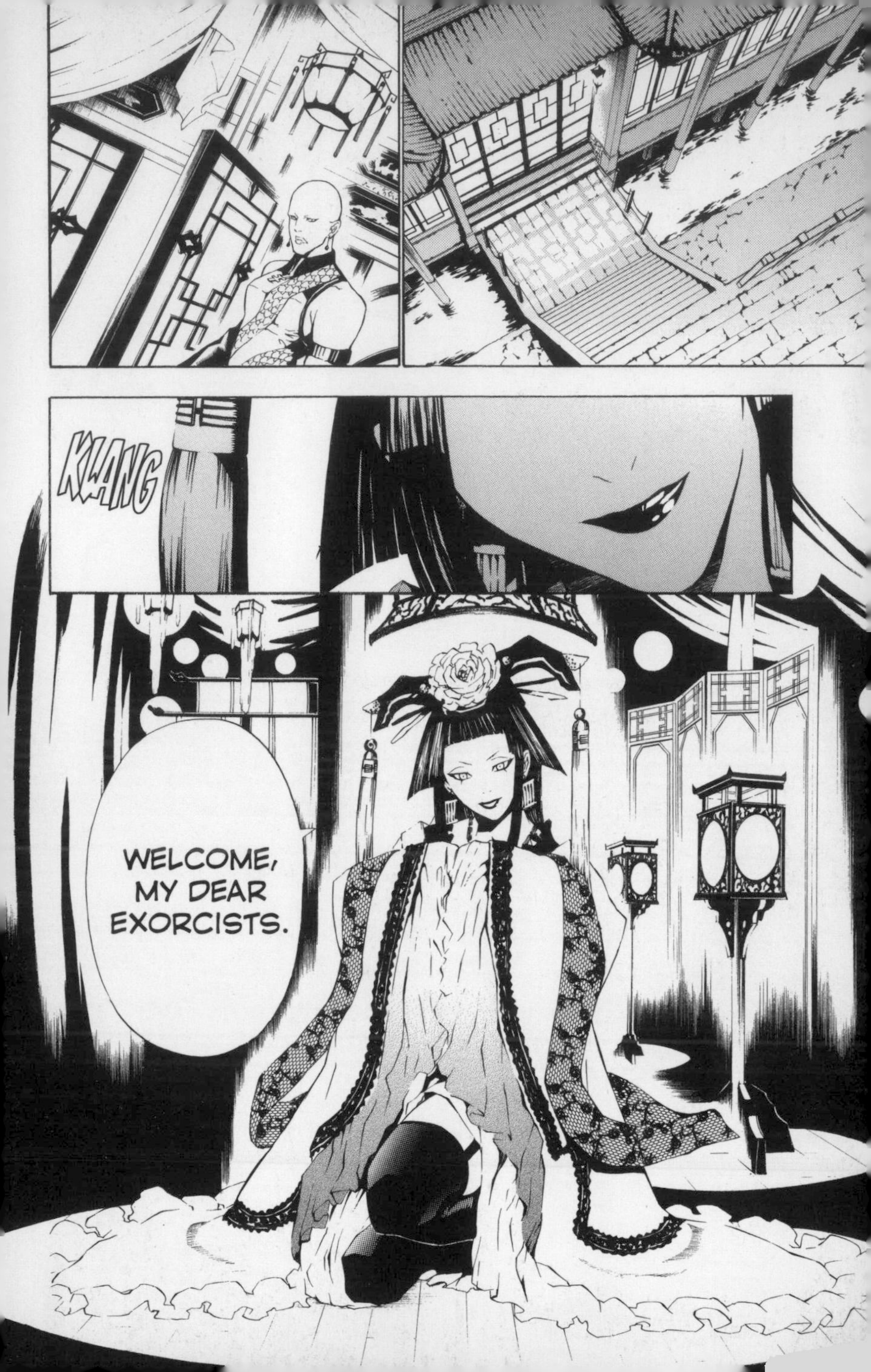
KLANG
WELCOME, MY DEAR EXORCISTS.

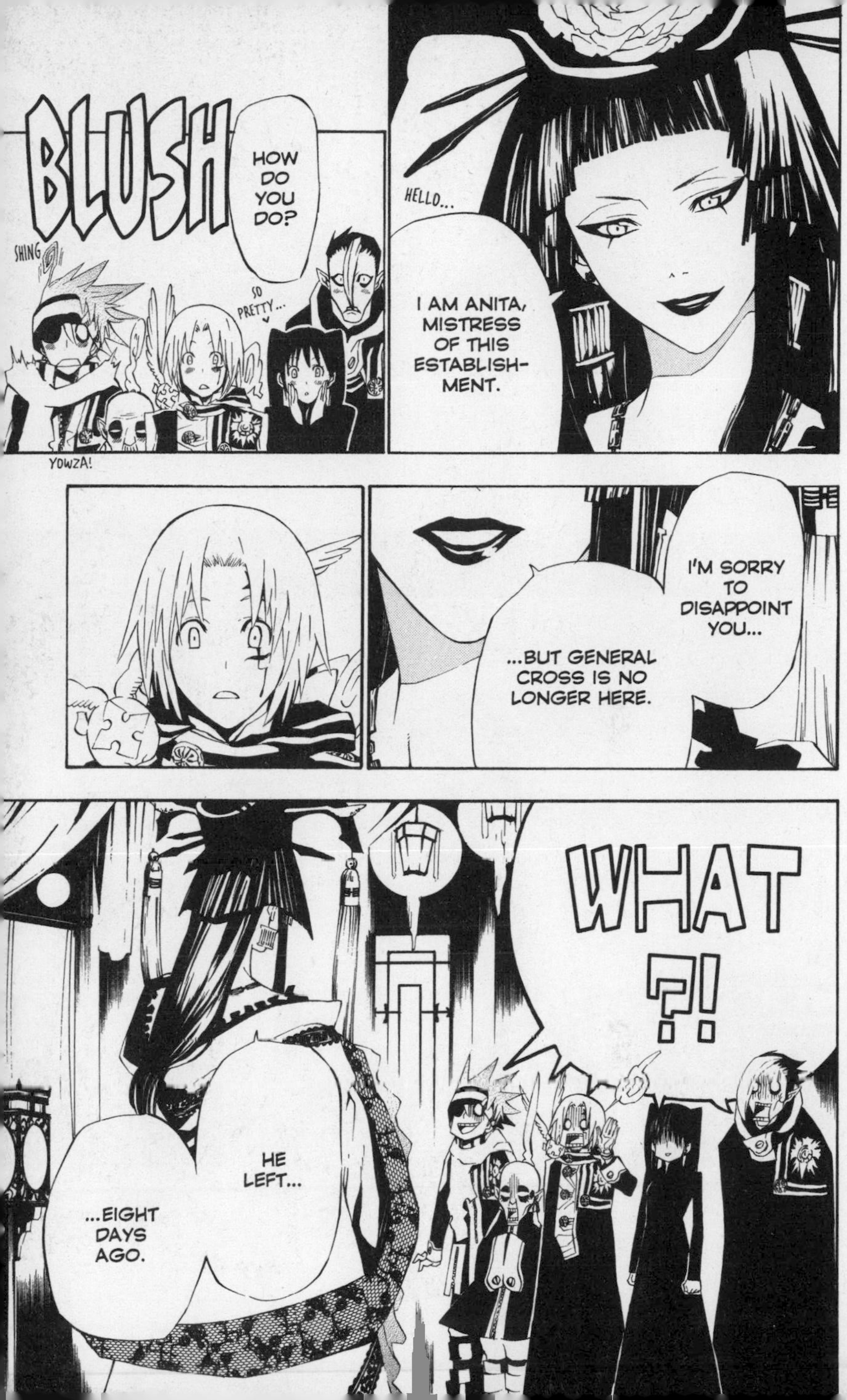
HELLO...
I AM ANITA, MISTRESS OF THIS ESTABLISH- MENT.
BLUSH
HOW DO YOU DO?
SHING
SO PRETTY...
YOWZA!
I'M SORRY TO DISAPPOINT YOU...
...BUT GENERAL CROSS IS NO LONGER HERE.
WHAT ?!
HE LEFT...
...EIGHT DAYS AGO.

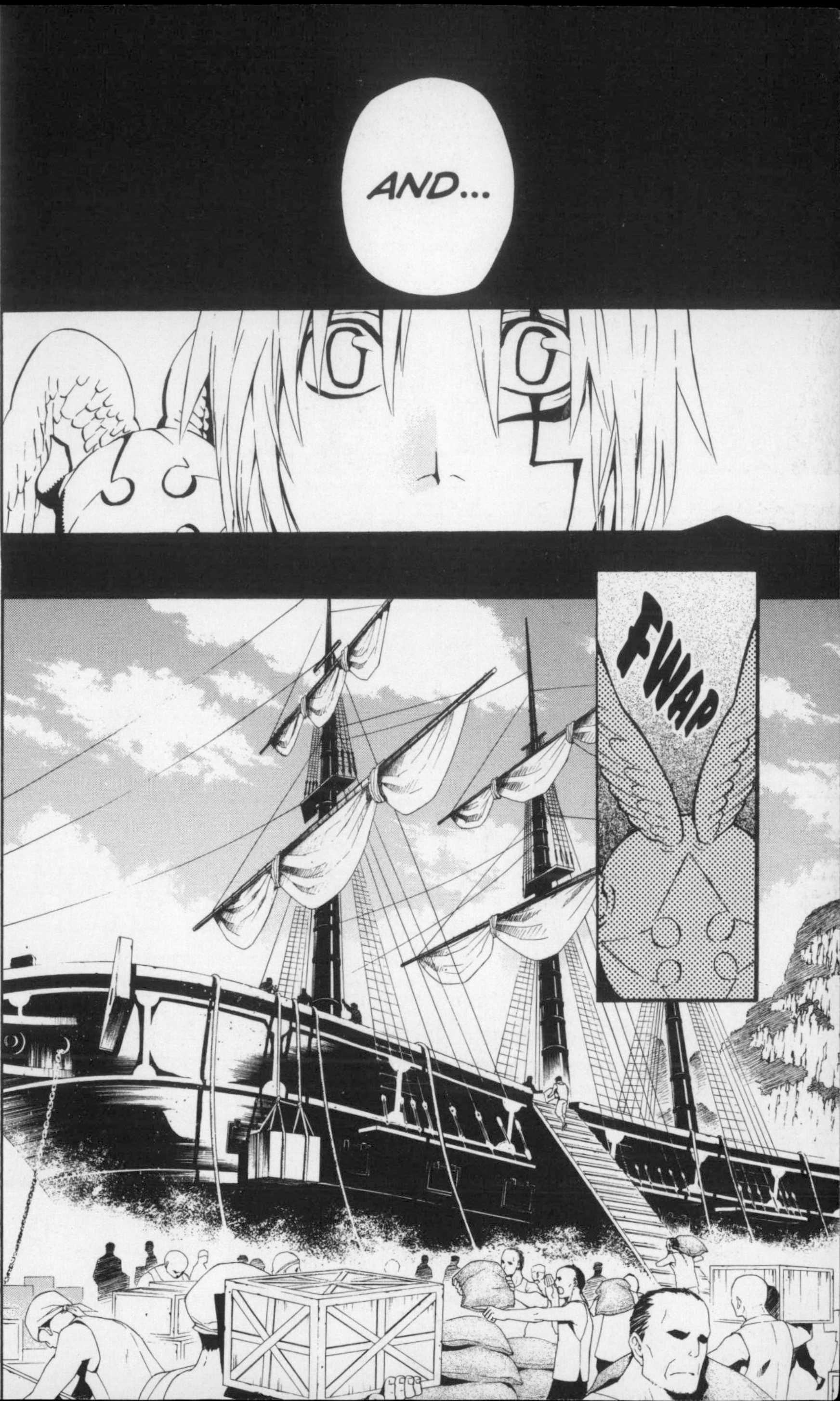
AND...
FWAP

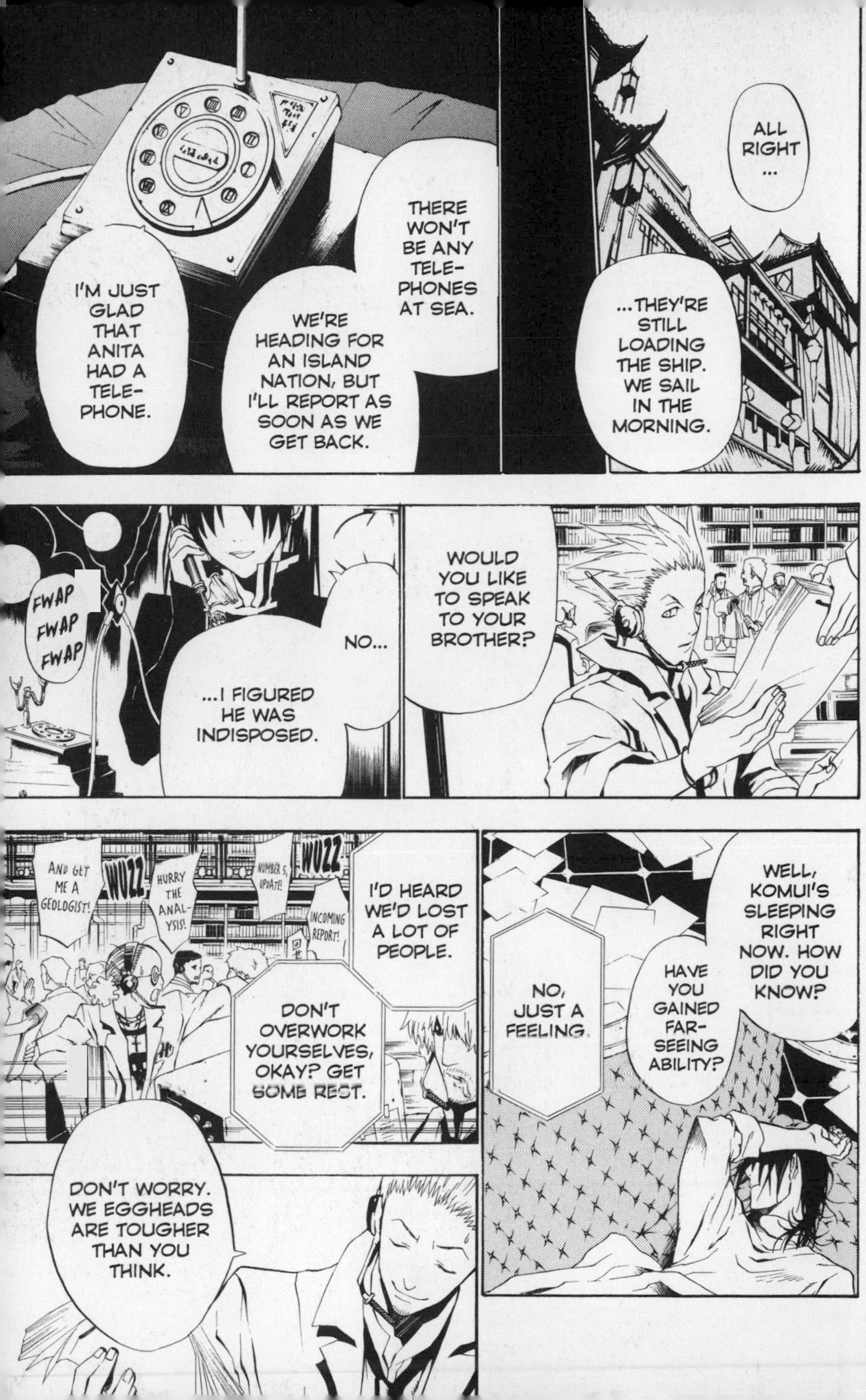
ALL RIGHT ...
...THEY'RE STILL LOADING THE SHIP. WE SAIL IN THE MORNING.
THERE WON'T BE ANY TELE-PHONES AT SEA.
WE'RE HEADING FOR AN ISLAND NATION, BUT I'LL REPORT AS SOON AS WE GET BACK.
I'M JUST GLAD THAT ANITA HAD A TELE-PHONE.
WOULD YOU LIKE TO SPEAK TO YOUR BROTHER?
NO...
...I FIGURED HE WAS INDISPOSED.
FWAP FWAP FWAP
WELL, KOMUI'S SLEEPING RIGHT NOW. HOW DID YOU KNOW?
HAVE YOU GAINED FAR-SEEING ABILITY?
NO, JUST A FEELING.
I'D HEARD WE'D LOST A LOT OF PEOPLE.
WUZZ
NUMBER 5, UPDATE!
INCOMING REPORT!
HURRY THE ANALYSIS!
WUZZ
AND GET ME A GEOLOGIST!
DON'T OVERWORK YOURSELVES, OKAY? GET SOME REST.
DON'T WORRY. WE EGGHEADS ARE TOUGHER THAN YOU THINK.

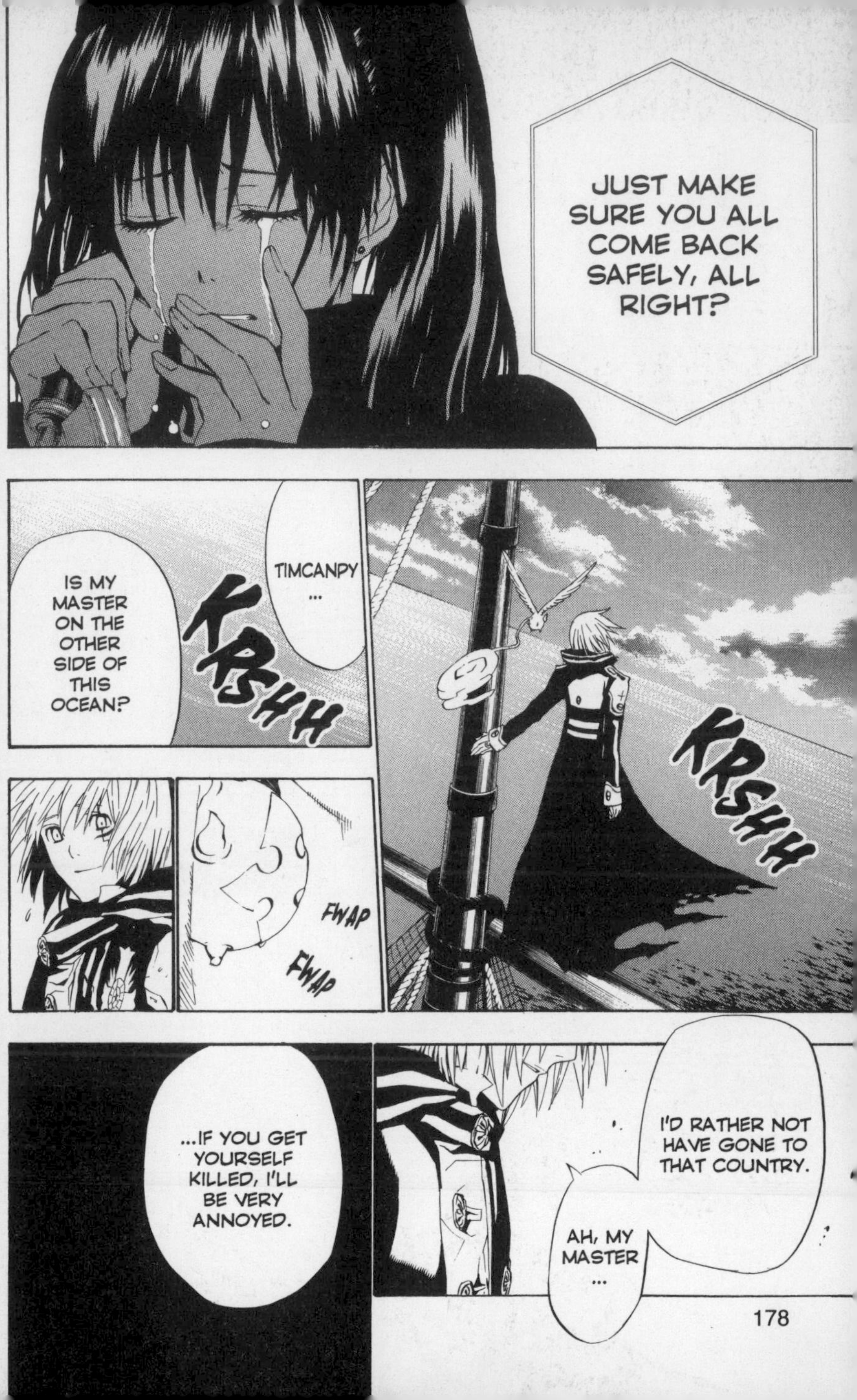
JUST MAKE SURE YOU ALL COME BACK SAFELY, ALL RIGHT?
KRSHH
TIMCANPY ...
KRSHH
IS MY MASTER ON THE OTHER SIDE OF THIS OCEAN?
FWAP
FWAP
I'D RATHER NOT HAVE GONE TO THAT COUNTRY.
AH, MY MASTER ...
...IF YOU GET YOURSELF KILLED, I'LL BE VERY ANNOYED.

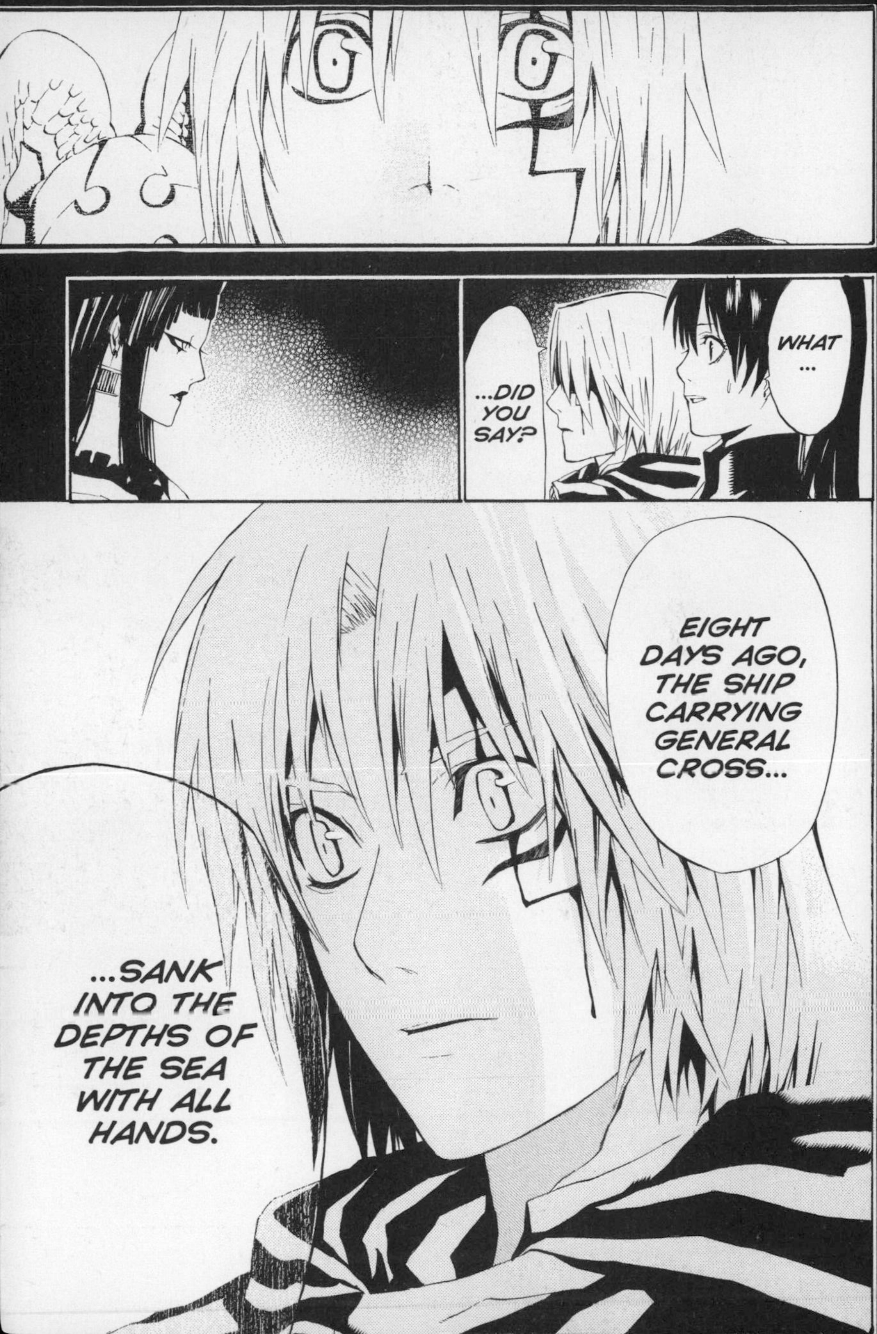
WHAT ...
...DID YOU SAY?
EIGHT DAYS AGO, THE SHIP CARRYING GENERAL CROSS...
...SANK INTO THE DEPTHS OF THE SEA WITH ALL HANDS.

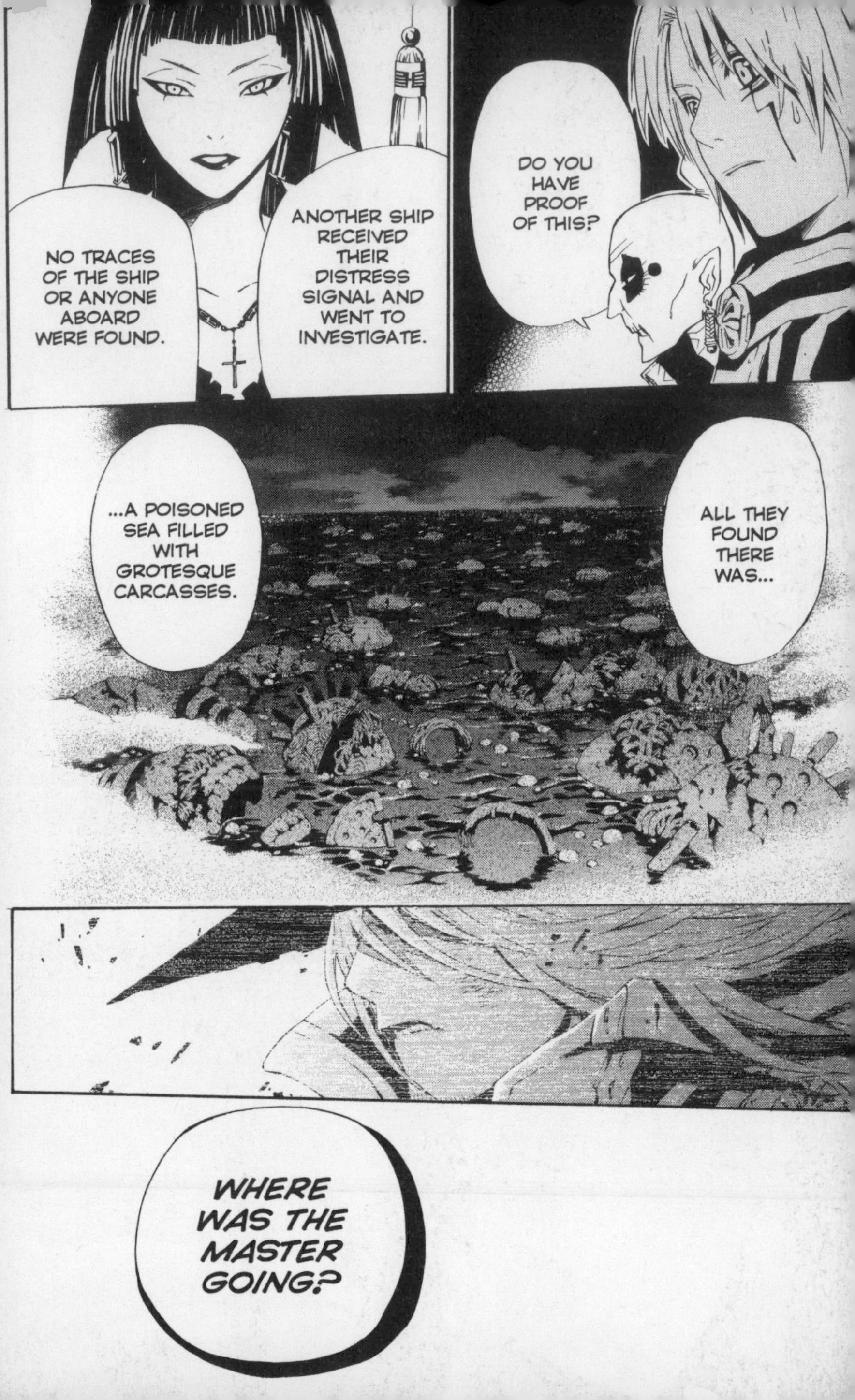
DO YOU HAVE PROOF OF THIS?
ANOTHER SHIP RECEIVED THEIR DISTRESS SIGNAL AND WENT TO INVESTIGATE.
NO TRACES OF THE SHIP OR ANYONE ABOARD WERE FOUND.
ALL THEY FOUND THERE WAS...
...A POISONED SEA FILLED WITH GROTESQUE CARCASSES.
WHERE WAS THE MASTER GOING?

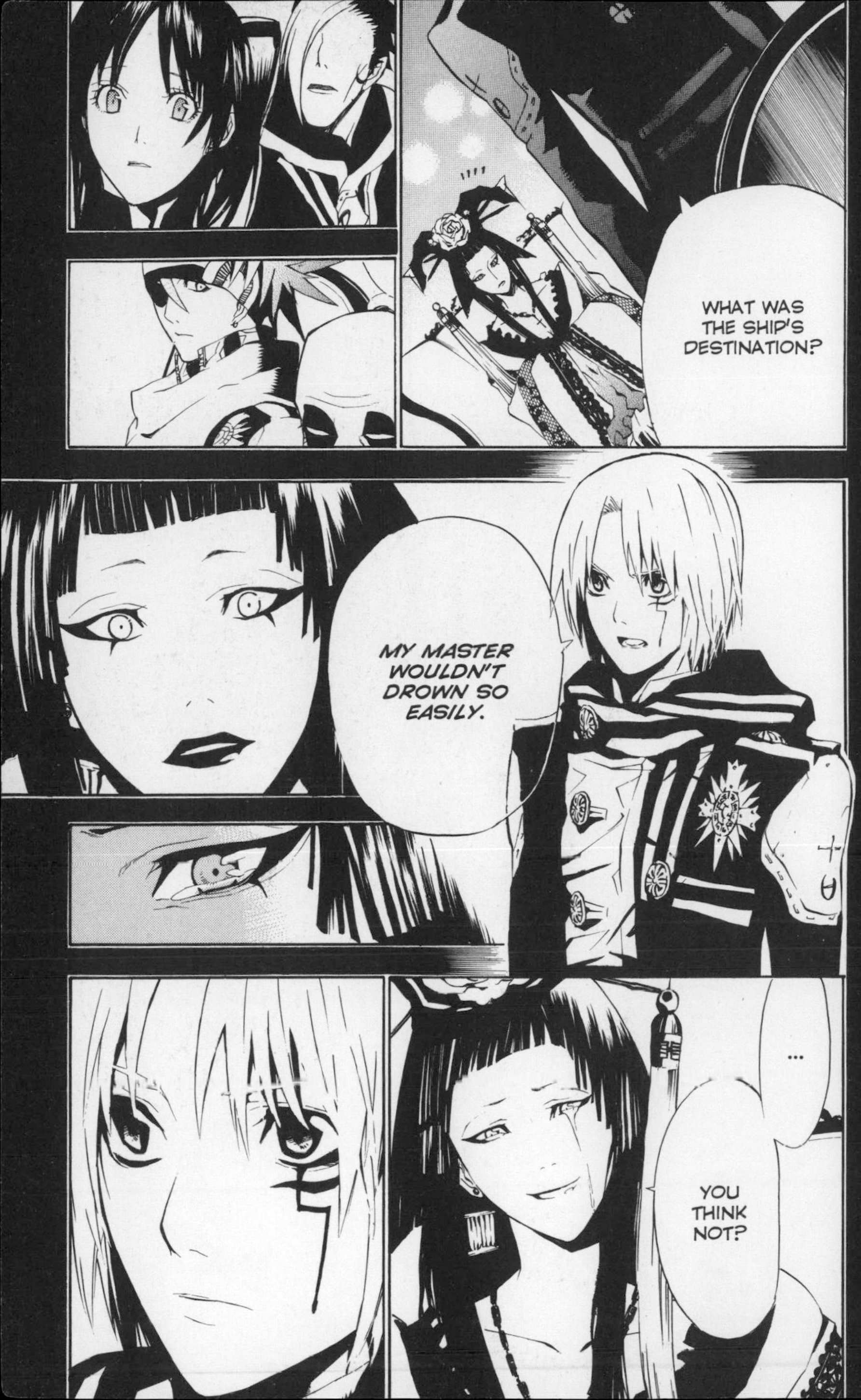
WHAT WAS THE SHIP'S DESTINATION?
MY MASTER WOULDN'T DROWN SO EASILY.
...
YOU THINK NOT?

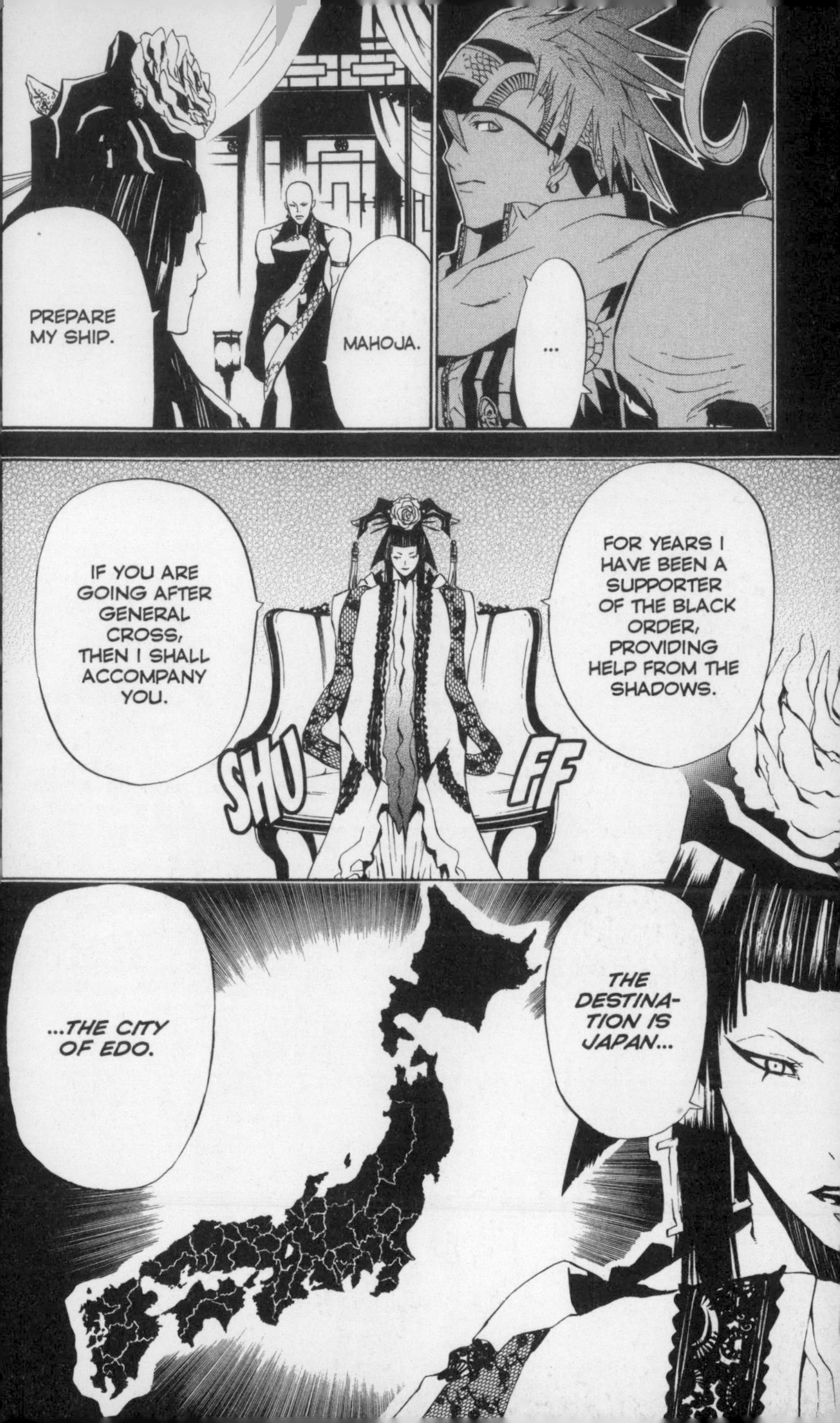
...
MAHOJA.
PREPARE MY SHIP.
FOR YEARS I HAVE BEEN A SUPPORTER OF THE BLACK ORDER, PROVIDING HELP FROM THE SHADOWS.
IF YOU ARE GOING AFTER GENERAL CROSS, THEN I SHALL ACCOMPANY YOU.
SHUFF
THE DESTINA-TION IS JAPAN...
...THE CITY OF EDO.

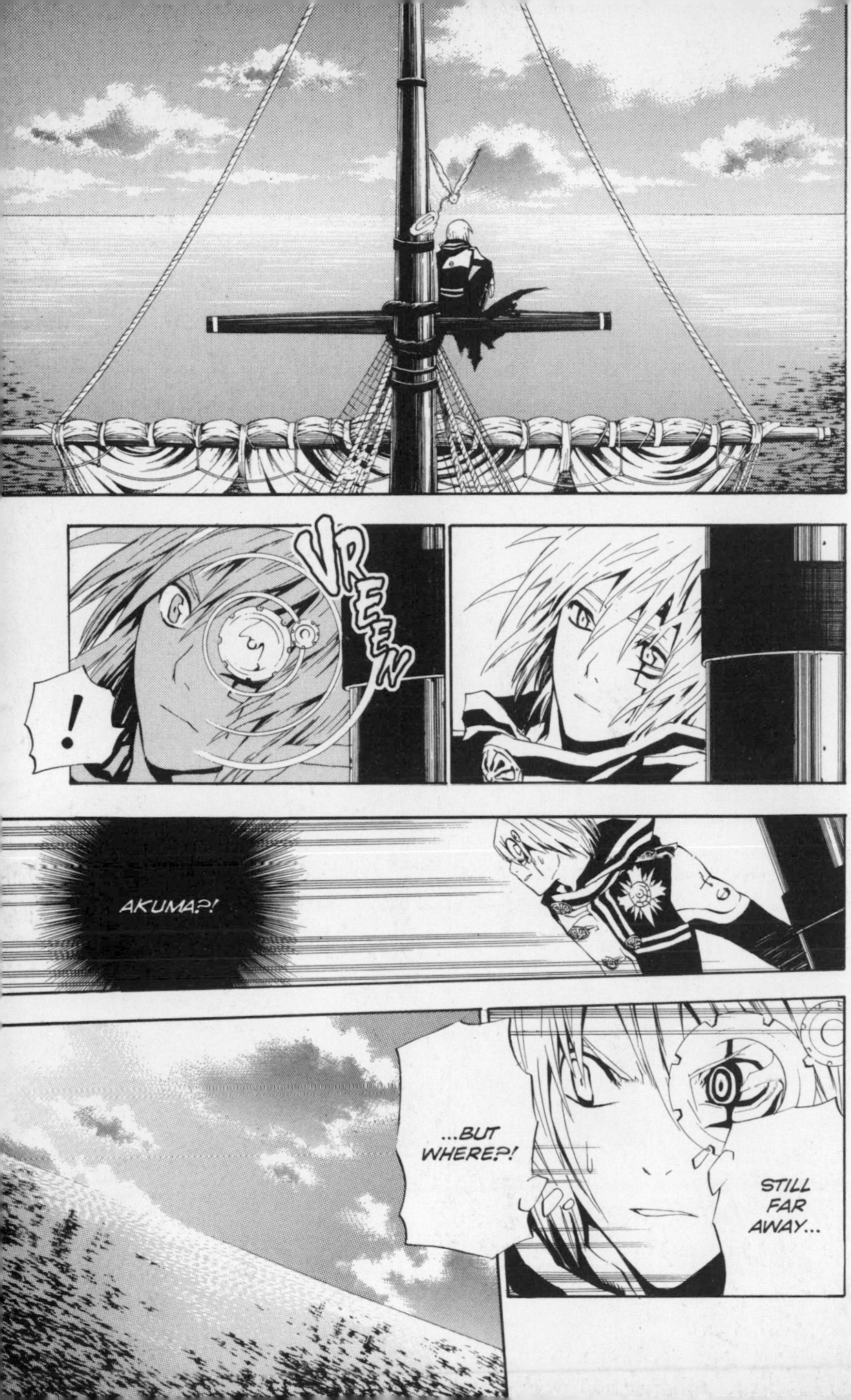
VREEN
!
AKUMA?!
STILL FAR AWAY...
...BUT WHERE?!

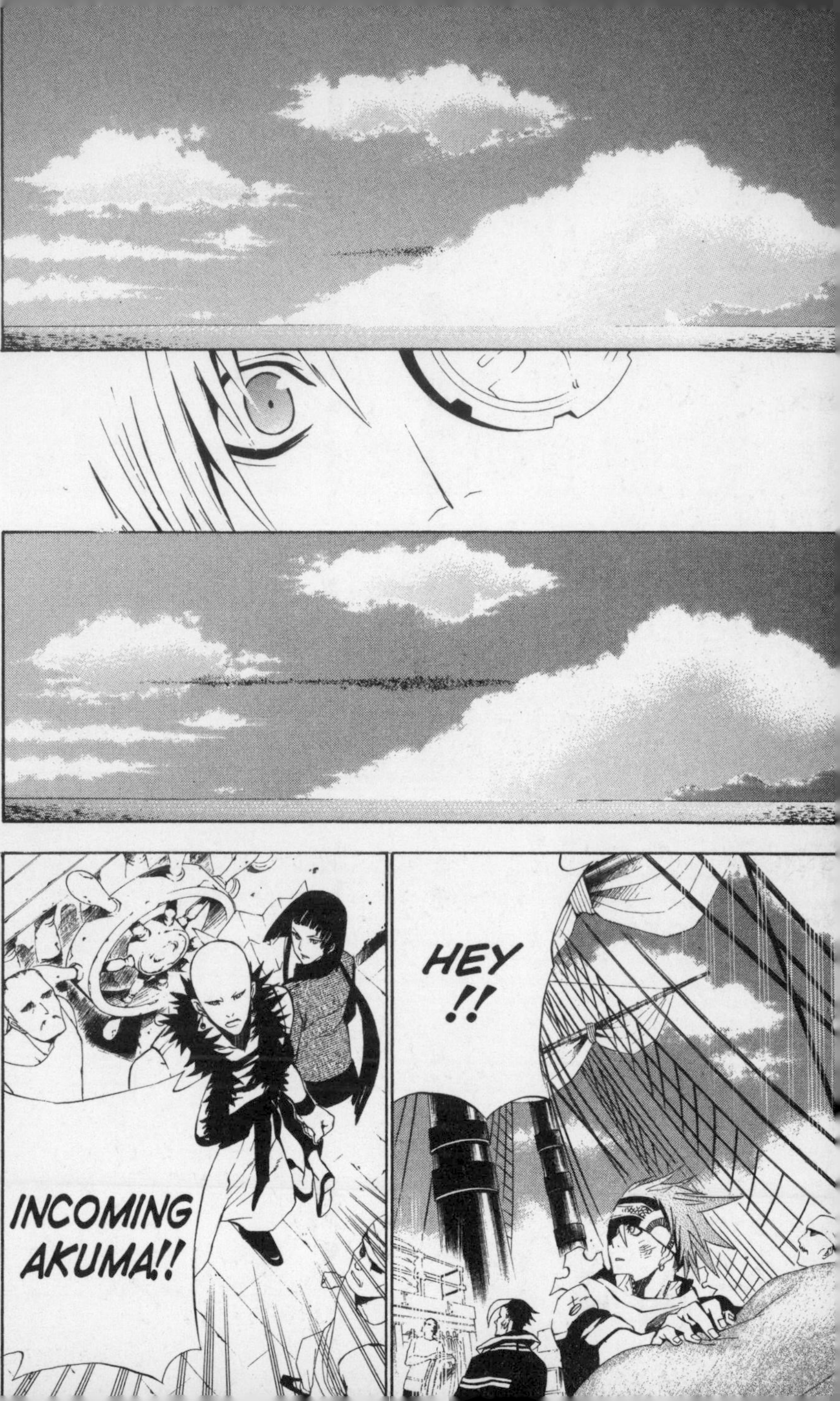
HEY !!
INCOMING AKUMA!!

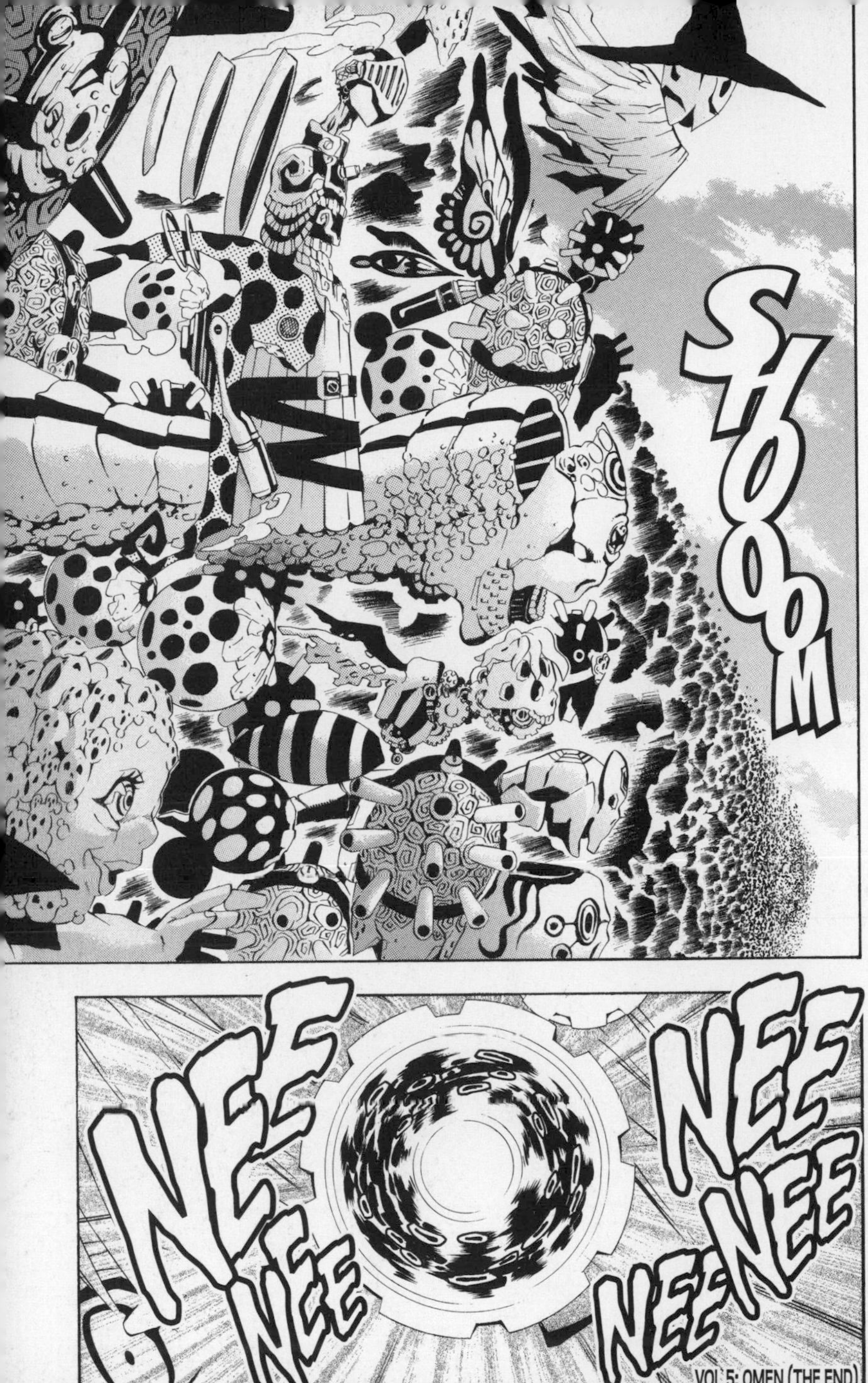
SHOOOM
NEE NEE-NEE-NEE
NEE NEE

VOL. 5: OMEN (THE END)

IN THE NEXT VOLUME...

A horde of Akuma close in on Allen, but they bypass him and head straight for another Exorcist, Suman Dark! His long tragic story and the secret of his unique "Innocence" is revealed, but in the process Suman's life is threatened. Allen tries his best to save his comrade, but his efforts put him in grave danger!

Available Now!

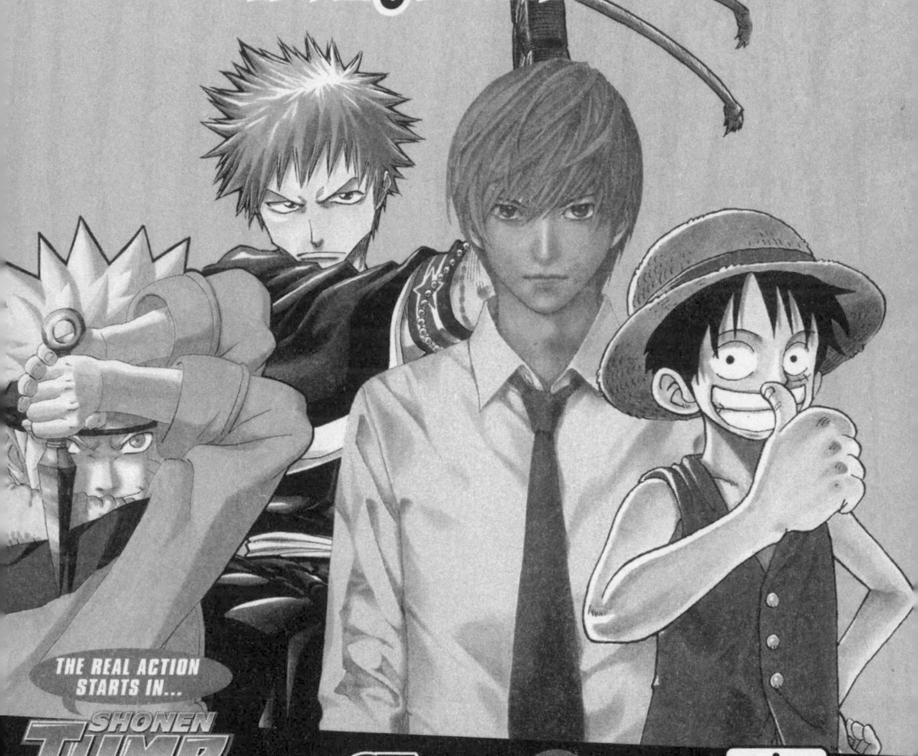

THE REAL ACTION STARTS IN...

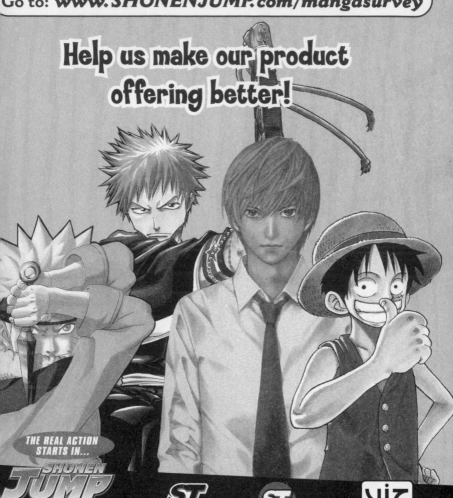

V/11